Constantinople and the West

Constantinople and the West

Essays on the Late Byzantine (Palaeologan) and Italian Renaissances and the Byzantine and Roman Churches

---

Deno John Geanakoplos

The University of Wisconsin Press

The University of Wisconsin Press
114 North Murray Street
Madison, Wisconsin 53715

The University of Wisconsin Press, Ltd.
1 Gower Street
London WC1E 6HA, England

5 4 3 2 1

Printed in the United States of America

Library of Congress Cataloging-in-Publication Data
Geanakoplos, Deno John.
Constantinople and the West:essays on the late Byzantine (Palaeologan) and Italian Renaissances and the Byzantine and Roman churches/Deno John Geanakoplos.
326pp. cm.
"Selected works by Deno J. Geanakoplos": pp. 295–300.
Includes bibliographical references and index.
1. Italy—Civilization—1268–1559. 2. Renaissance—Italy. 3. Byzantine Empire—Intellectural life. 4. Humanism—Italy—History. 5. Church history—Middle Ages, 600–1500. I. Title.
DG445.G43 1989
945—dc19 88-40434
ISBN 0–299–11880–0 cloth; ISBN 0–299–11884–3 (pbk.)

To my mother and to the memory of my father

Contents

Illustrations

Introduction

This volume owes its existence to the suggestion of several colleagues and students that, to mark my retirement after thirty-four years of almost uninterrupted teaching, a number of my essays of wider appeal be gathered together and published in a single accessible volume. I have chosen for inclusion in this book essays that reflect the primary research interest of my career, the broad theme of the cultural and ecclesiastical relations between the Byzantine East and Latin West during the Middle Ages and Italian Renaissance. It is this consideration—together with the relative unavailability of most of the essays—that constitutes the basis for this collection.

Part 1 deals with the influences on Italian Renaissance humanism of the so-called Byzantine Palaeologan "Renaissance," a fascinating but generally little-understood revival of Greek learning (and art) that took place in the Byzantine East somewhat before and during the Italian Renaissance. It has long been known of course that Greek manuscripts of the Palaeologan Renaissance, including those of authors until then unknown to the West, were brought to Italy by Byzantine scholars fleeing the Turkish conquest of their homeland. But what these essays demonstrate, for the first time systematically, I believe, is that through their knowledge of the Alexandrian and Byzantine traditions, the Byzantine émigrés alone were able to unlock and authentically interpret the more advanced treatises of Aristotle, Plato, and other Greek literary, philosophic, and scientific works. Through their teaching in Italy of the meaning, style, and nuances of the Greek texts (as well as their editing of texts for the press), the Byzantine refugees were thus able, if sometimes unwittingly, to promote a fusion of the Palaeologan Renaissance of Greek learning with the developing Latin, and later, Italian humanism. Accordingly, thus the essays in Part 1 attempt to restore a balance between the old, now entirely untenable, view that the coming of the Greek émigrés served to begin the Italian Renaissance, and the more recent but still exaggerated view of not a few modern Renaissance historians that they were merely transmitters of Greek learning to the West.

Through juxtaposition, so to speak, in these essays of both the Palaeologan and the Italian renaissances, it is hoped that the reader may comprehend more clearly the *process* of the broadening horizon and enrichment of Italian Renaissance thought and learning fostered by the émigré scholars from Byzantium.

Part 2 deals with the relations between the Byzantine and Roman churches, largely irenic in the earlier centuries of the undivided Christian church but turbulent in the period after 1054 and especially 1204, the date of the Latin conquest of Constantinople and beginning of the forced Byzantine conversion to "Roman Catholicism."[1] Any modern attempts to bring about a genuine reconciliation of the churches must be based on the mutual experience of the two ecclesiastical bodies in the medieval and Renaissance periods, some of the main encounters and phases of which are discussed in this volume. Most important for such a reconciliation is probably an understanding of the churches' last great encounter at the Council of Florence. There, after centuries of mutually recriminating schism and unsuccessful attempts at reunion, every religious difference of any significance was, finally and for the first time in a general council, publicly debated by theologians of East and West.

A few words about the nature of each essay: The first is an attempt at a broad synthesis reevaluating the vital question of the various aspects of the Byzantine émigrés' contribution to the Italian Renaissance. The second essay, on the same general theme, covers roughly the same period but with its argument organized according to the various intellectual fields or themes treated rather than by phases of the Italian Renaissance. Essays 3 and 4 concern two major Byzantine personalities who I think substantively influenced Italian Renaissance intellectual thought. The first is the polymath Theodore Gaza, a first-class Greek and Latin philologist and probably the leading secular Aristotelian of the earlier Italian Renaissance. His collaboration in Rome with Andrea Giovanni di Bussi and several others, editing for the first printers in Italy a corpus of classical *Latin* works, and his responsibility for what appears to be the first printed passage from a classical *Greek* author (Plato), have gone almost unnoticed by most modern historians. The second is the philosopher John Argyropoulos, a Byzantine humanist who, several authorities now believe, was primarily responsible for bringing about the reorientation of Italian (especially Florentine) humanism from emphasis on rhetoric and philology to Platonic philosophic thought.

Probably one of the most original contributions to the volume is the fifth essay, an attempt at a biography (the first in English) of the little known but widely influential Greek scholar Nicolaus Leonicus Tomaeus. His official appointment by the Venetian Senate in 1497 to teach Aristotelian philosophy in the original Greek text marked the ascendancy, if not the triumph, of the Greco-Byzantine Aristotle at the Renaissance's

1. The forced conversion lasted in Constantinople to 1261 when the Byzantines recovered their capital from the Latins.

leading university, Padua, over the hitherto prevailing Averroist (Arab) interpretation. As will be seen, essays 3, 4, and 5 focus on the cities of Rome, Florence, and Venice, each of which in turn became the major center of Greek learning in the Italian Renaissance (Florence being historically first).

Essay 6 examines the great eighteenth century historian Edward Gibbon's in many respects surprisingly accurate and vivid, if acerbic, treatment of the ill-fated schism between the Greek and Latin churches. The next essay is an analysis of the proceedings and intricate theology of the Second Ecumenical Council at Constantinople in 381, which in effect marked the emergence to leadership in the Greek East of the patriarchate of Constantinople that subsequently of course became the great rival to Rome. Essay 8 examines the interaction at the unionist Council of Lyons in 1274 of the Franciscan minister-general and theologian Bonaventura and other representatives of the mendicant orders with the legates of the Byzantine church and Emperor Michael VIII Palaeologus. The essay demonstrates, among other things, that the role of Bonaventura has been exaggerated by historians, the principal intellectual architects of the union being two little-known Franciscan friars, the sympathetic Greek Franciscan John Parastron and the Latin Franciscan Jerome of Ascoli.

The next essay, 9, deals with a neglected chrysobull of the same emperor. The document expresses the exultant Byzantine mood at the restoration of Constantinople to the Greeks in 1261 and the treatment accorded the Cathedral of Hagia Sophia by its Byzantine restorer Michael VIII. Essay 10, a shorter essay read to commemorate the 700th anniversary of the Sicilian Vespers (1282), delineates the attitudes of the Greek-speaking, in ritual still Orthodox, population of Sicily toward possibly the two most astute diplomats and implacable enemies of the medieval world, Charles I King of Sicily and the Byzantine ruler Michael Palaeologus.

Study 11, though published two decades ago, remains, I believe, essentially still valid in its interpretation of the Council of Florence. One of the first Western analyses to utilize, critically, the behind-the-scenes memoirs of the Byzantine cleric Sylvester Syropoulos, the essay is possibly the only article in English analyzing the preliminaries, proceedings, and problems of the famous council. The final essay, written for the 550th anniversary of the beginning of the councils of Basel (1431–49) and Florence (1438–39), will interest, I hope, not only church historians and theologians, but also ecumenists who look back to these last two medieval confrontations between Eastern and Western Christendom as the point of departure for any modern negotiations to reunite the two churches.

The Appendix, closely related to material in Part 1, is concerned with the vital but still rather neglected problem of the first editions of the Greek Church Fathers printed in the Renaissance.

I have endeavored to revise all the essays in the aim of correcting errors, enriching the text, and bringing the studies entirely up to date. Thus essay 11, in particular (on the Council of Florence) contains many changes and considerable additional material. Also, essay 4, on Argyropoulos, has in parts been rewritten in the light of the most recent scholarship, and the texts of the other essays (especially 3 on Gaza, 5 on Tomaeus, and the Appendix) have been reworked, along with their notes.

For the convenience of interested scholars and the general reader, more detailed recent bibliographical material is provided at the end of each essay. These bibliographical additions include not only works specifically relevant to each essay but also related material of a more general nature. It should be noted that I have incorporated into the text and notes any pertinent new information provided by the titles listed in the additional bibliographies. Full bibliographical material for works of my own that are cited in the text can be found in the list of Selected Works at the end of the volume.

Notes on the Provenience of the Essays

Essay 1 was originally read at the American Historical Association in 1978 and later published in the Italian journal *Rivista di studi bizantini e slavi,* festschrift in honor of the Italian scholar A. Pertusi, vol. 3 (1984): 129–57. This essay, titled "Italian Humanism and the Byzantine Emigré Scholars" and with updated documentation, has now appeared in A. Rabil, Jr., ed., *Renaissance Humanism: Foundations, Forms, and Legacy* (Philadelphia: Univ. of Pennsylvania Press, 1988), 1:349–81. It is reprinted here, with minor changes, with permission.

Essay 2 was the main address at the annual conference at Villanova University in 1976 and was later printed in that institution's *Proceedings of the Patristic, Medieval and Renaissance Conference* 3 (1978): 1–25. The third essay was delivered in 1980 at Thessalonica, Greece, on the fortieth anniversary of the Society of Macedonian Studies and published by that society in *Hē Thessalonikē Metaxy Anatolēs kai Dyseōs* (1982). It was later printed, with important changes, in *Medievalia et humanistica,* n.s., no. 12 (1984): 61–81. Essay 4 was read as a lecture at Ball State University and printed in *Focus on Biography,* ed. D. Hoover and J. Koumoulides, *Conspectus of History,* vol. 1, no. 1 (1974): 12–28. The fifth essay was published in the festschrift for J. Karagiannopoulos, *Byzantina* 13 (1985): 355–72. It had first appeared in shorter form and without footnotes in *Proceedings of the World Congress on Aristotle,* Thessalonica, 7–14 August 1978, vol. 2 (Athens, 1981), 15–20.

Essay 6 was read at the American Historical Association in 1965 and published in *Church History* 35 (1966): 1–16. Essay 7 was originally read at a symposium commemorating the Second Ecumenical Council (381) at Union Theological Seminary in New York in 1981 and published in *Greek Orthodox Theological Review* 27 (1984): 207–29. The eighth essay was published in the festschrift for George H. Williams, *Continuity and Discontinuity in Church History,* ed. F. Church and T. George (Leiden, 1979), 104–17. Essay 9 was read in 1982 at the Congress in Palermo, Sicily, commemorating the 700th anniversary of the Sicilian Vespers (1282) and printed in *XI Congresso di Storia del Corona d'Aragona: La società mediterranea all'epoca del Vespro,* April 1982, vol. 3 (Palermo, 1984), 177–82. Essay 10 was read before the British Ecclesiastical History Society in 1975 at its symposium on the Orthodox churches and the West. It was printed in *The Orthodox Churches and the West,* ed. D. Baker (Oxford: Blackwell, 1976), 182–211. The eleventh essay, on the Council of Florence, was presented at the American Society of Church

History in 1953 and printed in *Church History* 24 (1955): 324–46. It was subsequently printed, with changes, in my *Byzantine East and Latin West* (Oxford, 1966), 84–111.

Finally, essay 12 was originally read in English in Basel, Switzerland in 1981 on the 550th anniversary of the Council of Basel and first published in German in *Theologische Zeitschrift* 38 (1982): 330–59, under the title "Die Konzile von Basel und Florenz (1431–49) als Paradigma für das Studium moderner ökumenischer Konzile aus orthodoxer Perspektive." More recently it was printed with corrections, in English, in *Greek Orthodox Theological Review* 30 (1985): 311–34. The Appendix is a paper read in 1974 at Cambridge University at a conference sponsored by Professor R. Bolgar on new research in Renaissance humanism. It was published in rather different form as chap. 14 of my *Interaction of the Sibling Byzantine and Western Cultures.*

Part I

The Byzantine Palaeologan "Renaissance" and Italian Renaissance Humanism

One

Italian Renaissance Thought and Learning and the Role of the Byzantine Emigré Scholars in Florence, Rome, and Venice: A Reassessment

Any reassessment of the role of the émigré Byzantine scholars in the development of Italian Renaissance thought and learning must recognize that at the time of the development of the Italian Renaissance there was also a parallel "Renaissance" taking place in the Byzantine East.[1] The latter, more accurately termed the Palaeologan "revival of learning," had begun earlier, in the thirteenth century. This revival of culture under the Palaeologan dynasty was expressed in the emergence of certain "realistic" qualities in painting, a further development in mystical beliefs, and what we shall focus on exclusively here, a greater intensification than ever before of the study of ancient Greek literature, philosophy, and science.

1. The term Palaeologan "Renaissance" has been the object of much discussion. Unlike Latin in the Italian Renaissance, Greek learning (though undergoing several rather notable declines in its study) had never been lost to the Byzantines. And in the thirteenth to early fifteenth centuries (the Palaeologan period) Greek learning underwent a truly remarkable intensification ("renaissance") of study in all respects—literary, rhetorical, philological, philosophical, as well as mathematical and scientific (not to speak of artistic). Aside from a certain diminution in ecclesiastical opposition to study of the ancient classics, a basic, underlying cause of the revival was the tremendous outpouring of Greek sentiment after (and even before, in Nicaea) the reconquest of Constantinople from the Latin conquerors in 1261 by Emperor Michael Palaeologus. See below nn. 2 and 3.

Byzantinists disagree about the precise causes of the Palaeologan intellectual revival, which took firm hold, notably, after the Greek recovery of Constantinople from the Latins in 1261.[2] But there is no doubt that it was characterized by somewhat different and more intensive methods of study than earlier Byzantine revivals of classical Greek learning.[3] An understanding of the characteristics of this Palaeologan intellectual revival is vital, as I shall try to show, because the recovery of Greek learning in the Italian Renaissance was influenced not only by the content of Palaeologan learning but also by such considerations as its methods of teaching, curricula of study, and attitudes toward the corpus of disciplines in the Byzantine cultural tradition.

It is the principal thesis of this essay—in my view this is an important reason to reevaluate the role of the Byzantine scholars—that the development of Greek learning in the Italian Renaissance was the result primarily of the fusion, however imperfect in certain respects, of various elements of the Palaeologan Renaissance with those of the Italian. This is a consideration of which most Western Renaissance historians are unaware, often lacking a knowledge of Greek and, no less important, of late Byzantine cultural developments.

This thesis, however, must be qualified to take into account such considerations as Italian receptivity or lack thereof toward certain kinds of Greek learning on account of intellectual differences, ethnic prejudices, or even divergent methods of academic organization. My method in reassessing the significance of the Greek émigrés in Italy will be first to point out the historical Italian milieu for the reception of Greek learning and its agents of transmission, the émigrés, then to outline the main characteristics of this little-known Palaeologan revival of Greek literature, philosophy, and science, along with Byzantine attitudes toward such learning. Then, in the main body of the essay, I shall deal with the activities of the more important émigrés in the three principal centers of the Italian Renaissance: Florence, Rome, and Venice-Padua, each of which experienced a period of primacy in Greek studies. Finally, I shall

2. On causes of the Palaeologan revival, see Geanakoplos, *Interaction of the "Sibling" Byzantine and Western Cultures in the Middle Ages and Italian Renaissance,* 17–21, 85–91, 285–86; and essay 8 below. See also A. Vacalopoulos, *Origins of the Greek Nation: The Byzantine Period, 1204–1461* (New Brunswick, N.J., 1970), 1:46–57, 2:157–61; cf. S. Runciman, *The Last Byzantine Renaissance* (Cambridge, 1970), 55f. and 14f.

3. See esp. H. G. Beck, "Intellectual Life in the Late Byzantine Church," in *From the High Middle Ages to the Eve of the Reformation,* Handbook of Church History, ed. H. Jedin and J. Dolan, vol. 4 (New York, 1968), 505–12, who points out the greater intensity of study in the Palaeologan than in earlier Byzantine Renaissances and the apparently less constricting attitude of the Greek church. Cf. N. Wilson, "The Church and Classical Studies in Byzantium," *Antike und Abendland* 16 (1970): 68–77.

draw a few general conclusions about the significance of the Byzantine émigrés' contribution to Italian Renaissance thought and learning.

What was the state of Greek learning in Italy at the outset of the Italian Renaissance, roughly 1350? Scholasticism then held sway with its primary focus on Aristotelian logic and philosophy, and attempts were being made to reconcile Aristotle with Christian theology. But unless we understand the method, *verbum ad verbum* translation, and intent of Scholastic translators from the Greek such as William of Moerbeke, we shall fail to comprehend the need felt later by Italian humanists and the Byzantine émigré scholars to retranslate most of these ancient Greek texts.[4] The Scholastic versions had served to whet Western appetites for Greek logical, metaphysical, and scientific works, but virtually all the literary, rhetorical, and historical works, along with several important writings of Aristotle and most of Plato, were either unknown in the West or left untranslated by the Scholastics.[5]

With the dawn of the early Italian Renaissance and humanist emphasis on classical Latin literature, the receptivity of Italian men of letters to ancient Greek *literature* was accordingly intensified. In Florence in particular, the birthplace of so-called civic humanism with its focus on Roman republicanism, Greek works pertaining to the activities of civic life, the *vita activa,* were now welcomed, especially those concerning ancient Athens, the rhetorical qualities of whose statesmen were considered worthy of emulation. In this social ambience of the Italian urban areas, we see, then, a general readiness for appreciation of certain Greek works, especially rhetorical ones. But the degree of receptivity varied. Leonardo Bruni, for example, may well have considered making a Latin translation of Plato's *Republic.* Quite possibly, however, he was not sophisticated enough to appreciate the subtleties of the work, or he may have disliked its "communistic" concepts and praise of despotism, however benevolent.[6]

4. On Moerbeke's method of translation, see Geanakoplos, *Interaction of the Sibling Cultures,* 266; P. O. Kristeller, *Renaissance Concepts of Man* (New York, 1972), 69; and G. Holmes, *The Florentine Enlightenment* (New York, 1969), 115–17, who discusses the dispute between the Scholastic Bishop of Burgos, a critic of Bruni's humanist translations and supporter of the "accuracy" of Moerbeke's word-for-word rendering. Some modern scholars now prefer many of the Scholastic translations as being more faithful to the original. The humanist ones were often virtually copies of the Scholastic, but rendered only superficially more "rhetorical."

5. The principal Aristotelian texts translated after 1350 were the *Eudemian Ethics* and the pseudo-Aristotelian *Mechanica.* See E. Garin, "Le traduzioni umanistiche di Aristotele nel secolo XV," *Atti e memorie dell'Accademia fiorentina di scienze morali la Colombaria* 16 (1949–50): 55–103.

6. On Bruni, see C. Vasoli, in *Dizionario biografico degli Italiani* 14:618–33; and

As for the Byzantine émigrés, they found the Italian intellectual terrain well prepared for them, because the Italian humanist focus on the *studia humanitatis* was very similar to the rhetorical training so fundamental to the Palaeologan Renaissance. P. O. Kristeller has astutely remarked that the learning and interests of the Italian humanists had more links to the Byzantine didactic tradition than to their Western predecessors, the Scholastics.[7]

We now turn to a vital but inadequately explored area: Palaeologan methods of teaching and exegesis, curricula, and attitudes toward various ancient Greek writers. The young Byzantine student, after learning grammar and composition, a process requiring a great deal of memorization, advanced to the study of the Greek orators.[8] Rhetorical studies were important in Byzantium if simply to satisfy the government's need for a well-trained, articulate bureaucracy (not to speak of the inordinate Byzantine love for rhetorical expression), a situation comparable to the Italian cities' need for "professional" humanists. (Isocrates was more esteemed in Byzantium than Demosthenes, apparently because of his more "didactic" qualities.)[9] The most esteemed manuals on rhetoric used by the Byzantines were those of Hermogenes of Tarsus and his follower Aphthonius. Hermogenes' value lay in his pragmatic and highly effective analysis of the various kinds of rhetoric and in his concrete information on precisely how the rhetorician can create desired effects on his audience through observing specified rhetorical "forms."[10]

Holmes, *Florentine Enlightenment,* 30–31. Chrysoloras first in Florence and Uberto Decembrio later in Milan continued translation of Plato's *Republic.* It was completed by Pier Candido Decembrio: see E. Garin, "Ricerche sulle traduzioni di Platone nella prima metà del secolo XV," *Medioevo e rinascimento: Studi in onore di Bruno Nardi,* 2 vols. (Florence, 1955), 1:361–63. For Bruni's abhorrence of certain ideas in the *Republic,* see Bruni, *Epistolae,* ed. L. Mehus (Florence, 1741), no. 9, 4. On translations of Plato's *Republic* see, most recently, J. Hankins, "A Manuscript of Plato's *Republic* in the Translation of Chrysoloras and Uberto Decembrio with Annotations of Guarino Veronese," in *Supplementum Festivum: Studies in Honor of Paul Oskar Kristeller,* ed. J. Hankins, J. Monfasani, and F. Purnell, Jr. (Binghamton, N.Y., 1987), 149–88.

7. Kristeller, "Italian Humanism and Byzantium," in *Renaissance Concepts of Man,* 75.

8. R. Browning, "Byzantine Scholarship," *Past and Present* 28 (1964): 3–30; and Runciman, *Last Byzantine Renaissance,* 15–16.

9. See Geanakoplos, *Interaction of the Sibling Cultures,* 192, 240; and J. Monfasani, *George of Trebizond: A Biography and Study of His Rhetoric and Logic* (Leiden, 1976), 253, 288.

10. On Hermogenes in Byzantium, see esp. G. Kustas, "The Function and Evolution of Byzantine Rhetoric," *Viator: Medieval and Renaissance Studies* 1 (1970): 55–73; Kustas, "Studies in Byzantine Rhetoric," *Theologia* 45 (1975): 413ff. See also Monfasani, *George of Trebizond,* 248–55.

The Byzantine curriculum, then, strongly emphasized rhetoric, but unlike the parallel *studia humanitatis* of Italy, particularly in the earlier Florentine stage of humanism, it also included metaphysical philosophy, mathematics, and pure science. It was the Byzantine aim to impart an all-encompassing education (based on the traditional *enkyklios paideia*), the culmination of which lay, theoretically, in theology.[11] It attests to the organic unity of late Byzantine education that, so far as I can ascertain, every scholar who dealt with literature in the Palaeologan Renaissance also concerned himself with science.[12] Maximos Planudes, the great *literatus,* wrote a little-known work on mathematics and was even interested in Arabic numerals.[13] I stress this point because the huge scope of learning and interests manifested by such Byzantine émigrés in Italy as George of Trebizond, John Argyropoulos, and Bessarion, will contrast strongly with the narrower Italian interests of the *studia humanitatis,* which, for some time at least, excluded metaphysical philosophy and science.[14]

During the Palaeologan Renaissance there was a far more intensive and systematic study than ever before of the entire range of classical Greek works: literary, philosophical, and scientific. And the Byzantine church, in contrast to its earlier position, seemed not (or at least less) to object to the reading of such texts.[15] The works of the leading ancient commentators on Aristotle and Plato were now carefully analyzed.[16] In addition, Palaeologan scholars studied more closely the ancient historians, Thucydides in particular, possibly because of the very difficulty of

11. F. Fuchs, *Die höheren Schulen von Konstantinopel im Mittelalter* (rept. Amsterdam, 1964), 41–45; L. Reynolds and N. Wilson, *Scribes and Scholars* (Oxford, 1974), chap. 2 and pp. 130–42; Browning, "Byzantine Scholarship," 3–20; and Runciman, *Last Byzantine Renaissance,* 53–54, 31–33. In the later Byzantine period *enkyklios paideia* came to refer to the *general rudiments* of Byzantine education.

12. My friend the eminent scholar A. Turyn has expressed this view to me.

13. On Planudes' writings, see esp. A. Turyn, "Demetrius Triklinios and the Planudean Anthology," *Festschrift N. Tomadakes* (Athens, 1973), 403–50; also Geanakoplos, *Interaction of the Sibling Cultures,* 101 and bibliography 327 n. 17, including his interest in mathematics; also I. Ševčenko, "Theodore Metochites, Chora, et les courants intellectuels de l'époque," *Art et société à Byzance sous les Paléologues* (Venice, 1971), 29f.; Runciman, *Last Byzantine Renaissance,* 59–60; and H. Hunger, *Die hochsprächliche profane Literatur der Byzantiner* (Munich, 1978).

14. On the *studia humanitatis,* see P. O. Kristeller, *Renaissance Thought,* vol. 1 (New York, 1961), 9f., 19f.

15. See Beck, "Intellectual Life in the Late Byzantine Church," 505–12; Wilson, "The Church and Classical Studies in Byzantium," 68–77; and Runciman, *Last Byzantine Renaissance,* 33–34, cf. 29f.

16. Runciman, *Last Byzantine Renaissance,* 83, 17; B. Tatakis, *La philosophie byzantine* (Paris, 1949), 233, 251, 287, 299.

his text.[17] But the chief intellectual emphasis seems to have been on poetry, particularly the classical dramas and lyric poetry, perhaps owing to the greater challenge offered by the more refined style of these texts. Thus for the first time *systematic* study of the great tragedians and Aristophanes, along with attempts to correct and establish accurate texts, were now undertaken.[18]

In their teaching at Padua and Florence the Greek émigré scholars, and the Latins who followed them, taught the Greek dramas in the order they seem to have been read in Palaeologan Byzantium, in the case of Euripides first the easiest, *Hecuba,* and with Aristophanes first the *Plutus.*[19] In philosophy, Plato and Aristotle were both read in the Byzantine schools from at least the eleventh century on. There was no such polarization between them as was to some degree the case in the West during the Scholastic period and especially after the Byzantine Pletho's discourse on their differences in Florence.[20]

Finally, I note a unique Palaeologan scholarly technique used in poetry and prose which is rarely considered in discussing Byzantine influences on the Italian Renaissance of Greek learning, that termed *schedographia.* Following this technique, Byzantine scholars, after dividing the entire text before them into passages of several lines each, would write a comment or an elaborate paraphrase explaining each passage. This would include a careful analysis of terms employed, homonyms, antonyms, syntax, and so forth. Each passage of the original text would alternate with a schedographic passage. It seems safe to affirm that the fruits of this practice of *schedographia* were utilized by many of the Byzantine scholars (such as Musurus) in their teaching in Italy.[21]

17. View also expressed to me by Professor Turyn.

18. On Palaeologan study and edition of the tragedians and Aristophanes, see esp. the works of Turyn, *The Manuscript Tradition of the Tragedies of Aeschylus* (New York, 1943) . . . *of Sophocles* (Urbana, Ill., 1952), . . . *of Euripides* (Urbana, Ill., 1957). See also Hunger, *Die hochsprächliche profane Literatur* 1:37–41, 2:66–77.

19. Kristeller, *Renaissance Concepts of Man,* 74–75.

20. On their nonpolarization in Byzantium, see Tatakis, *La philosophie byzantine,* 250–58; also essay 3 below, text at nn. 47–49. On the enormous diffusion of Aristotle in Byzantium, see A. Wartelle, *Inventaire des manuscrits grecs d'Aristotle et de ses commentateurs* (Paris, 1963). The extent of the diffusion of Plato in Byzantium is less clear.

21. On *schedographia,* see Hunger, *Die hochsprächliche profane Literatur,* 29ff. He cites the example of Moschopoulos's use in Byzantium of *schedographia* in MSS known later to the Italian Renaissance.

Florence

Let us now consider the Byzantine émigrés' activities in Florence, the first center of Greek studies in Italy. The initial holder of the Greek chair in the Florentine *studium* was the south Italian Greek Leontius Pilatus, appointed in 1361 through the mediation of Boccaccio.[22] A. Pertusi has recently shown that Pilatus's translation of Homer into Latin, the first since antiquity, despite almost unanimous Renaissance and modern condemnation, was as accurate as could be expected for his time. It was not in the flowing humanist style of Bruni but rather *ad verbum,* as was then the fashion in Byzantine south Italy. Pertusi also demonstrates that Pilatus resided for years in Crete, whence probably came much of his remarkable knowledge of Greek mythology which he imparted to Boccaccio for composition of the latter's *Genealogia deorum.*[23] As for Petrarch's Greek teacher, Barlaam, perhaps only Byzantinists realize that his command of Greek was so good that he taught a course in Constantinople on the teachings of the difficult early Byzantine (or late ancient) mystical theologian, Pseudo-Dionysius the Areopagite.[24]

After Chrysoloras's arrival in Florence in 1397 to teach Greek at the invitation of the Signoria, the enthusiasm generated by his efforts became so contagious that a wave of interest in Greek studies spread over much of northern Italy.[25] Since Chrysoloras lacked adequate texts to teach properly, he first had to compose a Greco-Latin grammar. This, notably, was modeled on the typical Palaeologan type of grammar called *Erotemata.*[26] It is tantalizing to speculate on how Chrysoloras taught Greek. After rudimentary instruction in grammar utilizing the *Erotemata,* I believe he probably continued with the method of teaching literature utilized in Byzantium. After reading aloud in Greek a passage of an

22. G. Brucker, "Florence and Its University, 1348–1434," in *Action and Conviction in Early Modern Europe,* ed. T. Rabb and J. Seigel (Princeton, N.J., 1969), 231–33; Geanakoplos, *Interaction of the Sibling Cultures,* 66.

23. A. Pertusi, *Leonzio Pilatao fra Petrarca e Boccaccio* (Venice and Rome, 1964), 433–37; Pertusi, "Leonzio Pilato a Creta prima del 1358–59: Scuole e cultura a Creta durante il secolo XIV," *Krētika chronika* 15–16 (1961–72): 363ff.

24. See Barlaam's writings in Migne, *Patrologia graeca,* vol. 115, cols. 1239–1342. On his career, see J. Meyendorff, *A Study of Gregory Palamas* (London, 1964), 42–62; and Tatakis, *La philosophie byzantine,* 263–66.

25. G. Cammelli, *Manuele Crisolora* (Florence, 1941), 34ff.; Geanakoplos, *Greek Scholars in Venice,* 24f.; and K. Setton, "The Byzantine Background to the Italian Renaissance," *Proceedings of the American Philosophical Society* 100 (1956): 57.

26. On the *Erotemata,* see A. Pertusi, "*Erotemata:* Per la storia e le fonti delle prime grammatiche greche a stampa," *Italia medioevale e umanistica* 5 (1962): 329–51; cf. Geanakoplos, *Greek Scholars in Venice,* 219–20, 286.

ancient author, first alone and then with the class, he would then carefully analyze it, probably incorporating information drawn from Byzantine scholia (that is, marginal comments on manuscripts) or from *schedographia.*[27]

To Chrysoloras, it seems, goes the credit for first establishing the subsequently standard humanist method of Greek translation into Latin so expertly utilized by his student Bruni. Instead of *ad verbum,* he prescribed rendering a passage in the spirit of the text *(ad sententiam transferre),* while at the same time avoiding an overly free translation.[28] It is of interest also that Chrysoloras, probably for the use of his students, began to translate into Latin the *Republic* of Plato. Perhaps too busy, he did not finish the task. Translation of the *Republic* was later taken up by Chrysoloras and one of his pupils in Milan, Uberto Decembrio, who was then in the service of the despot Giangaleazzo Visconti of Milan. But this translation was unsatisfactory and the work was later corrected and refined by Uberto's son, the leading Milanese humanist, Pier Candido Decembrio.[29] A letter of Salutati's mentions that Chrysoloras in Florence began, in addition, to translate the *Geographia* of Ptolemy (further evidence of Palaeologan scientific interests transplanted to Italy). His translation was completed, not too accurately, however, by his pupil Jacopo Angeli da Scarperia, who dedicated the work to his patron, the later Cretan pope of Pisa, Alexander V. (There is another [perhaps earlier] dedication of the work by Scarperia also to Pope Gregory XII.)[30]

Inspired by Chrysoloras, almost all his Italian pupils—Vergerio, Guarino, Bruni, Rossi, Scarperia, Cencius de' Rusticci, and others—became humanists noted for their knowledge and promotion of Greek studies. Bruni in particular translated a number of Aristotle's works, notably the *Politics,* in humanist fashion to replace the *ad verbum* version

27. On Chrysoloras's teaching method in Florence, see Cammelli, *Manuele Crisolora,* 81–85. The evidence comes mainly from his students Cencius de' Rusticci and Guarino of Verona, whose Greek teaching (doubtless modeled on that of Chrysoloras) is described in his son's treatise, translated in W. Woodward, *Vittorino da Feltre and Other Humanist Educators* (New York, 1963), 159–78. On *schedographia,* see above, text at n. 21.

28. Cammelli, *Manuele Crisolora,* 88–92, esp. 91. See preface of Chrysoloras's pupil, Cencius de' Rusticci, to the *Bacchus* of Aristides, where Cencius explicitly cites the translating principle of Chrysoloras: L. Bertalot, *Studien zum italienischen und deutschen Humanismus,* ed. P. O. Kristeller (Rome, 1975), 2:132–33.

29. Cammelli, *Manuele Crisolora,* 89; on Uberto see M. Borsa, "Un umanista vigevanasco del secolo XIV," *Giornale ligustico* 20 (1893): 81–111; and on Pier Candido, see F. Gabotto, "L'attività politica di Pier Candido Decembrio," ibid., 5–75, 423–41. See also Hankins, "A Manuscript of Plato's *Republic.*"

30. See R. Weiss, "Jacopo Angeli da Scarperia," *Medioevo e rinascimento: Studi in onore di Bruno Nardi,* 2:811–12 and n. 50.

Maestro Manuel Chrysoloras teaching Greek letters at the *Studium* in Florence by an anonymous contemporary artist, perhaps his student. From G. Cammelli, *I dotti bizantini e le origini dell' umanesimo, I, Manuele Crisolora* (Florence, 1941). Drawing is in the Louvre Museum, Paris.

of Moerbeke.[31] At the end of his introduction to the *Politics,* Bruni stressed, in evident contrast to the Scholastics, the *flumen aureum* (golden stream) of Aristotle's style as well as thought.[32] It may have been from Chrysoloras that Bruni derived additional knowledge of the enormous range of Aristotle's works. Thus he translated (or in some cases retranslated) Aristotle's *Rhetoric, Ethics,* the pseudo-*Economics,* and logical writings. These versions were not always completely accurate (as the Greek Argyropoulos later put it, they were too freely rendered),[33] but in general they preserved the textual nuances and style more faithfully than did the Scholastic renderings. Bruni in addition translated several of Plato's less difficult works as well as Plutarch's *Lives,* probably again at the inspiration of Chrysoloras. According to Chrysoloras, Plutarch was the best author with whom to start Greek study, as he most successfully bridged the gap between Greeks and Romans. Indeed, owing primarily to the individual and civic virtues extolled in Plutarch (a very popular author in Byzantium), almost every Latin humanist who knew Greek tried his hand at translating him.[34]

In line with early Florentine humanist interest in what has been called civic humanism, Bruni sought out Greek rhetorical texts that might offer material to glorify the republicanism of his city. Thus in his *Laudatio* he drew heavily on the *Panathēnaikos* of the Greek orator Aelius Aristides. The main reason for his use of Aristides apparently was to draw the analogy between the democracy of Athens, which had saved Greek culture from the Persians, and the republicanism of Florence, then locked in struggle with the despotic Visconti of Milan. Moreover, Aristides provided new and more effective Greek rhetorical material for his purposes. H. Baron believes that Bruni was the first Italian humanist not merely to imitate Greek political ideals but also to apply them creatively to the contemporary events of his own epoch.[35]

31. Vasoli's article on Bruni in *Dizionario biografico degli Italiani* 14:618–33; Holmes, *Florentine Enlightenment,* 95.

32. See E. Garin, *Filosofi italiani del quattrocento* (Florence, 1942), 118, passage from the end of Bruni's preface to his Latin translation of Aristotle's *Politics.* But Bruni, basing his views on Cicero, in praising Aristotle's style was thinking of the popular writings of Aristotle now lost. Aristotle's preserved works are only the lecture notes of his students and not really eloquent.

33. Cammelli, *Giovanni Argiropulo* (Florence, 1941), 180, but cf. 93 where earlier Argyropoulos praises Bruni's person. Cf. Holmes, *Florentine Enlightenment,* 263.

34. Cammelli, *Giovanni Argiropulo,* 88–89. See also Chrysoloras's letter (in Greek) to Salutati: *Epistolario di Coluccio Salutati,* ed. F. Novati, 5 vols. (Rome, 1891–1911), 4:333 (quoted in Holmes, *Florentine Enlightenment,* 18). See Cammelli on Chrysoloras's reading of Plutarch with his students.

35. H. Baron, "Imitation, Rhetoric, and Quattrocento Thought in Bruni's *Laudatio,*" in *From Petrarach to Leonardo Bruni* (Chicago, 1968), 115–71, esp. 155–56, 151–53.

A catalytic event for Greek studies in Italy was the Council of Florence, assembled in 1438–39 to reunite the two churches. At this council, to quote a modern critic, a few Greek scholars in attendance conducted a kind of continuing "seminar" in Hellenic studies for the Latins.[36] An official interpreter for the Latins was the Calmaldolese monk Ambrogio Traversari, the first Latin since Burgundio of Pisa in the twelfth century to translate Byzantine church fathers into Latin.[37] The number of Latin scholars present at the council is remarkable, including many celebrated humanists, for example, Bruni, Traversari, Vergerio, Poggio, Valla, Alberti, Guarino, and briefly, Nicholas of Cusa. Opportunities for intellectual exchange were frequent. We know for instance that Mark of Ephesus, the most intransigent anti-unionist Greek bishop, permitted Traversari to examine the manuscripts he had brought with him from Constantinople.[38]

It is now more widely realized that the early Florentine humanists such as Niccolò Niccoli were as interested in the ancient church fathers (including the Greek) as in classical learning. When Leonardo Bruni, for instance, heard of the rediscovery in Rome of the text of St. Basil's *Discourse to Christian Youth on Study of the Greek Classics,* he pounced upon it, translating it into Latin. His version, which was subsequently widely disseminated, was the first or one of the first Greek patristic works in translation to be printed (c. 1470–71).[39] No wonder, for discovery of a work by the highly esteemed Basil supporting, though with qualification, the reading of pagan Greek literary works for their moral value and aid in interpreting the Greek Scriptures was powerful justification for combating the accusation of paganism levied against the early Italian humanists.[40]

The most remarkable humanist development at the Council of Flor-

36. See Setton, "Byzantine Background to Italian Renaissance," 71.

37. On Traversari, see C. Stinger, *Humanism and the Church Fathers: Ambrogio Traversari and Christian Antiquity in the Italian Renaissance* (Albany, N.Y., 1977), who stresses Traversari's indebtedness in learning Greek to the Greek monk Scaranus. On Burgundio, see M. Anastos, "Some Aspects of Byzantine Influence in Latin Thought," in *Twelfth-Century Europe and the Foundations of Modern Society* (Madison, Wis., 1961), 138–49; and esp. P. Classen, "Burgundio von Pisa," *Sitzungsberichte der Heidelberger Akademie der Wissenschaften: Philosophisch-historische Klasse* (1974): 128f.

38. See L. Mehus, *Ambrosii Traversarii . . . latinae epistolae* (Florence, 1959); and D. Traversari, *Ambrogio Traversari e i suoi tempi* (Florence, 1912). On contacts see Woodhouse (n. 45).

39. See, on Bruni's version of Basil, L. Schucan, *Das Nachleben von Basilius Magnus "Ad adolescentes"* (Geneva, 1973), 62–76. See also Geanakoplos, *Interaction of the Sibling Cultures,* 270 and nn. 15, 18. Basil's work is listed in *Gesamtkatalog der Wiegendrücke,* vol. 3 (Leipzig, 1928), no. 3700. See Geanakoplos, "St. Basil, Christian Humanist of the 'Three Hierarchs' and Patron Saint of Greek Letters" (1980).

40. Geanakoplos, *Interaction of the Sibling Cultures,* 270–72 and refs.

ence was the appearance of the Byzantine Platonist Gemistos Pletho of Mistra. At banquets hosted by Cosimo de' Medici Pletho held forth on the pagan philosophic doctrines not only of Plato but also of his Neoplatonic followers such as Iamblichus and Proclus, no few of whom the West now learned of for the first time. In addition, he introduced the occult, arcane works of the Pythagoreans, Hermes Trismegistos, and the Chaldaic oracles.[41] Many scholars maintain that Pletho's lectures and writing had a considerable immediate impact on his Florentine audience. That they were impressed, even enraptured, seems clear, but that they really understood the nuances of this highly sophisticated Byzantine philosophic exegete is, I believe, extremely doubtful.[42] It was during the council that Pletho wrote his famous treatise *On the Differences between Plato and Aristotle.* It was, according to Pletho himself, partly, because of the apparently excessive emphasis of the Italian scholars on Aristotle that Pletho denigrated Aristotle and exalted Plato, which tended to create a greater polarization between the two philosophers than existed in the Byzantine tradition, in which they were not viewed as genuinely antagonistic.[43] Pletho's treatise thus seemed to sharpen for the West the differences between the two and provided an impetus for an accurate translation of all of Plato as well as Aristotle. It is notable that Marsilio Ficino's later translation and interpretation of Plato were drawn from and based in considerable part on the Byzantine tradition, on Psellus, Pletho, Bessarion, and other Byzantine Platonists. Ficino even knew Pletho's tract *De fato.*[44] More concrete evidence of Pletho's direct contact with the Florentine humanists is offered by the corrections that still survive in his own hand on a manuscript containing Bruni's work in Greek on the constitution of Florence.[45]

41. On Pletho, see F. Masai, *Pléthon et le platonisme de Mistra* (Paris, 1956); A. della Torre, *Storia dell'accademia platonica di Firenze* (Florence, 1902), 438ff.; P. O. Kristeller, *Renaissance Thought and Its Sources,* ed. M. Mooney (New York, 1979), 156–58. Now esp. Woodhouse (n. 45 below).

42. Opinion of Kristeller, *Renaissance Thought and Its Sources;* and Monfasani, *George of Trebizond,* 203, based on della Torre, *Storia dell'accademia platonica,* 438ff.

43. See Tatakis, *La philosophie byzantine,* 250–58; Kristeller, *Renaissance Thought and Its Sources,* 157; and E. Garin, *Portraits from the Quattrocento,* tran. V. A. Velen and E. Velen (New York, 1972), 50, showing that Argyropoulos "did not set Pletho against Aristotle." See also Holmes, *Florentine Enlightenment,* 257–59. Cf. Woodhouse, 165–66.

44. Pletho's *De fato* constituted part of his *Laws.* See *Traité des Lois,* ed. C. Alexandre and A. Pelissier (rpt. Amsterdam, 1966), 64–78; Kristeller, *Renaissance Thought and Its Sources,* 156, 304 n. 42. Of course, Ficino's approach to Plato was heavily indebted to Augustine and other Western authors, and he used whatever earlier Latin translations were available.

45. Masai, *Pléthon,* 68. See now C. Woodhouse, *George Gemistos Plethon. The Last of the Hellenes* (Oxford, 1986) esp. 161–65.

The figure whose appearance in Florence helped most to reorient Florentine humanism away from its primarily rhetorical emphasis was not Pletho but the Byzantine professor John Argyropoulos, who later occupied a chair in Greek philosophy at the Florentine *studium* (1456–71).[46] It was during his teaching tenure that the Florentines began, for the first time I believe, fully to understand what Pletho had spoken about and especially, as E. Garin maintains, to view Greek learning in the total context of ancient Greek philosophy and civilization.[47] Ironically, Argyropoulos, who had taught in Constantinople at the higher school called the Katholikon Mouseion,[48] was brought to Florence by several young Florentine Aristotelians in order to expound not Plato but Aristotle. In the morning, Argyropoulos publicly taught and interpreted Aristotle's writings on natural science, notably physics, and on his metaphysics, ethics, and other subjects. In the afternoon, however, in his own home and to a select group of students, he expounded on the philosophical and "theological" doctrines of Plato, on the Pythagoreans, on the Chaldaic oracles, and on the various Neoplatonic successor schools.[49] So deep an impression did his Platonic teaching make that, according to E. Garin, J. Seigel, G. Holmes (and myself), Argyropoulos deserves primary credit for the shift in the focus of Florentine humanism from rhetoric, that is, eloquence, to metaphysical philosophy, particularly Platonism.[50] Argyropoulos's emphasis on understanding Plato as well as Aristotle was undoubtedly an expression of Palaeologan interest in both philosophers. Reflecting also his Byzantine sense of the wholeness of culture (the traditional *enkyklios paideia*), Argyropoulos taught Greek philosophy as a developing organic unity, beginning with the pre-Socratics, the Pythagoreans, and Orpheus, and proceeding systematically to Socrates, Plato, Aristotle, and their successors.[51] Moreover, he did not feel, as many Italian humanists might well have, that he was humbling himself intellectually in writing a small tract on logic modeled on Aristotle's *Organon.*

46. On Argyropoulos, see Cammelli, *Giovanni Argiropulo;* Garin, *Portraits from the Quattrocento,* chap. 3; J. Seigel, "The Teaching of Argyropoulos and the Rhetoric of the First Humanists," in *Action and Conviction in Early Modern Europe,* 237–60; and essay 4 below.

47. Garin, *Portraits from the Quattrocento,* 71, 75, and esp. 82.

48. At the so-called Xenon. Fuchs, *Die höheren Schulen von Konstantinopel,* 71.

49. See esp. Garin, *Portraits from the Quattrocento,* 68–83.

50. Ibid., 70, 80; Seigel, "Teaching of Argyropoulos"; Holmes, *Florentine Enlightenment,* 262–65; and the end of essay 4 below.

51. Garin, *Portraits from the Quattrocento,* 75–79. On Argyropoulos's teaching in Florence, see most recently A. Field, "John Argyropoulos and the 'Secret Teachings' of Plato," in *Supplementum Festivum,* ed. Hankins, Monfasani, and Purnell, 299–326. See also essay 4.

His profound knowledge of both Latin and Greek (he had received a doctorate from Padua University)[52] made him the ideal interpreter to explicate the teachings of Plato and Aristotle to the Latins. It remained for the Florentine Ficino, who apparently did not study formally with Argyropoulos but, I believe, was at least indirectly influenced by his teaching, to produce the Renaissance synthesis of Catholic Christianity and Neoplatonic thought.[53]

The importance of Florence under Ficino as a center for the radiation of Platonic thought is too well known to need repetition. I should mention, however, still another Byzantine, the Athenian Demetrius Chalcondyles, a student of Pletho's at Mistra, who in 1476 succeeded Andronicus Callistos's successor, Argyropoulos, in the Florentine *studium.* According to the German scribe Hartmann Schedel, who earlier in 1463 had copied down Chalcondyles's inaugural address on the establishment of the first Greek chair at Padua, Chalcondyles, when in Florence, had explained to Ficino (difficult) passages in Plato's *Dialogues.*[54]

Angelo Poliziano, who without doubt studied with Argyropoulos, is an outstanding example of a Florentine humanist who was able to take what the Byzantines offered and, fusing it with his deep knowledge of Latin literature, apply it to benefit his own works in Latin and even Italian, for example, in his important essay *Miscellanea;* in other pieces of criticism on Greek epic, lyric poetry, and rhetoric; and in his translations of Plutarch, Homer, and other Greek authors. What Poliziano gained particularly from Byzantine interpretations of ancient Greek literary and rhetorical works was a new awareness of the subtlety and nuances of classical style as well as content, both in poetry and prose. Poliziano was one of the first Italian humanists to give lectures on Aristotle on the basis of the Greek text, to which his attention was directed by the Venetian Ermolao Barbaro as well as by Argyropoulos.[55]

52. Cammelli, *Giovanni Argiropulo,* 23–26.

53. On the influence of the Byzantine tradition on Ficino, see Kristeller, *Renaissance Thought and Its Sources,* 161–62. Nothing concrete seems to be known about links between Ficino and Argyropoulos. See essay 4, p. 108.

54. Geanakoplos, *Interaction of the Sibling Cultures,* 254, 296. Ficino himself says he consulted Chalcondyles before publishing his Plato translation: see P. O. Kristeller, *Supplementum Ficinianum* (Florence, 1937), 2:105. Cf. below n. 94.

55. On Poliziano, see Garin, *Portraits from the Quattrocento,* chap. 6, esp. 171–73, for his relations with Argyropoulos and other Greeks. On his lectures (and MSS, esp. on Aristotle), see I. Maïer, *Les manuscrits d'Ange Politien* (Geneva, 1965), 189, 227–28, 323–24, 336–38, 432–34; I. del Lungo, *Florentia, uomini e cose del quattrocento* (Florence, 1897, (133f., 175f. See below, nn. 100–101 on Tomaeus and his work on Aristotle in Padua. Mention should be made of Francesco Filelfo, one of the quattrocento's best Hellenists (he even wrote Greek verse), who was in Florence only briefly, however, spending most of his life in Milan.

The Florentine humanist mastery of Greek style, together with an increasing knowledge of Greek vocabulary, syntax, and structure,[56] probably carried over into Florentine historical writing, especially after translation into Latin of the major Greek historians.[57] Bruni, in writing his *History of Florence,* was very likely influenced by the work of Plutarch and Polybius as well as by such Romans as Livy, and the Florentine Villani. And Machiavelli, as has been shown by G. Sasso, also drew upon the work of Polybius, though far more, of course, on the Latin and vernacular Italian historical traditions.[58]

Rome

While Florence's primacy in Greek letters extended to the end of the quattrocento, Rome's rise to prominence in Greek studies began in the mid fifteenth century, during the pontificate especially of Nicholas V, and continued for about one and a half decades, that is from about 1440 to 1455.[59] The principal "institution" in Rome for Greek scholarship was the so-called academy founded by Pope Nicholas and Bessarion, the Byzantine cardinal of the Roman church. Its prime purpose was the translation into Latin of classical Greek writings as well as Byzantine church fathers.[60] Bessarion's academy included, besides Greeks, learned Latins of the Curia who knew Greek, such as Giovanni Tortelli, who journeyed to Byzantium to study there even before Constantinople's fall, as did a number of other Latins in this period.[61]

56. Kristeller, *Renaissance Thought and Its Sources,* 142–43.

57. Thucydides and Herodotus were translated by Valla, and Polybius by Perotti (earlier paraphrased by Bruni), while Xenophon's *Cyropaedia* was translated by Filelfo and paraphrased by Poggio, and his *Hellenica* paraphrased by Bruni.

58. Bruni was influenced by Polybius, as shown by B. L. Ullman, "Leonardo Bruni and Humanist Historiography," *Medievalia et humanistica* 4 (1946): 50. Also on Polybius's influence on Bruni, see H. Baron, *Crisis of the Early Italian Renaissance* (Princeton, 1966), 410, 508 n. 14; and on Machiavelli, see C. Sasso, "Polibio e Machiavelli: Costituzione, potenza, conquista," *Giornale critico della filosofia italiana* 40 (1961): 51–86, esp. 86, 50.

59. In 1380–81 the Byzantine Simon Atumano seems to have briefly taught Greek in Rome to Raoul de Rivo, evidently for ecclesiastical purposes. See G. Fedalto, *Simone Atumano monaco di studio* (Brescia, 1968), 105; Setton, "Byzantine Background to Italian Renaissance," 49–50.

60. On Bessarion, see L. Mohler, *Kardinal Bessarion als Theologe, Humanist und Staatsmann,* 3 vols. (Paderborn, 1923–42), esp. vol. 3; H. Vast, *Le Cardinal Bessarion* (Paris, 1878); and the entry on him by L. Labowsky in *Dizionario biografico degli Italiani* 9:686–96.

61. On Tortelli, see Holmes, *Florentine Enlightenment,* 251; Monfasani, *George of*

The major translators in the papal court were two Byzantines, the polemical Cretan George of Trebizond and the more irenic Theodore Gaza from Thessalonica, intense rivals but each highly competent. A biography of George has recently been written which elucidates many obscure points in this period of Roman primacy while revealing new aspects of the career of a truly major humanist.[62] From Crete in 1415, George of Trebizond, at the age of twenty, came to Venice, invited by his patron, the Venetian patrician Francesco Barbaro, for whom he probably translated manuscripts and to whom he probably taught Greek in exchange for Latin lessons. It was George's primary aim to learn and then to teach *Latin* rhetoric in Italy, enriched by his background of Palaeologan Greek studies. George studied Latin with the greatest Latinist of the day, Vittorino da Feltre. With his wide background of interests, derived at least in part from the influence of the broad scope of Palaeologan education, he engaged in a very wide range of intellectual activities, including rhetoric, logic, Greek and Latin apocalyptic literature, philosophy, and theology.

Most important, through his Latin treatise *Rhetoricorum libri V,* he brought to the awareness of Western humanists the writer whom Bessarion called "the greatest glory of Greek rhetoric," Hermogenes.[63] (None other than Lorenzo Valla wrote that George was generally considered the most learned rhetorician of Italy in the Latin language.) In the *Rhetoricorum libri V,* George set forth the contents of Hermogenes' masterful analysis of ways to move an audience. In this work he was able to fuse the Byzantine Hermogenean rhetorical tradition with the Latin tradition of Cicero, which he greatly esteemed.[64] Some Byzantine scholars, however, tended to denigrate Ciceronian rhetoric, notably John Argyropoulos,[65] perhaps because Cicero was the only authority for most Latins, who did not know the Greek sources of rhetoric.

George's treatise on rhetoric, after its gradual assimilation by the Italian humanists, became the leading Italian and, later, northern Renaissance rhetorical text, supplementing or even supplanting the rhetorical writings of Cicero and Quintilian. George, along with Valla, also was one

---

Trebizond, 38, 80–81; and esp. G. Mancini, "Giovanni Tortelli Cooperatore di Niccolò V," *Archivio storico italiano* 78 (1920): 161–268.

62. Monfasani, *George of Trebizond,* 69–179. On Gaza see below essay 3.

63. E. Legrand, *Cent-dix lettres de F. Filelfe* (Paris, 1892); Monfasani, *George of Trebizond,* 254.

64. Monfasani, *George of Trebizond,* 80, 249–55, 265, 272, 290ff.

65. Garin, *Portraits from the Quattrocento,* 82; Cammelli, *Giovanni Argiropulo,* 176–78. See essay 4 below.

of the first humanists in Italy to write a treatise (in Latin) on logic, a field generally considered the domain of the Scholastics.[66]

At the request of Pope Nicholas V and Bessarion, George turned into Latin no fewer than eleven major Greek texts, some never before translated, others translated for the first time in the humanist manner. His versions were not infrequently criticized, but they were on the whole well executed, the flaws in most cases being attributable to factors over which he had little or no control. For example, George's papal patron insisted that in his translation of the Greek church father Eusebius's *De praeparatione evangelica,* he delete any statements reflecting Eusebius's Arian beliefs.[67] George's method of translation was sensible: to adhere closely to the original in the case of scientific texts (Aristotle and Ptolemy especially) but to provide a more flexible rendering in the case of the Greek historians and the fathers of the Byzantine church.[68]

His translation of Ptolemy's capital work on astronomy and mathematics the *Almagest (Mathēmatikē syntaxis),* which was already available in the faulty twelfth-century Latin version of Gerard of Cremona, was of extraordinary importance for the future development of mathematics and astronomy. Believing that Ptolemy's text had been corrupted by his Arab translator, George, at the personal suggestion of Bessarion, appended a lengthy commentary to his translation explicating Ptolemy's astronomic theories on the basis of, or rather often in disagreement with, the ancient Greek commentary of Theon of Alexandria, hitherto unknown in the West. George's commentary but not his translation was then evaluated but sharply condemned by the Italian scholar in the Curia, Jacopo da Cremona, who had previously translated Archimedes.[69] George's version of Ptolemy's *Almagest,* nevertheless, subsequently became standard, although, surprisingly, the Greek text was not printed until much later, in 1538.[70] In addition, George rendered into Latin for the first time Pseudo-Ptolemy's work, the *Centiloquium,* containing one hundred aphorisms dealing primarily with astrology,[71] a subject contrib-

66. Monfasani, *George of Trebizond,* 306, where Monfasani says Valla perhaps completed his work one year before George finished his manual. Even before 1400 the humanist Vergerio had taught logic in Padua, though apparently writing no work on it.

67. Geanakoplos, *Interaction of the Sibling Cultures,* 272 and n. 22; Monfasani, *George of Trebizond,* 78.

68. Monfasani, *George of Trebizond,* 76nn.

69. Ibid., 232–33, 104–5. On Bessarion's suggestion, see ibid., 108 and n. 165.

70. See E. Sandys, *A History of Classical Scholarship* (New York, 1964), 2:490. The text was edited by Grynaeus at Basel.

71. Discussed in J. Monfasani, *Collectanea Trapezuntiana: Texts, Bibliographies, and*

uting no little to the development of Renaissance astronomy. For Nicholas of Cusa, George translated into Latin Plato's *Parmenides.*[72] Cusanus, though very interested in Platonism and the Dionysian writings, probably never learned Greek well. He himself relates that, when, before the Council of Florence, he represented the papacy in Constantinople, he there sought out Greek manuscripts (probably of Plato)[73] and that it was during his boat trip back home from Constantinople that he conceived the main philosophical ideas for his chief work, *De docta ignorantia.*[74]

In addition to scientific and literary translations, George turned into Latin more of the Greek church fathers than is generally realized, including works of Gregory of Nazianzus, Basil, Gregory of Nyssa, Athanasius, and more striking, works of Cyril of Alexandria and Eusebius's *De praeparatione evangelica,* the last of which soon became very popular in Italy. He also produced a Latin version of the extremely valuable homilies of Chrysostom on Matthew, then hardly known in the West except for a small portion of an ancient Latin version and the little-used rendering of the twelfth-century Burgundio of Pisa. George's many translations had a far wider dissemination than has hitherto been recognized.[75] He therefore played a major role in promoting a greater knowledge of both ancient Greek classical and Byzantine ecclesiastical learning

Documents of George of Trebizond (Binghamton, N.Y., 1985). The *Centiloquium* is now believed to be an Arabic work.

72. See, on Plato's *Parmenides,* R. Klibansky, *The Continuity of the Platonic Tradition . . . with Plato's Parmenides* (Millwood, N.Y., 1982). P. O. Kristeller, "A Latin Translation of Gemistos Pletho's *De fato* by Johannes Sophianos dedicated to Nicholas of Cusa," in *Nicolò Cusano agli inizi del mondo moderno: Atti del congresso internazionale in occasione del V centenario della morte di Nicolò Cusano Bressanone, 1964* (Florence, 1970), 175–93.

73. See M. Honecker, "Nikolaus von Cues und die griechischen Sprache," *Sitzungsberichte der Heidelberger Akademie der Wissenschaften: Philosophisch-historische Klasse* 28 (1938): 13. Also, on reports of the conciliar and papal envoys in Constantinople, see E. Cecconi, *Studi sul concilio di Firenze* (Florence, 1869), dix ff. and dixxvi ff. Finally, on the *Docta ignorantia,* see E. Vansteenburghe, *Le Cardinal Nicolas de Cues* (Paris, 1920), 27–28. (On Cusanus and his ms. at the Council of Florence see essay 11 below.)

74. P. Watts, *Nicolaus Cusanus: A Fifteenth Century Vision of Man* (Leiden, 1982), 5. Greeks with whom Cusanus had conversations on the boat while returning to the council may possibly have helped inspire or develop some of his ideas.

75. See Monfasani, *Collectanea Trapezuntiana.* It is also shown in his *George of Trebizond.* For the Byzantine émigrés and the Greek church fathers see Geanakoplos, "The Last Step: Western Recovery and Translation of the Greek Church Fathers and Their First Printed Editions in the Renaissance," chap. 14 of *Interaction of the Sibling Cultures,* 265–80, which, in revised form, constitutes this book's Appendix.

in Italy. (On Theodore Gaza's important activity in Rome see below essay 3.)

Striking advances have recently been made in the study of New Testament textual criticism in the Renaissance. These advances are concerned primarily with the Greek scholarship of Lorenzo Valla, secretary in the papal Curia during the mid-fifteenth century. In 1444, in Naples, even before he went to Rome, Valla had undertaken a comparison (*Collatio,* he entitled his work) of Jerome's Vulgate text and the Greek New Testament, a work, we are told, that was read by the Byzantine cardinal Bessarion, an intimate of Valla's.[76] Valla himself notes that he had heard from "quidam Graeci" ("certain Greeks")—probably Gaza and Bessarion—of errors existing in a passage or rather passages of Jerome's Latin Vulgate version.[77] S. Camporeale admits Bessarion's influence on Valla in at least one important textual reading, that of John 21.22.[78] It seems almost certain, then, that the Byzantine émigrés—"some learned scholars," as M. Fois puts it—exercised no slight influence on the development and possibly even the genesis of Valla's thought with regard to a Latin New Testament text corresponding more closely to the Greek original than the several existing Latin Vulgate versions—a process of thought later resulting in Valla's epoch-making *Annotationes* (or *Adnotationes*).

Valla is also credited with suspecting the authenticity of the apostolic authority of the "Dionysian" corpus of mystical writings.[79] These works were already suspect in the eyes of certain early Byzantine theologians such as the sixth-century Hypatius of Ephesus.[80] Valla himself, in his *Annotationes,* refers to the suspicions of "certain very learned Greeks of our time" who (in accord with one Byzantine view) associated the Dionysian writings with the fourth-century Apollinaris of Laodicea. It is therefore again plausible to believe, without gainsaying any of Valla's remarkable historical acumen, that he was probably influenced in his suspicions

76. Lorenzo Valla, *Collatio Novi Testamenti,* ed. A. Perosa (Florence, 1970). For Bessarion's help on special passages in the *Collatio,* see xxiv, xlix. See also S. Camporeale, *Lorenzo Valla* (Florence, 1972), 366, 389; and M. Fois, *Il pensiero cristiano di Lorenzo Valla* (Rome, 1969), 416–19.

77. On "quidam Graeci," see Fois, *Il pensiero cristiano,* 417.

78. Valla, *Collatio,* xxxiv.

79. In his *Opera,* 1:852b, Valla wrote, "De libris Dionysii nemo veterum habuit mentionem neque Latinorum neque Graecorum." See Camporeale, *Lorenzo Valla,* 429–30. Now also Monfasani, cited in next note.

80. See *Oxford Dictionary of the Christian Church* (Oxford, 1963), 402; Runciman, *Last Byzantine Renaissance,* 44; also J. Monfasani, "Pseudo-Dionysus the Areopagite," in *Supplementum Festivum,* ed. Hankins, Monfasani, and Purnell.

by Greek scholars in the papal Curia such as the erudite Theodore Gaza, though evidently in this case not by Bessarion, who in contrast held to the traditional view of authorship of the Dionysian writings.[81]

The increasing availability of Byzantine texts and commentaries on the New Testament may well have contributed also to the Western interest in St. Paul, as evidenced by the almost simultaneous study of the Pauline writings on the part of Ficino, Colet, Lefèvre, Reuchlin, and, later, Erasmus.[82] One cannot help wonder whether certain Greek commentaries on Paul, the very important ones of Origen in particular, now made known to Italian humanists in the original Greek version, did not foster questions about the accuracy of the Latin text and Western interpretations thereof.[83]

The manuscripts used by George of Trebizond, Gaza, Perotti (Bessarion's secretary), perhaps Valla, and others for making translations from ancient Greek authors or Greek Fathers very often came from Bessarion's Greek manuscript collection, the greatest in the Renaissance.[84] Of course, Bessarion was not alone in collecting Greek codices; Corbinelli, Cencius (who secured Chrysoloras's library), Aurispa, and Giorgio Valla, among other Latins, assembled an impressive number.[85] Yet through his many codices on Greek mathematics in particular, Bessarion was able to promote mathematical study considerably. Euclid and Archimedes had already been translated by the indefatigable Scholastic Moerbeke. But, as Paul Rose has shown, Bessarion was instrumental in inculcating in Regiomontanus, a German humanist who later became the Renaissance's leading mathematician, an intense interest in Archimedes and in the Pseudo-Aristotle's *Mechanica,* both works of first importance for dealing with, among other things, stresses and balances, and in the treatise of the fourth-century Byzantine Pappus, who also wrote on

81. Camporeale, *Lorenzo Valla,* 428–30. See also essay 3 below, p. 86 and nn. 58, 59.

82. My view. Also see N. Robb, *Neoplatonism of the Italian Renaissance* (New York, 1968).

83. On Origen's commentaries on St. Paul, see E. Wind, "The Revival of Origen," *Studies in Art and Literature for Bella Costa Greene,* ed. D. Miner (Princeton, N.J., 1954), 412–24. For other Italians (such as Traversari), see Stinger, *Humanism and the Church Fathers,* 33, 152.

84. On Bessarion's collection, see L. Labowsky, "Bessarion Studies," *Medieval and Renaissance Studies* 5 (1961): 108–62; Labowsky, "Il Cardinale Bessarione e gli inizi della Biblioteca marciana," *Venezia e l'Oriente fra tardo medio evo e rinascimento,* ed. A. Pertusi (Florence, 1966), 159–82.

85. On most of these, see Stinger, *Humanism and the Church Fathers;* R. Blum, *La Biblioteca della badia fiorentina e i codici di Antonio Corbinelli, studi e testi,* vol. 155 (Vatican, 1951); R. Sabbadini, *Carteggio di G. Aurispa* (Rome, 1931); and J. B. Heiberg, "Beiträge zur Geschichte Georg Vallas und seiner Bibliothek," *Centralblatt für Bibliothekswesen* 16 (1896): 1–129.

mechanics.[86] Partly as a result of Bessarion's patronage, mathematics in time became among the humanists a veritable appendage to the *studia humanitatis.*[87] Rome's less-important period of efflorescence in Greek studies in the late fifteenth and early sixteenth centuries I shall have to pass over here.[88]

Venice

Venice and its satellite city Padua, with its great university, constituted in many ways a single nucleus of culture. I shall therefore deal with them together. In Venice there existed the largest of the Greek émigré communities in Italy, one reason that Bessarion called Venice *alterum Byzantium.* But despite Venice's centuries-long connections with the Greek East, Venetian humanism did not clearly emerge until intellectual influences flowed to Venice from nearby Padua and Florence. Nevertheless, with the coming of the Greek exiles before and especially after 1453, there was a genuine intensification of Venetian humanist interests.[89] At Padua (as in other Italian universities) the medical school and the school of letters constituted a single faculty, hence Paduan interest in employing professors who could teach not only literary but scientific subjects as well. At Padua, from the time at least of the "Averroist" Peter of Abano, the scientific and other writings of Aristotle above all were studied but, notably, for a long time not from the original Greek text but in the Arab "Averroist" translations and interpretations.[90]

The long supremacy at Padua of the so-called Averroist tradition—I

86. See P. Rose, *The Italian Renaissance of Mathematics* (Geneva, 1975), esp. 44–46, noting Bessarion's influence on Regiomontanus; Geanakoplos, *Byzantine East and Latin West* (Oxford, 1966), 23, 26, on Moerbeke's translations; and P. Rose and S. Drake, "The Pseudo-Aristotelian *Questions of Mechanics* in Renaissance Culture," *Studies in the Renaissance* 18 (1971): 75–76.

87. Rose, *The Italian Renaissance of Mathematics,* 44–46, 49, 56. Cf. E. Cochrane, "Science and Humanism in the Italian Renaissance," *American Historical Review* 81 (1976): 105–6, on science and the *studia humanitatis.*

88. On this period, see Geanakoplos, *Greek Scholars in Venice,* 215–17, 248–49.

89. Ibid., 70, 33–40.

90. Nevertheless, Peter of Abano, who spent most of his life in Paris, being only briefly in Padua at the end of his life, had sought Greek MSS of Aristotle in Constantinople and had translated his pseudo-*Problemata.* See L. Norpoth, "Zur Biobibliographie und Wissenschaftslehre des Pietro d'Abano," *Kyklos: Jahrbuch für Geschichte und Philosophie der Medizin* 3 (1930): 293–353; L. Thorndike, *A History of Magic and Experimental Science* (New York, 1929), vol. 2, chap. 70, 874–947; Thorndike, "Peter of Abano and Another Commentary on the *Problems* of Aristotle," *Bulletin of the History of Medicine* 29 (1955): 517–23.

personally prefer Kristeller's less ambiguous and more accurate term, "Italian secular Aristotelianism"[91]—which flourished especially during the mid and later fifteenth century, began seriously to be challenged with the coming of the Byzantine émigrés with what they considered to be their more authentic texts of Aristotle and other scientific authors. Yet the Greek versions of Aristotle did not make any really effective impact in Padua—they were in fact resisted—until espousal of their cause by the leading Venetian humanists Ermolao Barbaro and Girolamo Donato, both of whom had studied with Greek teachers. Partly under the influence of the Byzantines, especially Theodore Gaza, with whom he had studied in Rome, Ermolao—who had contempt for Scholastic philosophy but was enamored of Greek literature, philosophy, and science—began to insist at Padua on recognition of the greater authority of the ancient Greek and early Byzantine commentators for explicating Aristotle.[92] As recently shown by Kristeller in his translation of the Byzantine commentator Themistius, Ermolao, despite his antipathy for the Scholastics, still utilized the old Scholastic translation but interpolated interlinearly material drawn from other Greek commentators.[93]

Earlier in 1463, as noted above, the Venetian Senate, at the urging primarily of Bessarion and perhaps Filelfo, had established the first chair for the teaching of Greek at Padua University, to which it appointed the Byzantine Demetrius Chalcondyles. In his inaugural orations (which I recently edited), Chalcondyles, like virtually all the Byzantines, lamented the corrupt manuscripts and translations of Aristotle and other Greek authors in use in Italy.[94] (The Byzantine émigrés, Pletho for example, also criticized Averroës' versions of Aristotle, and some liked to point out that Averroës knew no Greek.)[95] With medicine and letters so closely

91. P. O. Kristeller, *Renaissance Thought,* vol. 2 (New York, 1965), 111–18; Kristeller, "Renaissance Aristotelianism," *Greek, Roman and Byzantine Studies* 6 (1965): 163. But Averroism continued to be taught at Padua even through the sixteenth century.

92. For Ermolao's study with Gaza while Barbaro's father was Venetian ambassador to Rome, see *Dizionario biografico degli Italiani* 6:96–99. For Donato, see V. Branca, "Ermolao Barbaro and Late Quattrocento Humanism," in *Renaissance Venice,* ed. J. Hale (London, 1973), 227f. Now see V. Branca, "L'umanesimo veneziano alla Fine del quattrocento: Ermolao Barbaro e il suo circolo," *Storia della cultura veneta,* vol. 3, pt. 1 (Vicenza, 1980), 123–75.

93. P. O. Kristeller, *Studies in Renaissance Thought and Letters* (Rome, 1956), 352–53. See also Branca, "Ermolao Barbaro," 225–27.

94. Geanakoplos, "The Discourse of Demetrius Chalcondyles" (1974), 235; expanded in *Interaction of the Sibling Cultures,* chap. 13, esp. 246, 299. For the most accurate Latin text of the discourse see the Greek translation of *Interaction* entitled *Byzantio kai dysē,* 430–41.

95. Kristeller, *Renaissance Thought and Its Sources,* 161.

associated at Padua, it seems very probable that Chalcondyles taught there not only Greek grammar and literature but also scientific treatises, especially those of Aristotle.[96]

In 1470 the Venetian Senate received from George of Trebizond, then in Rome, the dedication of his Latin translation, the very first, of Plato's important treatise the *Laws*. In his dedicatory letter, George hyperbolically affirmed that the founding fathers of the Venetian state must have known Plato's *Laws* when they drew up their mixed constitution![97]

The rivalry between the entrenched Averroist tradition at Padua and the increasing support for the Greek versions of Aristotle grew more intense in the last decade of the fifteenth century. At this time, not long after Ermolao began teaching there, the leading Averroists were Nicoletto Vernia and his pupil and successor Agostino Nifo. E. Mahoney has shown that seven years before his death in 1499, Vernia sharply attacked Averroës' interpretation of Aristotle's views on the immortality of the soul, going so far as to condemn Averroës' view as the "perversam opinionem Averrois."[98] In his reversal of opinion Vernia had evidently been gradually influenced by the activities of Barbaro, the Byzantine exiles, and in particular the manifest superiority of the Greek texts of the ancient commentators now at hand. Already in 1472 Bessarion had bequeathed to Venice his entire library of Greek manuscripts, which contained many of Aristotle's scientific treatises.[99] In any case, as a result of Vernia's semidefection, the changing view of his successor Nifo, certainly Barbaro's efforts, and, not least, the impact of the new Greek manuscripts put forward by the Byzantines, the Venetian Senate in 1497 appointed a Greek, Nicolaus Leonicus Tomaeus, born in Venice, to a chair at Padua to read Aristotle "in the Greek [text]."[100]

This was a veritable triumph for the Greek text, meaning the traditional Byzantine interpretation, of the Aristotelian corpus. For what Tomaeus began above all to emphasize in his lectures was the Aristotelian texts as explicated by the ancient Greek and early Byzantine commentators.[101] These included Simplicius, Philoponus of sixth-century Alexandria (who anticipated the fourteenth-century impetus theory of

96. Geanakoplos, *Interaction of the Sibling Cultures,* 246.

97. Monfasani, *George of Trebizond,* 102–3.

98. E. Mahony, "Nicoletto Vernia on the Soul and Immortality," in *Philosophy and Humanism: Festschrift for Paul Oskar Kristeller,* ed. E. Mahoney (New York, 1976), 144, 149ff.

99. Geanakoplos, *Interaction of the Sibling Cultures,* 177–78; and Labowsky, "Il Cardinale Bessarione," 159–82.

100. For document of appointment, see J. Facciolatus, *De gymnasio patavini,* vol. 1 (Padua, 1752), under a. 1497, and pp. 56–57.

101. See essay 5 on Tomaeus.

projectile motion), Themistius, and, finally, the philosopher Alexander of Aphrodisias, who is noted particularly for his commentary on Aristotle's *De anima.*[102] The questions of the unity of the intellect and the immortality of the soul had for some time been burning issues at Padua among the so-called Averroists, not least because Aristotle himself was not always clear on certain points.[103] Averroës' hitherto prevailing commentary on Aristotle's *De anima* now began to be challenged by the interpretation provided by Alexander of Aphrodisias. The Greek commentators, who had been increasingly studied during the Palaeologan Renaissance, left a large range of materials on Aristotle's works.[104] Also in this period of the Italian Renaissance certain pseudo-Aristotelian writings were studied—the pseudo-*Economica,* pseudo-*Mechanica,* and pseudo-*Problemata.*[105] The idea finally had taken firm hold at Padua not only that the Greek manuscripts provided surer texts than those coming second-hand via Arab translations, but also that ancient Greek commentators could provide more-authentic interpretations of Aristotle's works.

The significant role of the Byzantines in the Greek academy and the publishing house of Aldus Manutius I have discussed in detail elsewhere.[106] I shall restrict myself here to only a few observations. The Cretan Marcus Musurus, Aldus's leading collaborator and also professor of Greek at Padua University, edited a very large number of first editions of Greek authors, including the complete works of Aristophanes and the writings of Plato. Even better known and hardly less impressive was Aldus's edition in 1495–98 of the *Opera* of Aristotle in Greek, possibly as a response to the earlier publication in Latin, in 1472, of Aristotle's works with all of Averroës' commentaries.[107] This Greek edition was of the highest importance because it provided for the first time reasonably accurate *Greek* texts of Aristotle. During the following years Aldus edited for the first time (probably with the aid of Musurus) Greek texts of the commentators Themistius and Alexander of Aphrodisias, while Musurus, evidently alone, edited the Greek authors Pausanias and Hesychius,

102. For translation of Philoponus see Geanakoplos, *Byzantium: Church, Society, and Civilization Seen through Contemporary Eyes,* no. 324. On Aristotle's *De anima,* see F. E. Cranz on Alexander of Aphrodisias, in *Catalogus Translationum et Commentariorum,* ed. P. O. Kristeller and F. E. Cranz, vol. 1 (Washington, D.C., 1960), 77–135.

103. Kristeller, "Renaissance Aristotelianism," 131.

104. See the example of George Scholarios, cited in Runciman, *Last Byzantine Renaissance,* 83.

105. "Pseudo" usually means that a work was probably not by Aristotle but by one of his students. For Aristotelian commentaries, see *Commentaria in Aristotelem graeca,* ed. Berlin Academy (1882–1909).

106. Esp. in Geanakoplos, *Greek Scholars in Venice,* 116–66, 226ff., and passim.

107. See A. Renouard, *Annales de l'imprimerie des Alde,* 3d ed. (Paris, 1834), 1:7–16.

though, perhaps surprisingly, not the historian Polybius.[108] Polybius was popular in Venetian and Florentine humanist circles, especially with Machiavelli and Guicciardini, and not only because of his analytical power, style, and stress on the theory of the mixed constitution. He was also, as Vergerio had put it earlier, "that Greek who alone tells us so much about an early period of Roman history."[109]

The teachings of Musurus and Tomaeus at Padua, though overlapping in time, evidently differed somewhat in scope. As successor to Chalcondyles' Greek chair, Musurus's primary emphasis was apparently on Greek literature, especially the poets and dramatists, including Planudes' noted collection of poetry, the *Greek Anthology.* As inheritor of the Palaeologan methods of textual criticism established by Demetrius Triklinios, Thomas Magister, and Manuel Moschopoulos, Musurus doubtless analyzed for his students the complex meters of ancient drama following the views of Triklinios, who in the fourteenth century had rediscovered a manuscript of Hephaestion explaining this technique.[110] This recently recovered knowledge of metrics, so vital for understanding ancient Greek poetry, Musurus applied to his own "Hymn to Plato," which prefixed his famous *editio princeps* of Plato in 1513.[111]

Tomaeus, whose name is probably unfamiliar to most Renaissance historians, must have stressed Aristotle's philosophy in his teaching at Padua, but to judge from his published editions of Greek texts and his translations into Latin,[112] this was philosophy in the broad sense, including Aristotle's metaphysics, moral and natural philosophy (that is physics), and biology and logic. Special mention should be made of Tomaeus's translation (which became standard) of Pseudo-Aristotle's *Mechanica.* Like Archimedes' *Mechanica,* this work, with its emphasis on the new "quantitative" physics (based on mathematics) rather than the older

108. On Pausanias and Hesychius see Geanakoplos, *Greek Scholars in Venice,* 154, 149, 154–55. Simplicius was first edited by the Greek Calliergis, p. 208. The Greek text of Polybius was not published until 1530, edited by Obsopoeus: see Sandys, *History of Classical Scholarship,* 2:105.

109. Woodward, *Vittorino da Feltre and Other Humanist Educators,* 106.

110. See Reynolds and Wilson, *Scribes and Scholars,* 66–67, 40–41, and Turyn on the manuscript traditions of Aeschylus, Sophocles, and Euripides.

111. For translation of part of this poem, considered, exaggeratedly, by E. Legrand the best poem in Greek since antiquity, see Geanakoplos, *Greek Scholars in Venice,* 152–53. On a pupil of Musurus, see M. Sicherl, *Johannes Cuno* (Heidelberg, 1978).

112. For these, see E. Legrand, *Bibliographie hellénique ou description raisonnée des ouvrages publiés en grec par des grecs au XVe et XVI^le^ siècles,* 4 vols. (Paris, 1885–1906), 3:281–84, 336–39, 438–44, etc. Tomaeus's most important manuscript is his letter-book in the Vatican, published in great part by Cardinal Gasquet in *Cardinal Pole and His Early Friends* (London, 1927). See essay 5.

Italy during the Italian Renaissance

"qualitative" Aristotelian physics, occupies a place leading to the development of early modern science.[113] Philology also interested Tomaeus, as we see by his contribution to the textual tradition of Plutarch's *Moralia*.[114] The Venetian government named Tomaeus preceptor to the many high-ranking English students studying at Padua, including the

113. Rose and Drake, "The Pseudo-Aristotelian *Questions of Mechanics*," 79–80, 68; Kristeller, "Renaissance Aristotelianism," 173–74.

114. See A. Turyn, *Dated Greek Manuscripts of the Thirteenth and Fourteenth Centuries in the Libraries of Italy*, 2 vols. (Urbana, Ill., 1972), 1:xx, 85–87.

later-famous Cardinal Pole. In a letter to the latter, Tomaeus requested a copy of More's *Utopia* in exchange for one of his own writings.[115]

Renouard believes the most valuable of all Aldine editions was the *Rhetores graeci,* which included Aristotle's *Rhetoric* and *Poetics* (both omitted from Aldus's Greek *Opera* of Aristotle). The *Rhetores graeci* was edited in 1508, primarily by the Cretan Demetrius Ducas.[116] Hermogenes' works occupy at least half of the edition, in contrast to the *Rhetoric* of Aristotle, which has a distinctly minor place. This difference reflects the differing attitudes of Byzantium and the West toward Aristotle's *Rhetoric.* In Byzantium it could not compete with Hermogenes' much more impressive treatises. In the medieval West, however, where Aristotle's *Rhetoric* was relatively little known (through Moerbeke's Scholastic translation), it was, because of its extensive discussion of the emotions, read by Scholastic philosophers in connection with Aristotle's *Ethics* and *Politics.*[117] The *Rhetoric* was later retranslated in humanist fashion and thereafter rather widely read by Renaissance rhetoricians, although it was subsequently displaced in popularity by Hermogenes' works.

As for Aristotle's *Poetics,* which also had been translated by Moerbeke, its contents were misinterpreted by Western medieval and early Renaissance scholars, who read the work in conjunction with Aristotle's *Organon,* that is, logical writings.[118] Not apparently until the impact of the Byzantine émigrés and the work of the Renaissance humanists Ermolao Barbaro and Giorgio Valla was it interpreted as a treatise of aesthetics, as Aristotle had evidently intended.

To return to the little-known Tomaeus: As a youth he had studied with his compatriot Chalcondyles in Florence.[119] Thus he too was to some extent in the Palaeologan tradition, as well as constituting a link between Florentine and Paduan humanism. Tomaeus was very open-minded; in explicating Aristotle he several times admitted that Aristotle was wrong on certain points. Once he even affirmed his preference for Averroës' interpretation over Aristotle's position on a particular question. Tomaeus's views on the debated questions of the unity of the intellect and

115. On Thomas More (and other English students), see Gasquet, *Cardinal Pole,* 11ff., 66ff.

116. Renouard, *Annales de l'imprimerie des Alde,* 54; Geanakoplos, *Greek Scholars in Venice,* 227.

117. Monfasani, *George of Trebizond,* 254. On Aristotle, the emotions, and rhetoric, 246.

118. E. Tigerstedt, "Observations on the Reception of Aristotelian 'Poetics' in the Latin West," *Studies in the Renaissance* 15 (1968): 12–14, 21.

119. Cammelli, *Demetrio Calcondila* (Florence, 1954), 36; Paolo Giovio, *Elogia doctorum virorum,* trans. F. A. Gragg (Boston, 1935), 129.

The Byzantine Empire during the Palaeologan Renaissance (1355)

immortality of the soul helped to lead to those of Pomponazzi, who in 1516 declared his belief in the concept of the immortality of the individual soul while affirming he could not prove it.[120] Like the Palaeologan scholars, Tomaeus was interested in both Plato and Aristotle and tried (rather like Bessarion, who really favored Plato) to conciliate them.[121] Tomaeus's career, then, marks the end of the conflict among the Greeks (though certainly not among the Latins) over the relative merits of Plato and Aristotle begun at Florence almost a century before. His career, finally, may be taken as a kind of capstone to the contribution of the Byzantine scholars in Italy. For at his death in 1531 virtually all the literary, philosophic, and scientific Greek works had been transmitted to Italy, and by the end of the century were either published in the original Greek text, translated into Latin, or in some cases even translated into Italian.[122]

Conclusion

It was not until the Italian Renaissance that the complete range of the ancient Greek writings, including many of the more profound and complex works of the ancients, and, in part, of the Byzantine period, came to the West. In particular there were now brought for the first time all the philosophical writings of Platonism, the remainder—much more than we realize—of Aristotle and Aristotelian-inspired writings, and the Greek sources of Stoicism and Epicureanism. Even more striking and numerous were the works of literature transmitted by the Byzantines: the tragedians and Aristophanes; all the lyric poetry of Pindar, Theocritus, and others; and the epic poems of Hesiod and especially Homer, as well as the great Greek historians and the Greek orators, especially Lysias, Isocrates, and Demosthenes. In rhetoric the entire Byzantine corpus was brought, notably Hermogenes and Aphthonius, the importance of whose new translations, along with the commentary on Ptolemy, has been discussed above. All these writings constitute a remarkably broad range of literary,

120. On Pomponazzi, see Kristeller, *Renaissance Concepts of Man,* 18–19, 38–41. On Tomaeus's connection with Pomponazzi, see P. Sherrard, *Greek East and Latin West* (London, 1959), 173–75. For the first biography of Tomaeus in English, see essay 5 below.

121. See Legrand, *Bibliographie hellénique,* 3:283, quoting a contemporary Padua professor referring to Tomaeus as "doctus disciplinae Platonicae et Aristotelicae"; and essay 5 below, 124.

122. See the end of essay 5. Janus Lascaris, another important Byzantine scholar, died in 1534.

scientific, and philosophic masterpieces without which modern Western culture would be quite different from what it is today.

In the transmission of almost all these works it was, as we have seen, the Byzantine émigrés who were the main protagonists, although of course Latins too made a considerable contribution. But were the Byzantines simply transmitters of the ancient Greek legacy for which, as several modern scholars put it, Constantinople was merely the "custodian" and its scholars simply the "world's librarians"?[123] We have seen that the transmission of Greek learning was not a simple process, but one that should be viewed in its many ramifications, including the problems of its reception, assimilation, and diffusion throughout Italy. In this process the émigrés were not merely transmitters but also interpreters in matters of textual meaning and nuances of style. Indeed, in the case of the more-complex works, the Byzantine tradition alone could unlock and authentically interpret the treasures brought to the West.

But the fundamental criterion, I believe, for evaluating the Byzantine scholars' contribution to the learning of the Italian Renaissance is whether or not their work of teaching, editing, and publishing texts resulted in any way in altering the patterns of thought current in Italy at the time of each of the three periods we have discussed. At the beginning of Florence's period of primacy the desire to learn the long-neglected Greek language and literature was, through Chrysoloras's inspired teaching, transformed into a veritable mania that spread rapidly from Florence throughout much of Italy. And during the latter half of the Florentine period the shift in the orientation of Florentine humanism from rhetoric to metaphysical philosophy was not so much the work of the Italian humanists or of Pletho's banquet speeches in Florence as, primarily, the result of the teaching of the bilingual Argyropoulos, a true representative of the Palaeologan Renaissance. It was his teaching that proved decisive for shifting the axis of Florentine humanism, thus paving the way, as Garin puts it, "for the triumphant entry into Florence of the Platonic 'theology.'"[124] This does not mean, of course, that in this change of direction Argyropoulos alone was responsible. The change in the Florentine government from republicanism to Medici "despotism" certainly lessened the opportunities for "civic" humanism, and of course in the educational backgrounds of Ficino and especially Pico, Aristotelian Scholasticism had a very firm place.

123. See, e.g., Setton, "Byzantine Background to Italian Renaissance," 76, citing C. Neumann, "Byzantinische Kultur und Renaissance Kultur," *Historische Zeitschrift* 91 (1903): 227, and also N. Baynes, *Byzantine Studies and Other Essays* (London, 1955) 71–72.

124. Garin, *Portraits from the Quattrocento,* 80. On Argyropoulos see essay 4.

During the period of Roman primacy it was Bessarion's leadership that not only produced the first translations of many important Greek works, but also substantiated the view that, in the search for the most authentic interpretation, whether in ancient science, philosophy, or Biblical studies, the preferred interpreters were generally the ancient Greek or early Byzantine commentators, those closer in time to the original. Bessarion, a pupil of Pletho at Palaeologan Mistra, was probably the most able of the Greek émigrés, especially in terms of his vision and ability to combine Byzantine and Latin patterns of thought and methods.[125] Indeed, his widespread patronage and influence can be detected in almost every endeavor notable for the advancement of Greek learning in the quattrocento. Through the force of his personality and his patronage of both Byzantine and Italian scholars, the size and quality of his manuscript collection,[126] his treatise demonstrating the easier assimilability to Christianity of Plato over Aristotle,[127] his probable inspiration of Valla in Biblical scholarship and certainly of Regiomontanus in mathematics, his role in founding the chair of Greek at Padua, and, not least, his feeling for the organic unity of the entire Christian church of both East and West as in patristic times,[128] Bessarion played a greater and more wide-ranging role than any other Byzantine émigré in the development of Italian Renaissance learning.

Finally, in the period of Venetian-Paduan preeminence, we have seen that the émigrés edited for the Aldine press virtually all the major Greek authors in the original text. Moreover, the Byzantine scholars, with the aid of Barbaro, as evidenced by Tomaeus's subsequent appointment at Padua, were able to promote recognition of the greater authority of the Greek text of Aristotle and the interpretations of his Greek commentators over, and, finally even in place of, the medieval Greco-Latin and Arabo-Latin versions of Aristotle.

Can we say that the Byzantine émigré scholars were very original? Probably not, I think, except for Bessarion, Gaza, and perhaps George of

125. On Bessarion's achievements, see L. Mohler, *Kardinal Bessarion als Theologe, Humanist und Staatsmann;* and Vast, *Cardinal Bessarion.* Also essay 11 below.

126. Tomaeus was an admirer of Bessarion and used his MSS: see Rose and Drake, "The Pseudo-Aristotelian *Questions of Mechanics,*" 97f.; also essay 5.

127. See the Latin text with Italian translation in Garin, *Filosofi italiani del quattrocento,* 276–83; also Geanakoplos, *Byzantium,* no. 300, for partial English translation.

128. Geanakoplos, *Interaction of the Sibling Cultures,* 14, 293; also Runciman, *Last Byzantine Renaissance,* 81, says Bessarion wanted to combine Greek and Latin cultures. Perhaps the only Greek émigré scholar whose career as humanist, diplomat, and "protector" of the Greek scholars can match that of Bessarion was Janus Lascaris (d. 1534). On him see Geanakoplos, *Greek Scholars,* 148 and passim.

Trebizond and Argyropoulos.[129] They were generally uncreative, as was typical of Byzantine scholars of the Palaeologan period, upon whose shoulders the ancient Hellenic tradition weighed all too heavily. But how many quattrocento Latin humanists and philosophers were truly original in thought? Aside from Nicholas of Cusa (himself inspired by, among others, Plato and the Pseudo-Dionysius) and perhaps Valla, Pico, and Poliziano, very few were truly original thinkers until Leonardo da Vinci and Galileo.

In our reevaluation we should not forget that the Byzantine accomplishments would have been impossible without certain basic considerations or qualities present in Renaissance Italian life: especially the growing desire, initially at least, of Italian humanists within the increasingly sophisticated context of urban Florence and other city-states to find perfected models for imitation and justification of their intensified secular values. Later, the generous patronage of the papacy, and then the economic strength of Venice, provided the opportunity for Aldus and the Greeks to exercise their talents. Let us not forget, too, the Italian scholars who even before 1453 went to Constantinople to learn Greek, such as Guarino, Scarperia, Filelfo, and Tortelli. Nor should we neglect the fundamental contribution of Italian humanists with knowledge of Greek, such as Bruni, Poliziano, Ficino, and Barbaro, who, along with the relatively few Byzantines with an acute knowledge of Latin, were in the main responsible for adapting the new Greek learning and concepts to their own native Latin and Italian traditions. I must mention also the invention of printing itself, which, fortunately for the fate of Greek learning, occurred at almost the very moment that the Byzantine state was being extinguished by the Turks.

Finally, it should be stressed that, despite the basic significance of Greek, in the last analysis it was a foreign language to the Italian humanists and that only a relatively small minority of them actually mastered it.[130] Yet this minority, it appears, included almost all the major formative Italian thinkers in the Renaissance. And these, on the basis of the assimilation of the rich Greek cultural inheritance to their Latin and native vernacular tradition, were able, at least in part, to inspire and lead to the more genuinely creative efforts that followed from the early six-

129. Argyropoulos, besides his work of synthesizing Greek philosophy and culture into an organic whole in his teaching in Florence, wrote a treatise on tyranny: see Garin, *Portraits from the Quattrocento,* 69–80. Also essay 4 below on Argyropoulos, and on Gaza, essay 3.

130. P. O. Kristeller, *The Classics and Renaissance Thought* (Cambridge, Mass., 1955), 16.

teenth century onward in the works of Leonardo, Machiavelli, Galileo, and others.

Bearing in mind the various achievements of the Byzantine émigré scholars and the qualifications I have pointed out, I think that our reassessment of the significance of the Byzantine contribution to Italian Renaissance thought and learning serves to reinforce what I stated in an earlier work: the revival of Greek learning in Italy, which was carried out primarily by the Byzantine émigrés and cannot easily be separated from them, probably did more than any other single factor not to begin but, once it had begun on the basis of *Latin* literature, to widen the intellectual perspective of the Italian Renaissance. And this, as I have tried to show, was accomplished by the émigrés essentially through their making possible the fusion, sometimes imperfect, of many elements of learning of the Palaeologan Renaissance with those of the emerging Italian Renaissance.

Additional Bibliography for Essays 1 and 2

I. Ševčenko, "The Palaeologan Renaissance," chap. 7 in *Renaissances before the Renaissance: Cultural Revivals of Late Antiquity and the Middle Ages,* ed. W. Treadgold (Stanford, 1984), 144–76, the most recent work on Greek scholars in Byzantium during the Palaeologan Renaissance (rather than their activity in Italy). N. Wilson, *Scholars of Byzantium* (London, 1983), chap. 12, "The Palaeologan Revival," and chap. 13, "The Epigoni," the best treatment of the philological aspects of the Palaeologan Renaissance in Byzantium. H. Beck, *Theodoros Metochites: Die Krise des byzantinischen Weltbildes im 14. Jahrhundert* (Munich, 1952), on Theodore Metochites' outlook in Byzantium. J. Thomson, "Manuel Chrysoloras and the Early Italian Renaissance," *Greek, Roman and Byzantine Studies* 7 (1966): 63–82. D. Nicol, *Church and Society in the Last Centuries of Byzantium* (Cambridge, 1979), delineating some intellectual trends in late Byzantium. C. Patrinelis, *Hellēnes kodikographoi tōn chronōn tēs Anagennēseōs* in Epetēris tou mesaionikou archeiou, vols. 8–9 (1958–59): 63–121. C. Constantinides, *Higher Education in Byzantium in the Thirteenth and Fourteenth Centuries* (1204–c. 1310) (Nicosia, 1982). P. Mastrodemetre, *Hellēnes logioi,* vol. 1, on the fifteenth to nineteenth centuries (Athens, 1979), especially three unpublished letters of the Byzantine Nicholas Secundinus. M. Manousakas, "Una prefazione greca inedita di Giovanni Gregoropoulos per una edizione veneziana del 1498," in *Bisanzio e l'Italia* (Milan, 1982), 218–28. Also *To hellēniko biblio 1476–1830,* by C. Koumarianou, L. Droulia, and E. Layton (Athens, 1986). I have long been preparing a biography of the Cretan pope Alexander V (Peter Philarges, d. 1410), who, in many respects, played a role in Renaissance Italian humanism.

For Byzantine Palaeologan scholars and study in the Western Renaissance of the Greek church fathers, an important but still comparatively neglected field of research, see my "The Last Step: The Recovery and Translation of the Greek Church Fathers and Their First Printed Editions in the Renaissance," chap. 14 of *Interaction of the Sibling Cultures,* and in the new Greek edition *Byzantio kai dysē* (Athens, 1985), with corrections and updated bibliography, 553–54. For this article, now revised, see below, Appendix.

For the benefit of scholars and interested readers the following comprehensive note is reprinted, with slight modifications, from my essay "Italian Humanism and Byzantine

Emigré Scholars," in *Renaissance Humanism: Foundations, Forms, and Legacy,* ed. A. Rabil (Philadelphia: Univ. of Pennsylvania Press, 1988), 1:628–82.

The question of the Byzantine émigré scholars' influence on Italian Renaissance humanism, especially those representing the late Byzantine Palaeologan "Renaissance," has not hitherto been studied systematically. Yet several centuries ago it was believed, erroneously, that the emigration of Byzantine refugee scholars from Constantinople and the Byzantine East after 1453 actually began the Italian Renaissance. Together with the present essay, the most recent study of the Byzantine Palaeologan contribution to Italian Renaissance humanism is my essay 2, "A Reevaluation of the Influences of Byzantine Scholars," and my *Interaction of the "Sibling" Byzantine and Western Cultures in the Middle Ages and Italian Renaissance* (revised ed. in Greek trans., 1985). See further, S. Runciman, *The Last Byzantine Renaissance* (Cambridge, 1970), which focuses on Palaeologan learning within Byzantium; and the pioneer American work of K. Setton, "The Byzantine Background to the Italian Renaissance," *Proceedings of the American Philosophical Society* 100 (1956): 1–76.

A valuable tool for study is still E. Legrand, *Bibliographie hellénique ou description raisonnée des ouvrages publiés en grec par des grecs au XVe and XVIe siècles,* 4 vols. (Paris, 1885–1906), which includes sketches of the more important Greek refugee scholars and an analytical catalog of their publications. But Legrand omits biographical treatment of some leading Byzantine émigrés, including Leonicus Tomaeus, and has no treatment whatever of Demetrius Ducas. For Ducas's biography (and others, especially in Venice-Padua), see my *Greek Scholars in Venice,* republished as *Byzantium and the Renaissance.* On late Byzantine learning, see B. Tatakis, *La philosophie byzantine* (Paris, 1949); R. Bolgar, *The Classical Heritage and Its Beneficiaries* (Cambridge, 1958); and L. Reynolds and N. Wilson, *Scribes and Scholars* (Oxford, 1974). On Byzantine and Italian humanists in Italy as well as France and Spain up to 1600, see my *Byzantine East and Latin West,* which includes a biography of Maximos Margounios and other little-known Greek humanists. For the Greek dramatists, see A. Turyn, *The Manuscript Tradition of the Tragedies of Aeschylus* (New York, 1943); Turyn, *The Manuscript Tradition of . . . Sophocles* (Urbana, Ill., 1952); and Turyn, *The Manuscript Tradition of . . . Euripides* (Urbana, Ill., 1957). See, more recently, H. Hunger, *Die hochsprächliche profane Literatur der Byzantiner* (Munich, 1978), references to the Palaeologan period.

On individual Byzantine humanists in Italy, see A. Pertusi, *Leonzio Pilato fra Petrarca e Boccaccio* (Venice and Rome, 1964); the pioneering G. Cammelli, *Manuele Crisolora* (Florence, 1941); Cammelli, *Demetrio Calcondila* (Florence, 1954); Cammelli, *Giovanni Argiropulo* (Florence, 1941); F. Masai, *Pléthon et le platonisme de Mistra* (Paris, 1956); P. O. Kristeller, "Byzantine and Western Platonism in the Fifteenth Century," in *Renaissance Thought and Its Sources,* ed. M. Mooney (New York, 1979), 150–63; Kristeller, "The Renaissance and Byzantine Learning," in *Renaissance Concepts of Man* (New York, 1972), 64–100; L. Mohler, *Kardinal Bessarion als Theologe, Humanist und Staatsmann,* 3 vols. (Paderborn, 1923–42); H. Vast, *Le Cardinal Bessarion* (Paris, 1878); J. Monfasani, *George of Trebizond: A Biography and Study of His Rhetoric and Logic* (Leiden, 1976); C. Stinger, *Humanism and the Church Fathers: Ambrogio Traversari and Christian Antiquity in the Italian Renaissance* (Albany, N.Y., 1977). And also, see my "The Discourse of Demetrius Chalcondyles on the Inauguration of Greek Studies at the University of Padua in 1463" (1974); and essays 3, 4, and 5 in this volume. For a very recent work in this area, see J. Hankins, "A Manuscript of Plato's *Republic* in the Translation of Chrysoloras and Uberto Decembrio with Annotations of Guarino Veronese," in *Supplementum Festivum: Studies in Honor of Paul Oskar Kristeller,* ed. J. Hankins, J. Monfasani, and F. Purnell, Jr. (Binghamton, N.Y., 1987), 89–110. Also V. Branca, "L'umanesimo veneziano alla fine del quattrocento: Ermolao Barbaro e il suo circolo," in *Storia della cultura veneta,* vol. 3, pt. 1 (Vicenza, 1980), 123–75; and A. Pertusi, "L'umanesimo greco dalla fine del secolo XIV agli inizi del secolo XVI," ibid., 174–264. Finally, *Renaissance Humanism: Foundations, Forms, and Legacy,* ed. A. Rabil, Jr., 3 vols. (Philadelphia, 1988), particularly vol. 1, chaps. 7–14, esp. chap. 9, "Humanism in Venice," by M. King, 209–43; chap. 2, "The Renaissance Idea of Christian Antiquity: Humanistic Patristic Scholarship," by E. Rice, 17–28. D. Zakythinos, "Mikhaēl Maroullos Tarkhaniōtes. Hellēn Poiētēs tōn Khronōn tēs Anagennēseōs," 344–410 and Zakythinos, "Anagennēsis kai anagennēseis. Hellēnikai Anakefalaiōseis," in *Metabyzantina kai Nea Hellēnika* (Athens, 1978) 130–228. C. Woodhouse, *Gemistos Plethon. The Last of the Hellenes* (Oxford, 1986) esp. for translations of Pletho's works. P. Canivet-N. Oikonomides, "(Jean Argyropoulos) La comédie de Katablattas. Invective byzantine du XVe s.," *Diptycha,* 3 (1982–3) 5–97, important new information on Argyropoulos's early life. And finally, very recently, published by the Greek Ministry of Culture, M. Manoussakas and K. Staikos, *The Publishing Activity of the Greeks during the Italian Renaissance (1469–1523),* translated from the Greek by W. W. Phelps (Athens, 1987), catalogue with short concise summaries of careers of Greek scholars and their important publishing activities, (with bibl., without notes). For additional bibliography, see the notes and bibliographical supplements to essays 3–5 below.

Two

A Reevaluation of the Influences of Byzantine Scholars on the Development of the Studia Humanitatis, *Metaphysics, Patristics, and Science in the Italian Renaissance (1361–c. 1531)*

The problem of the role of the Byzantine scholars in the Italian Renaissance, in particular the extent of their contribution to Italian humanism and thought, has, not surprisingly, never been the subject of systematic analysis devoted to the many complex facets of this question. In G. Voigt's famous book in German, *The Revival of Classical Antiquity,* published in 1859, one year before that of J. Burckhardt, *The Civilization of the Renaissance in Italy,* the idea was suggested that the revival of interest in Greek letters was the key to the Renaissance revival of classical antiquity. And earlier in the seventeenth and eighteenth centuries the view was common that it was the Byzantine scholars who, fleeing to the West from the Turkish conquest of Constantinople in 1453, set in motion the great movement of the Italian Renaissance. Setting aside the now obvious facts that the Greek émigré scholars, even those of the stature of Manuel Chrysoloras, had been active in Italy long before 1453, and that the most notable medieval encounter of Italian and Byzantine intellectuals had already taken place in 1438–39 at the Council of Florence, this hypothesis fails even to consider the possibility, universally accepted as correct, that it was instead the internal developments in Italian society that turned the earliest Italian humanists toward a renewed awareness of the importance of classical learning. In other words, it was above all the growing self-awareness of Italian middle-class society *within the context of the more sophisticated urban environment* that impelled the nascent humanists to see in Greek learning a rationale, even a justification, for the emerging secular life-style of the Italian city-states. In the writings of the ancient Greek and Latin classics these humanists saw perfected models worthy of imitation for their own increasingly complicated urban society and culture.[1]

Thus the earlier medieval focus on Scholasticism, with its heavy emphasis on dialectic and its close ties with theology, was no longer able to satisfy the interests of the more adventurous humanist intelligentsia. Indeed, in Florence after the pioneer contribution of Petrarch, the humanism of the early Florentine circle of the first decades of the quattrocento—which included such scholars as Coluccio Salutati, Leonardo Bruni, and Niccolò Niccoli—was severely criticized by ecclesiastical authorities for what the latter considered its pagan orientation. As is not always realized, it was not without a good deal of censure that the early Italian humanists won acceptance from the local ecclesiastical or, at times, even the civil authorities. Opposition to their views came not only from San Antonino, the very vocal bishop of Florence, but also from ecclesiastical scholars such as the Spanish Bishop of Burgos, who in a case that soon became classic criticized the more flowing humanist translation of Aristotle's *Politics* made by Leonardo Bruni as being inferior to the much more literal *verbum ad verbum* translation of the Scholastic William of Moerbeke.[2]

No wonder that, when in about 1400 the work of the Greek Father St. Basil, *Discourse to Christian Youth on Study of the Greek Classics*, was rediscovered in Rome, the Florentine humanist Leonardo Bruni not long afterward pounced on it, translating it into Latin.[3] And this for the precise reason that one of the greatest Fathers of the early church (who

1. See G. Voigt, *Die Wiederbelebung des classischen Altertums* (Berlin: Reimer, 1859); J. Burckhardt, *Die Kultur der Renaissance in Italien* . . . (Basel: Schwabe, 1860). On the Council of Florence see essay 11 below. And for more detail, J. Gill, *The Council of Florence* (Cambridge: Cambridge Univ. Press, 1959).

2. On the Florentine "environment" and attitude (including opposition to the early humanists) see G. Holmes, *The Florentine Enlightenment, 1400–1450* (New York, 1969), chaps. 1 and 2, esp. 30–35 on the conflict between the puritanical Dominican monk Giovanni Dominici, who, in his *Lucula noctis,* c. 1405, violently criticized Salutati and Bruni as anti-Christian.

3. On Basil's treatise "Address to Young Men on the Right Use of Greek Literature," trans. F. Padelford (New York: Henry Holt, 1902), see Geanakoplos, *Interaction of the "Sibling" Byzantine and Western Cultures in the Middle Ages and Italian Renaissance,*

lived long before the religious schism between East and West) was here advising, even urging—although to be sure, with qualification—the study of classical Greek literature and philosophy in order to further a clearer understanding of the teachings and moral values of Christianity.

The Western terrain, intellectually, was therefore at least in part already prepared for the contribution of the Byzantine émigré scholars in Italy, with their centuries-long tradition of the study of classical Greek literature and the Greek church fathers.

But the event which marks the first *systematic* teaching of Greek language and literature in the West was the arrival in Florence in 1397 of the aristocratic Byzantine Manuel Chrysoloras to teach at that city's *studium.* His coming was the result of a formal invitation issued by the Florentine Signoria, headed by its humanist chancellor Coluccio Salutati, who, like the humanist Petrarch before him, realized the value of Greek as a basic source for Latin learning. Already before Chrysoloras's coming, Boccaccio, Petrarch's pupil, had secured the appointment of the south Italian Greek Leontius Pilatus to the Florentine *studium* (1361). But Pilatus's tenure had evidently produced few results, though he was far from the inadequate Greek scholar too many modern specialists believe him to have been.[4] It was Chrysoloras's lectures, attended by virtually all the leading humanists then in Florence, for example, Vergerio, Guarino, Niccoli, and Leonardo Bruni, the latter of whom even abandoned his study of law to attend, that stamps his three-year tenure at the Florentine *studium* as the real beginning of Greek studies in Western Europe.[5] Bruni's famous remark, a bit exaggerated but more or less correct, expresses something of the contagious enthusiasm with which Chrysoloras was greeted: "This is the first time in 700 years that the Greek language has been taught in the West."[6] (What Bruni looked back at here was probably the career of Boethius in late sixth-century Ostrogothic Italy.)

With even these few facts in mind, it should be clear that the Greek

---

chap. 14, "The Last Step: Western Recovery and Translation of the Greek Church Fathers and Their First Printed Editions in the Renaissance," 265–80, esp. 270–74.

4. On Pilatus see A. Pertusi, *Leonzio Pilato fra Petrarca e Boccaccio* (Venice: Fondazione Cini, 1964); and Geanakoplos, *Greek Scholars in Venice,* 21–22, and Bibliography.

5. On Chrysoloras's career see G. Cammelli, *Manuele Crisolora* (Florence: Vallecchi, 1941); R. Sabbadini, "L'ultimo ventennio della vita di Manuele Crisolora (1396–1415)," *Giornale ligustico* 17 (1890): 43–98; and Geanakoplos, *Greek Scholars in Venice,* 24–28. The most recent related article is J. Hankins, "A Manuscript of Plato's *Republic* in the Translation of Chrysoloras and Uberto Decembrio with Annotations of Guarino Veronese," in *Supplementum Festivum: Studies in Honor of Paul Oskar Kristeller,* ed. J. Hankins, J. Monfasani, and F. Purnell, Jr. (Binghamton, N.Y., 1987), 89–110.

6. See Geanakoplos, *Greek Scholars in Venice,* 24, and references there.

scholars coming to Italy before and after 1453 had little to do with the *origins* of the humanist movement in Italy, which was instead the product of the interplay of internal factors in Italian society. The only place Greek learning could have come from was its repository in the Byzantine East, especially the capital city Constantinople, Thessalonica, and to a lesser extent south Italy, which during the earlier medieval centuries had always constituted more a part of the Byzantine than of the Western world.

Are we justified, then, in saying that Greek learning played no really important role in the development of Italian humanism? This is a view which a number of recent Renaissance historians, oriented primarily toward social and economic developments in the Renaissance West, seem at least tacitly to support. The pendulum has now apparently swung back to the opposite extreme: from the initially highly distorted view that Byzantine refugees brought about the Renaissance itself, some contemporary historians seem to have come to an almost total denial of, or probably more correctly, disregard for, any significant role for the Byzantine émigrés in Renaissance intellectual life.[7]

How can this difference of opinion be resolved? The best way, it seems to me, to determine the degree to which Greco-Byzantine learning actually influenced the thought-world of the Italian Renaissance is to make a systematic, or an attempt at a reasonably systematic, analysis of the various fields of humanistic endeavor influenced by Greek scholarship during the Italian Renaissance from say about 1390, the beginning of Salutati's chancellorship in Florence, to 1531 or 1534, the death of the last two major Greek humanists in Italy, the little-known Nicolaus Leonicus Tomaeus, and Janus Lascaris.[8] We may thereby be able to determine not only what new Greek literary, philosophic, or scientific works they brought to the West but, more important, what intellectual ideas or patterns of thought new to the period were brought by, or induced as a result of the activity of, the Byzantine refugees.

Since a systematic analysis of this kind has not, to my knowledge, hitherto been attempted, this inquiry cannot be much more than a broad overview. The categorization of fields to be considered will include the more important areas of learning, first the humanistic cult of the *studia humanitatis,* that is grammar, rhetoric, history, ethics, and poetry; then, insofar as time will permit, also metaphysical philosophy, writings of the

7. One might cite such fine historians as M. Becker, G. Brucker, or R. Lopez, whose interests of course lie elsewhere, in social-economic history primarily.

8. On Tomaeus see essay 5 below; and for Janus Lascaris see B. Knös, *Un ambassadeur de l'hellénisme: Janus Lascaris et la tradition greco-byzantine dans l'humanisme française* (Uppsala and Paris: Almquist & Wiksell, 1945).

Byzantine church fathers, mathematics, astronomy, physics, and, finally, medicine.

Before we begin our survey we should recall that what was known of Greek learning in the late Roman period was almost entirely lost in the West during the so-called Dark Ages. True, certain Byzantines did appear in the Western world as members of diplomatic or ecclesiastical embassies to discuss the problem of the competing Roman empires or the growing differences between the two churches. But such contacts were sporadic and ephemeral at best.[9] Greek texts in the original, especially in literature, were not to be recovered in substantial quantity by the West until the late fourteenth century with the advent of the humanist movement. To be sure, as E. Gilson rightly reminds us, the Scholastic movement of the twelfth and thirteenth centuries was itself based primarily on ancient Greek learning, on the logical, ethical, and certain scientific texts of Aristotle.[10] These had first come to the West from Spain in Arabic versions, second- and third-hand, as it were. But after the Latin conquest of the Greek East in 1204, the Latin scholar-bishop of Corinth in Greece, William of Moerbeke, translated Aristotle's *Politics* into Latin from the original Greek text and, as is all too little realized, his *Poetics,* not to forget several of the mathematical and "mechanical" treatises of Archimedes. It was Moerbeke's intent to translate into Latin the *entire* corpus of Aristotle (in much the same manner, centuries before, Boethius had sought to translate all of Aristotle *and* Plato).[11] Thus, a relatively small but significant amount of Greek learning was already available in the West before the coming of Chrysoloras. However, this Greek learning, except for Aristotle's *Poetics* (which, though available, was evidently not studied),[12] was primarily of a logical or scientific nature, not literary—and primarily appropriate to the interests of the Scholastics. Moreover, it often came from corrupted Greek manuscript sources.[13] Our study must therefore also deal with the Byzantine émigrés' role in bringing to the West not only unknown ancient works (whether pagan or Christian) but also more accurate and reliable texts of those Greek works already known.

9. On such contacts see Geanakoplos, *Interaction of the Sibling Cultures,* esp. Prologue and Epilogue.

10. See esp. E. Gilson, *History of Christian Philosophy in the Middle Ages* (New York: Random House, 1955), 540, 542.

11. On Moerbeke's translations see Geanakoplos, *Byzantine East and Latin West,* 22–23 and bibliography cited.

12. Ibid., 23 and note. See E. Tigerstedt, "Observations on the Reception of Aristotle's *Poetics* in the Latin West," *Studies in the Renaissance* 15 (1968): 7–24.

13. On corrupt manuscripts see below, text at nn. 88–92.

Let us begin with that touchstone of Italian humanism, the most fundamental subject in the *studia humanitatis,* rhetoric. (Grammar, the sine qua non for the expression of any scholarly thought, it goes without saying, is subsumed under this category.) The primary texts for the teaching of rhetoric in the early Italian Renaissance in Florence were the Latin works of Cicero and Quintilian.[14] And when Plato's *Dialogues* were brought forcefully and *in toto* to the attention of the West by the Greeks at the Council of Florence, the Italian humanists had the opportunity to learn something of Greek rhetoric from Plato's brilliant critique of rhetoric in his *Gorgias.*[15] But the Latins were not to realize the full benefits of Greek rhetoric until the translation in Italy by the Byzantine George of Trebizond of Byzantium's primary authority on rhetoric, Hermogenes. George of Trebizond, who came to Venice in 1416 and studied there primarily with Vittorino da Feltre, and with Guarino, Francesco Barbaro, and others, was, with his Byzantine compatriot John Argyropoulos, one of the extremely few Greeks who studied Latin at an Italian institution. He learned the language so well that in maturity he spoke it better than his native Greek. His own treatise, the *Rhetoricorum libri V,* introduced to the Latin West for the first time on a large scale the Byzantine rhetorical tradition based on Dionysius of Halicarnassus, Maximus the Philosopher, and, most of all, the highly analytical works of Hermogenes of Tarsus. In his text George set forth and expatiated in elegant Latin on Hermogenes' treatment of the twenty-one stylistic forms or types of rhetorical effect a good rhetorician should be able to achieve, and more important, *how* to achieve such effects. These forms included above all the quality of *deinotēs,* literally meaning power but implying "effective" eloquence in the highest humanistic sense of the term—that is, how to move people or affect them emotionally as well as logically.[16] Such an extremely analytical and especially very pragmatic approach to the study

14. See Holmes, *The Florentine Enlightenment,* for Cicero, passim, and on Quintilian, esp. 18–20. Also R. Bolgar, *The Classical Heritage and Its Beneficiaries* (Cambridge: Cambridge Univ. Press, 1958), 266–68, 346, and passim; P. O. Kristeller, *Studies in Renaissance Thought and Letters* (Rome: Edizioni di storia e letteratura, 1956), passim.

15. See J. Monfasani, *George of Trebizond: A Biography and a Study of His Rhetoric and Logic* (Leiden: Brill, 1976), 242–43, and 258–59 on George of Trebizond's (actually he was from Crete) use of the *Gorgias* in Italy in the early 1430s.

16. On George see the old work of G. Tiraboschi, *Storia della letteratura italiana* (Naples: Muccis, 1780), 6:268–78; R. Sabbadini, "Briciole umanistiche: Giorgio da Trebisonda," *Giornale storico della letteratura italiana* 18 (1891): 230–41; and 43 (1904): 253–54; G. Castellani, "Giorgio da Trebisonda, maestro di eloquenza a Vicenza e a Venezia," *Nuovo archivio veneto* 11 (1896): 123–43; and esp. Monfasani, *George of Trebizond,* esp. chap. 9 on rhetoric, in particular 248–55 on Hermogenes and the Byzantine rhetorical tradition; also 318–27 on the diffusion of Hermogenes.

of rhetoric was not yet available to the Italian humanists, whose favorites were Cicero and especially Quintilian. If the definition of the quattrocento Florentine humanists as professional rhetoricians is valid (as I think it is), one can imagine their excited reactions to these brand-new insights provided by Hermogenes. To which specific Florentine humanists George's rhetorical treatises were known (it took time for them to be "assimilated" by the humanists) has now been investigated. It has been shown that George's own (Latin) treatise, *Rhetoricorum libri V,* became in time the standard guide for rhetorical style not only in late quattrocento and all of cinquecento Italy but, even more so, in the North, where Budé and Erasmus among others utilized it.[17] As it is, we know through a study by H. Baron that Leonardo Bruni, the Florentine chancellor in the early years of the quattrocento, was highly influenced even by the rhetorical work of the Athenian rhetorician Aelius Aristides. Bruni's famous *Laudatio,* or panegyric, on the city of Florence draws directly on material from Aristides' *Panathēnaikos,* an oration that expounds on the virtues of ancient Athens. Indeed, in his *Laudatio* Bruni was one of the first to draw an analogy between the cities of Athens and Florence, as scores of other Italian humanists were later on to do.[18]

Greek rhetoricians and philosophers had stated that the city-state's population should not be so large that it could not make its will known through a democratic assembly and that the inhabitants should be able to see the walls from every point in the city. Aristides in particular stressed the beauty of Athens' layout, extending in concentric circles from the rural area to the suburbs, the walls, and the inner city. Such considerations as these were utilized by Bruni in his own description and praise of Florence. Making the analogy between Athens and Florence particularly effective was Bruni's affirmation that Florence, because of its republican constitution which preserved civic freedom, triumphed over the Milanese tyrant Giangaleazzo Visconti in the same manner that Athens, according to Aristides, had saved Greek freedom from Persian despotism.[19]

In connection with the Florentine constitution, so often a theme for

17. Monfasani, *George of Trebizond,* 318–28, on the treatise's influence in the Renaissance. George's influence might perhaps be compared to that exerted on the formation of elegant Latin style by Valla's treatise *De elegantia latinae,* which drew heavily on Quintilian.

18. H. Baron, *From Petrarch to Leonardo Bruni: Studies in Humanistic and Political Literature* (Chicago: Univ. of Chicago, 1968), chap. 5, "Imitation, Rhetoric, and Quattrocento Thought in Bruni's *Laudatio,*" 151–72. Baron mistakenly terms Aristides a minor rhetorician.

19. Ibid., 156ff.

Florentine humanist discussion, it is interesting to note that the Byzantine Pletho, during his sojourn in Italy at the Council of Florence, made corrections in the manuscript of Bruni's own Greek treatise on the constitution of Florence. It would be hard to find two more striking examples than these of the direct influence of Byzantine scholars on the ideas and actual writings of Italian humanists.[20]

According to A. Renouard the most valuable of all publications of the celebrated Aldine Greek press of Venice was its edition of the rhetoricians, the *Rhetores graeci.* Edited principally by the Cretan Demetrius Ducas and probably his compatriot Marcus Musurus (in addition to Aldus himself), this work was published in 1508.[21] It included not only the writings of Hermogenes and his important follower Aphthonius (which took up over half the entire volume) but also the *Rhetoric* of Aristotle, hitherto almost unknown in the West, but which, when read by the Scholastics, was read as part of his psychological works rather than as rhetorical theory. Nevertheless, Aristotle's *Rhetoric,* if only for the great name attached to it, was soon to have no little impact upon Western scholars, indeed far more than it had had in Byzantium, where it was looked upon as less instructive and useful than the *Rhetoric* of Hermogenes. At least it was not an integral part of the Byzantine Palaeologan oratorical tradition of the last two centuries of Byzantium's life.[22] It was probably to override this Byzantine attitude (and to cater to the Western mania for Aristotelian works) that Ducas, in his prefatory letter attached to the *Rhetores graeci,* advised Musurus, then teaching at the great University of Padua, "to include in your lectures besides the *Rhetoric* of Hermogenes, the rhetorical treatise of that genius *[tou daimoniou]* Aristotle, whom to praise and recommend is, it seems to me superfluous."[23]

We turn now to history. In 1402 the humanist Pier Paolo Vergerio wrote what is considered the first truly humanist treatise on education, *De ingenuis moribus.* In this work he affirmed that history was the chief subject of the *studia humanitatis.* "I accord first place," he wrote, "to history among the liberal studies on grounds both of its attractiveness and its utility, qualities which appeal equally to the scholar and to the

20. See F. Masai, *Pléthon et le platonisme de Mistra* (Paris: Les Belles Lettres, 1956), 337 n. 2, 320, 332–33. Cf. Geanakoplos, *Interaction of the Sibling Cultures,* 192–93.

21. A. Renouard, *Annales de l'imprimerie des Alde,* 3 vols., 3d ed. (Paris: Renouard, 1834), 1:128. Cf. Geanakoplos, *Greek Scholars in Venice,* 227.

22. See Monfasani, *George of Trebizond,* 260, 262 (in the West); on Byzantine rhetoric see also G. Kustas, *Studies in Byzantine Rhetoric* (Thessalonica: 1973); and Kustas, "The Function and Evolution of Byzantine Rhetoric," *Viator: Medieval and Renaissance Studies* (1970): 55–74.

23. See Geanakoplos, *Greek Scholars in Venice,* 227–28.

statesman. . . . History . . . gives us concrete examples of the precepts inculcated by philosophy. The one shows what men should do, the other what men have said and done in the past and what practical lessons we may draw therefrom for the present day."[24] (As he and other humanists put it more succinctly elsewhere, "History is philosophy teaching by example.")[25]

In this period of Florentine humanistic primacy, history indeed held an important place. Most widely read were the works of the Latin historians of republican Rome, especially Livy, whose work best reflects the "civic" republicanism of early fifteenth-century Florence. Manuscripts of Herodotus and Thucydides, the leading Greek historians, were also brought in by Byzantines in this period, Herodotus first becoming known in Latin translation through the version made by Perotti, secretary of the Byzantine cardinal Bessarion (and later by Lorenzo Valla).[26] Thucydides became available again primarily through Valla's translation (1450–53). It is impossible to gauge the impact of Thucydides on Italian humanism until a careful study is made. But his powers of historical analysis, objectivity, and the rhetorical excellence of the speeches included would have impressed any humanist, in particular Valla, whose acute awareness of the importance of historical criteria for evaluating documents permits historians to call him the father of modern historical criticism and of critical philology as well. In the latter connection one cannot resist mentioning that several scholars, S. Camporeale, J. Monfasani, myself, and others, are now convinced that Bessarion was responsible for, or at least inspired, some of the textual readings or ideas contained in Valla's famous *Annotationes,* which provided new textual readings of the New Testament (different from manuscripts of Jerome's Vulgate version) and a new philological technic for evaluating texts of the Bible.[27] Valla's work, still in manuscript, was of course later utilized to the full by Eras-

24. On Vergerio and his treatise *De ingenuis moribus* see W. Woodward, *Vittorino da Feltre and Other Humanist Educators* (New York: Teachers College Columbia, 1963), 93–118, esp. 106.

25. This kind of aphorism quoted by Vergerio and even Erasmus would help explain the tremendous popularity of Plutarch's *Lives* and especially his essays, collectively entitled the *Moralia.* Many humanists tried to translate single Plutarchean essays.

26. For Perotti see R. Oliver, *Niccolò Perotti's Translation of the Version of the Enchiridion of Epictetus* (Urbana: Univ. of Illinois, 1954), which lists his works; R. Cessi, "Notizie umanistiche tra Niccolò Perotti e Poggio Bracciolini," *Giornale storico della letteratura italiana* 60 (1912): 79. Perotti also translated Polybius later. The Byzantine rhetorical tradition was really a union of rhetoric with other disciplines (called together *enkyklios paideia,* that is, "encompassing education").

27. See S. Camporeale, *Lorenzo Valla: Umanesimo e teologia* (Florence: 1972), esp. 234–76; and G. Napoli, *Lorenzo Valla, filosofia e religione nell'umanesimo italiano*

mus in his own first edition of the Greek text of the New Testament in 1516.[28]

Plutarch's famous *Lives,* a biographical kind of history, was particularly valued by humanists such as Vittorino, Valla, and Erasmus as a prime example of history as "philosophy teaching by example."[29] Plutarch's *Lives* fascinated the humanist world, the Italians especially, who took delight in debating who was greater, Alexander or Caesar, Hannibal or Scipio. (The future Pope Alexander V, elected at the Council of Pisa in 1409, relates that while serving in a diplomatic capacity at the Venetian court he heard a discussion one evening over the relative merits of the strategy of Hannibal and Scipio.)[30]

Other major Greek historical texts brought to Italy by Greek émigrés and translated into Latin were those of Xenophon and Polybius. Xenophon's *Hellenica* and the *Apologia Socratis* were paraphrased by Leonardo Bruni before 1440, and the *Cyropaedia* was paraphrased by Poggio in 1437 and first actually translated by Filelfo in 1471.[31]

Polybius was especially attractive to the Italians because he had sought to explain how Rome, originally an insignificant city-state, had in a relatively short time become master of the world, including far more cultured Greece. Moreover, as Vergerio wrote, referring to Polybius, "It is strange that no small portion of Roman history is known through the work of one Greek, and in Greek."[32] The similarity between the relation-

---

(Rome: Edizioni di Storia e Letteratura, 1971). Also see Valla's *Collatio Novi Testamenti,* ed. A. Perosa (Florence: Sansoni, 1970), the first redaction of his work, conceived in Naples, comparing the Vulgate and Greek New Testament texts. See also Monfasani, *George of Trebizond,* 92, 96–97, on Bessarion and Valla. In the second redaction (the *Annotationes*) Bessarion's (and possibly Theodore of Gaza's) influence was exercised. If Valla (a close friend in Bessarion's circle in Rome) heard the (Greek) liturgy performed in Bessarion's house (he had special papal permission), he might well have noted differences in meaning and text from MSS of Jerome's Vulgate translation.

28. On Erasmus and the New Testament see Geanakoplos, *Interaction of the Sibling Cultures,* 275ff. Erasmus had the *Annotationes* published in 1505.

29. See ibid., 278–79.

30. Cited in a manuscript, to be included in my forthcoming biography of Alexander V (Peter Philarges, also known as Peter of Candia), who was born in Crete and studied as a boy in Padua-Venice. On translations of some of Plutarch's *Lives* done by Scarperia (and redone by Vergerio), see R. Weiss, "Jacopo Angeli da Scarperia (c. 1360–1410–11)," *Medioevo e rinascimento: Studi in onore di Bruno Nardi,* 2 vols. (Florence, Sansoni, 1955), 2:804.

31. On Xenophon translated by L. Bruni in 1439 see Holmes, *Florentine Enlightenment,* 13, 95. On Polybius see also 95 and 250 for Nicholas Perotti's version. Plutarch was most popular among the Latins, with perhaps Xenophon second. On Poggio and Filelfo see 253, and on Filelfo, 98–99.

32. Woodward, *Vittorino da Feltre and Other Humanist Educators,* 106.

ship of the situations of ancient Rome and Athens, on the one hand, and that of Byzantium and Renaissance Italy, on the other, was not lost on some of the Italians and certainly not on the Greek humanists. Thus the Cretan Michael Apostolis, in a discourse addressed to the Italian humanists, commented on the passing of primacy in intellectual matters from "the moribund Byzantine world" to the intellectual world of "youthful, vigorous Italy"—a phenomenon Apostolis rationalized, however, by affirming, not without a certain justification, that the humanistic culture of Italy was at bottom based on the Greek.[33] It is curious to note that, despite considerable Italian humanist interest in Polybius—we know for example that Vittorino used his work—the *editio princeps* was not printed until as late as 1530 in Hagenau, and that Leonardo Bruni in 1421 paraphrased parts of Polybius in his *Commentarium de bello punico.*[34] Since one of the few major Greek literary texts not printed by Aldus was Polybius, one wonders why Aldus's Byzantine friends such as Musurus or Leonicus Tomaeus did not suggest its publication. Perhaps no adequate manuscripts were then available, especially from Bessarion's great manuscript collection, which, left in his will to Venice, served as the principal quarry for the Aldine editions as well as for George of Trebizond's translations in Rome of Ptolemy and the Greek fathers of the church.[35]

As for the study of ethics, Aristotle's *Ethics* was of course already well known to the Scholastics, notably to Aquinas, who used the Aristotelian ethics as a framework for his own work on Christian ethics. But Greek moral ideas were certainly drawn upon by Italian humanists from other Greek literary works also, notably Homer. This held true also for Hesiod, whose *Works and Days* is exemplary for its ethical content, stressing what we might call the "work ethic." Though Hesiod's work in manuscript was already to be found in medieval south Italian Greek monastic libraries and, during the late fifteenth century, in the library of the Venetian humanist Giorgio Valla, so far as I can determine, the work was not, or very little, studied.[36] I have found evidence indicating that the *Works and*

33. Geanakoplos, *Greek Scholars in Venice,* 101–6; and Geanakoplos, "A Byzantine Looks at the Renaissance: The Attitude of Michael Apostolis toward the Rise of Italy to Cultural Eminence" (1958) 157–62.

34. On Polybius's MSS in Italy see Bolgar, *Classical Heritage,* 487. On Bruni, see Holmes, *Florentine Enlightenment,* 95. On Polybius's *editio princeps,* by Obsopoeus in 1530 in Hagenau, see J. Sandys, *A History of Classical Scholarship* (Cambridge: Cambridge Univ. Press, 1908), 2:105.

35. On Bessarion's library see Geanakoplos, *Greek Scholars in Venice,* 35; and esp. L. Labowsky, "Il Cardinale Bessarione e gli inizi della Biblioteca marciana," in *Venezia e l'Oriente fra tardo medio evo e rinascimento,* ed. A. Pertusi (Florence: Sansoni, 1966), 159–82.

36. On Hesiod and Giorgio Valla see Bolgar, *Classical Heritage,* 279.

Days was taught in the West for the first time in a course given at the University of Padua by the Athenian Demetrius Chalcondyles—a fact mentioned by the scribe Hartmann Schedel, who copied down Chalcondyles' discourse delivered in 1463 before the Venetian Senate on the occasion of the establishment of the first Greek chair of letters at that great university.[37] Evidence indicates that almost half a century later Musurus also read Hesiod in his courses at the same university. (In his discourse Chalcondyles also stressed the importance of history, but the precise historical texts read in his classes are not known.)[38]

The importance of ethics in the works of the Christian fathers and their view on the proper utilization of Greek classical learning we have already seen in Basil's *Discourse to the Christian Youth.* As observed, after its initial translation by Bruni the work had considerable impact on many other Italian and northern humanists.

The Greek Plutarch's major work on ethics, the *Moralia,* a collection of essays, was also introduced to the West by the Byzantines in the fifteenth century.[39] Since it was unknown to the medieval Scholastic West, its use was, according to all remaining evidence, of first importance for Italian humanist thought of the earlier quattrocento, especially in Florence. There where the type of humanism known as "civic" humanism flourished, those qualities of mind and character praised by Plutarch as conducive to the good and actively useful life in the polis were held in high esteem. The history of the transmission or *fortuna* of Plutarch's *Moralia* is not yet clearly known, but there can be no doubt of the work's popularity not only in early quattrocento Florence but also later in Venice. Though many of the ethical ideas presented were certainly not new to the West, the attractive style of the *Moralia* and the luster of Plutarch's name imparted to his work a special authority which made it even more influential.[40]

37. On Schedel and Chalcondyles see Geanakoplos, "The Discourse of Demetrius Chalcondyles on the Inauguration of Greek Studies at the University of Padua in 1463" (1974), 128 and n. 32. Also see the English translation of Chalcondyles's entire text in Geanakoplos, *Interaction of the Sibling Cultures,* 254; Latin text, 296: "Demetrius Atheniensis qui publice Padue primo *Erothimata* deinde Hesiodum nobis exposuit." There is now a new Greek translation of this book, with a more accurate Latin text of this discourse: *Byzantio kai dysē,* 430–41.

38. Geanakoplos, *Greek Scholars in Venice,* 137, in the biography of Musurus; and Geanakoplos, *Interaction of the Sibling Cultures,* 298.

39. See Bolgar, *Classical Heritage,* 485–86, on the presence of this work in the libraries of Filelfo, Traversari, Nicholas V, and Bessarion.

40. Ibid., 485–86. On Tomaeus's important contribution to the *Moralia*'s manuscript tradition see below and esp. A. Turyn, *Dated Greek Manuscripts of the Thirteenth and Fourteenth Centuries in the Libraries of Italy,* 2 vols. (Urbana: Univ. of Illinois Press, 1972), 1:xx, 85.

The *studia humanitatis* at first included only literary and rhetorical subjects, not the logic, metaphysics, and science stressed by the Scholastics. Nonetheless, with the growing interest in Plato on the part of later Florentine humanists such as Ficino and Pico, an abiding interest was generated for the study of philosophy as a metaphysical system. As E. Garin, J. Seigel (and I) have stressed, it was the teaching of the Byzantine John Argyropoulos that was *chiefly* responsible for the major shift in the emphasis of Florentine humanism away from rhetoric to metaphysical philosophy, in particular Platonism.[41] In accordance with his contract with the Signoria of Florence Argyropoulos taught Aristotelianism at the *studium* in his morning lectures. But in the afternoon, to a select group of disciples, he would discourse on Plato and Neoplatonism, drawing out all the meanings and implications, literal, esoteric, or occult. His instruction followed the traditional Byzantine didactic practice of first reading a passage aloud, studying its grammar, structure, and syntactical position in the sentence, then analyzing its meaning. Finally, by means of analogies and utilizing concrete examples, he would point out various interpretations in the text and seek to apply these to contemporary life.[42] It was Argyropoulos then, and not Ficino, who was primarily responsible for bringing about the transformation in the orientation of Florentine humanism.[43] This major change in turn paved the way, as Garin rightly maintains, for the triumph of Ficino's Neoplatonic teachings as expressed in his *Teologia platonica.*

These Platonic doctrines were soon carried to northern Europe by scores of humanists who came to Florence to study with Ficino and participate in the life of the so-called Platonic academy. It should again be stressed that the methodology utilized by Argyropoulos in his teaching was essentially a continuation of the method he had used in the higher school at the Xenon in Constantinople, where he taught during the Palaeologan Renaissance and before its fall to the Turks in 1453.[44] More-

41. On Argyropoulos's role in this Florentine shift from rhetoric to philosophy see E. Garin, "Donato Acciaiuoli, Citizen of Florence," in *Portraits from the Quattrocento,* trans. V. A. Velen and E. Velen (New York: Harper & Row, 1972), chap. 3; Holmes, *Florentine Enlightenment,* 262–65; essay 4 below, 104f.; and the old but still useful work of G. Cammelli, *Giovanni Argiropulo* (Florence: Le Monnier, 1941). See also n. 43 below on the important qualification regarding Medici despotism and also Scholasticism and their connection with Florentine humanism's shift to metaphysics. Most recently see A. Field, "John Argyropoulos and the 'Secret Teachings' of Plato," in *Supplementum Festivum,* ed. Hankins, Monfasani, and Purnell, 229–326.

42. See essay 4 below.

43. Garin, "Donato Acciaiuoli," 78, esp. 80. Of course Lorenzo's despotism, displacing Florence's republican government, lessened opportunities for "civic" humanism. Also, both Ficino and Pico had Scholastic backgrounds.

44. Cammelli, *Giovanni Argiropulo,* 30–35ff.; and Geanakoplos, *Greek Scholars in Venice,* 75; also P. O. Kristeller's penetrating article, "Byzantine and Western Platonism

over, the famous treatise on education written by Guarino of Verona's son Battista was based, it is generally accepted, on the teaching methods of his father, a pupil of the Byzantine Manuel Chrysoloras, with whom he had studied in Florence and later even in Constantinople.[45] These two cases further the argument that one of the major accomplishments of the period of the Italian Renaissance was to fuse together the interests and characteristics and qualities of the Byzantine (that is, the so-called Palaeologan) "Renaissance" with the humanism and thought of the Italian Renaissance.[46]

Let us turn to a consideration of poetry. As is well known, the first real Italian humanist in the true sense of the word—one who began to look upon the world through the eyes of the ancients, in particular the Romans—was Petrarch. Petrarch had already realized the need for devotees of ancient Latin literature to recognize Virgil's indebtedness to Homer. (One may recall his railing at Virgil himself in one of his *Letters to the Illustrious Ancient Dead* for the latter's lack of recognition of his debt to Homer.) Hence Petrarch's successful attempt to secure a manuscript of Homer from Sigeros, the Byzantine envoy to the Avignonese papal court.[47]

But Petrarch's inability to read this precious manuscript prompted him to take lessons in Greek from Barlaam and Pilatus, two south Italian Byzantines. Pilatus, in fact, under the influence of Petrarch and even more of his pupil Boccaccio, made a Latin verse translation of the *Iliad* and *Odyssey,* which had been known to the West only in a very inadequate brief Latin summary. Contrary to the erroneous belief of most scholars who repeat this story, Pilatus's Latin versions were, if not "humanistically" flowing, of reasonably good quality.[48]

Pilatus aided Boccaccio to produce what is sometimes called the first modern work of critical philology. In his *Genealogia deorum* Boccaccio sought to explain the genealogy of the gods through a study of the ancient Greek myths. It was his aim to present the gods as they were in classical

---

in the Fifteenth Century," in *Renaissance Concepts of Man* (New York: Harper & Row, 1972), 86–109. On Argyropoulos see essay 4.

45. For Guarino's treatise see Woodward, *Vittorino da Feltre and Other Humanist Educators,* 129–78.

46. See Geanakoplos, *Greek Scholars in Venice,* e.g., 110: "[The Byzantine émigrés] made possible the emergence of a cultural synthesis combining the new and youthful spirit of the Italian Renaissance with the older, disciplined learning of Byzantium." Also cf. the similar view of Monfasani, *George of Trebizond.*

47. *Petrarch's Letters to Classical Authors,* trans. M. Cosenza (Chicago: Univ. of Chicago Press, 1910), letter to Homer, 148–71; see Geanakoplos, *Greek Scholars in Venice,* 21 n. 24, on Nicholas Sigeros.

48. On Pilatus see Pertusi, *Leonzio Pilato;* also Cammelli, *Manuele Crisolora,* 8, 44.

Greek times, freed of the Christian or even at times pseudo-Christian accretions of the medieval world. In this venture Pilatus's acute knowledge of the myths via the Byzantine tradition was invaluable.[49]

Other Greek poets who were read and studied by the Italian humanists were Pindar and Theocritus. Editions of both were first published by one of the pioneer Cretan printers and editors, Zacharias Calliergis, in Rome, although they were unknown to the West before this.[50] His compatriot Musurus, as may be ascertained from his epistolary prefaces to these *editiones principes,* taught and interpreted these texts at the University of Padua and subsequently in Venice.

Musurus, a pupil of the Byzantines Chalcondyles and Janus Lascaris in Florence, was one of the extremely few Byzantines (certainly not to speak of Latins) who knew much about quantitative meter of the ancient Greek poets and tragedians. Actually this technique had been resurrected in Byzantium only in the fourteenth century during the Palaeologan Renaissance by Demetrius Triklinios, who discovered an ancient treatise by Hephaestion on the subject.[51] Musurus was the chief editor in Venice of the Renaissance's leading publisher, Aldus Manutius, who perhaps conceived the idea of printing for the first time all the great works of classical Greek antiquity. (It is my own opinion, rather, that Calliergis, the Cretan, first had this idea, as I believe we may deduce from his first work, the huge lexicon *Etymologicum magnum.)*[52] It was Musurus's deep knowledge of the science of metrics which, more than anything else, enabled him to make valuable emendations and permitted him to become the prime editor of ancient Greek poetic texts and dramas in the entire Renaissance.[53] In his poem "Apostrophe to Plato," prefixed to his great edition of the original Greek text of Plato's *Dialogues* which has

---

The *editio princeps* of Homer was first edited by the Greek Demetrius Chalcondyles and printed by the Cretan Demetrius Damilas in Milan in 1488.

49. Pertusi, *Leonzio Pilato,* 35, 371, and elsewhere; and Geanakoplos, *Interaction of the Sibling Cultures,* 66. Pertusi believes that Pilatus visited Crete and learned much there on this matter: "Leonzio Pilato a Creta prima del 1358–59: Scuole e cultura a Creta durante il secolo XIV," *Krētika chronika* 15–16 (1961–62): 363ff.

50. Geanakoplos, *Greek Scholars in Venice,* 214, 217–18.

51. See Reynolds and Wilson, *Scribes and Scholars,* 66–67.

52. Reasons given in Geanakoplos, *Greek Scholars in Venice,* 146, esp. nn. 133, 156; see also Geanakoplos, *Interaction of the Sibling Cultures,* 180, on Calliergis's edition of the *Etymologicum magnum.*

53. Geanakoplos, *Greek Scholars in Venice,* 151. Also see A. Turyn, *The Manuscript Tradition of the Tragedies of Euripides* (Urbana: Univ. of Illinois Press, 1957), passim, and his works on the other Greek dramatists (see additional bibliography at end of essay 1).

learned son, Pier Candido Decembrio.[63] It is well known that Marsilio Ficino in Florence (from 1463 to 1482) translated and disseminated all of Plato's *Dialogues,* including the *Republic.* But the chief event for the wider diffusion of Plato's political ideas (also to the North, for example, to Thomas More) was surely publication of Musurus's edition of the original *Greek* text by the Aldine press in 1513.[64]

As for Plato's other great political tract, the *Laws,* we have a bit of evidence of its direct impact on the government and humanists of Venice. George of Trebizond, believing that Plato's *Laws* with its treatment of the various kinds of governments could benefit the Venetian state, translated the work (in about 1450) and dedicated it (c. 1460) to the doge of Venice.[65] In a letter of his to the Venetian humanist Francesco Barbaro, George, comparing the Venetian constitution and the ideas expounded in Plato's *Laws,* expressed amazement at his discovery that the founding fathers of Venice had evidently studied Plato![66] In his preface to the doge alluded to above, he noted that the Venetian Grand Council represented the plebs without any of the lowliness of the *vulgus,* and that the Council of Ten provided the best form of aristocratic control, while the doge held the position of monarch.[67] F. Gilbert refers to George's letter and preface as the first working out of the concept of the ideal mixed constitution of Venice. As he notes, George had already absorbed the concept of the mixed constitution from Polybius and Aristotle. But Gilbert has identified a passage in Plato's *Laws* in praise of the Spartan constitution as the actual passage where George found this idea. Thus, to quote another modern historian, J. Monfasani, "the political myth of Sparta gave birth to the Renaissance political myth of Venice through the midwifery of the Byzantine George of Trebizond."[68]

63. What the role of Peter of *Candia,* godfather of Pier *Candido* (and later Pope Alexander V), was is not known, although he was the patron of Uberto and knew Chrysoloras. See Sandys, *History of Classical Scholarship,* 2:70. Pier sent his translation of the fifth book to the Duke of Gloucester, Humphrey and finished the translation in 1440. On translation of the *Republic* see now Hankins, "A Manuscript of Plato's Republic."

64. See Geanakoplos, *Greek Scholars in Venice,* 149–53.

65. Monfasani, *George of Trebizond,* 103. George had originally planned to dedicate it to Pope Nicholas V.

66. F. Barbaro, *Epistolae,* ed. A. Querini (Brescia: Rizzardi, 1743), 290–91. Cf. Monfasani, *George of Trebizond,* 102.

67. Monfasani, *George of Trebizond,* 102–3.

68. F. Gilbert, "The Venetian Constitution in Florentine Political Thought," in *Florentine Studies,* ed. N. Rubenstein (Evanston: Northwestern Univ. Press, 1968), 463–500, esp. 468ff.; Monfasani, *George of Trebizond,* 103.

The work of Demosthenes that would seem to posses the most relevance for Venetian politics of quattrocento Italy was his *On the Crown,* a speech addressed to King Philip of Macedon, the enemy of Athenian liberty. The analogy of Philip symbolizing Emperor Charles V and Athens representing republican Venice comes readily to mind here. Yet even more relevant for and appealing to the practical-minded Venetians would seem to be Isocrates' defense of Alexander, with the analogy of Venice and her influence over her empire, on the one hand, contrasted to that of Alexander and his beneficent influence over the Greek areas on the other.[69]

As would naturally be expected, the Byzantine exiles brought with them a thorough knowledge of the writings of the Byzantine church fathers. And because of the ecclesiastical interest engendered in these writings at the Council of Florence, there was a parallel interest among such humanists as Niccoli, Valla, and Ambrogio Traversari, the Italian Camaldolese monk who had already translated some of the Greek fathers into fairly "humanistic" Latin partly for use by the papacy. But the chief scholar responsible for their wider diffusion in the West was George of Trebizond, who, in the circle of the Byzantine cardinal Bessarion in Rome, translated for Pope Nicholas V and several other popes some writings of Gregory of Nazianzus, Gregory of Nyssa's *Life of Moses,* Basil's *Adversus Eunomium* (important for *seeming* to be closer to the Latin than the traditional Greek view of the *filioque*), also Athanasius, even Cyril's *Thesaurus against Heretics,* and the remarkable commentary of John Chrysostom on Matthew. The latter had been known in the West only in an ancient translation by Anianus. Burgundio of Pisa had rendered it into Latin in the twelfth century, but his version was virtually unknown. George of Trebizond's Latin translations had, as a modern scholar has only recently shown, a far wider diffusion in his time than has hitherto been believed.[70]

Let us turn finally to the realm of science. In the chief scientific field to be examined here, astronomy, the major Greek writer was Ptolemy. His *Almagest (Mathēmatikē syntaxis)* first appeared in the West in the twelfth century as a gift to King Roger II of Sicily from the Byzantine emperor Manuel I Comnenus.[71] But as with most Greek works first turned into

69. V. Branca, "Ermolao Barbaro and Late Quattrocento Venetian Humanism," in *Renaissance Venice,* ed. J. Hale (London: Faber & Faber, 1973), 218; and C. Dionisotti, "Aldo Manuzio Umanista," in *Umanesimo europeo e umanesimo veneziano,* ed. V. Branca (Florence: Sansoni, 1963), 220–43.

70. Monfasani, *George of Trebizond,* 69–79, and passim.

71. Geanakoplos, *Byzantine East and Latin West,* 15; and on the Greek Fathers,

Latin, this version was faulty. Moreover, the Arab version most in use was itself very corrupt. Thus in the academy which Bessarion formed in Rome under several popes specifically to translate Greek works into Latin, he commissioned George of Trebizond to make another. Despite the standard view that George's "shady" character and enmity for Bessarion impelled him to make a faulty translation, or even to omit entire passages, one scholar has recently shown that George's work, on the contrary, was generally accurate not only because of his expertise in both Latin and Greek but because of his use of new and better manuscripts—codices undoubtedly made available to him from Bessarion's own library. More important still, George's commentary on the *Almagest* made use of a certain hitherto unused ancient Greek commentator, Theon of Alexandria.[72] We may assume, then, that George's version had a certain impact on the development of modern Western astronomy.

Ptolemy's other principal work was his *Geography,* the first Latin translation of which was made by Jacopo Angeli da Scarperia, the Italian humanist who, in his mania to learn Greek, like Guarino followed Manuel Chrysoloras from Florence back to Constantinople to study with him.[73] Scarperia's translation was dedicated to the Cretan Peter Philarges (Pope Alexander V) and also, strangely enough, to his rival pope in this period of the Great Schism, Gregory XII.[74] (Evidently in the great papal sweepstakes Scarperia did not wish to bet on the wrong horse!) Scarperia's translation made Ptolemy's *Geography* accessible to the West, although the Greek text was apparently not to be published until as late as 1533 at Basel, edited by Erasmus. The reason for the great popularity of Ptolemy's *Geography,* then and in the next century, and the enormous influence it exercised was in part its content. Following his ancient Greek

---

Geanakoplos, "The Last Step: Western Recovery and Translation of the Greek Church Fathers and Their First Printed Editions in the Renaissance," chap. 14 of *Interaction of the Sibling Cultures,* 265–80 (revised here in Appendix).

72. On George and his translation of and commentary on Ptolemy's *Almagest* see Monfasani, *George of Trebizond,* 104–8. George, under Bessarion's influence, used the commentary of the ancient Greek Theon of Alexandria (the father of Hypatia), though he objected strongly to some of Theon's statements and corrections of Ptolemy. This was the cause of a quarrel between Bessarion and George. Later, Regiomontanus, the German astronomer, defended Theon (196) but soon came to use George's version.

73. See Weiss, "Jacopo Angeli da Scarperia," 806–7. Weiss, 811, shows that Chrysoloras had already begun a translation of Ptolemy's *Geography* and handed over what he had begun to Scarperia (including perhaps his Greek MS of the text).

74. On Peter Philarges see ibid., 819. Also see *Claudii Ptolemaei Geographiae: Codex urbinus graecus* no. 82, vol. 1, pt. 1, p. 206, and my forthcoming biography on Peter of Candia.

predecessor Hipparchus, Ptolemy divided the equator into 360 parts (that is, degrees) for map projection. His idea that Asia extended much further East than is the case strengthened Columbus's belief that Asia could be reached by traveling westward. Strabo, too, had been translated during this period and probably had some effect on the type of thinking that led to the discovery of America.[75]

Mathematics, important per se but usually ancillary to astronomy and geography, was much utilized in Ptolemy's works. For a long time in the Renaissance mathematics was excluded from the *studia humanitatis* as not partaking of literary or, we would say, humanistic significance. The basic mathematical works of Euclid and a few of Archimedes had been known to the Latin Scholastic world already in the twelfth and thirteenth centuries. But the humanists exhibited little interest in this field until Bessarion began to make available to Italian and Northern humanists important mathematical texts from his great library of Greek codices, the greatest in the world of the Renaissance. Especially significant were codices of Archimedes, the greatest ancient mathematician and writer on mechanics. As a result of his long association in the 1460s with Bessarion in Rome, the great German Renaissance mathematician Regiomontanus began to study the Archimedean manuscripts in Bessarion's collection.[76] Indeed, these particular manuscripts, unknown or hitherto unused in the West (despite Moerbeke's earlier attempts at a partial translation), it has been shown by Rose, led to a revival of mathematical studies. Interest in mathematics soon became so popular that from the 1470s onward mathematics was in effect generally included by the humanists in the *studia humanitatis*.[77]

We move briefly to the sphere of physics. Aristotle's *Physics* was already known to the Scholastics through Arab transmission or through Byzantine versions. So important were Aristotelian ideas of physics in the West that certain scholars place the preparation for early theoretical science or dynamics at the University of Paris in the later fourteenth century with the work of Buridan and Oresme, work stimulated primarily

75. See Sandys, *History of Classical Scholarship,* table on 2:105; and s.v. "Ptolemy," *Encyclopaedia Britannica,* 14th ed.; M. Anastos, "Pletho, Strabo, and Columbus," in *Mélanges H. Grégoire* 4 (1953): 1–18; and P. O. Kristeller and A. Diller, "Strabo," in *Catalogus Translationum et Commentariorum,* ed. P. O. Kristeller and F. Cranz, vol. 2 (Washington, D.C.: Catholic Univ. Press, 1971), 225–33.

76. See P. Rose, "Humanist Culture and Renaissance Mathematics: The Italian Libraries of the Quattrocento," *Studies in the Renaissance* 20 (1973): 48–105; and Rose, "The *Mechanica* in the Renaissance," *Studies in the Renaissance* 18 (1971): 76–77.

77. Rose, "*Mechanica* in the Renaissance"; cf. E. Cochrane, "Science and Humanism in the Italian Renaissance," *American Historical Review* 81 (1976): 1056.

by Aristotle's ideas of impetus.[78] We shall shortly turn to the Renaissance development of physics at the University of Padua.

In medicine Hippocrates and Galen, the ancient world's leading physicians and writers in the field, had been directly known since the thirteenth century through Moerbeke's translation and, particularly with respect to Hippocrates, from Arabic versions in Islamic Spain. But it was not until the early cinquecento that original Greek texts of Byzantine versions of Greek medical and scientific works began to be published in Venice at the Aldine press and elsewhere in Italy. Aldus and probably Musurus edited the Greek text of Aristotle's *Opera* in 1503, and Hippocrates was published in 1526. Soranus, the Greek gynecologist of the second century A.D. also then first became known to the Italian Renaissance world.[79]

This brings us to the third major center of Italian cultural activity besides Florence and Rome—Venice and its satellite university city, Padua. It was there, especially in connection with science, medicine, and philosophy, in the last decades of the fifteenth and early sixteenth centuries, that the activity of the Byzantine scholars attained a new and significant peak of activity. The history of the development of Venetian and especially Paduan humanism and scientific thought (both cities constituted a single nucleus of cultural activity), though much worked on, is only now becoming fully clarified.[80] What is clear is that the University of Padua, because of its great medical school—which by the end of the fifteenth century became the finest in Europe—was primarily science oriented. The one author whose works were revered above all was Aristotle, not so much for his logical or literary works as for his scientific treatises—his physics, his biology, and, notably, his treatise on the soul *(De anima).* In vogue there, however, were not the Byzantine versions

78. See P. O. Kristeller, "Renaissance Philosophy and the Medieval Tradition," in *Renaissance Concepts of Man,* 141–42.

79. See Galen (1525), Hippocrates (1526) in chart of Sandys, *History of Classical Scholarship,* 2:105. Also see complete list of Aldine publications in Renouard, *Annales de l'imprimerie des Alde.*

80. See, for overview of the period up to 1536, Geanakoplos, *Greek Scholars in Venice;* also Pertusi, *Venezia e l'Oriente;* and the many recent publications of the Fondazione Cini in Venice: *La civiltà veneziana del quattrocento, la civiltà veneziana del cinquecento,* etc., esp. V. Branca, "L'umanesimo veneziano alla fine del quattrocento: Ermolao Barbaro e suo circolo," 123–75; and A. Pertusi, "L'umanesimo greco dalla fine del secolo XIV agli inizi del secolo XVI," 174–265, both in *Storia della cultura veneta,* vol. 3, pt. 1 (Vicenza, 1980). Also M. King, *Venetian Humanism in an Age of Patrician Dominance* (Princeton, N.J., 1986); and J. Ross, "Venetian Schools and Teachers Fourteenth to Early Sixteenth Century, a Survey and a Study of Giovanni Battista Egnazio," *Renaissance Quarterly* 39 (1976): 521, 560.

which are presumably closer to the original Greek texts, but primarily those interpreted by the Arabs, in particular "the" commentator, Averroës. Indeed, from one major point of view the history of the University of Padua and of Paduan-Venetian humanism in this period may be symbolized or rather summarized in the rivalry between the Islamic tradition of Aristotle, which long held sway there, and the Byzantine tradition, which ultimately, in great part, displaced it.[81] From here on our discussion will focus on this third great Italian Renaissance center, in part on its literary activities but more on its scientific achievement. Greek exiles played a prominent part in both areas.

In literature Padua University was influenced by the course taken by Florentine humanism with its emphasis on the *studia humanitatis.* Though Vittorino da Feltre, Francesco Filelfo, and the young Argyropoulos had all earlier taught Greek privately at the university, Chalcondyles was the first lecturer appointed *officially* by the Venetian Senate to a public chair not of rhetoric but of Greek [letters], an appointment instigated primarily by the urgings of Bessarion and perhaps Filelfo.[82] In view of the University of Padua's preeminence in medicine, and also (as in other Italian universities) because its faculty of medicine and of letters constituted a single faculty, it seems very likely that a consideration of importance in Chalcondyles' appointment was his ability to teach not only Greek literature but also Aristotle's scientific texts in physics, biology, and other subjects relating to medicine.[83]

The humanist to whom credit should chiefly go for seeking to introduce at Padua the original Greek texts of Aristotle and of other ancient Greek authors as well is the Venetian scholar Ermolao Barbaro. But Barbaro did not yet have available the best Byzantine manuscripts of Aristotle, nor, as has recently been demonstrated by Kristeller and Branca, did he succeed in completely assimilating the Greek Aristotle. Rather, in the earlier Scholastic versions or translations he used of Aristotle, he inserted many interlinear changes drawn from the Byzantine interpretations.[84] Ermolao had to fight a decisive battle against the Averroist faction, led at this time by the energetic Averroist philosophers

81. A great deal has been written on Padua and its Aristotelian, especially its "Averroist" tradition, by B. Nardi and others. See P. O. Kristeller, "Paduan Averroism and Alexandrism in the Light of Recent Studies," *Renaissance Thought,* vol. 2 (New York: Harper & Row, 1965), esp. 117ff., who objects to use of the term Averroism and prefers "Italian secular Aristotelianism," certainly a much more exact term.

82. See Geanakoplos, "The Discourse of D. Chalcondyles on the Inauguration of Greek Studies at Padua" (1974), 123–25; text in Geanakoplos, *Interaction of the Sibling Cultures,* 241; and for a more accurate edition of the Latin text see my *Byzantio kai dysē,* 430–31.

83. Geanakoplos, *Interaction of the Sibling Cultures,* esp. 251.

84. See, e.g., Branca, "Ermolao Barbaro and Venetian Humanism," 226.

Nicoletto Vernia and his pupil Agostino Nifo.[85] Ironically, only a few years before his death Vernia, persuaded probably by the more authentic Byzantine texts, even wrote a work attacking that "perverse" commentator's (Averroës!) version of Aristotle's ideas on the immortality of the soul.[86]

Finally, Ermolao's views—and the manuscripts of the Byzantine scholars of the ancient Greek commentators on Aristotle—prevailed, and in 1497 the Venetian Senate appointed a Greek scholar born in Venice, Nicolaus Leonicus Tomaeus, to a lectureship or chair "to read [in the philosophy of] Aristotle in the Greek [text]."[87] This phrase almost certainly did not mean that he would teach in Greek but rather that the Aristotelian materials were to be studied in the *original Greek text.*

When the Byzantines came to Italy we know that they were amazed and horrified by the corruption of the Greek (and Latin) manuscripts of Greek works utilized by the Scholastics and even by the humanists.[88] So bad were most of these texts that not only was the text inaccurate but the meaning was often distorted. The Byzantine émigrés complained repeatedly, but for some time little was done to rectify the situation. For some time, in fact, Western scholars preferred the second- or even third-hand Arab versions to the Greek texts of Byzantium. (The Byzantines of course were considered schismatics, even heretics, by the general Western public. But the émigrés became Roman Catholic upon coming West, though they retained their Greek liturgy and their ethnic Greek sentiment.) Bessarion, the Greek cardinal of the Roman church, was among those scholars in the West who fully understood the situation; Chalcondyles and George of Trebizond were others. It is for this reason (among others) that Bessarion established his academy in Rome under several popes: to render the Greek classics (and the Greek Fathers too, as is not always realized) in correct Latin versions.[89]

85. Branca, "Ermolao Barbaro"; P. Ragnisco, *Nicoletto Vernia: Studi storici sulla filosofia padovana nella seconda metà del secolo decimoquinto* (Venice: Tip. Antonelli, 1891); and B. Nardi, *Saggi sull'aristotelismo padovano del secolo XIV al XVI* (Florence: Sansoni, 1958).

86. See E. Mahoney, "Nicoletto Vernia on the Soul and Immortality," in *Philosophy and Humanism: Festschrift for Paul Oskar Kristeller,* ed. E. Mahoney (Leiden: Brill, 1976), esp. 149ff.

87. Geanakoplos, *Greek Scholars in Venice,* 137–38; and Branca, "Ermolao Barbaro," 225. On the document of appointment, see J. Facciolatus, *Fasti gymnasii patavini,* vol. 1 (Padua: Seminarii, 1752), under a. 1497.

88. See, e.g., Chalcondyles's own words in his oration(s), in Geanakoplos, *Interaction of the Sibling Cultures,* 246: "The texts of Aristotle have been rather badly and improperly translated into the Latin language." George of Trebizond also inveighed against the condition of manuscripts (Monfasani, *George of Trebizond).* See n. 72, above.

89. On Bessarion see esp. L. Mohler, *Aus Bessarions Gelehrtenkreis, Abhandlungen,*

Nor were all Western humanists (or even Scholastics) unaware of the more authentic versions of the Greek codices, some still to be found in the Greek East. The medieval West's greatest physician, the late thirteenth-, early fourteenth-century Peter of Abano (near Venice), it is now known, had brought back with him from a visit to Constantinople sometime before 1285 a Greek manuscript on the *Problemata* of Aristotle (now considered pseudo-Aristotelian), a series of questions and answers on science, including astrology.[90] Nonetheless, the ascendancy, virtually complete domination, of the Averroist interpretation of Aristotle continued at Padua, especially in medicine and philosophy.

This raises the more difficult question of what *were* the interpretations, that is, the views of Aristotle himself, since as we know, his works, at least some, survive primarily through notes of his students.[91] Logic dictates that the most-authentic surviving manuscripts were those possessed by the Byzantines, these presumably having descended in a more or less direct line from Aristotle's school in Athens, the Lyceum, and from Greek Alexandria. In the dual problem at Padua of determining (1) the most authentic texts, and (2) the best interpretations of Aristotle, a new step was taken through recourse to the ancient Greek and early Byzantine commentators or exegetes on Aristotle—texts which were part of the legacy of the Palaeologan Renaissance.[92] One of the most important ways to determine the accuracy of his texts, certainly of the meaning, would seem to be to use these commentaries by the ancient scholars, Alexander of Aphrodisias of the third century, and several early Byzantines, Simplicius of Athens and Philoponus of Alexandria, both of the sixth century, and earlier, Themistius of the fourth.

Already Ermolao Barbaro, who had himself studied with Byzantine teachers, had occupied himself with the study of Themistius (a work of

---

Rede, Briefe von Bessarion . . ., vol. 3 of *Kardinal Bessarion als Theologe, Humanist und Staatsmann* (Paderborn: Schoning, 1942); H. Vast, *Le Cardinal Bessarion* (Paris: Hachette, 1878); Geanakoplos, *Greek Scholars in Venice,* 91, 280. On works of Greek Fathers translated by George into Latin, see Monfasani, *George of Trebizond,* 55ff., which is the best treatment of this Roman period and its Greek translations under Bessarion.

90. Actually c. 1310 he completed an *Expositio* of the *Problemata.* See L. Thorndike, *History of Magic and Experimental Science,* vol. 2 (New York: Macmillan, 1929), 874–947.

91. On Aristotle's students see P. O. Kristeller, chap. 2, on Aristotelianism, in *Renaissance Thought,* vol. 1 (New York: Harper, 1961).

92. P. O. Kristeller (see above n. 81) suggests, wisely, substitution of the term "Italian secular Aristotelianism" for the many ambiguities of the term "Averroism," since all Averroists did not share all the same "Avveroist" views.

whose he was the first Latin to translate into Latin),[93] but it was the Greek Leonicus Tomaeus who fully revealed the true significance of most of the Greek and Byzantine commentators for interpreting Aristotle, and probably of his principal commentator (in certain aspects, especially on *De anima*), Alexander of Aphrodisias.[94] To take but one example of the usefulness of these ancient commentators: Philoponus showed the incorrectness of Aristotle's position on the impossibility of the existence of a vacuum and also corrected or modified his views on two bodies of different weights dropping to the ground at the same time (thus anticipating the fourteenth-century impetus theory of projectile motion).[95]

Tomaeus, despite his appointment at Padua in Aristotelian philosophy, did not restrict himself to the Stagirite's philosophy. As may be seen from his many editions and publications, he was interested in Plato as well as in Aristotle, especially in lessening the extreme polarization the two philosophers had been forced into by the Scholastics and to some extent by the early quattrocento humanist Platonists at Florence. Indeed, his career, I think, combines both Florentine humanism with its emphasis on the metaphysical philosophy of Plato (as a youth Tomaeus had studied in Florence under Chalcondyles) and the Paduan preference for science, medicine, and Aristotle.[96] His career of teaching and editing for the Aldine and other Venetian and also Florentine presses lasted from 1497 to 1531, longer than that of any other Byzantine scholar in Italy except for Chalcondyles and Argyropoulos. Both Italian and Northern humanists attest to his deep fund of knowledge, keen mind, sense of literary style, and interest in science, and inspiration in teaching. He was especially known as the mentor of foreign, in particular English, students who came to Padua because of its medical school, liberal policies, and the sophistication of its environment. These included several subsequently noted English statesmen, ecclesiastics, and humanists, such as Cardinal Pole, Thomas Tungston, and Richard Pace. Tomaeus loaned various

93. Ermolao was a devoted student and follower of Theodore Gaza (see Branca, "Ermolao Barbaro," 222) and a friend to Leonicus Tomaeus (Geanakoplos, *Greek Scholars in Venice,* 137–38). On Ermolao see also P. O. Kristeller, *Studies in Renaissance Thought and Letters,* 343.

94. On Alexander see F. Cranz, "Alexander of Aphrodisias," in *Catalogus Translationum et Commentariorum,* ed. P. O. Kristeller and F. Cranz, vol. 1 (Washington, D.C.: Catholic Univ. Press, 1960), 77–135.

95. See *Source Book in Greek Science,* trans. M. Cohen and I. Drabkin (New York: McGraw Hill, 1948), 217–21; the same text is printed in Geanakoplos, *Byzantium: Church, Society and Civilization,* no. 324.

96. See G. Cammelli, *Demetrio Calcondila* (Florence: Le Monnier, 1954), 36.

Greek authors in manuscript to his English students along with his own recent publications. For example, he sent to Pole, at the latter's request, a certain Greek edition he had just finished and, interestingly enough, asked in return for a copy of More's *Utopia.* His work in helping to establish the original text of Plutarch's *Moralia* is well known to philologists. Several letters written by Erasmus attest to his high respect for Tomaeus's scholarship and personality.[97]

Among the editions Tomaeus published are several of purely literary significance which reveal the broad humanist cast of his mind. In addition to an edition of Plutarch's *Moralia,* he published an edition of the work of the Greek traveler Pausanias (the *editio princeps* was done earlier by Musurus). More interesting was his publication of works of the physician Galen in Latin translation—something which should not surprise us since some commentaries on Aristotelian logic and philosophy were imbedded by Galen in his various works on medicine.

These last few remarks are among the first to evaluate the contributions of Tomaeus and his career to Italian Renaissance culture. Although Ermolao Barbaro paved the way for Tomaeus, it may properly be said that it was during Tomaeus's official tenure of the post in Aristotelian philosophy at Padua that the "triumph" of the Byzantine, that is, the original Greek, Aristotle occurred. Tomaeus's activities along with the more important ones of Chalcondyles, Musurus, Calliergis, and other Greek émigrés helped to make Venice-Padua in the last decade of the fifteenth and the early sixteenth century the chief center of Greek studies in the European world, thus displacing Florence as well as Rome, each of which could earlier claim primacy in Greek studies.

In certain respects Tomaeus's career, besides combining the best of Florentine and Venetian humanism, marks the culmination of the contribution of the Byzantine scholars in Italy. Through the work of the Byzantines, as well as the Venetians Ermolao Barbaro and his fellow scholar Girolamo Donato, the way was prepared at Padua as well as Venice for the emergence of a new phase in the Paduan-Venetian philosophic school to be climaxed by the great Pomponazzi. Pomponazzi was able to explain the problem of the immortality of the soul through the improved texts of,

97. Cardinal F. Gasquet, *Cardinal Pole and His Early Friends* (London: G. Bell, 1927), esp. 11ff., 66ff.; Turyn, *Manuscript Tradition of Euripides;* on Tomaeus and science, P. Rose and S. Drake, "The Pseudo-Aristotelian *Questions of Mechanics* in Renaissance Culture," *Studies in the Renaissance* 18 (1971): 79. I read a paper on Tomaeus at the International Aristotelian Congress in 1978 in Greece and also at the International Neo-Latin and Renaissance Conference at Bologna, 1979. Essay 5 below is a longer treatment.

and commentaries on, Aristotle's *De anima,* among others.[98] Pomponazzi's work in turn helped, in certain ways, to pave the way scientifically for the advent of Galileo and, finally, even for Copernicus, who, some scholars claim, was helped to reach his conclusions about a heliocentric universe by the Pythagorean mathematical material contained in Plato.[99]

To conclude: many half-true statements are still frequently made about the Byzantine contribution to Italian Renaissance culture, some of them fulsome, more often slightly denigrating or at least grudgingly laudatory. In this essay I hope that I have been able to show that the Byzantine émigré scholars—far from serving merely in the capacity of blind transmitters of ancient Greek learning as is often affirmed—through the many new manuscripts they brought westward, through their restoration and correction of Greek manuscripts already known, through their recourse to exegeses on both Aristotle and Plato of both the Byzantine and Alexandrian traditions, through the many *editiones principes* they edited for the Aldine and other leading presses, and through the teaching they did, sometimes highly inspirational, at all three major centers of learning, Florence, Rome, and Venice, exerted a remarkably formative influence on the development of Italian quattrocento thought and learning. Indeed, in the light of the material presented, I think it may be affirmed that they were *primarily* responsible for bringing about three major shifts in Renaissance thought: (1) in early quattrocento Florence, from the early, central emphasis on rhetoric to one on metaphysical philosophy by means of their introduction and interpretation of Platonic materials; (2) in Venice-Padua, by reducing the dominance of the Averroist Aristotle in science and philosophy, and supplementing (but not completely replacing) it with the Byzantine tradition which utilized ancient and Byzantine commentators on Aristotle; and (3) earlier in the mid fifteenth century in Rome, through emphasis not on any particular philosophic school but through the production of more authentic and reliable versions of Greek texts relevant to all fields of humanism and science and with respect to the Greek fathers of the church. Hardly less important was their influence, direct or indirect, on exegesis of the New Testament itself through Bessarion's inspiration of Valla's biblical emendations of the Latin Vulgate in the light of the Greek text.

98. On Pomponazzi see P. O. Kristeller, "Renaissance Aristotelianism," *Greek, Roman and Byzantine Studies* 6 (1965): esp. 170–73.

99. See Geanakoplos, *Interaction of the Sibling Cultures,* 64, based in part on E. Burtt, *Metaphysical Foundations of Modern Physical Science* (London: Kegan Paul, 1925), 40ff.

By means of their contributions to virtually all spheres of learning—to rhetoric, history, politics, poetry, ethics, and metaphysical philosophy, to astronomy, geography, physics, and medicine, and finally to the fathers of the church and the Bible itself—these Byzantine literati, and the manuscripts they brought with them, provided the inspiration for changing prevailing humanistic and scientific interpretations and bringing about new ones. In this way they played a definite, though to be sure not easily measured, part in the very complex and still inadequately understood process of the transformation of Italian, and to a lesser degree, Northern society from medieval values and views to a greater secularity approximating in many ways that of the ancient Greco-Roman world and even our own.

Were there any truly creative thinkers among the Byzantine émigré scholars? As may also, I believe, be said in general about the Latin scholars of the Italian Renaissance (with the possible exception of Cusanus and Pico), there were probably very few if any. Many Byzantines, certainly, were only transmitters of knowledge and manuscripts, but, as we have seen, some figures such as Chrysoloras, Argyropoulos, George of Trebizond, Gaza, and Tomaeus were largely responsible for creating changes in the very direction of Italian humanism and thought. In my own view, Bessarion was at once the most original and most pragmatic mind among the Byzantine exiles who came to the West. He gathered together the most valuable library of Greek manuscripts in the entire Renaissance; he founded an academy in Rome for translation, or more-accurate translation, of ancient Greek texts and also, as is sometimes forgotten, of the works of the Byzantine church fathers; through his Archimedean codices and his patronage he inspired the revived study of mathematics; and through application of the Byzantine tradition of theological exegesis, he (and probably Theodore Gaza) helped to inspire Lorenzo Valla to formulate a new kind of critical methodology for explication of the New Testament itself.[100] Let us not forget also that, as a Greek patriot, a main reason for his bequeathing his manuscript collection to Venice was that he hoped that, through use of his collection, his Greek countrymen could prevent themselves from falling into the bar-

100. Perhaps Bessarion, with his *In calumniatorem Platonis,* a Latin translation of which he sent to Ficino in 1469, may even have inspired Ficino to try to conciliate Plato and Christianity in his *Theologica platonica* (see Holmes, *Florentine Enlightenment,* 259–60). On Theodore Gaza and his influence on Valla's biblical scholarship see esp. M. Fois, *Il pensiero cristiano di Lorenzo Valla* (Rome: Università Gregoriana, 1969), 416–18; and J. Monfasani, "Pseudo-Dionysius the Areopagite in Mid-Quattrocento Rome," in *Supplementum Festivum: Studies in Honor of Paul Oskar Kristeller,* ed. J. Hankins, J. Monfasani, and F. Purnell, Jr., 189–220 (Binghamton, N.Y., 1987). See also essay 3.

barism then threatening them. Thus the Byzantine émigré scholars, on the basis of their activity in the transmission and interpretation of the rich experience of classical and patristic Hellenism as mediated by the primarily rhetorical tradition of the Palaeologan Renaissance of Byzantium—a tradition gradually combined with that of the developing "Italian" culture—may be said to have made a fundamental, if not the key contribution to *broadening* the horizon of Italian Renaissance thought and learning.

Additional Bibliography

See the bibliographical note at the end of essay 1.

Three

Theodore Gaza, a Byzantine Scholar of the Palaeologan "Renaissance" in the Early Italian Renaissance (c. 1400–1475)

The general outlines of the career of the famous Byzantine scholar Theodore Gaza of Thessalonica (Theodoros Gazes in Greek), who was active in Renaissance Italy during the second and third quarters of the fifteenth century, have long been known to scholars. But in spite of the now old researches of A. Gercke, H. Hody, E. Legrand, A. Kyrou, and, more peripherally, of L. Mohler and H. Vast, no comprehensive modern biography has ever been attempted.[1] And this despite Gaza's considerable importance for the development of Italian Renaissance Greek studies in the crucial decades after Manuel Chrysoloras's seminal work of teaching in Florence in 1397–99. What makes a new biography of Gaza especially desirable are the many recent advances in our understanding of certain intellectual problems concerning the Italian Renaissance, particularly the

1. See accounts in H. Hodius, *De Graecis illustribus* (London, 1742), 55–101; A. Gercke, *Theodoros Gazes* (Greifswald, 1903), 1–46; L. Stein, *Der Humanist Gaza als Philosoph,* Archiv für Geschichte der Philosophie, vol. 2 (Berlin, 1889), 426ff.; E. Legrand, *Bibliographie hellénique ou description raisonnée des ouvrages publiés en grec par des grecs au XVe et XVIe siècles,* vol. 1 (Paris, 1885), xxxi–xlix; K. Sathas, *Neohellēnikē philologia* (Athens, 1868), 37–40; A. Kyrou, *Hoi Hellēnes tēs anagennēseōs* (Athens, 1938), 91–93; texts and references in L. Mohler, *Kardinal Bessarion als Theologe, Humanist und Staatsmann,* 3 vol. (Paderborn, 1923–42), esp. vol. 3 (1942), 253–68; and H. Vast, *Le Cardinal Bessarion* (Paris, 1878). For more recent bibliography, see below nn. 10, 16, 58, 59, and bibliographical note to this essay.

development of the parallel Palaeologan "Renaissance" of the last Byzantine period and the attempts made by Byzantine scholars and, to a lesser extent, Latin Hellenists toward a fusion of qualities of *both* of these Italian and late Byzantine Renaissances.[2] In this historical process Gaza was a key figure. It is the aim of this chapter, then, to discuss some of the more important aspects of his life and thought within the context of recent Italian and Palaeologan scholarship and, at the same time, to raise certain questions not hitherto considered by scholars.

That Gaza was born in Thessalonica seems clear from the epithet *Thessalonicensis* (in Latin) or *Thessalonikeus* (in Greek) found in his own treatises as well as in those of Italian humanists.[3] The date of his birth is not at all clear, nor even that of his arrival in Italy. K. Sathas, for example, adduced the certainly erroneous birthdate of c. 1370; others probably more correctly have suggested 1400.[4] No facts whatever of his early life in Thessalonica have emerged although, given his lifelong interests in classical Greek literature and science, he was undoubtedly subject in his early education to the still-lingering influences of the remarkable literary renaissance taking place in fourteenth-century Thessalonica, of which Demetrius Triklinios, Demetrius Cydones, and Thomas Magister had been the principal protagonists.[5] This renaissance, more correctly

2. On attempts, conscious or otherwise, of the Byzantine scholars to fuse qualities of both Renaissances, see Geanakoplos, *Interaction of the "Sibling" Byzantine and Western Cultures in the Middle Ages and Italian Renaissance,* esp. 13–24, 284–95; J. Monfasani, *George of Trebizond: A Biography and Study of His Rhetoric and Logic* (Leiden, 1976), 248–55; S. Runciman, *The Last Byzantine Renaissance* (Cambridge, 1970), esp. 98–103; A. Vacalopoulos, *Origins of the Greek Nation: The Byzantine Period, 1204–1261* (New Brunswick, N.J., 1970), 241–45, and his *The Greek Nation, 1453–1669* (New Brunswick, N.J., 1976), 157–61; and, more recently, essays 1 and 2 above.

3. E.g., Sassuolo da Prato wrote in 1443, "Nacti sumus nuper Graecum hominem Thessalonicensem Theodorum, cum doctum, tum hac aetate in sua lingua paene principem." See W. Woodward, *Vittorino da Feltre and Other Humanist Educators* (Cambridge, 1905), 53; and Legrand, *Bibliographie hellénique* 1:xl, quoting from Matthias Palmieri, *Opus de temporibus suis,* in *Rerum italicarum scriptores . . . ex florentinarum bibliothecarum codicibus* (Florence, 1748), fol., vol. 1, col. 259: "Theodorus Thessalonicensis."

4. Sathas, *Neohellēnikē philologia,* 38 (he says, probably correctly [n. 13 below], Gaza taught Greek first in Siena, before Ferrara). The article on Gaza in the *Thrēskeftikē kai ēthikē egkyklopaideia,* vol. 4 (Athens, 1964), 142–43, says that Gaza was born in 1400, while not affirming he went to Constantinople after 1430. See also Gercke, *Theodoros Gazes,* 22. Cf. L. Stein, "Der Humanist Teodor Gaza als Philosoph," *Archiv für Geschichte der Philosophie,* vol. 2 (1889) 426–58, esp. 431–32, who quotes a letter of Gaza showing he was in Constantinople during Sultan Murad's siege in 1422. Stein, 433, also believes Gaza became a priest already in Constantinople. Certainly he had to be a priest of the Roman church when Bessarion later gave him a *sacerdotium* in Italy (Stein, 458).

5. On the Renaissance in Thessalonica, see B. Laourdas, *Hē klassikē philologia eis tēn*

intensive revival, of ancient Greek literature, philosophy, and science in Thessalonica was correlative with the perhaps even more significant revival also taking place in Constantinople.[6] Indeed, Gaza was probably the beneficiary of the cultural legacy of both Palaeologan centers, since evidence indicates he was active in Constantinople before going to Italy. Taylor, Stein, and Legrand assert that Gaza not only went to Constantinople just before the Turkish siege of the capital in 1422 but, as seems very likely, also opened his own school of higher education there.[7] A striking characteristic of the Palaeologan revival of letters was that virtually an equal emphasis was placed on both literature and science. This emphasis was typical of the traditional Byzantine concept of the *enkyklios paideia,* a complete cycle of study which included not only letters, philosophy, mathematics, and science, but also theology, the latter considered to be the capstone of all studies.[8]

Up to the mid fifteenth century Italian Renaissance humanism centered on the so-called *studia humanitatis*—that is, primarily rhetoric, as well as history, poetry, and ethics—subjects whose study was thought to

---

Thessalonikēn (Thessalonica, 1960); G. Schirò, *Ho Barlaam kai hē philosophia eis tēn Thessalonikēn* (Thessalonica, 1959); Geanakoplos, *Interaction of the Sibling Cultures,* 205; Runciman, *Last Byzantine Renaissance,* 62–66, 72–74; D. Nicol, *Church and Society in the Last Centuries of Byzantium* (Cambridge, 1979), 34, 56. On Triklinios, Cydones, and Magister, see esp. A. Turyn, "Demetrius Triclinius and the Planudean Anthology," *Festschrift N. Tomadakes* (Athens, 1973), 403–50, and his books *The Manuscript Tradition of the Tragedies of Aeschylus* (New York, 1943), . . . *of Euripides* (Urbana, Ill., 1957), and . . . *of Sophocles* (Urbana, Ill., 1952). Finally, see essays 1 and 2 above.

6. On the Palaeologan Renaissance in Constantinople see, in addition to the works listed above, B. Tatakis, *La philosophie byzantine* (Paris, 1949), 232–306; Geanakoplos, *Greek Scholars in Venice,* esp. 22–24 (also the Greek ed., trans. Ch. Patrinelis, *Hellēnes logioi eis tēn Benetian* [Athens, 1965]); R. Bolgar, *The Classical Heritage and Its Beneficiaries* (Cambridge, 1958), 82–90; H. Hunger, *Die hochsprächliche profane Literatur der Byzantiner,* vol. 2 (Munich, 1978); and S. Runciman, *Last Byzantine Renaissance.* Also see below, essays 1 and 2.

7. Several important private higher schools then existed in Constantinople. See Geanakoplos, *Byzantium: Church Society, and Civilization,* 402–3. J. W. Taylor, *Theodore Gaza's "De fato"* (Toronto, 1925), 5, says (with no note) that Gaza seems to have entered holy orders in Constantinople. Sathas, *Neohellēnikē philologia,* 40, notes that Gaza wrote from Italy to his two brothers in Constantinople. It is very possible that at this time in Constantinople Gaza knew leading Byzantine scholars, but Bessarion was only c. 19 then. On Gaza in Constantinople see Stein's evidence (n. 4). J. W. Taylor, *Theodore Gaza's "De fato"* (Toronto, 1925) 5, follows Stein.

8. F. Fuchs, *Die höheren Schulen von Konstantinopel* (Leipzig and Berlin, 1926), 41–45; essay 1 above; L. Reynolds and N. Wilson, *Scribes and Scholars* (Oxford, 1974), chap. 2 and pp. 130–37; and R. Browning, "Byzantine Scholarship," *Past and Present* 28 (1964): 3–20.

be conducive to effective participation in the civic life of the state. Only in the later fifteenth century was this humanist curriculum expanded to include metaphysical philosophy, science, and mathematics—an expansion perhaps to a small degree the result of the philosophic influence of Gemistos Pletho at the Council of Florence but much more directly of the teaching of John Argyropoulos, who lectured in Florence systematically on Aristotle and privately at his home on the metaphysical philosophy of Plato.[9]

The influence of Theodore Gaza on this important shift in the orientation of Italian humanism has been completely overlooked. Gaza's interests and activities, like those of Argyropoulos, reflected most aspects of the traditional Byzantine *enkyklios paideia* rather than the narrower ones of the Latin *studia humanitatis.* This breadth of interest may be seen in Gaza's work of translation (sometimes rather of paraphrasing) of Aristotle's scientific as well as philosophic works (including the *Problemata* and *De animalibus*), in his translation of Theophrastus's *De plantis,* in his work in grammar and oratory (Demosthenes above all), and in his translations of several of the Greek church fathers. It is interesting to note that Gaza was one of the very few fifteenth-century Byzantines—following Planudes of the late thirteenth century—to translate Latin literary works into Greek, among them Cicero's *Somnium Scipionis* and *De senectute* and works of Claudian.[10]

Gaza is often cited as one of the very few Byzantine scholars with an excellent knowledge of Latin, a skill he acquired after only about three years (one writer affirms after only eighteen months!) of study under the

9. Of course, other background factors were no less important: the Medici control in Florence, which prevented truly republican government, and the Scholastic interests of Ficino and Pico. For Argyropoulos's role in the metaphysical revival, see essay 4 below; E. Garin, *Portraits from the Quattrocento,* trans. V. A. Velen and E. Velen (New York, 1972), 59–81; J. Seigel, "The Teaching of Argyropoulos and the Rhetoric of the First Humanists," in *Action and Conviction in Early Modern Europe,* ed. T. Rabb and J. Seigel (Princeton, N.J., 1969), 237–60; and essay 2 above.

10. Gaza's main works of translation are listed in *Tusculum Lexicon,* ed. W. Buchwald et al. (Munich, 1963), 170–71; Legrand, *Bibliographie hellénique* 1:xlvi–xlix; Sathas, *Neohellēnikē philologia,* 39–40; and Gercke, *Theodoros Gazes,* 26. Bolgar, *Classical Heritage,* 283, notes that Gaza translated, beside Aristotle's *Problemata, De animalibus,* and *De caelo,* other medical works—including Hippocrates' *Aphorisms* and Aelian's *Tactica*— and owned a MS of Isocrates. Taylor, *Gaza's "De fato,"* 5, says Gaza translated Cicero's *Somnium Scipionis,* although the *Tusculum Lexicon,* 171, and Legrand, lxvi, differ. To be noted is that Gaza also translated the *Problemata* of Alexander of Aphrodisias, an ancient commentator on Aristotle: see esp. J. Monfasani, "Pseudo-Dionysus the Areopagite in Mid-Quattrocento Rome," in *Supplementum Festivum: Essays in Honor of Paul Oskar Kristeller,* ed. J. Hankins, J. Monfasani, and F. Purnell, Jr. (Binghamton, N.Y.: 1987), pp. 206–214, for Gaza's translations and editing.

most famous Italian humanist teacher, Vittorino de Feltre.[11] According to epistolary evidence, Gaza had already become intimate with Francesco Filelfo in Constantinople, the Italian humanist then serving as personal secretary to the Byzantine emperor John VIII, and, very possibly, it was as a result of Filelfo's influence that Gaza went to Italy.[12] After his arrival in Italy, evidently several years before 1440, and probably in 1434, it was certainly Filelfo's recommendation that secured him entrée in Mantua to study Latin with Filelfo's close friend the famous teacher, Vittorino da Feltre. Among Gaza's fellow-students was Giovanni de Bussi, who would later collaborate with Gaza in Rome, editing classical Latin works for the press.[13]

It seems certain that in exchange for Latin lessons Gaza in turn helped Vittorino with his Greek. With Gaza's help Vittorino doubtless made progress in learning the texts of certain hitherto unknown Greek writings and in practicing Greek composition to improve his style.[14] Under Vittorino's tutelage Gaza mastered Ciceronian Latin rhetoric, characterized by its flexibility of style and freedom from pedantry.[15]

Several scholars have affirmed that around this time Gaza appeared at Ferrara at sessions of the ecclesiastical council which met there and later in Florence in order to unite the Byzantine and Latin churches.[16] Evidence for this assertion, according to these scholars, is found in the Paris manuscript B. N. Graecus 1287, drawn up by Gaza, which analyzes the problems of the *filioque* and purgatorial fire after death, both of which had been discussed at Ferrara. A careful analysis of these tracts might shed more light on how, or whether, Gaza's views differed from those of other Byzantine pro-unionists such as Bessarion or Dorotheos of Mytilene, who probably drew up the Greek pro-unionist record of the council,

11. Woodward, *Vittorino da Feltre,* 54; Legrand, *Bibliographie hellénique* 1:xxxii.

12. Legrand, *Bibliographie hellénique* 1:xxxi, also discussing relations of Filelfo's son and Gaza. Cf. Stein, "Der Humanist T. Gaza," 435f. See also n. 36 below.

13. Legrand, *Bibliographie hellénique,* 1:xxxi–xxxii, for Filelfo's letters on Gaza in Pavia 1440. E. Pinto, *Teodoro Gaza Epistolae* (Naples, 1975) 13, says Gaza taught in Siena between 1434–35. On de Bussi see below.

14. A theory of Woodward's, *Vittorino da Feltre,* 53.

15. Hermogenes' (Greek) rhetoric, so popular in Byzantium, was almost unknown in Italy until Trapezuntius "popularized" it. Monfasani, *George of Trebizond,* 26–27 chap. 9. Quintilian's (Latin) rhetoric was not yet as widely popular as it would later be.

16. Legrand, *Bibliographie hellénique* 1:xxxi, cites G. Giraldi, *De poetis nostrorum temporum* (Florence, 1551), 56, on Gaza at the Council of Florence (not mentioned in J. Gill, *Council of Florence* [Cambridge, 1959]). Vacalopoulos, *Origins of the Greek Nation,* 244, affirms Gaza was with the Greek delegation at Florence. Woodhouse, 21 (see my p. 113) says at Florence Gaza and Bessarion (with Pletho) discussed the Latinity of St. Jerome. Ibid., 160, that Basinius, poet, learned Greek from Gaza in Mantua. On Gaza at Ferrara Council [not Florence?] see Pinto, *Epistolae,* 15.

the so-called *Acta graeca.*[17] Relevant is Gaza's later remark that the Greeks were so interested in showing the Latins wrong theologically that "I am afraid that they will still be engaged in religious arguments and the writing of diatribes against the Roman church while the few cities that are left are being taken [by the Turks] and their wives and children sold into slavery."[18] This judicious remark, however, should not cast Gaza in the role of a "Latinophron" in the usual pejorative Byzantine sense of the term. For I believe that Gaza, like Bessarion, far from denigrating his Greek or Byzantine heritage, simply desired a return to the historical ecclesiastical unity characteristic of East and West in the earlier patristic period, something which in turn, hopefully, would lead to Western military aid against the Turks.[19] Indeed, I have found much evidence of Gaza's pride in his Greek race and heritage in such references to himself as "Graecus de natione."[20] A. Vacalopoulos, with much justice I believe, affirms that the Greek émigré scholars, Gaza in particular, constitute one of the first examples of a modern sense of "nationality" to be found in Europe.[21]

From 1440 to 1449, as successor to the Byzantine Nicholas Secundinus, Gaza taught Greek to students at the *studium* of Ferrara.[22] His tenure there constitutes a genuine landmark in the dissemination of Greek letters in the West, for it occurred only a few decades after Chrysoloras's first systematic teaching of Greek in the Renaissance at Florence's *studium.* So successful was Gaza's teaching that in 1449 he was named the first rector of the university of Ferrara after its reconstitution by Duke Lionello d'Este.[23] Gaza's inaugural address, *De litteris graecis,* is preserved, along with his oration on his later assumption of the office of rector and a third address given upon retirement from the rectorship.[24] In these discourses his main aim was always to kindle or promote interest in

17. See Gill, *Council of Florence,* ix, x, xiv. See essay 11.

18. See Sp. Lampros, *Palaiologeia kai Peloponnēsiaka,* vol. 4 (Athens, 1926), 46–47 (translated in Vacalopoulos, *Origins of the Greek Nation,* 187). Pinto, *Epistolae,* 31.

19. On the views of Bessarion and other intellectual pro-unionists, see esp. Geanakoplos, *Interaction of the Sibling Cultures,* 292–93. Also essay 11 below.

20. See J. Irmscher, "Theodoros Gazes als griechischer Patriot," *Parola del passato* 16 (1961): 161–73. Also see Gercke, *Theodoros Gazes,* 13.

21. Vacalopoulos, *Origins of the Greek Nation,* 257.

22. Legrand, *Bibliographie hellénique,* vol. 1, xxxii f. There is no mention in P. Mastrodemetres, *Nikolaos Sekoundinos* (Athens, 1970), of Secoundinos's second period of teaching at Ferrara (see below 88).

23. Legrand, *Bibliographie hellénique* 1:xxxi; and W. Gundersheimer, *Ferrara, the Style of a Renaissance Despotism* (Princeton, N.J., 1973), 103, 114ff., 154.

24. For text of Gaza's three orations see Gercke, *Theodoros Gazes,* 3–9; L. Mohler, *Aus Bessarions Gelehrtenkreis: Abhandlungen, Reden, Briefe von Bessarion, T. Gazes, M. Apostolios, A. Kallistos, G. Trapezuntios, . . .,* vol. 3 of *Kardinal Bessarion* (Paderborn,

Greek studies. These addresses, known but not yet thoroughly studied, reveal several interesting features: for example, his indebtedness (perhaps for his appointment as professor) to his teacher Vittorino, to the Sicilian humanist and manuscript collector Giovanni Aurispa, to the famous Guarino (a colleague of his at Ferrara), and, not least, to the duke of the Ferrarese court Lionello d'Este.[25] They also seem to indicate that, besides teaching elementary Greek grammar, he gave a course in Greek literature, including the reading of such authors as Demosthenes, especially his oration *On the Crown.*[26]

Gaza's *De litteris graecis* is, I believe, the earliest surviving inaugural discourse on the importance of Greek studies given by a Byzantine émigré scholar in Italy. (The earlier address given by Manuel Chrysoloras in Florence has not survived.) Moreover, Gaza's oration offers for the first time arguments for the study of Greek by Latins that were to recur in similar speeches given later by both Byzantine and Latin scholars and, above all, in the famous oration of his student Demetrius Chalcondyles, delivered at the inauguration of Greek studies at the great University of Padua in 1463.[27] Chalcondyles, Gaza's student earlier in Constantinople and later a lifelong friend, makes some of the same points as Gaza, especially that the ancient Romans too had found knowledge of Greek literature of inestimable value for effective participation in political life. (Indeed, the leading Roman political figures sent their sons to study in Greece.) In his own discourse Chalcondyles has of course expanded this and other ideas more fully. In my view the inaugural discourses of Gaza at Ferrara, of Chalcondyles at Padua, of Argyropoulos at Florence, and of the Venetian cardinal Bembo delivered in Venice about 1539 rank among the finest (surviving) tributes to the study of Greek letters in the entire Italian Renaissance.[28]

1942), 253–68; and scattered references in Monfasani, *George of Trebizond* (see his index).

25. On Ferrara's humanist circle see G. Bertoni, *Guarino da Verona fra letterati e cortigiani a Ferrara* (Geneva, 1921), esp. chaps. 2–3; and Gundersheimer, *Ferrara,* 92–127 (but with little on Gaza). Gundersheimer does not analyze Gaza's discourses and laments we know so little about him.

26. Legrand, *Bibliographie hellênique* 1:xxxiii, citing evidence. Cf. Mohler, *Aus Bessarions Gelehrtenkreis,* 256.

27. For complete Latin text, translation, and analysis of Chalcondyles' oration at Padua see Geanakoplos, *Interaction of the Sibling Cultures,* 254–64, 296–304, 241–53; and Geanakoplos, "The Discourse of Demetrius Chalcondyles on the Inauguration of Greek Studies at the University of Padua in 1463" (1974). See the Greek translation of Geanakoplos's *Interaction of the Sibling Cultures, Byzantio kai dysē,* esp. 430–41, for a more accurate text of Chalcondyles' Latin oration.

28. On Bembo's discourse see Geanakoplos, *Greek Scholars in Venice,* 279. For

Praise for Gaza's teaching was common among contemporary humanists, but little concrete evidence is available about his methods of teaching. Well known, of course, was his Greek grammar, *Introductiva grammatica (Grammatikē eis merē tessara)* which he wrote in Ferrara for his students and which has been recognized as the ablest of all manuals of Greek grammar compiled by humanists, Byzantine or Latin, for learning Greek in the fifteenth and early sixteenth century. Erasmus had so high an opinion of it that he introduced it to Cambridge University, editing a version for his classes there. As Erasmus later wrote in his *De ratione studii:* "Among the Greek grammarians everyone assigns first place to Theodorus Gaza; Constantine Lascaris, in my opinion, rightly lays claim to second place."[29] Important to note is that Gaza's grammar was composed essentially in the Palaeologan tradition, drawing directly on such works as the *Erotemata* of Manuel Moschopoulos of the fourteenth century and on earlier manuals of grammar by Maximos Planudes and the ninth-century Michael Syncellos.[30]

Gaza's students in Italy included some later famous humanists. Aside from the Byzantines Demetrius Chalcondyles and Demetrius Sgouropoulos (the latter had studied under Gaza in Constantinople) and his Latin teacher Vittorino, Gaza instructed at Ferrara, among others, Ludovico Carbone, who came to be head of the humanist circle there.[31] Subsequently, during his years of residence in Rome, Gaza gave instruction to the (later) preeminent Venetian humanist Ermolao Barbaro (whose father was serving there as Venetian ambassador) privately to Chalcondyles, and, probably informally, as the result of their friendly relationship, to the great Renaissance philologist Lorenzo Valla. (It is very possible that, as is sometimes affirmed, he taught a leading German Hellenist, Rudolf Agricola, who later first taught Greek at Heidelberg University.) Gaza also taught Leonardo da Bologna and the Venetian

---

Argyropoulos's, see K. Müllner, *Reden und Briefe* (Vienna, 1899), 3ff. Also esp. 4. On Chalcondyles see esp. G. Cammelli, *Demetrio Calcondyla* (Florence, 1954).

29. Translated from Erasmus, "On the Method of Study," *Collected Works of Erasmus, Literary and Educational Writings,* ed. C. Thompson, vol. 2 (Toronto, 1978), 667. Gaza's Greek grammar was first printed in Venice in 1495 by Aldus.

30. A. Pertusi, "*Erotemata:* Per la storia e le fonti delle prime grammatiche greche a stampa," in *Italia medioevale e umanistica* 5 (1962): 321–51. See also D. Donnet, "Théodore de Gaza, Introduction à la grammaire, Libri IV," *Byzantion* 49 (1979): 133–55, who shows Gaza drew directly from the grammatical works of Maximos Planudes and Michael Syncellos for composition of his grammar. On the difference between Gaza's and Moschopoulos's grammars, see esp. Pertusi, *"Erotemata."* Cf. Hunger, *Die hochsprächliche profane Literatur,* 17–18.

31. Taylor, *Gaza's "De fato,"* 5. Cf. Sathas, *Neohellēnikē philologia,* 40; Gundersheimer, *Ferrara,* 165.

Giovanni Lorenzi and, in Naples, the principal court humanist, Antonio Panormita.[32]

There is clear evidence that in Rome (where he arrived probably in late 1449 or 1450) Gaza gave advice on the Greek text of certain Greek mathematical treatises to the great quattrocento astronomer and mathematician, the German Regiomontanus. Indeed, it was in part as a result not only of the capital influence of Cardinal Bessarion but also, to a lesser and undetermined degree, of Theodore (and, of course, of other Italian humanists such as Toscanelli) that Regiomontanus was able to play perhaps the leading role in propagating the Renaissance revival of mathematical and astronomical studies.[33] Notably, Regiomontanus made very profitable use of the rare Greek mathematical treatises contained in Bessarion's manuscript library, including those of Ptolemy, Euclid, Hero, Apollonius, Diophantus, and Archimedes, the ancient world's leading mathematician whose works on mechanics in particular were hitherto unknown to the West in the original Greek text. Regiomontanus himself (later in 1474 in Nuremberg) outlined an ambitious program for the revival of mathematical studies in which he announced a new edition of Ptolemy's *Geographia* (earlier inadequately translated from the Greek by Jacopo Angeli da Scarperia), a project for which Theodore Gaza was explicitly named by Regiomontanus as a consultant.[34]

32. See *Dizionario biografico degli Italiani,* s.v. "Ermolao Barbaro," 6:96–99. For Valla, see below, nn. 55, 57. On Agricola see L. Spitz, *The Religious Renaissance of the German Humanists* (Cambridge, 1963), 25, who says Agricola came to Ferrara in 1475 after Gaza's death and that he studied Greek with Gaza's student Ludovico Carbone. But on Gaza's second stay in Ferrara Pinto, 22, says Agricola heard him. Also see Legrand, *Bibliographie hellénique* 1:xl. For Lorenzi, see King, *Venetian Humanism,* 390.

33. On Regiomontanus see P. Rose, *The Italian Renaissance of Mathematics* (Geneva, 1975), chaps. 3–4, pp. 76–118. On 94–95 he notes specific contacts between Gaza and Regiomontanus through Bessarion. Gaza was the leading translator of a closely knit "Academy" of scholars in Rome and a dear friend of Bessarion's, and it is therefore inconceivable that Gaza was not in close connection with Regiomontanus, with whom Bessarion had very close relations. According to Monfasani, *George of Trebizond,* 81, "Valla . . . along with Gaza and Cremonensis formed part of the inner circle of humanists associated with Bessarion" (based on Mohler, *Aus Bessarions Gelehrtenkreis,* 320ff., 399ff.). To be noted is that from 1450 to 1455 Bessarion was papal legate in the papal city of Bologna, where he reorganized the university curriculum along humanist lines, even establishing a Greek chair: see E. Raimondi, "Umanesimo e università nel quattrocento Bologna," *Studi e memorie per la storia dell'Università di Bologna,* n.s., 1 (1956): 325–56. Given Bessarion's sojourn there, Gaza's association with him during these years was probably through visits or letters exchanged. Of course they were together in Rome on Gaza's return to Rome from Naples.

34. On Greek mathematicians mentioned, see Rose, *Italian Renaissance of Mathematics,* 94–95, 99. On Gaza's help with Ptolemy's *Geographia,* see ibid., 104–5, 108. The time of Gaza's aid referred to was certainly earlier, in Rome (or possibly later in Ferrara

I suspect—as has not hitherto been noted—that in his teaching Gaza utilized a common Palaeologan didactic device, *schedographia,* that is, the close reading of specific passages of classic authors interpreted with the aid of (generally short) commentaries called *schede.* These commentaries, which were inserted between the lines of text or in the margins, analyzed vocabulary, etymology of words, historical references, and syntax in each passage. (*Schedographia* had been used by the Byzantines at least from the time of Anna Comnena of the early twelfth century, who in fact complained about its excesses.) *Schede* on passages from classical Greek authors composed by Manuel Moschopoulos and other Palaeologan writers of the last two centuries of Byzantium still survive, and Gaza may well have utilized these to broaden his teaching and make it more effective. There is no reason to believe that Gaza, so well trained in the schools of the Palaeologan "renaissances" of both Thessalonica and Constantinople, did not continue to utilize their methods of teaching and philological scholarship.[35]

While in Ferrara in 1447, Gaza declined an invitation from Cosimo de' Medici to assume what was still the most coveted Greek chair in Italy, that of Manuel Chrysoloras in Florence.[36] But in the fall of 1449, probably because of his need for more permanent and munificent patronage, he accepted an invitation from the humanist Pope Nicholas V to come to Rome.[37] There he became a member of the learned papal literary circle of Greek studies under the aegis of the most influential of all Byzantine émigré scholars, Cardinal John Bessarion. It was the aim of Pope Nicholas and Bessarion (the latter also a product of the Palaeologan revival) to have translated into Latin as accurately as possible the great classical Greek literary and scientific authors, especially Aristotle, as well as the

---

when Gaza returned there): see text below and nn. 60–63. According to J. Sandys, *A History of Classical Scholarship,* vol. 2 (New York, 1967) 105, a Latin translation of the *Geographia* apeared in Rome in 1462 and the Greek *editio princeps* was edited by Erasmus in 1533 at Basel with the Froben press aided by the Greek Nicholas Episcopius.

35. My good friend the eminent Byzantine philologist Alexander Turyn has informed me that he has found Byzantine manuscripts containing *schede* in the possession of Byzantine scholars teaching in Italy in the fifteenth century. Hence his view that Byzantine scholars like Gaza utilized *schede.* On *schedographia* see Hunger, *Die hochsprächliche profane Literatur,* 29ff. On Anna Comnena see *Alexiade,* ed. B. Leib, vol. 3 (Paris, 1945), 218. Translated in Geanakoplos, *Byzantium,* 406–7.

36. T. Klette, *Die griechischen Briefe des Franciskus Philelphus* (Greifswald, 1890), 64; and Legrand, *Bibliographie hellénique* 1:xxxiii.

37. Monfasani, *George of Trebizond,* 80, citing letter of Guarino (from R. Sabbadini, *Epistolario di Guarino Veronese,* vol. 3 [Venice, 1919], 480–81). In 1451 Pope Nicholas V had Gaza write a letter on aid against the Turks to the Byzantine emperor Constantine XI (Legrand, *Bibliographie hellénique* 1:xxxiv).

The Byzantine humanist Theodore Gaza. From E. Legrand, *Bibliographie hellénique,* vol. 3 (Paris, 1903).

ancient Greek historians and the Byzantine church fathers. Bessarion's circle included many learned Italian humanists, among others the papal intimate and erudite Greek scholar Giovanni Tortelli (who from 1433 to 1438 had been one of the few Italian humanists to study Greek in

Constantinople and who, after 1449 in Rome, seems to have exerted an influence on Gaza); also the Florentine humanist Poggio Bracciolini, Bessarion's secretary Nicholas Perotti, the mathematician Jacopo da Cremona, and the great philologist and humanist Lorenzo Valla.[38] Gaza, with his impeccable knowledge of Greek and Latin, became in time the principal translator of the circle, being referred to by Nicholas Perotti as "princeps Academiae Bessarioneae."[39] According to Vast, Gaza served as Bessarion's private secretary, though perhaps in rather an informal capacity since Perotti seems to have held that position officially. Vast affirms plausibly that Gaza even handled the pensions that Bessarion, as self-appointed patron of his Greek compatriot scholars, was in the habit of distributing to these often near-indigent refugees.[40]

Gaza's work of translation in Bessarion's group was particularly important since the West at this time needed not only translations of the many still unknown classical Greek and Byzantine writings but, perhaps even more important, more-accurate versions of Aristotle, Ptolemy, and the Greek Fathers than those already executed by the Latin Scholastics. Though very valuable in many ways, the Scholastic versions were sometimes inadequate, not only in failing to preserve the spirit of the original Greek text but, more serious, in often being based on very faulty manuscripts. For these reasons the perspicacious Bessarion early realized the necessity of collecting a huge library from all parts of the old Byzantine world. Bessarion's Greek manuscripts often served as the basis for the translations made by Gaza (and by others, especially his predecessor in Bessarion's group, George of Trebizond). Later, after Bessarion had bequeathed his library to Venice, his manuscripts provided the texts from which the famous Greek first editions of the Aldine press were printed.[41]

38. On Bessarion's circle see G. Holmes, *The Florentine Enlightenment* (New York, 1969), 250–56, who notes that the actual product, however important, was not very large. See also esp. Mohler, *Aus Bessarions Gelehrtenkreis;* and recently Monfasani, *George of Trebizond,* chaps. 3–5. On Tortelli, see esp. G. Mancini, "Giovanni Tortelli, cooperatore di Niccolò V nel fondare la biblioteca vaticana," *Archivio storico italiano* 78 (1920).

39. Vast, *Cardinal Bessarion,* 321; A. della Torre, *Storia della accademia platonica di Firenze* (Florence, 1902), 151. Gaza was asked by Bessarion and Nicholas V to retranslate many of the Greek works previously translated by the Cretan George of Trebizond (esp. the works of Aristotle and the *Almagest* of Ptolemy with Theon's commentary), who thus became Gaza's implacable enemy. Trebizond left the papal Curia (see esp. Monfasani, *George of Trebizond,* chaps. 3–4).

40. Vast, *Cardinal Bessarion,* 321, citing J. Boissonade, *Anecdota graeca* (Paris, 1833), 5:402, 408. In 1450 Bessarion was sent by the pope to Bologna, where he reorganized the university curriculum (see above, n. 33).

41. On Bessarion's library, see L. Labowsky, "Il Cardinale Bessarione e gli inizi della Biblioteca marciana," *Venezia e l'Oriente fra tardo medio evo e rinascimento,* ed. A.

Bessarion, the most influential Byzantine émigré scholar, patron of the Greek scholars, and Cardinal of the Roman Church

It is rarely recognized that Bessarion thus vigorously collected Greek manuscripts not only for the benefit of Western scholars but, more important, as he himself states in a letter to the Cretan scholar Michael Apostolis, one of his chief collectors, "for the benefit of my Greek countrymen who are left now [*ta leipsana tōn Hellēnōn*—"remnants of

---

Pertusi (Venice, 1966), 158–82. It contained 482 Greek MSS. (later Bessarion added more).

the Greek people," a famous phrase then often used of the Greeks] who, without these few vestiges of these excellent and divine [Greek] authors which have been preserved, would differ in no way from barbarians and slaves."[42] As noted, Gaza expressed similar patriotic sentiments elsewhere in his writings.

Gaza's work of translation for Pope Nicholas is of capital significance for the history of Aristotelian studies in the West. For his improved readings of the texts, together with his various translations of the Aristotelian writings, served to point the way to the eventual subordination four decades later at the leading Italian university, Padua, of the Arab-Averroist interpretation of Aristotle to the Hellenistic and early Byzantine interpretation. Gaza, for example, translated the *Problemata* of the Hellenistic commentator Alexander of Aphrodisias and mentions the many Greek commentators on Aristotle in his work *Antirretikon* (see nn. 10, 49). This gradual transformation in the interpretation of Aristotle at Padua was climaxed in 1497 by the Venetian Senate's appointment of the Venetian-born Greek Nicolaus Leonicus Tomaeus "to lecture for the first time on the Greek [text] of Aristotle."[43] It is noteworthy that the chief link with Gaza in firmly establishing the "Greco-Byzantine" interpretation and text of Aristotle at Padua was Gaza's student, the great Venetian humanist Ermolao Barbaro, who, as noted above, had studied Greek with Gaza when his father was serving as Venetian envoy to Rome. Like his teacher Gaza, Barbaro, in seeking to establish the most authentic interpretation of Aristotle's works, made use of the exegeses of the Hellenistic and early Byzantine commentators on Aristotle, such as Themistius, Philoponus, Simplicius, and Alexander of Aphrodisias, whose *Problemata,* as we have noted, had been previously translated by Gaza himself.[44]

42. Quoted in Geanakoplos, *Interaction of the Sibling Cultures,* 172, from Bessarion's letter, in Mohler, *Aus Bessarions Gelehrtenkreis,* 478–79. For the phrase "remnants of the Greeks," see Geanakoplos, *Greek Scholars in Venice,* 103, quoting from letter of Michael Apostolis.

43. See Geanakoplos, "The Little-Known Greek Aristotelian-Humanist at Padua: Nikolaos Leonikos Tomaeos," in *Proceedings of the World Congress on Aristotle,* Thessalonica, 7–14 August 1978, vol. 2 (Athens, 1981), 15–20, esp. 15, a short version of my paper read to the congress but without footnotes. For the completed paper see below, essay 5. On Tomaeus's (Latin) document of appointment by the Venetian Senate, see J. Facciolatus, *Fasti gymnasii patavini,* vol. 1 (Padua, 1752), 56 and 110, under a. 1497: "Leonicus de Tomaeis qui primus huic Gymnasio [Padua] veram Aristotelis faciem ostendit, et Graeco sermone, . . . ejus doctrinam explicuit."

44. On Barbaro and certain Hellenistic commentators of Aristotle see P. O. Kristeller, *Studies in Renaissance Thought and Letters* (Rome, 1956), 337–53; also *Dizionario biografico degli Italiani* 6:96. Cf. V. Branca, "Ermolao Barbaro and Late Quattrocento Venetian Humanism," in *Renaissance Venice,* ed. J. Hale (London, 1973); also essay 2,

The question of exactly which works Gaza translated for Pope Nicholas V and Bessarion is complex. Another Byzantine, the Cretan George of Trebizond, had previously been designated to translate Greek texts, especially Ptolemy's *Mathēmatikē syntaxis (Almagest)* and the ancient commentary thereon by Theon of Alexandria. But George's translations were considered—unjustly in some respects, as we now know—inaccurate or misleading.[45] As a result, Gaza was commissioned to retranslate much of George's work, including, as noted, Aristotle's *Problemata,* his *De animalibus,* and Theophrastus's *De plantis.*

Gaza's method of translation from Greek to Latin evidently resembled that of his predecessor Manuel Chrysoloras in that he often translated not *verbum ad verbum* (word for word) as the Scholastic William Moerbeke had done, but *ad sententiam ferre;* that is, he sought primarily to render the *spirit of the text* while preserving insofar as possible the style and nuances of meaning. Thus in many cases, especially in works of a *philosophic* nature, he rendered into Latin almost a paraphrase of the Greek text. But Gaza's translation of Aristotle's *De animalibus (Peri zoōn)* provides, on the other hand, a concrete example of the precision of his method in translating *scientific* texts. As may be deduced from a letter of Bessarion's, in this particular work of Aristotle Gaza sought to find precisely equivalent Latin terms to render the technical Greek ones of the original text (rather, it seems, than rely on the transliterations from the Greek made by the earlier Scholastic translators).[46]

In Rome Bessarion, Gaza, and Trapezuntius all became involved in the famous dispute over the relative merits of Aristotle and Plato, first begun at the Council of Florence (1439) by Gemistos Pletho with his treatise *Peri hōn Aristotelēs pros Platona diapheretai,* which defended Plato and castigated Aristotle, though rather unjustly.[47] Gaza took the

---

n. 80, for articles by Branca and Pertusi. For Gaza's translation of Alexander of Aphrodisias's *Problemata,* see *Tusculum Lexicon,* 71; and Gercke, *Theodoros Gazes,* 26.

45. Monfasani, *George of Trebizond,* 109ff. Some work comparing Trapezuntius's work and Gaza's retranslations has been done (see Monfasani, who cites it, 76–77, noting also that in some cases Trapezuntius used better MSS than Gaza).

46. On this see L. Labowsky, "An Unknown Treatise by Theodorus Gaza," *Medieval and Renaissance Studies* 6 (1968): 173–98, esp. 176. Bessarion's copy of Theophrastus's *Historia plantarum* is full of marginalia in his own hand giving Latin equivalents for Greek names of plants (ibid., 176). Monfasani, *George of Trebizond,* 153, says Gaza translated the technical Greek terms of Aristotle's *Problemata* by Latin approximations. Trapezuntius, of course, claimed Gaza's translation perverted Aristotle's *Problemata.*

47. On this complex conflict see Geanakoplos, *Greek Scholars in Venice,* 85–88. George Scholarios, also present at the Council of Florence, in 1443 wrote a detailed attack against Pletho's treatise and in defense of Aristotle (*Oeuvres complètes,* vol. 4, ed. L. Petit, Ch. Siderides, and M. Jugie [Paris, 1935], 1–116). Here he speaks con-

first step to revive this conflict. Primarily an Aristotelian, he apparently feared that the true Aristotle was being obscured not only by Pletho's work but also by the late Scholastic interpretations of his works, by the Arab-Averroist interpretations favored in Venice and Padua, and, perhaps not least, by the Italian humanists' increasing preference for Plato, especially in Florence.[48] Thus in about 1459 Gaza wrote his treatise *Peri ekousiou kai akousiou (De fato)* to rebut certain aspects of Pletho's attack on Aristotle.[49] Gaza's was not, however, an acrid response, his aim being (possibly under Bessarion's influence) rather to show to the Italian scholars that these two ancient philosophers could be reconciled in many, if not most respects. Indeed, during the Palaeologan Renaissance the Byzantines had not considered the two philosophers really antithetical.

This spirited defense of Aristotle by Gaza, made in the context of Greek philosophy and apparently without reference to the Scholastic *theological* argument, has led the modern scholar L. Stein to affirm that Gaza should be viewed as the first pure (i.e., secular) Aristotelian of the fifteenth-century Italian Renaissance. (Stein also affirmed, with probably no exaggeration, that, along with Pletho and Marsilio Ficino, there was no more genuine "philosopher" than Gaza in that century.)[50] Stein's view should be qualified by consideration of a tract of Gaza's recently found and analyzed by L. Labowsky. In this work Gaza discusses three Christian theological doctrines which he found particularly difficult to recon-

---

temptuously of Pletho's Italian friends who admire Plato for his *literary* talent and are unable to judge the philosophical merit of Aristotle: see P. O. Kristeller, "Byzantine and Western Platonism in the Fifteenth Century," in *Renaissance Thought and Its Sources* (New York, 1979), 158. On the Pletho–Scholarios conflict see Woodhouse, *Plethon,* 129ff. Also T. Zisis, *Gennadios Scholarios* (in Greek) (Thessalonica, 1980) who believes some earlier works attributed to Scholarios are not authentic.

48. Actually Bessarion, concerned over Trapezuntius's violent attack on Plato (in response to Gaza's *Antirretikon* [text in Mohler, *Aus Bessarions Gelehrtenkreis,* 207–35] vis-à-vis Pletho's earlier treatise) and fearing that the Italian humanists, who yet knew little of Plato, would then depreciate him, wrote a letter to Gaza between 1456 and 1459 indicating that he had begun to write a work (later to become the famous *In calumniatorem Platonis*) to represent both Aristotle's and Plato's views objectively. And Bessarion asked Gaza for his views on the conciliation of Christian doctrine with Plato and Aristotle. Monfasani, *George of Trebizond,* 220, says Bessarion had the aid of Gaza (and Perotti) in writing his *In calumniatorem Platonis.*

49. Text published in Mohler, *Aus Bessarions Gelehrtenkreis,* 239–46. Gaza's treatise *Antirretikon* was later acrimoniously attacked by Michael Apostolis: text also in J. Powell, "Michael Apostolios gegen Theodorus Gaza," *Byzantinische Zeitschrift* 38 (1938): 71–86. Actually Gaza wrote two other little-known tracts against Pletho before his *De fato:* See Taylor, *Gaza's "De fato,"* 6. The *Antirretikon (Rebuttal)* was Gaza's chief philosophical tract.

50. Stein, "Der Humanist T. Gaza," 427, 429 (quoted in Taylor, *Gaza's "De fato,"* 6).

cile with Aristotelian philosophy: that of the Trinity, of the immortality of the individual soul, and especially of the incarnation. He also explained how he himself would seek to reconcile the doctrines.[51]

The chain reaction on the problem of the supremacy of Aristotle or Plato, set off among the Byzantines by Gaza's *Peri ekousiou kai akousiou,* came to involve many Western as well as Byzantine scholars. Among the Byzantines the conflict was decisively calmed by the appearance in 1469 of Bessarion's great work, *In calumniatorem Platonis.* In this remarkable treatise, aided and influenced to no little degree by the views of the Aristotelian Gaza (who, as noted, was actually sympathetic to Plato), Bessarion skillfully responded to George of Trebizond's violent criticism of Plato. At the same time he sought to harmonize the views of the two great Greek philosophers while reconciling Plato with and putting him at the service of Christianity.[52]

After Pope Nicholas's death in 1455, another phase of Gaza's career took place in Naples, to which he was invited in the same year to teach Greek by the Neapolitan king Alfonso the Magnanimous. There Gaza also translated certain Greek authors for Alfonso, including a work of Chrysostom, and he assisted the Italian humanist Bernard Facio to edit (in Latin translation) Arrian's *Taktika.* He also had a flattering epigram dedicated to him by an admirer in the court, the noted Neapolitan humanist Giovanni Pontano. Alfonso's court contained a remarkable humanist circle of scholars, which had originally been founded by the humanist Antonio Panormita. Cardinal Bessarion had resided there for a time as papal envoy, and George of Trebizond had only recently departed after a not entirely satisfactory sojourn of teaching at the Neapolitan court. Two decades before Gaza's arrival, the humanist philologist Lorenzo Valla had come to Naples to serve as secretary to Alfonso.[53] And it

51. For Gaza's attempt to reconcile Christian doctrine with Aristotle and Plato in *De fato,* see Labowsky, "An Unknown Treatise by Gaza," 180–84 (English translation of text in Taylor, *Gaza's "De fato,"* 19–29).

52. See Bessarion's text in Mohler, *Aus Bessarions Gelehrtenkreis.* In *De fato* Gaza wrote: "To assume a multitude of irreconcilable differences in Plato and Aristotle, to quarrel with the partisans of either, is anything but a worthy proceeding. On the contrary, it is better to reconcile them in whatever aspect they seem to have differed, and following both as though one excellent leader in knowledge and wisdom, to delineate the truth in harmony with both, since both are wise and worthy of reverence (trans. Taylor, *Gaza's "De fato,"* 29). See also Mohler, *Aus Bessarions Gelehrtenkreis,* vol. 3, for epistolary exchanges between Bessarion and Gaza on Aristotle, Plato, and Christianity. Gaza also criticized Pletho in his *Adversus Plethonem pro Aristotele de substantia* (Mohler, III, 140–50).

53. C. De Frede, *I lettori di umanità nello studio di Napoli* (Naples, 1960), 80ff. On the Neapolitan circle, see M. Fuiano, *Insegnamento e cultura a Napoli nel rinascimento* (Naples, 1976), 65–69, with very little on Gaza. On Pontano's poem, ibid., 67.

was in Naples that Valla had begun to work on his important *Collatio,* a comparison of the Greek text and the Latin versions of the New Testament. This work of Valla was to lead in 1444 to composition of his celebrated *Annotationes,* a treatise often considered to mark the beginning of modern Western Biblical textual criticism.[54]

In a passage of the *Annotationes* Valla referred pointedly to "quidam nostrae aetatis eruditissimi Graeci" who, presumably, had aided him in his work of achieving a more accurate Latin version of the New Testament on the basis of the Greek. Included among these "very erudite Greeks" was, it is now certain, Cardinal Bessarion, several of whose specific contributions to Valla's work on the New Testament are textually well attested.[55] It would be tempting to include Gaza among the learned Greeks referred to here by Valla, for Gaza's own acute interest in biblical and patristic studies is clearly reflected in, among other things, his translation of Chrysostom's *Commentaries on the Incomprehensible Nature of God,* and in his later letter to Cristopher Persona urging him to turn Origen's *Contra Celsum* into Latin.[56] But it has been shown that Valla's composition of the *Annotationes* had been accomplished in Naples c. 1444, a decade before Gaza's arrival there. It now seems certain that Valla came to know Gaza later in Rome, to which, by invitation of Pope

---

Trapezuntius, expelled from the papal court, went to Naples under patronage of Alfonso (Monfasani, *George of Trebizond,* 112–13). Legrand, *Bibliographie hellénique* 1:xxxiv–v, quotes Filelfo's letter to Alfonso praising Gaza as "virum quo nemo est in universo Graecorum genere neque doctior nec eloquentior nec modestior." In 1444 Alfonso inaugurated teaching of Greek at Catania, and both he and Pope Eugenius IV sought to bring educated Greeks to replenish Orthodox monasteries in Calabria, Apulia, and Sicily (Vacalopoulos, *Origins of the Greek Nation,* 244). On Chrysostom see n. 56.

54. See Lorenzo Valla, *Collatio Novi Testamenti,* ed. A. Perosa (Florence, 1970). The second recension of Valla's *Collatio,* the *Annotationes,* was discovered and edited for publication in 1505 by Erasmus. This consisted primarily of suggestions for the correction of textual readings in the Latin Vulgate as compared to the Greek New Testament. It was of great value to Erasmus in his publication of the Greek New Testament text in 1515 in Basel (see Geanakoplos, *Greek Scholars in Venice,* 245–46). On the first printed edition of the New Testament Greek text by the Greek Demetrius Ducas for Cardinal Ximenes, see biography of Ducas, ibid., chap. 8.

55. For Valla and Bessarion, see M. Fois, *Il pensiero cristiano di Lorenzo Valla* (Rome, 1969), 415–19. We know that Bessarion read through Valla's *Collatio* and made many suggestions on textual readings and interpretations, e.g., on St. John 21.22 (cf. Camporeale, *Lorenzo Valla,* esp. 366, noting Valla finished the additions and corrections to the *Collatio* which had been suggested particularly by Bessarion in 1449).

56. On Chrysostom see Legrand, *Bibliographie hellénique* 1:xliv. For letter to Persona, ibid., 3:51. In this letter (see also ibid., 1:xxxviii) Gaza writes that at his urging Pope Nicholas procured from Constantinople a copy of Origen's *Contra Celsum.* Persona's version was printed in Rome in 1481.

Nicholas V, Valla moved in 1448 after the death of his patron Alfonso. Valla and Gaza's close association is attested to by their becoming active members of the "inner circle" of Bessarion's academy. It would be surprising indeed, therefore, if Valla did not at this time draw upon Gaza's expertise in the subtleties of the Greek language, both textually and interpretatively, in order to benefit his long-standing interest in biblical studies. This argument is all the more persuasive since we know from a letter from Gaza to Giovanni Tortelli dated 1449 that after his removal to Rome, Valla, still seeking to improve upon the accuracy of his *Annotationes,* sought out "anyone who could offer suggestions or possessed any special competence in this [biblical] material, such as . . . Rinuccio Aretino or Theodore Gaza."[57]

A related problem in New Testament studies concerns Valla's criticism of the authenticity of the famous corpus of mystical works attributed to Dionysius "the Areopagite." What the specific influence of Gaza (and also of Bessarion) may have been here on Valla's thinking is only now being thoroughly investigated.[58] We do know that, while Bessarion favored the traditional Byzantine and Western view that accepted the Dionysian corpus's authenticity, Gaza, exercising a freer and more independent judgment, opposed the accepted view (though only privately). As is today too little realized, centuries before this period a few individual Byzantine theologians had already harbored suspicions of the authenticity of Dionysius and his corpus.[59] And it is now certain that

57. On Aretinus and Gaza (as well as Aurispa and Tortelli) see Camporeale, *Lorenzo Valla,* 362–63. Also esp. passage in Sabbadini, *Epistolario di Guarino* 3:480–81, quoting from Gaza's letter to Tortelli, dated 1449, saying he wanted to come to Rome to see the rest of his dear friends, including Lorenzo Valla ("non modo cum reliquis amicis et cum Laurentio Vallensi, *meis deliciis*" [emphasis added]). See also Monfasani, *George of Trebizond,* 80–81.

58. See Camporeale, *Lorenzo Valla,* esp. 362, 428–29. For Valla's own words on the inauthenticity of "Dionysius" see his *Opera* (Paris, 1498–99), 1:852b (cf. Camporeale, 428–30), where in connection with Dionysius, Valla mentions the "eruditissimi Greci" he knew in Rome. See most recently the notable article of Monfasani, "Pseudo-Dionysius," esp. 206, 209–13, concluding that Gaza primarily influenced Valla's view on Pseudo-Dionysius but restrained his view out of respect for Pope Nicholas V and Bessarion.

59. In the sixth century the Byzantine ecclesiastic Hypatius had rejected Dionysius's authorship of the "Dionysian" corpus (see *Oxford Dictionary of the Christian Church* [Oxford, 1963], 402; and Runciman, *Last Byzantine Renaissance,* 45). Camporeale, *Lorenzo Valla,* 429–30, says certain Byzantines identified Dionysius with the heretic Apollinaris of Laodicea (a view attacked by Maximos the Confessor), but that Bessarion did not (he accepted the traditional view), while Gaza, though not publicly, also identified Apollinaris with the author of the Dionysian corpus. On 430 Camporeale quotes a striking remark of Valla in his *Annotationes:* "De libris Dionysii nemo veterum

Gaza and Bessarion made these views known to Valla, with whom they were both on intimate terms.

At the death of his patron King Alfonso in 1458, Gaza withdrew for some years to the monastery of San Giovanni a Piro near Salerno. Later, in 1464, he was once again recalled to Rome, to the beneficent patronage of his close friend and patron Cardinal Bessarion and, of course, to the latter's superiors in the papal court, the pontiffs Pius II and then Sixtus IV. In the service of these persons he continued his work of copying Greek manuscripts in his elegant hand[60] and especially under the aegis of Sixtus IV, again took up the task of translating Aristotle's works into Latin. It is reported that on one occasion, when Sixtus paid him a number of gold pieces (not so much, it seems, for his elegantly rendered Latin version of Aristotle's *De animalibus* as for the cost of the expensive gold binding of the manuscript), Gaza angrily cast the money into the Tiber river.[61]

It was at this last phase of his career in Rome that Gaza, as has been almost unnoticed by modern historians, participated in the publishing enterprise undertaken in Rome by Italy's first printers, the Germans Conrad Sweynheim and Arnold Pannartz (who had earlier set up their press in Subiaco). With his friend Bishop Giovanni de Bussi of Aleria, Gaza, in 1469, helped to edit for Sweynheim and Pannartz the *editio princeps* (in Latin) of the *Noctes atticae* of Aulus Gellius. In the preface, de Bussi writes that the work was issued with the collaboration and advice of Gaza. More significant even is perhaps the second work Gaza edited with de Bussi (1470), the *Natural History* of Pliny the Younger. For Gaza included in the edition of the work an excerpt in Greek taken from the original text of Plato's *Gorgias.* This excerpt quite possibly constitutes the very first specimen of Greek (apart from titles or isolated words) to be printed in the Italian Renaissance.[62]

---

habuit mentionem neque Latinorum neque Graecorum." On the question of Pseudo-Dionysius's authenticity and Bessarion's circle see esp. Monfasani, "Pseudo-Dionysius." Photius in his *Bibliotheca* had also impugned the authenticity of Dionysius.

60. Legrand, *Bibliographie hellénique* 1:xxxvi. Gaza made a magnificent copy of the *Iliad* for Filelfo (Legrand, xxxviii, xlvii: see *Homērou Ilias meta palaias paraphraseōs ex idiocheirou tou Theodōrou Gazē,* ed. N. Theseus [1811]). On S. Giovanni, Legrand, xxxvi.

61. Legrand, *Bibliographie hellénique* 1:xxxviii, who also cites Gaza's letter to his cousin Andronicus Callistos complaining that his hopes for advancement were not realized under Sixtus. See also L. von Pastor, *History of the Popes,* vol. 4 (London, 1949), 444, esp. note, evidence based on a work of Perotti.

62. For Aulus Gellius see Legrand, *Bibliographie hellénique*, 1, xlix and 3, 5–6. For Pliny, *ibid.*, 3, 6–7; and Stein, "Der Humanist T. Gaza," 455, esp. n. 67, where Stein says he learned of Gaza's ed. of Pliny from a MS in the Angelica library in Rome, something

After the death of his patron Bessarion in 1472, Gaza in early 1473, at the invitation of Ercole d'Este returned to Ferrara to his old chair where he lectured for a few months on Aristotle.[63] But soon Gaza, now old himself and resuming his sacerdotal function, went again to live in south Italy on the revenue, which had been assigned to him by Bessarion. There in Calabria, historically so long tied to the Byzantine East, Theodore Gaza died obscurely, doubtless in 1475, and was buried in the Basilian monastery of San Giovanni da Piro.[64]

Research in the Italian archives, especially in those of Naples, Rome, and perhaps Siena, will doubtless help to fill in some of the remaining lacunae in Gaza's career in Italy. Meantime we may conclude that this essay has served to strengthen the view that Gaza was without doubt one of the most influential of all Byzantine émigré scholars to the West. He was important not only because he appeared in Italy at an early, formative phase of the Renaissance, but because he was one of the very few Byzantine exiles (along with John Argyropoulos, George of Trebizond, Demetrius Chalcondyles, Marcus Musurus and Janus Lascaris) who possessed a really expert knowledge of Latin as well as Greek. It was this ability, as should again be emphasized, that enabled him to draw upon and accurately interpret for Italian humanists the texts, methods, even the spirit of the Byzantine Palaeologan "Renaissance," instead of merely acting as a passive transmitter of texts, as was so often the case with other Greek exiles.

The text of Gaza's inaugural addresses on the occasion of his appoint-

---

he says was yet unknown before his discovery. Also see A. Pollard, *Catalog of Books Printed in the Fifteenth Century,* 4 (Oxford, 1900) 44f., on collaboration of Gaza and de Bussi and their publications. Also see M. Miglio's article on de Bussi in *Dizionario biografico degli italiani,* v. 15 (1972) 565–74. M. Miglio ed., *Le prefazioni alle edizioni di Sweynheym e Pannartz prototipografi romani* (Milan, 1978) 44ff., and M. Manoussakas and N. Staikos, *The Publishing Activity of the Greeks during the Italian Renaissance* (Athens, 1987) 24–31 on Gaza.

63. His presence again in Ferrara (under Duke Hercules) is noted by Stein, "Der Humanist T. Gaza"; Sathas, *Neohellēnikē philologia,* 39, and Kyrou, *Hoi Hellēnes,* 93, but not by Legrand or Gundersheimer, *Ferrara.* Pinto, *Epistolae,* 22, supports his second, brief stay in Ferrara teaching Aristotle. He says Gaza was there when Agricola came and heard him. Cf. n. 32.

64. See Legrand, *Bibliographie hellénique* 1:xxxix, for discussion of dates. Stein, "Der Humanist T. Gaza," 458, dates his death in 1458. *Thrēskeftikē kai ēthikē engk.,* vol. 4, 142 says that before his death, Gaza lived in Calabria in the monastery of St. John. For poetic encomia on Gaza by the Greek scholars Michael Marullus Tarchaniotes, Demetrius Chalcondyles, and Constantine Lascaris see Legrand, 1, xli. Kyrou, *Hoi Hellēnes,* 92. Pinto, *Epistolae,* 22, dates his death in 1475.

ment to teach Greek at the *studium* of Ferrara evidently served as the model for subsequent orations of the same kind delivered by Byzantine humanists in Italy on the importance of Greek studies for acquiring a broad education, one effective and conducive to active participation in civic life.

At Ferrara, Rome, and Naples Gaza transmitted a knowledge of Greek (formally or through a variety of informal relationships) to a considerable number of subsequently famous Italian humanists. Most notable among these were the leading humanist educator Vittorino da Feltre, the preeminent Venetian humanist Ermolao Barbaro, the Cremonese Ludovico Carbone in Ferrara, the Sicilian Antonio Panormita in Naples and, very probably, the Roman Lorenzo Valla. In Rome Valla associated with Gaza in the inner circle of the famous academy of Cardinal Bessarion, and as noted, it seems very likely that at this time he profited from Gaza's knowledge of Greek patristics in connection with his own important philological work on the New Testament. Also to be mentioned here is Gaza's expert philological (and apparently interpretative) aid to Regiomontanus in his work on some difficult but highly significant mathematical and scientific texts.

Moreover, in the history of printing he occupies a not unimportant niche as coeditor (with Andrea Giovanni de Bussi and others) of perhaps not only the first corpus of *Latin* books published in Italy but, perhaps no less important, of probably the first excerpt from a classical *Greek* author to be printed. This episode, then, provides a vivid example of the increasingly effective and impressive symbiosis of the culture and learning of the Palaeologan Renaissance with that of the Italian Renaissance. Indeed, in certain respects the episode prefigures by several decades the achievement of Aldus Manutius in Venice.

One of Gaza's most lasting contributions to Italian Renaissance humanism lay in his utilization (following the Byzantine Palaeologan tradition) of the Hellenistic and early Byzantine commentators in order to establish the most accurate text and therefore interpretation of Aristotle's works—efforts on his part which (as we shall see in essay 5), along with his own more accurate translations of Aristotle, would lead to recognition of the superiority of the Greco-Byzantine tradition over the Arab-Avveroist interpretation of Aristotle several decades later at Italy's greatest citadel of Aristotelianism, the University of Padua.[65] Finally, the example of Gaza's Olympian demeanor and irenic personality (not to over-

65. In 1497 the Greek (born in Venice) Nicolaus Leonicus Tomaeus was officially appointed at the University of Padua "to read" and explain Aristotle "in the original Greek [text]." On Tomaeus see below, essay 5.

look his vast learning in rhetoric, literature, natural science, Greek patristics, and not least Latin literature and philology) served to enhance the reputation of his not always admired fellow Byzantine exiles, who, as refuges in an alien land, often had to endure suspicion and jealousy before some (but far from all) could secure employment in universities or humanist courts.[66]

66. On Gaza's translations (sometimes paraphrases) of the *Iliad* and of the "Homeric school's" *Batrachomyomachia,* Xenophon's *Cyropaedia,* two sections of Dionysius of Halicarnassus's *Rhetoric* (all into Latin), and of works on baths of Michael Savonarola (into Greek), as well as his own writings (in Greek): *On the Origins of the Turks, On Praise of a Dog* (i.e., Sultan Mehmet II), *On the [Ancient] Months,* see esp. Legrand, *Bibliographie hellénique* 1:xli–xlix. For Greek texts see Migne, *Patrologia graeca,* vols. 161 and 19, cols. 973–1014 and 1156, respectively. Cf. on Gaza's works also C. Patrinelis, *Thrēskeftikē kai ēthikē engk.,* vol. 4, 142–43.

Additional Bibliography for Essay 3

See above, bibliographical note to essays 1 and 2. Also L. Labowsky, "Bessarione," *Dizionario bibliografico degli Italiani* 9:686–96. Most recently, J. Monfasani, "Pseudo-Dionysius the Areopagite in Mid-Quattrocento Rome," *Supplementum Festivum: Studies in Honor of Paul Kristeller,* ed. J. Hankins, J. Monfasani, F. Purnell, Jr. (Binghamton, N.Y., 1987), 189–220 (used here). E. Pinto, *Teodoro Gaza epistolae* (Naples, 1975), a new edition of Gaza's letters. C. Stinger, *The Renaissance in Rome* (Bloomington, Ind., 1985), with references to Gaza. My *Byzantio kai dysē: He hallēlepidrasē tōn amphithalōn politismōn* (Greek translation, with corrections and revisions of *Interaction of the Sibling Cultures*), with references to Gaza; and my *Byzantium: Church, Society, and Civilization Seen Through Contemporary Eyes,* with translations of documents on Byzantine education, the university, and private schools in the Palaeologan period, 399–400, 407–8, 435–38, 717–18. J. Monfasani, ed., *Collectanea Trapezuntiana: Texts, Documents and Bibliographies of George of Trebizond* (Binghamton, N.Y., 1984), references to Gaza, Bessarion, and others. Finally, M. Manoussakas and K. Staikos, *The Publishing Activity of the Greeks during the Italian Renaissance* (Athens, 1987) 24–31, concise summary of Gaza's career and publishing activity with bibliography but no footnotes.

Four

The Career of the Byzantine Humanist Professor John Argyropoulos in Florence and Rome (1410–87): The Turn to Metaphysics

Our knowledge of the activities of the Byzantine-scholar émigrés to the West in the period of the Italian Renaissance has in recent years been increasing. Nevertheless, the careers of many, including even some of the most important, are still insufficiently known. More precisely, their contribution to the Renaissance has not yet adequately been integrated into the mainstream of the development of Italian humanism. Such is the case with the Byzantine John Argyropoulos. Although his name is as well known as that of the most famous of the Byzantine humanist émigrés—Bessarion, Chalcondyles, Chrysoloras, Musurus, and Lascaris—no biography has been written on him since the single, pioneering, but now in some ways outdated work of G. Cammelli, nor has anyone yet attempted to delineate his entire career in English. Yet, his career is of genuine significance not only because his teaching of Greek philosophy brought a special éclat to Medici Florence but, more important, because it was primarily his influence on Florentine humanism that served to transform its original emphasis on rhetoric to a broader interest in metaphysical philosophy.

The career of Argyropoulos may be divided into three broad phases: the first (obscure because of the extreme poverty of the sources) in Constantinople, where he taught in the decade or more before its fall to the Turks in 1453; the second period, longest by far and most meaningful for the Italian Renaissance, that of his tenure of instruction in Florence when that city was at the height of its fame as a humanistic center; and third, the brief period of his sojourn in Rome, where for some years he taught at its university and where he died in 1487.

The precise place of Argyropoulos's birth has only recently been definitely established as the Byzantine capital, Constantinople, and his date of birth fixed as c. 1393–4. Of his family we know that he came of respectable, wealthy parents who died when John was still a boy. Whereupon his uncle undertook to take care of him, sending him in c. 1403–4 to a school in Thessalonica in order to study under the protonotory Alexios Phorvinos. At the age of 17 Agyropoulos returned to Constantinople, where he continued his higher studies under a very distinguished professor, possibly John Chortasmenos. That Argyropoulos early revealed aptitude and ardor for study, with a particular bent toward philosophy, is evident from his own remarks in a letter he later sent to the Italian humanist Francesco Filelfo.

Argyropoulos's professor took a distinct liking to him and even brought him to live in his own house. That they were on intimate terms is also revealed by the fact that he found a spouse for the young man and introduced him to the circle of ecclesiastics at the Great Church, Hagia Sophia. Argyropoulos also studied with other teachers, as is indicated in a letter he later wrote to a fellow-Byzantine humanist George of Trebizond, referring to the famous teachers he had studied with in his youth. Because of Argyropoulos's acute interest in Plato, especially his familiarity with the more occult doctrines of that philosopher, it has long been speculated that one of his teachers must have been the celebrated Byzantine Neoplatonist Gemistos Pletho, with whom we know him, definitely, to have associated later in life.

In this period Byzantine secular ("outer") learning, though in decline from the eminence it had attained in the fourteenth century under Theodore Metochites and Nicephorus Gregoras, nonetheless, still carried on its long tradition of emphasis on classical Greek literature, science, and mathematics.

Argyropoulos, finally, finished his advanced studies sometime before 1425, at the age of c. 31, when he was officially appointed by Emperor Manuel II, and then John VIII, to head a public school in the capital city. In the meantime, the scope of his interests was broadened by his ordination to the priesthood and about this time his appointment as an imperial judge.[1]

1. These facts about his early life come from a manuscript presented by N. Oikonomides and published by him and P. Canavet: "(Jean Argyropoulos) La Comédie de Katablattas. Invective byzantine du XVe s." *Diptycha* 3 (Athens, 1982–83) 5–97.

The next definite notices we have on Argyropoulos's career relate to his first appearance in Italy as part of the Greek delegation attending the church Council of Ferrara-Florence (1438–39), that greatest confrontation of Greek and Latin intellectuals (as well, of course, as theologians) of the entire medieval period. If, as seems accepted by modern scholars, Argyropoulos was present at this council, it may be assumed that he shared the various experiences and vicissitudes of the Greek delegation in general. Thus, together with the rest of the huge 700-man delegation, he spent some weeks in Venice, whence he went to Ferrara and ultimately to Florence, where the meetings of the council continued. There he had the remarkable opportunity to become acquainted with some of the most illustrious Italian humanists of the day. Many of these had been assembled there by Pope Eugenius IV in order to act as interpreters or otherwise to engage in theological debate with the Greeks. The disputations which took place over the course of a year and a half between some good minds of Byzantium and Italy were beneficial in many ways to both sides: to the Latins, among other things, because they could now learn something of the philosophy of Plato as expounded by the great Platonic specialist Gemistos Pletho. (Argyropoulos is in fact specifically mentioned by the contemporary historian Ducas as being present at Florence "together with Pletho and other Greek intellectuals.")

The Greeks, too, were struck by the achievements of Latin civilization with which they were confronted in Florence. So much so, in fact, that the Byzantine delegate (and later cardinal of the Roman church) Bessarion later wrote that in order to reinvigorate the dying Byzantine state, young Greeks should be sent to Italy to learn the advanced Western techniques in engineering and shipbuilding, and even to study ancient Greek literature under Italian Hellenists. To emphasize the shift in attitude among some Greeks toward Latin culture, we may cite the opinion of the Byzantine judge George Scholarios, who wrote, "The Italian race which we once ranked among the barbarians now not only turns its attention to the arts but creates new intellectual edifices beside the old ones."[2] His intercourse with the Italian scholars thus affected Argyropoulos's intellectual outlook. Hardly less important for his career must have been the realization that here, among these Italian humanists so eager to imbibe classical Greek learning, was a land of future opportunity and refuge in case he might some day be forced to flee his homeland.

Argyropoulos returned to Constantinople with the Greek delegation, whereupon, he seems to have set himself up as a private teacher. In this period of deep Greek anxiety and dislocation as the result of the Turkish

2. But Scholarios a few years later in Constantinople seems to have had a different view than at the Council.

threat the intellectual life of Byzantium continued. Some teachers in fact were instructing publicly in the "higher school" of Constantinople, though more often they taught in various private schools around the capital city. We know that one of Argyropoulos's students at this time was the son of Francesco Filelfo, his lifelong Italian humanist friend, who had himself come to Constantinople before the Council of Florence and who, after learning Greek well, had become official interpreter and secretary to the Byzantine emperor John VIII Palaeologus. In a letter written in this period to Argyropoulos, Filelfo deplored his young son's attitude toward learning and his sloppy habits.

In 1441, a more mature, seasoned Argyropoulos returned to Italy, but this time to the university city of Padua, which, as noted, he may well have visited on his earlier trip. Now he was in the employ of the celebrated Florentine Maecenas, Palla Strozzi, who had been living in exile in Padua for many years. Staying in Palla's home, Argyropoulos, along with another learned, younger Greek, Andronicus Callistos, served as teacher of Greek for the intellectually insatiable Florentine. Strozzi's interest in Greek should come as no surprise, since several decades earlier in 1397 it had been Palla himself who had taken the primary responsibility for bringing to teach in Florence the great Byzantine teacher and aristocrat Manuel Chrysoloras. Under Chrysoloras, Palla had to be sure learned considerable Greek, but now he wished to continue his studies, especially in the philosophic and other writings of Aristotle.

In these years it cannot be said that Padua was barren of Greek knowledge. Indeed, a virtual cult of Greek letters was in the early stage of development—owing especially to the generous patronage of Strozzi. At nearby Venice, too, (for which Padua served as its university and both of which together constituted one intellectual nucleus) the Venetian humanist Ermolao Barbaro was teaching. And earlier even than that, Vergerius, a former student of Chrysoloras, had begun teaching Greek privately in Venice. It is notable, then, that despite the surge in interest in Greek studies in both Padua and Venice, all the teaching had hitherto been on a private basis. No professor of Greek was in fact *officially* appointed to the famous public *studium* of Padua University until 1463 with the coming of the Byzantine Demetrius Chalcondyles.

The relations between Palla and his protégé, Argyropoulos, were close—the Florentine becoming a stimulating friend as well as a munificent host. We are told that Palla frequently guided him around the city, and they may well have visited Venice together. Along with his instruction of Strozzi, Argyropoulos in his spare time probably also gave private lessons in Greek language and philosophy to other pupils, including Paduan aristocrats as well as copying manuscripts.

When Argyropoulos was not teaching and interpreting the philosophy of Aristotle to Palla—not the "Scholastic" Aristotle but that based on the original Greek texts, which is what his eager host was most desirous of hearing—Argyropoulos was enabled to attend, as a student, classes at the famous University of Padua. No doubt the alert Greek had, quickly enough, realized that a degree from an Italian university could prove very useful if the threatened Turkish conquest of Constantinople were to force him ultimately to seek shelter in the West. Subsequent events would prove the correctness of his reasoning. For, along with his own remarkable erudition in Greek literature and philosophy, his ability, rare among the Greeks, to lecture in fluent Latin played a considerable role in the success of his later teaching career. He was, it seems, the only important Greek refugee among those who came west just before and soon after the fall of Constantinople who earned a doctorate from an Italian university. It was probably for this reason that, along with Chalcondyles and perhaps Bessarion, his Latin style was among the best of all the Byzantine humanists.

Argyropoulos remained in Padua for three years, both teaching and studying. At last in 1444, after less than three years of study, he received his doctorate in both letters and medicine, a double major, as it were, that would be of value later in his exegesis of natural philosophy in Florence and Rome. At Padua, as in other Italian Renaissance universities, the arts and medicine were united into one school or curriculum.

The date of Argyropoulos's departure from Padua is again uncertain, but definite evidence remains that he was teaching (that is, holding a professorship) in 1448 at the *Katholikon Mouseion,* the higher school or "university" of Constantinople, at the so-called Xenon. Why he left Padua is unclear, but it was probably owing to a combination of factors: the attainment of his doctorate, perhaps the offer of a position at the *Mouseion* on the part of the Greek emperor, and, probably not least, a desire to see again his family and fatherland, all deeply endangered by an imminent Turkish siege. At any rate, his four years of instruction at Constantinople, however brief, are important for the development of his career.

The situation of the old and famous "university" of Constantinople at the time of his return is difficult to envisage precisely. But a short summary of the history of that institution during the last two centuries of its existence would be helpful. After the fall of Constantinople to the Latins in 1204 as a result of the Fourth Crusade and during the period of Latin rule there is little evidence of any *Latin* intellectual activity in Constantinople. True, the Latin emperor Baldwin evidently planned to establish a (Western-style) university there (mainly in the aim of proselytizing the Greeks), but this never materialized. With the capture of Constantinople in 1261 by troops of the Greek emperor Michael Palaeologus, that ruler refounded the old "university," establishing it in an outer building of the Cathedral of Hagia Sophia. The first head of this re-established institution was George Acropolites, who taught mathematics as well as philosophy, the main courses being on Euclid, Nicomachus, and Aristotle. Under Michael's son Andronicus II, the higher school of Constantinople was enlarged and placed under the care of the grand logothete Theodore Metochites, under whom it prospered greatly. A number of famous professors (such as the scholar-historian Nicephorus Gregoras) instructed there or nearby in semiprivate schools. At the end of the fourteenth century, Manuel II Palaeologus again reorganized Byzantine higher education, moving the "university" itself to the Monastery of St. John (in Petrion), where there was a good library—always a desideratum in the life of the "university." (It was, incidentally, at this time that the patriarchal academy, a school for training clerics, was located in the Monastery of St. John in Studius.) The higher school was now called the *Katholikon Mouseion* and as such it maintained itself as an institution until the very fall of the city in 1453.[3]

It was over this higher school, or rather its reorganization, that Argyropoulos now formally presided, with the support of Emperor John VIII. As noted, the school was located in the Xenon (literally "guest rooms"), a building constructed back in the late thirteenth or early fourteenth century by the Serb Kral Stephen Uroś. Some specific evidence remains about Argyropoulos's teaching and his pupils. A surviving Greek manuscript of the period contains a sketch depicting him lecturing from the *cathedra* (the professorial "chair") of the *Mouseion* at the Xenon.[4] Listed here below also are the names of some of his students, several of whom themselves were later to become prominent in the development of Italian humanism. One of these was the subsequently celebrated scholar, at this time a precocious boy of twelve, Constantine Lascaris. In an epistle of the latter's he affectionately refers to his "wise and beloved teacher" John Argyropoulos. Another pupil, who also later became well known, was older, the humanist Michael Apostolis, who had in fact possibly studied with Argyropoulos even before the latter had gone to Padua. Apostolis himself succeeded Argyropoulos in teaching at the Xenon.

The names of others of Argyropoulos's Greek students, many of them interested primarily in medicine, have survived: Antonios and Manuel Piropoulos, John Panaretos, Demetrius Angelus, and Vranos, all medical

3. On the characteristics and development of the "higher school" (or "university") in Constantinople, and of the patriarchal school, see D. Geanakoplos, *Byzantium: Church, Society, and Civilization,* nos. 301–306, esp. 306.

4. See accompanying illustration.

The Byzantine John Argyropoulos teaching from the cathedra of the Katholikon Mouseion at the Xenon in Constantinople, a drawing probably made by one of his students during class. From E. Legrand, *Bibliographie hellénique,* vol. 3 (Paris, 1903).

men; Agallone Moschus, and a certain Andreas. Besides these young Greeks (as Argyropoulos himself tells us in a later letter of his to George of Trebizond), many others came to hear his lectures not only from various parts of Greece but also "from outside Greece, and from Italy itself." Who these Italians were we do not know specifically, although it is well known that in these few decades before the fall of Constantinople it was not particularly remarkable (though certainly not common) for Italians desirous of learning Greek well to undertake the journey to Constantinople for purposes of study, for example, Guarino of Verona, Giovanni Tortelli, and also Francesco Filelfo, who, as already noted, had become secretary to the emperor himself. Aeneas Silvius Piccolomini (later Pope Pius II) made the remarkable but revealing statement that in this period one could not be considered truly educated unless he had studied in Constantinople.

In his same letter to George of Trebizond, Argyropoulos relates, interestingly enough, that his teaching consisted of "ta physika kai tous syllogismous" ("the physics and the syllogisms") of Aristotle. The latter term probably referred to Aristotle's logic in general rather than to the Latin-type, Scholastic syllogistic method of reasoning which Argyropoulos, among other things, had certainly studied at Padua. It is known that in his courses at the Xenon he discussed and compared views based on Aristotle and on the Bible relating to the nature of man and his creation. In the fourteenth century mathematics and astronomy, along with the quadrivium, had been taught in Constantinople, all within the framework of the seven branches of learning, and there is no reason to believe that this tradition did not continue at the Xenon during the period of Argyropoulos's instruction.

Among other teachers instructing in the *Katholikon Mouseion* at the Xenon were, or recently had been, George Chrysokokkes (under whom Bessarion and George of Trebizond had studied) and this same George of Trebizond. From a satire recently published, it is clear that Argyropoulos and George of Trebizond then had a falling out. The satire, recently edited primarily by N. Oikonomides, provides many interesting, even scatological, details on their clash. Certainly the known litigious character of George and the sometimes excessive hauteur of Argyropoulos may well have helped to create an atmosphere of suspicion and sharp rivalry between the two scholars.

Little more is known of this phase of Argyropoulos's teaching at the Xenon, except the important fact that in this period he was a strong proponent of ecclesiastical union with Rome. The fundamental question —whether to support or to oppose union with the Latin church—permeated the thinking of virtually all the Greek ecclesiastical and intellectual leaders of the later fourteenth and early fifteenth centuries. After all, many Greeks believed that Constantinople's salvation from the Turkish peril depended upon the success of such a union. Argyropoulos thus espoused the unionist cause. When exactly he had become a pro-unionist is unclear, but it seems certain that his early exposure to the lengthy, formal theological debates at the Council of Florence and to the more informal private discussions with many Latin intellectuals in Florence–as also later at Padua—must early have made him aware not only of the theological points at issue but also of the broader political and cultural implications of the problem as well. It is evident that by about 1448, or certainly 1451, he had actively joined the unionist side. In the former year he once again made an appearance in Italy, at the court of Pope Nicholas V. In a very adulatory petition directed to Pope Nicholas, Argyropoulos notes that it was for the sake of the religious union of the two churches that he had left behind wife and children, fatherland and friends, in order to accompany the papal legate, the Greek cardinal Isidore, back to Rome. This information is important, as is obvious, not only because it provides clear corroboration of his marriage and the birth of his children, but also because it is evidence of his now definitive conversion to the Roman faith. Indeed, here he explicitly affirms his dogmatic beliefs, indicating his acceptance of the procession of the Holy Spirit "from the Father through the Son, that is, from both Father and Son as from one essence." These words constitute in effect the solution to the famous dogmatic problem of the *filioque* which had been fixed upon, finally, at the Council of Florence. In any case Argyropoulos now became known both in Constantinople and in Italy during the years of his instruction at the Xenon as a partisan of religious union. The full theological implications of his views on this issue are known from a detailed dogmatic tract he wrote in this period. Yet it may well be that for him, as for some other contemporary Greek intellectuals such as Bessarion and the fourteenth-century Demetrius Cydones—all called derisively by many Greeks "Latinophrones"—the broader cultural question of rapprochement with the West and especially the need for Western military aid to save their capital city from the Turks, played as much if not more of an influential role in their support of religious union than the theological aspects of the question.

In this final period of Byzantium's existence, there was a searching among both Greek and Latin intellectuals for the fundamentals of the original Christian faith. And thus the concept of the unity of Christendom as it had existed in the early church before the schism (that is, before 1054) was now increasingly appealed to. Of course, it does not need to be pointed out that the vast bulk of the (much diminished)

Byzantine population bitterly opposed religious union on any grounds, tenaciously believing, rightly or wrongly, that union would quickly lead to political domination by the Latins, which, in turn, would sooner or later bring about a considerable cultural assimilation or even absorption of the culture of the Greek East by the now much more powerful West. Thus for many Byzantine anti-unionists union with Rome seems essentially to have been a matter of preservation of their "sense of identity" as a people distinct from the Latins. For some of the Greek intellectuals, however, who saw how preoccupation with ancient Greek learning was fast spreading in Italy and who probably even looked forward to a kind of merger of the two civilizations, the fear of cultural assimilation must have seemed of considerably less importance. Indeed, ancient Greek culture, now so popular in the humanist circles of Italy, might well become *the* superior element capable of welding both cultures together! It was in these years in fact that Argyropoulos urged the (last) Byzantine ruler, Constantine XI, to proclaim himself "King of the Hellenes" [Greeks], thus attesting both to John's love of his country and his attitude toward the legacy of ancient Greek culture—an emphasis which could help to strengthen a sense of patriotism based no longer on the ideal of imperial Byzantium but, more realistically, on that of a contemporary "Greek" ethnicity.

The political and military situation of Constantinople was now reaching the truly critical stage. Catastrophe was in fact almost upon the Greeks. Increasingly desperate, the new emperor, Constantine XI Palaeologus, now intensified his negotiations with the Western powers for military aid. And of course this always entailed the matter of religious union with Rome. But so intransigent did the bulk of the ecclesiastics, not to speak of virtually all the Greek common people, continue to be that the patriarch of Constantinople, Gregory Mammas, a pro-unionist, had to abdicate his throne and seek sanctuary in Rome. In response to imperial requests for aid, Pope Nicholas V, in order to secure what the papacy always demanded as a precondition to military aid, now sent to Constantinople an embassy headed by the Byzantine Isidore, a prelate who had previously been metropolitan of Kiev (and all Russia) and was now a Cardinal of the Roman church. In the grave events which ensued in Constantinople, Argyropoulos (again in Constantinople) ranged himself at the side of Isidore. On 12 December 1452, only five short months before the city's fall to the Turks, union was officially proclaimed by Isidore in the Cathedral of Hagia Sophia, but still with the sharp opposition of the bulk of the population. Only a few months now remained before the end. That in these events Argyropoulos was personally deeply involved is attested by a report of the Italian prelate Leonardo Giustiniani of Chios to the pope which refers to "Argyropoulos, Master of Arts."

On 29 May, at long last, Constantinople fell into the hands of the Turks. And in the tragic sack, looting, and other traumatic events which followed in the capital city, Argyropoulos lost not only all his wealth and possessions, but also his family, all of whom were captured by the Turks. He was to spend the next three years of his life in long, initially futile efforts to recover them through ransom, if possible. His efforts were ultimately to prove successful, but only after a vast expense of energy How he himself escaped from the Turks is not told us. But we know that Cardinal Isidore managed to escape the invaders disguised as a slave and flee to Crete. Other learned men, along of course with scores of thousands of common people, were captured.

Now began a most difficult and anxious period in the life of Argyropoulos when, as noted, his overriding objective was the raising of a ransom to secure the release of his family. Agitated and harassed in mind, not knowing which way to turn, Argyropoulos made constant peregrinations, traveling, when he could secure the funds, to Italy to appeal in particular to friends in Florence. But, equally important, he also sought a teaching position so that when he had finally managed to free his family, they could all settle permanently and peacefully with some degree of security.

It was during his stopover in Florence that there occurred a meeting that was to have the most profound influence on his entire future career. There he encountered a young Florentine intellectual, Donato Acciaiuoli. About this fateful meeting we learn from a detailed epistle of the young Donato himself. As he relates, conversation between the two concerned Donato's proposal that Argyropoulos submit his candidacy for a teaching professorship (of Greek) at the famous *studium* of Florence.

The intellectual situation in mid-fifteenth- century Florence, despite the glorious achievements of the early fifteenth century, was not encouraging. With the advent of the Byzantine teacher Manuel Chrysoloras in 1396/7 to the *studium* to teach Greek, intellectual life in Florence had quickened remarkably. Indeed, as a result of his teaching Florence soon held unquestioned primacy in the West for the study of Greek. A host of students, Florentines and outsiders, headed by Leonardo Bruni and Palla Strozzi, had studied with Chrysoloras. But by the middle of the fifteenth century the situation had changed drastically. The important old protagonists of Florentine humanism, that is, of the rhetorical type initiated by Salutati and continued and intensified (but in Greek studies) by Chrysoloras, were now dying off: Niccolò Niccoli, Ambrogio Traversari, and Leonardo Bruni. Only Marsuppini was left and he too soon died (1453).

As for Poggio, he was now very old, and the only other important Florentine humanist of the first rank, Gianozzo Manetti, had been exiled as the result of his political opposition to Cosimo de' Medici's regime.

Thus by the mid 1450s a vacuum existed in Florentine intellectual life and it may be said that it was about as poor intellectually as it had been rich several decades before. Added to the disappearance of many humanists through natural causes was the departure of the entire papal court from Florence (where it had resided for years) to the city of Rome. This meant the severe loss of papal patronage and, intellectually, also of a number of eager humanists who served professionally as secretaries of the papal Curia—Poggio and Flavio Biondo, for example.

It was to rectify this situation that several young Florentines, themselves already exposed to the old humanistic rhetorical interests, now sought to induce the Florentine Signoria to appoint capable new teachers to fill the vacancies in the *studium* and thus to restore some life to the intellectual scene in Florence. Chief among these intellectual zealots was the young Donato Acciaiuoli. Donato, a precocious young man (whose family name, Acciaiuoli, was well known in the East as being that of the rulers of Latin-held Athens in the fourteenth century) was the beloved grandson of none other than Palla Strozzi, the grand, old Florentine exile still living in Padua. Though residing in Padua, Strozzi had continued to exert a strong influence not only on the upbringing and education of his grandson (who with his mother, Palla's daughter, had remained behind in Florence), but through him, indirectly at least, on the cultural life of Florence itself.

It is not at all improbable that the name Argyropoulos had first become known to young Donato earier in Padua when the Greek scholar had been living in the home of his grandfather, or that Palla himself had written to Donato about the remarkable abilities of John Argyropoulos. In any event, it was Donato who sought out and arranged an interview in Florence with Argyropoulos during the latter's last trip to the city while seeking aid for his captive family. Donato himself was later to write, enthusiastically explaining how some time after Chrysoloras's departure Greek studies had begun to lag, that he had now found a Greek "worthy of the ancients" with whom he had conversed. By every possible argument he could muster, Donato sought to persuade Argyropoulos to become a candidate for an academic post in the Florentine *studium.*

As noted earlier, Chrysoloras, and especially his pupils Leonardo Bruni, Roberto Rossi, Guarino, and others, were interested primarily in rhetorical studies, in the so-called *studia humanitatis,* which stressed eloquence above all. (To be sure, Chrysoloras had earlier sought to introduce some Platonic philosophy to Florence but had had only little success in this effort.) Bruni himself, after learning Greek very well from Chrysoloras, undertook to make some translations of Aristotle, translations which differed from the earlier Scholastic versions in that they were not word-for- word translations but emphasized instead elegance of style. They thus often arrived closer to the original meaning of the Greek texts, but not always. Bruni, who, characteristically, emphasized the "golden stream" not only of Cicero's eloquence but (surprisingly perhaps) that of Aristotle as well, now became the hero of the early quattrocento Florentine humanists. It should be stressed that the focus on Aristotle was much more on his eloquence and ethics than on his speculative, metaphysical philosophy.

It might at first glance seem remarkable that Argyropoulos did not jump at Donato's proposal. Instead, after a short stay in Florence, he departed for Rome, then for Bologna and Venice, whereupon he returned to the Peloponnesus in Greece. One reason for his apparent reluctance is perhaps that he did not feel certain enough that the intellectual ambience of Florence was as yet sufficiently conducive to his appointment. More important, he had evidently heard a report of the escape of his wife and children from servitude and naturally wished to go at once to find them. The Peloponnesus was at this time virtually the only piece of Greek territory remaining unoccupied by the Turks, and his family may have fled there. Nonetheless, to judge by his subsequent actions there can be little doubt that he nurtured the hope that, once having recovered his family, he would be offered the appointment at the Florentine *studium.*

In the same year, 1454, an event of prime intellectual significance occurred in Florence— the formation of the so-called Florentine academy. This was not a formal society but rather a loosely organized group of intellectuals, primarily young men, led by the aristocrats Alamanno Rinuccini and his friend Donato Acciaiuoli. Gathering daily, they would read texts together and then engage in long, often fruitful discussions on primarily literary and sometimes philosophic problems. Rinuccini knew Greek well; he had even translated into Latin some of the lives of Plutarch which he dedicated to Piero di Cosimo. This Florentine academy, incidentally, with its primary emphasis on the "old style" (one might say) rhetorical humanism of Bruni, should not be confused with the more famous Platonic academy, later established (reportedly under the much earlier inspiration of Gemistos Pletho) by Cosimo de' Medici, which devoted itself almost exclusively to the discussion of Platonic and Neoplatonic philosophy.

It was through the influence of the members of this recently formed academy of Florence that on 24 February 1455 a decree was promulgated by the government providing for the immediate filling of two vacant chairs in the *studium,* specifically, of oratory and poetics. It was, however, also prescribed that the selection be limited to Florentines, which would of course (as Donato and his friends certainly realized) militate against the appointment of the Greek Argyropoulos, whose candidacy by now they passionately supported. The candidacy which in particular threatened the nomination of Argyropoulos was that of the Florentine Cristoforo Landino. And it was not until after a rather acute two-year struggle that the partisans of Argyropoulos triumphed, and he was, in October 1456, elected to the post of *lettore* of Greek philosophy, with the splendid yearly stipend of 400 florins. Decisive in his election, however, seems to have been the support thrown to him, at the end, by Cosimo and his son Piero de' Medici, both of whom had originally opposed his candidacy.

Shortly before his election, that is, earlier in the same year (1456), Argyropoulos had once again come to Rome, this time on a mission for Thomas Palaeologus, the Byzantine despot of the Peloponnesus. His visit this time was for the purpose of securing from Pope Calixtus III some kind of military aid against the Turks, in particular in the form of a crusade, an expedition for which Bessarion had for some time been preparing the way in the Curia. However, besides the military and political aspects of the problem, it was for Argyropoulos still another opportunity to plead the cause of himself and his family in the West. From Rome he continued on his mission to Milan, where he visited the Sforza duke, and from there he proceeded to France (then ruled by Charles VIII) and even to England. Of the specific instructions carried by Argyropoulos we have no knowledge. All that is clear is that, politically at least, he succeeded in obtaining nothing. Nor, apparently, did he secure any form of aid for his family, except possibly vague promises. Meantime, in Italy Argyropoulos did hear again from Donato (with whom he was doubtless in close correspondence) about his election to the new academic post in Florence. Whatever the order of these various events, before his going to Florence it was imperative that Argyropoulos first return to Greece to gather up his family.

At long last, on 4 February 1457, in the humanistic style of the age, Argyropoulos delivered in Florence his inaugural lecture at the *studium.* It was the first of a long series of public lectures that, according to a very plausible view, would lead to a significant change in the orientation of Florentine and hence of Italian humanism. For through his teaching (both formal and informal) in Florence Argyropoulos was to be instrumental in initiating the transition from the humanism typical of Petrarch and Bruni, with its emphasis on rhetoric, to the new, more strictly metaphysical phase of Renaissance humanism. Thus, through his own interests (he always referred to himself as a "philosopher") Argyropoulos helped to shift the axis of Florentine learning from the rhetoric of the early humanists to the philosophical speculation of the later period—a shift which in turn would have a great impact on the emerging humanism of the North.

Argyropoulos disagreed from the outset with the earlier Italian humanist belief in the small utility of speculative philosophy for daily life (shades of the ancient conflict between Plato and Isocrates). Thus in the introductory lecture (in November 1458) to his course on Aristotle's *Physics* (that is, on "natural philosophy")—a rather grandiloquent discourse, by the way, not untypical of the period—Argyropoulos indicated the great usefulness for life of ancient Greek philosophy. Dividing philosophy into its various component parts, he then turned to consider that specific part called Ethics. He spoke particularly of Aristotle's *Nicomachean Ethics,* praising in passing (it should be noted) Bruni's Latin translation of Aristotle. This must have been a gesture particularly pleasing to his Florentine audience. Through Bruni, Chrysoloras's favorite student, he thus drew a straight line from himself back to Chrysoloras, separated from him by some fifty years but the mention of whose name could still thrill his audience.

His lectures became increasingly popular, to the point that he became the heart and soul of the Florentine *studium.* His students came from near and far and included the most brilliant youths of Florence: Pier Filippo, Pandolfo di Giannozzo Pandolfini, Domenico di Carlo, Francesco de Lorenzi Filarete, Vespasiano da Bisticci (who wrote the famous *Biographies of Illustrious Men,* which includes a sketch of Argyropoulos), Bartolommeo della Fonte, of course Donato Acciaiuoli and Rinuccini, and finally Bernardo Platina, who, we are told, gave up the idea of going to Greece to learn Greek in order to study instead with Argyropoulos in Florence.

But most important of all his students was the (later) celebrated humanist Angelo Poliziano, then still a boy but a prodigy. Poliziano developed a deep respect, even affection, for his Greek teacher; he became so expert in Greek, in fact, that, as is well known, he later boasted (and in some but certainly far from all cases correctly) that he knew Greek better than any of the Greek émigré humanists. But except for Argyropoulos, Poliziano seemed to have had a general distaste for the Byzantines, and this probably serves in part to explain his remark. Besides Argyropoulos's students proper, there were of course many others who came simply to hear some of his lectures.

Curiously, at the same time that Argyropoulos was reaping his great success in the *studium,* Christoforo Landino (who had learned Greek earlier when George of Trebizond had taught at the Florentine *studium*) was also teaching there. But little seems to be known of their relations, though Landino undoubtedly participated in activities of the Florentine academy.

In seeking to assess the impact of Argyropoulos's instruction on the intellectual life of Florence, it must be made clear that his teaching was not limited to formal daily presentations at the *studium.* These took place in the morning and were devoted primarily to Aristotle, to his *Ethics,* then to his *Politics,* to his ideas on economy and on moral and natural philosophy, to his *De anima* and, after all this preparation, finally to his *Metaphysics.* Later, evidently in the afternoon, however, Argyropoulos also taught at his home, but privately, for a select group of students, and here unlike, or certainly to a far greater degree than, in the *studium,* animated discussions took place directly between professor and students. It was here that Argyropoulos emphasized the logical works of Aristotle to which he attached special importance. And here he even began to expound on the philosophy of Aristotle's teacher, the "Divine Plato," beginning with his dialogue the *Meno.* The *Meno* had of course been available to the West for centuries in the elventh-century Latin translation of Henry Aristippus of the Sicilian, Norman court. But Argyropoulos's exposition was so lucid, so penetrating, and in some ways so novel (he would on occasion make references to the Greek pre-Socratic philosophers as well as to Plato and Aristotle) that, we are told, his audience followed his presentation as if transfixed. Obviously, Argyropoulos had one advantage contributing to his enormous success lacking to virtually all other Greek exile professors: an excellent command of Latin (and presumably Italian) and of Western philosophic thought, especially of Scholasticism, to which he had been exposed in his course of study at Padua University.

Evidence of Argyropoulos's success in expounding Plato comes to us from Donato Acciaiuoli, his loyal student, and also from Vespasiano, who praises his teaching and his profound understanding of Plato. So persuasive was his teaching, it seems, that he was even able to turn the young Donato Acciaiuoli and Alamanno Rinuccini from their original chief interest in rhetoric to philosophy. His instruction, therefore, was definitely not, as is sometimes stated, a continuation of the old Florentine tradition but rather a sharp break with it. Far more than Pletho, Argyropoulos, then, should be given credit for turning the orientation of mid-fifteenth-century Florentine humanism from a rhetorical to a philosophical interest in Plato—no mean achievement. One should not of course overlook in this change the despotic rule of the Medici, which by now was not conducive to the kind of activities existing under a republican form of government, nor should one forget the still-existent intellectual influence of late medieval Scholasticism.

Though Argyropoulos developed in his students a genuine enthusiasm for Plato, he himself never really expressed a preference for Plato or Aristotle or attempted to declare one superior to the other. Thus while discussing Aristotle's *Ethics* and his *De anima,* he would include sympathetic recitals of the related doctrines of Plato. Nor, more surprisingly, did he directly participate in the celebrated conflict begun by the Byzantines at the Council of Florence, and continued thereafter in Constantinople and Italy, over the respective merits of Plato and Aristotle. Argyropoulos, to be sure, often compared the doctrines of the two philosophers, but he seemed to take pleasure in the dissimilar but, as he put it, not truly contradictory doctrines of both. Not even with respect to Plato's unique theory of ideas did he seem to believe that there existed an absolute contrast between the two. Indeed, his only entrance, and that indirect, into the Aristotle-Plato conflict was in response to a treatise sent to him by Bessarion. This was a copy of Bessarion's famous *In calumniatorem Platonis,* which he had written in reply to George of Trebizond's scathing attack on the supporters of Plato. But Argyropoulos merely congratulated Bessarion for his brilliant defense of Plato and went no further.

Granted Argyropoulos's attraction to both Aristotle and Plato, it should be recalled that, while he was fond of and often brilliantly expounded informally to the audience at his home the fascinating and sometimes complex doctrines of Plato, Argyropoulos's chief activity in the Florentine *studium*—and the purpose for which he had originally been hired—was to lecture publicly on the philosophy of Aristotle. For Argyropoulos, the evidence seems to indicate, it was Aristotle, the pupil of Plato, who marked the climax in Greek philosophical development.

Concomitant with his teaching of Aristotle at the *studium,* Argyropoulos himself composed many translations into Latin of Aristotle's works, a number of which between 1464 and 1469 he dedicated to Cosimo and his son Piero de' Medici. Cosimo, in fact, became so fond of Argyropoulos that he presented him with a house on the Via Larga in Florence. More important, to show that he had been completely won over, Cosimo had his young grandson, the brilliant Lorenzo, become a student of Argyropoulos's, though whether in his public or private class (or both) is not certain. It may well have been Cosimo's close relationship with Argyropoulos that induced him finally to actuate his old resolve to found, in 1462, the Platonic academy in Florence. Argyropoulos reciprocated Cosimo's affection and was deeply grieved at his death in 1464. Cosimo's son and heir, Piero, himself an old student of Argyropoulos's, continued his patronage of Argyropoulos.

One question that arises concerns the kind of relationship that existed between Argyropoulos and the person who would become Florence's, indeed the West's, greatest Neoplatonist, Marsilio Ficino. But whether Argyropoulos's teaching had any really decisive influence on Ficino, then a young man in his early twenties, is not clear. Certainly Argyropoulos much more than Ficino deserves the major credit for opening the way to the intensive study of the philosophy of Plato—and for the first time, it should be stressed, in the context of a systematic exposition of the entire history of Greek philosophy. Argyropoulos's method of presenting Greek philosophy as a unified whole is surely one of the major contributions to the study of Greek philosophy during the Renaissance.

Earlier, of course, during his tenure at the *studium* in Florence, Chrysoloras had at least introduced the Florentines to Plato, but he had only been able to whet their appetites. Ficino had indicated his own preference for philosophy over rhetoric before the arrival of Argyropoulos in Florence. But it was not until 1462/3 that Ficino learned Greek sufficiently well to begin translating the *Dialogues* of Plato. Thus, though he had already indicated his desire to undertake his great enterprise of the translation of Plato, it seems almost impossible to believe that the example of Argyropoulos (about whom Ficino must certainly have heard much talk) and perhaps that of Bessarion (who, as noted, wrote the *In calumniatorem Platonis* supporting Plato and had sent copies of the treatise to both Ficino and Argyropoulos) did not in some way affect him. It seems logical, then, to affirm that in 1463, when Ficino was translating the most difficult of the Platonic dialogues for his old patron Cosimo, the ground had already been well prepared among the Florentine intelligentsia by Argyropoulos for the new type of "metaphysical humanism," especially Plato. It is of interest that after completion of his translation of Plato, Ficino evidently submitted his work for criticism not to Argyropoulos but to another leading Byzantine scholar, the emigré Demetrius Chalcondyles who, as we shall see, would later teach in Florence simultaneously with Argyropoulos. Evidence for this is found in the (Latin) introduction to the Latin text I recently published of Chalcondyles's inaugural oration on the establishment of the first Greek chair at the University of Padua in 1463 (see above essay 1, text and notes 94 and 100).

The crowning point of Argyropoulos's brilliant career in Florence came in 1466, some two years after Cosimo's death, when, as a testimonial to nine years of beneficent influence on the cultural life of Florence, he was presented, together with his entire family, with all the privileges of citizenship in the Florentine republic. It was a fine attestation to his endeavors and to the intellectual progress made under his tutelage by the Florentine youth. Truly, by now Florence had become a second homeland for him. It appeared that Argyropoulos, basking in the glory and tranquillity of his life on the Arno, wanted to remain permanently in Florence. Indeed, the government granted him a five-year extension of his teaching contract. But, alas, it would be Argyropoulos himself who, all too soon, would seek to leave Florence.

What interrupted this happy period of his life was the loss in only two years time of three of his four sons. Of the four, only Isaac would survive (later to become a famous musician at the Sforza court in Milan). To add to this tragic loss of his beloved children in so brief a period was the death also of his great patron Piero de' Medici. Saddened beyond measure by the deaths of these people dearest to him, Argyropoulos now decided to leave Florence. Thus in mid 1471 the *cathedra* which he had occupied in the *studium* so auspiciously for fifteen long years was vacant.

But his departure to Rome had been preceded by some indecision on his part. For his reputation, which had by now spread over much of western Europe, had reached even to Budapest and the ears of the humanist patron King Matthias Corvinus of Hungary. Thus through the Hungarian humanist Giano Pannonius, who had come to know Argyropoulos on a visit to Florence, Corvinus now extended an invitation to Argyropoulos to come teach in Budapest. But though tempted, Argyropoulos did not, finally, succumb to the blandishments of the Hungarian king. His change of mind was in large part owing to the election to the papal throne of his old friend from his student days in Padua, Sixtus IV. Pope Sixtus had grand ideas: he planned, it seems, to resurrect the famous old academy in Rome of Pomponio Leto. To head this renewed center of humanistic studies he chose the most prominent and famous of the Greek exiles, the long-time patron of many of the Byzantines, Cardinal Bessarion, with whom, as we have seen, Argyropoulos was and had always been on excellent terms. It was the irresistible combination, then, of the election of Sixtus IV and the promise of suitable employment held out by the position of Bessarion that now attracted Argyropoulos to the papal court in Rome.

Soon after his arrival in the Curia (1471) Argyropoulos wrote to his friend and student Lorenzo de' Medici in Florence, requesting him to have sent to Rome his books, which he had left behind until he could properly settle himself in the papal capital. Specifically, Argyropoulos requested his own translations of Aristotle, which members of the Curia interested in the "new" Aristotle now wished to see. Under Bessarion's leadership, the Curia had been virtually transformed into a kind of center or "Academy" of humanist, especially Greek studies. Bessarion had in fact summoned a number of his compatriots to Rome—among them conspicuously George of Trebizond—to make, systematically, Latin versions of the ancient Greek literary and scientific works as well as of the Greek church fathers.

Thus began in Rome the third and final phase of Argyropoulos's career. But all too soon he was to find conditions in Rome quite different from those in Florence. True, for three years he seemed to find favor in Rome, but shortly thereafter his dreams of a quiet, relaxed old age were rudely shattered. Nevertheless, during his initial three years of teaching he attracted some outstanding students with whom he achieved a considerable success. Most notable of these was the later-famous German humanist Reuchlin. It was of him that his grandnephew, the humanist Melanchthon, could make the famous remark that when Argyropoulos first heard Reuchlin reading from the Greek text of Thucydides, he exclaimed, "Greece has flown across the Alps."

In Rome Argyropoulos taught both Greek language and philosophy, but in contrast to Florence (where, as noted, at his home he often engaged in intense discussion with his students), there were few opportunities for the forming of close relationships between teacher and student. Moreover, the interests of the Curia absorbed too much of the energies of the several Greeks teaching there, including Argyropoulos himself. In addition, more time was taken up with the tasks of translation allotted by the academy than in teaching. And, as the reader must have noted, Argyropoulos's chief love and talent lay in teaching, in communicating ideas to his students. There seems to be no evidence that he participated in editorial work for any printing house in Rome. It is of interest, however, that the printer Giacomo Mazzocchi, later in Rome in 1515, published Argyropoulos's Latin translation of St. Basil's *Hexameron* and his (Latin) *Commentary on St. Basil's Hexameron.* Finally, though Sixtus himself was not niggardly, the constant preoccupation of the papacy with wars and diplomatic affairs soon served to diminish the stipends that could be paid to the professors of his academy. It is not surprising therefore, that, especially with the disappearance of his patron Bessarion from the scene, Argyropoulos resolved once more to move. (Bessarion died in 1472 soon after he was sent as papal ambassador to France and only six months after Argyropoulos's arrival in Rome.) The loss of Bessarion created a void that for Argyropoulos could not be filled.

Argyropoulos bent all his efforts to recover, if possible, his old position in Florence. Several years before this, he had been replaced in the *studium* by another very able Greek refugee scholar, his younger colleague of Padua, Andronicus Callistos. But at this very moment Callistos had decided to abandon his Florentine chair in preference for one offered him in Milan by Duke Galeazzo Sforza. It was therefore an opportune moment for Argyropoulos. Nonetheless, despite a letter of recommendation written to Florence on his behalf by his old friend Filelfo, Argyropoulos was unable to secure the chair. Still another no less able Byzantine refugee scholar, Demetrius Chalcondyles, was also striving to secure the same chair, and it is possible that the Florentines preferred Chalcondyles, who had already been among them for a short time. It is reported that in order to push his own candidacy personally, Argyropoulos now paid a visit to Florence, where to the amazement, indeed near shock, of his old Florentine friends, he appeared with his beard shaved off—a "Latinization" ("Latinizzamento") as the Florentines termed it.

In still another reversal, Argyropoulos was, in 1477, reappointed to his old post in Florence. This time, however, he held it for only three years. Remarkably enough, he was teaching there at the same time as Chalcondyles. It must have been a unique sight to have seen these two celebrated Byzantine refugee scholars both teaching simultaneously at the *studium*. But, once again, Argyropoulos decided to move. Why is again not known. Was it rivalry with the younger Chalcondyles, who by then had succeeded in becoming very popular with the Florentines? Or more likely, his agitated and disturbed spirit, so common a characteristic among almost all the exiled Greek refugees, full of nostalgia for their lost homeland and continually seeking self-assurance, that did not permit him to rest in peace? And so, finally, we find him again in the city of Rome where he spent his remaining years.

Of these last years, from 1481 to 1487, we know little. Taking up his lectureship again, he apparently still could evoke an attentive audience, among whom were Lefèvre d'Etaples and John Reuchlin, later to become, respectively, outstanding French and German humanists. Their tutelage must have afforded some degree of satisfaction. But that he was unhappy in this last phase of his life is strongly suggested by a remark by a student of his youth at the *Katholikon Mouseion* of Constantinople, Constantine Lascaris. Lascaris, who by now had become a famous humanist himself in Italy, living in distant Messina, Sicily, wrote a moving letter to his friend Giovanni Pardo, in which he lamented the melancholy fate of himself and his fellow Greek exiles. As he wrote, "Callistos has died friendless in distant England, Gaza has passed away obscurely in distant Calabria, and my learned teacher Argyropoulos lives in poverty in Rome and has even to sell his books in order to secure his daily bread." Whether this statement can be taken literally or not, Argyropoulos's last years seem indeed to have been bitter ones. Bereft of family and evidently of close friends, an exile, he died in Rome in 1487 at the very advanced age of c. 93, burdened with many debts as well as by the enmity of Paolo Giovio, a vituperative Italian writer who was never slow to calumniate anyone with whom he had the slightest difference of opinion. And Argyropoulos, unfortunately, had become involved with Giovio in the famous quarrel over Ciceronianism. But to counter Giovio's words about Argyropoulos's character we have only to cite those of the often "difficult" Filelfo, who had known Argyropoulos almost all of his life. Filelfo had a high opinion not only of the scholarship of his friend (he called him a "true phoenix in learning") but of his character as well.

Argyropoulos, like all men, had his defects of character but these were apparently minor—notably a kind of self-conceit or hauteur that was in fact the natural hallmark (a defensive mechanism?) of almost all the Greek exiles. But the virtually unanimous testimony of students (both Italian and Greek), of friends and patrons, attests to the high quality, even nobility, of his character. True, he was sometimes carried away by a sense of his own importance and learning and was perhaps inordinately proud of his Greek heritage. This latter quality in particular made him, on occasion, critical of the Latin intellectuals. Thus when he first came to Florence he made the egregious error of attacking Cicero as being "ignorant not only in philosophy but also in Greek letters," much to the displeasure of the Florentine humanists as a whole to whom Cicero was by then virtually a god. (Subsequently he showed more respect for Cicero.) It should be noted that of almost all the Latins the one most universally disliked by the Greek intellectuals was Cicero, for the Italians were fond of constantly holding him up to the Greek exiles as a model of rhetorical excellence and as one who, though influenced in the extreme by the Greeks had, so to say, surpassed them at their own game. This lack of tact on the part of Argyropoulos, which occasionally revealed itself in his career, was also evidenced in his early criticism of another Florentine humanist hero, the great chancellor Leonardo Bruni. Despite these few lapses, it may be said with certitude that the relations between Argyropoulos and the Florentine humanists during the principal phase of his career, his eighteen-year sojourn of teaching in the Florentine *studium,* were on the whole remarkably smooth and fruitful and constitute a landmark in the study of Greek philosophy in the Italian Renaissance.

As several modern authorities have affirmed, in the development of Florentine humanism the shift in orientation from a rhetorical to a more strictly philosophical emphasis owed its origins in Florence primarily to the Byzantine school. And it was in particular through the courses of the Byzantine professor John Argyropoulos that this renewed interest in metaphysics prepared the way for the triumphant entry into Florence of the Platonic and Neoplatonic "theology" which was to become so important to Renaissance humanism under Ficino.

Bibliography for Essay 4

This essay was originally presented as a much shorter lecture and printed with only a bibliographical note, an updated longer version of which is published here.

On the career of Argyropoulos see especially G. Cammelli, *I dotti Bizantini e le origini dell'umanesimo: Giovanni Argiropulo* (Florence, 1941), with bibliography; more recently, E. Garin, "Donato Acciaiuoli, Citizen of Florence," in his *Portraits from the Quattrocento,* trans. V. A. Velen and E. Velen (New York, 1972), 55–117. J. Seigel, "The Teaching of Argyropoulos and the Rhetoric of the First Humanists," in *Action and Conviction in Early Modern Europe,* ed. T. Rabb and J. Seigel (Princeton, N.J., 1969), 237–60. On the Byzantine émigré scholars in general see my *Byzantium and the Renaissance* (rpt. of *Greek Scholars in Venice*).

E. Bigi, "Giovanni Argiropulo," *Dizionario biografico degli Italiani* 4:129–31. E. Garin, "Le traduzioni unmanistiche di Aristotele nel secolo XV," *Atti e memorie dell'Accademia fiorentina di scienze morali la Colombaria* 16 (1949–59, 1951): 50–104. Garin, "Platonici bizantini e platonici italiani: Nuove indagini sul Pletone," *Studi sul platonismo medievale* (Florence, 1958), 153–90. G. Zippel, "Per la biografia dell'Argiropulo," *Storia e cultura del rinascimento* (rpt. Padua, 1979). S. Lampros, *Argyropouleia* (in Greek) (Athens, 1910). A. Vacalopoulos, *Origins of the Greek Nation: The Byzantine Period, 1204–1461* (New Brunswick, N.J., 1970), references to Argyropoulos; Vacalopoulos, *The Greek Nation, 1453–1669* (New Brunswick, N.J., 1976), see references. J. Monfasani, *George of Trebizond* (Leiden, 1976), 375–78, short note on Argyropoulos's birth date. More recently, see A. Field's notable article, "John Argyropoulos and the 'Secret' Teachings of Plato," *Supplementum Festivum: Studies in Honor of Paul Oskar Kristeller,* ed. J. Hankins, J. Monfasani, and F. Purnell, Jr. (Binghamton, N.Y., 1987), 299–326 (used here). Field, "The Studium Florentinum Controversy, 1455," *History of Universities* 3 (1983):31–59. C. Woodhouse, *Gemistos Plethon, The Last of the Hellenes* (Oxford, 1986) a few references to Argyropoulos. MPG, 157, cols. 992–1008, Argyropoulos's tract on the Holy Spirit. P. Canavet, N. Oikonomides, "(Jean Argyropoulos) La comédie de Katablattas. Invective Byzantine du XVe s." *Diptycha* 3 (Athens, 1982–3) 5–97, important new evidence on Argyropoulos's early years. M. Manoussakas, K. Staikos, *The Publishing Activities of the Greeks during the Italian Renaissance* (Athens, 1987) 44–53, sketch of Argyropoulos's career with information on his printed works. Also E. Garin, "Endelecheia e Entelecheia," *Atene e Roma,* 3d ser. (1937): 177–87.

Five

The Career of the Little-Known Renaissance Greek Scholar Nicolaus Leonicus Tomaeus and the Ascendancy of Greco-Byzantine Aristotelianism at Padua University (1497)

In Venice and at the adjoining University of Padua the Arabic Averroistic interpretation of Aristotle had become entrenched in the curriculum since as early as the later fourteenth century. And the struggle at Padua to restore the original Greek texts and interpretations of Aristotle and to substitute them for the Arabic (not only for Aristotle's philosophic and scientific but also for his literary works) was a long and arduous one.[1] It culminated finally in 1497 with the official appointment by the Venetian Senate of the Greek humanist Nicolaus Leonicus Tomaeus "to read [as the document of appointment puts it] in the Greek [text]" of Aristotle's philosophy.[2]

1. This is the first biography in English of this very important but little-known scholar. On the rivalry between the Greek and Averroist interpretations of Aristotle at Padua, see B. Nardi, *Saggi sull'aristotelismo padovano dal secolo xiv al xvi* (Padua, 1958); J. Randall, *The School at Padua and Emergence of Modern Science* (Padua, 1961); P. O. Kristeller, "Renaissance Aristotelianism," *Greek, Roman and Byzantine Studies* 6 (1965): 157ff., 163–72; G. Saitta, *Il pensiero italiano nell'umanesimo e nel rinascimento,* 2d ed. (Florence, 1961), 415ff., esp. 449; E. Ferrai, *L'ellenismo nello studio di Padova* (Padua, 1876); and C. Schmitt, *Aristotle and the Renaissance* (Cambridge, Mass., 1983).

2. See Latin text in J. Facciolatus, *Fasti gymnasii patavini,* vol. 1 (Padua, 1752), 56,

Born in Venice in 1456 of Greek parents from Epirus (wrongly termed Albania by some scholars), Tomaeus as a youth was sent to study in Florence, where at its *studium* he read Greek literature and philosophy with his famed compatriot Demetrius Chalcondyles. The latter, along with other Greek associates, imbued him with a devotion for the ancient Greek and Byzantine texts and especially the works of Aristotle.[3] This was of particular significance because at that time in Florence, and even earlier, the use of the Scholastic versions of Aristotle's *Ethics* and *Politics* had evoked the censure of such leading humanists as Leonardo Bruni and later of Angelo Poliziano. Both of these recognized the superiority of the Greek texts for providing the best interpretations of Aristotle.[4] Tomaeus's period of study and association with leading Florentine scholars permit him to be considered one more, though almost entirely overlooked, link between the humanism of Florence and that of Venice-

---

under a. 1497; J. Sandys, *A History of Classical Scholarship,* vol. 2 (Cambridge, 1908), 110f. On Tomaeus, besides references mentioned in n. 1, see references or brief sketches in F. Gasquet, *Cardinal Pole and His Early Friends* (London, 1927); G. Tiraboschi, *Storia della letteratura italiana,* vol. 3 (Milan, 1833), 467ff.; Geanakoplos, *Greek Scholars in Venice,* 137, 38, 228; K. Sathas, *Neohellēnikē philologia* (Athens, 1868), 92–94; A. Kyrou, *Hoi Hellēnes tēs anagennēseōs* (Athens, 1938), 112–13; and esp. Paolo Giovio, *Elogia doctorum virorum,* trans. F. Gragg, *An Italian Portrait Gallery* (Boston, 1935), 129–30. D. De Bellis, "Niccolò Leonico Tomeo interprete di Aristotele Naturalista," *Physis* 17 (1975): 70–93. E. Legrand's famous work *Bibliographie hellénique ou description raisonnée des ouvrages publiés en grec par des grecs au XVe et XVIe siècles,* 4 vols. (Paris, 1885–1906) on Greek scholars in Italy and esp. their publications, contains no biographical sketch of Tomaeus, though he lists his publications. Tomaeus wrote a large number of works, some of which are hardly known today.

3. A. King, *Venetian Humanism in an Age of Patrician Dominance* (Princeton, N.J., 1986), 433, says Tomaeus's father emigrated to Venice, from Negropont but cites no evidence. See D. De Bellis, "La vita e l'ambiente di Niccolò Leonico Tomeo," *Quaderni per la storia dell'Università di Padova* 13 (1980): 37 (an article I saw when this book was in press and which I was able to profit from). See G. Cammelli, *Demetrio Calcondila* (Florence, 1954), 36, esp. n. 3; also cf. G. Tiraboschi, *Storia della letteratura italiana,* vol. 7 (Venice, 1796), 386. Most authorities base the view of Tomaeus's study with Chalcondyles on Giovio, *Italian Portrait Gallery,* 129. Tomaeus himself wrote of a lecture on Homer he presumably heard in Florence by Chalcondyles in 1496. See Gasquet, *Cardinal Pole,* 11, who affirms (on the basis of Tomaeus's letters) that as a boy Tomaeus studied at Montecassino and that before settling at Padua he had apparently lived in Bergamo. Cf. De Bellis, quoting Tomaeus's MS on Bergamo and saying Tomaeus followed Chalcondyles also to Milan and to Padua.

4. On Bruni's criticism see G. Holmes, *The Florentine Enlightenment* (New York, 1969), esp. 114; also *Dizionario biografico degli Italiani,* s.v. "Leonardo Bruni," 14: esp. 625, 629–30. On Poliziano see Holmes, 263; and E. Garin, "Il Poliziano e il suo tempo," in *Miscellaneorum centuria secunda,* vol. 1 (Florence, 1972), 13–14; and Garin, *Portraits from the Quattrocento,* trans. V. A. Velen and E. Velen (New York, 1972), 161–90.

Padua.[5] The twin centers of Padua and Venice, which in effect constituted a single nucleus of learning, evinced no little interest in belles lettres, but their activities were most famous for the medical school at Padua, which by the late fifteenth century had become the most prominent in all Europe.

Venice, and to a lesser extent Padua before 1405, had long had contacts with the Greek East, before 1204 with Constantinople, and afterward through Venetian possession of the islands of Crete and Euboea and of Coron and Modon. A continual mercantile traffic passed between Venice and its Greek colonies. More important were the hundreds, even several thousands, of Greek émigrés who poured into Venice soon before and especially after the fall of Constantinople to the Turks. There in time they organized themselves into a cohesive community which in 1494 was officially recognized as a Confraternità by the Venetian Senate.[6] To this Greek community in Venice, and also to another, though far smaller and more amorphous community in Padua, came many Greeks, some of whom were well educated in the Byzantine literary and rhetorical tradition. As the Venetian cardinal Bembo put it much later in c. 1531 on the occasion of his oration before the Venetian Senate extolling Venice's primacy in Greek studies, the city's preeminence in this respect was at least in part owing to the presence of the many cultured Greeks living in the midst of the Venetians.[7]

These émigré Greeks, of course, did not have to be instructed in the greater authenticity and therefore superiority of the original Greek versions of Aristotle's multifarious writings. Indeed, the sources are full of references to the dismay, even shock, felt by learned Greeks of the Italian Renaissance when they saw the mutilated versions of Aristotle—not only manuscripts replete with scribal errors but also inadequate Scholastic translations into Latin, especially when accompanied by the interpretations or commentaries of the Arab Averroës[8] —which were used generally throughout Renaissance Italy instead of the original Greek texts of

5. For Florentine humanist influences in Venice-Padua see Geanakoplos, *Greek Scholars in Venice,* 37–40 (republished as *Byzantium and the Renaissance*).

6. On the Greek colony in Venice see Geanakoplos, *Greek Scholars in Venice;* Geanakoplos, *Interaction of the "Sibling" Byzantine and Western Cultures in the Middle Ages and Italian Renaissance,* chaps. 9–10; also G. Fedalto, *Ricerche storiche sulla posizione giuridica ed ecclesiastica dei greci a Venezia nei secoli XV e XVI* (Florence, 1967).

7. Quoted in Geanakoplos, *Greek Scholars in Venice,* 279.

8. On the Byzantine protest against such mutilated manuscripts note, e.g., Chalcondyles' dismay as expressed in his inaugural oration at Padua, in Geanakoplos, *Interaction of the Sibling Cultures,* 257–58; see Greek translation of this book with better text of Chalcondyles' oration in *Byzantio kai dysē* (Athens, 1985), 430–41. Bessarion

which the Byzantines had for centuries been the custodians. Rarely would the Byzantines recognize any legitimacy in the Averroist tradition. Indeed, several Greek scholars thought that Averroës' knowledge of Greek was simply inadequate.[9]

The significance of the Byzantine claim of authenticity for the Greek Aristotelian texts was certainly not lost on most of the Italian humanists, including those of Padua University. As early as the late fourteenth century Peter of Abano, the greatest of medieval Western physicians, had eagerly sought to acquire Greek texts of Aristotle's scientific and medical works. He had even traveled to Constantinople whence, it is known, he brought back to the West for the first time the pseudo-Aristotelian *Problemata.* Nonetheless, the Averroist tradition (which Peter reputedly founded at Padua's school of medicine), was undeniably a rich and varied one which in some ways even made advances on Aristotle's theories.[10] In any event, it early took firm hold at Padua University's medical school and, to a lesser extent, in the school of letters. Both of these schools, as was common in Italian universities of the time, constituted a single faculty of learning,[11] and hence they developed a common interest in establishing the most accurate versions of Aristotle's works.

It was at the urging especially of the Greek cardinal of the Roman church Bessarion that the Athenian Demetrius Chalcondyles was appointed, in 1463, to the first chair of Greek studies to be established at Padua. In a recent study in which I published the Latin text of his inaugural oration, I discussed the significance of this appointment for the development of Greek letters in Italy. Most relevant here is the importance of Chalcondyles' Greek instruction for Padua's medical school, with its vigorous interest in Aristotle's scientific works.[12] Chalcondyles'

---

complained about this in many of his works; it is one reason he collected his great library of Greek manuscripts.

9. See P. O. Kristeller, "Byzantine and Western Platonism in the Fifteenth Century," in *Renaissance Thought and Its Sources* (New York, 1979), 161. Yet note Tomaeus's use of Averroës, at n. 22 below. Also see S. Runciman, *The Last Byzantine Renaissance* (Cambridge, 1970), 83, on the Byzantine George Scholarios's knowledge of Averroës. Gemistos Pletho (see essay 11) had attacked Averroës: Migne, *Patrologia graeca,* vol. 60, col. 890A.

10. On Peter of Abano's career see L. Thorndike, *A History of Magic and Experimental Science,* vol. 2 (New York, 1964), 874–947; also Thorndike, "Peter of Abano and Another Commentary on the Problems of Aristotle," *Bulletin of History of Medicine* 29 (1955): 317–23. For some careful distinctions on use of the term "Averroism" see P. O. Kristeller, *Renaissance Thought and Its Sources,* 39, 42ff.

11. See Geanakoplos, *Interaction of the Sibling Cultures,* 246.

12. Ibid., 246–47. For more accurate Latin text of his oration see the Greek translation, *Byzantio kai dysē,* 430–41.

appointment may therefore be considered an important step in the development of the competition between the Averroist and Greek, or more accurately Byzantine, textual tradition of Aristotle at Padua.

The growing awareness at Venice-Padua of the importance of the Greek texts was considerably facilitated by two native Venetian humanists, Girolamo Donato and especially the anti-Scholastic Ermolao Barbaro.[13] Barbaro, now generally recognized as the greatest of the Venetian humanists, had been bringing pressure to bear on the Padua faculty to displace, or at least to supplement, the dominant Averroist versions with the Greek. Earlier Barbaro had studied in Rome with the noted Byzantine humanist exile Theodore Gaza, who, some modern scholars affirm, was the first Renaissance scholar to study Aristotle's texts apart from the context of Christianity or Islamic Averroism, that is, to interpret the pure texts.[14] As a result of Gaza's influence (and of course his own studies) Barbaro soon became convinced that the truest Aristotelian interpretations were to be found not in the Arab Averroës or in the similar views of the Latin Averroists, not in the syllogisms of the Western Schoolmen but—and this is notable—above all in the late ancient Greek and early Byzantine commentators on Aristotle such as Simplicius, Themistius, Philoponus, and Alexander of Aphrodisias.[15]

Barbaro was the first Italian humanist to translate into Latin a commentary on Aristotle by the fourth-century Byzantine Themistius. And his teacher, Theodore Gaza, had utilized all or most of the commentators in his own writings on Aristotle.[16] Though Barbaro died in 1485, it was, indirectly at least, partly as a result of his efforts and those of his fellow Venetian humanist Girolamo Donato, together with the even earlier activity of Cardinal Bessarion in Rome, that induced the Venetian Senate, finally, in 1497, to take the capital step of appointing Nicolaus Tomaeus as lecturer in Aristotelian philosophy "in the Greek [text]" at Padua University. Tomaeus, after receiving his doctorate of arts at

13. On Donato and Barbaro see esp. V. Branca, "Ermolao Barbaro and Late Quattrocento Venetian Humanism," in *Renaissance Venice,* ed. J. Hale (London, 1973); and Branca, "L'umanesimo veneziano alla fine del quattrocento: Ermolao Barbaro e il suo circolo," in *Storia della cultura veneta,* vol. 3, pt. 1 (Vicenza, 1980), 123–75. See also P. O. Kristeller, "Un codice padovano di Aristotele postillato da Francesco ed Ermolao Barbaro," in *Studies in Renaissance Thought and Letters* (Rome, 1956), 337–53.

14. S.v. "Ermolao Barbaro," *Dizionario biografico degli Italiani* 6:96. Barbaro's father was then (1462) serving as Venetian ambassador to Rome, and Gaza was a member of Bessarion's circle in the papal court. See also essay 3, above; and T. Gercke, *Theodoros Gazes* (Greifswald, 1903), 26, citing others also.

15. See *Dizionario biografico degli Italiani* 6:96–97.

16. See Kristeller, "Un codice padovano," 343. On Gaza see essay 3 above.

Padua in 1485, had established his residence there by 1497, when he inherited property from his family.[17]

Support for the Greek Aristotle also came from a completely unexpected quarter, from the Venetian scholar Nicoletto Vernia, for many years the leading proponent at Padua of Averroës' commentaries on Aristotle. Near the end of his life, Vernia himself succumbed to the interest being generated in the newly translated Greek commentators. Thus, some years before 1489 he went so far as to write a work, *Contra perversam opinionem Averrois,* in which he castigated Averroës for his interpretation of the Aristotelian questions of the immortality of the soul and the unity of the intellect.[18] It is hard to believe that Vernia's "defection," even if only on one or two aspects of Averroës' thought, did not exert a certain influence in the official establishment of a chair for exegesis of the Greek text of Aristotle.[19]

By the time of Tomaeus's official appointment at Padua in 1497 the way had therefore already been cleared for the reception of Greek letters relating not only to the *studia humanitatis* but especially to medicine and science, in all fields of which Aristotle had left important writings. Yet the conflict between the Aristotelian interpretation and the Averroist was far from over. After Vernia, his student and successor at Padua, Agostino Nifo, continued, in the last decade or so of the fifteenth century, to expound to Padua audiences the Averroist interpretation of Aristotle's scientific works, though he too finally began to see the value of the numerous Greco- Byzantine commentators. It was Tomaeus's appointment by the Venetian Senate prescribing explicitly that he was to lecture "on the Greek [text]" that finally seemed to tip the scales in favor of the

17. See Facciolatus, *Fasti gymnasii patavini* 1:56: "Qui primus huic Gymnasio veram Aristotelis faciem ostendit et graeco sermone . . . ejus [Aristotelis] doctrinam explicuit." Also see Giovio, *Italian Portrait Gallery,* 129–30. Also De Bellis, "La vita di Tomeo," 41, n. 13, for the senatorial decree. Also King, *Venetian Humanism,* 432.

18. On Vernia see P. Ragnisco, *Nicoletto Vernia studi storici* (Venice, 1891), and esp. E. Mahoney, "Nicoletto Vernia on the Soul and Immortality," in *Philosophy and Humanism: Festschrift for Paul Oskar Kristeller,* ed. E. Mahoney (Leiden, 1976), 144–63, esp. 149ff. Actually Vernia reversed himself on the important Aristotelian question of the unity of the intellect, writing his "Contra perversam Averrois opinionem de unitate intellectus"—a change probably at least in part the result of the introduction of more-correct Byzantine manuscripts of Aristotle.

19. On the significance of Tomaeus's appointment see, besides nn. 2 and 17 above, also P. Sherrard, *Greek East and Latin West* (Oxford, 1959), 173–75. See also E. Mahoney, "Neoplatonism, the Greek Commentators, and Renaissance Aristotelianism," in *Neoplatonism and Christian Thought,* ed. D. O'Meara (Norfolk, Va., 1982), 170–72, for Vernia and his pupil Agostino Nifo. Actually Nifo dedicated his version and commentary of (part of) Aristotle's *Parva naturalia* to Tomaeus (published in Venice in 1523).

The Greek humanist Nicolaus Leonicus Tomaeus in Venice. From E. Legrand, *Bibliographie hellénique,* vol. 3 (Paris, 1903).

Greek text. But even then, Averroism was hardly moribund at Padua, for it was still being taught there past the sixteenth century.[20]

20. On Agostino Nifo see previous note, and Giovio, *Italian Portrait Gallery,* 130–31. On later Averroism at Padua see, among others, Nardi, *Saggi;* and Saitta, *Pensiero*

In his instruction at Padua, Tomaeus taught not only Aristotelian philosophy and other scientific treatises such as the pseudo-*Mechanica* of Aristotle (which B. Vitali had published with his Latin translation and commentary in 1525 in Venice) but some belles lettres as well. Thus he expounded on Aristotle's *Rhetoric* and even on the Platonic *Dialogues.*[21] He even preferred certain of Plato's metaphysical ideas to those of Aristotle. Such was Tomaeus's open-mindedness, we are told, that he accepted and in fact preferred certain ideas and textual interpretations of Averroës to those of Aristotle himself.[22] Regarding the Greek commentators on Aristotle, we have concrete evidence that Tomaeus lectured on the sixth-century Byzantine John Philoponus.[23] Philoponus had contradicted Aristotle on the possibility of the existence of a vacuum and had also attacked his position on the laws regulating falling bodies. Philoponus showed that, despite a difference in weight, two objects dropped from the same height fall at the same rate of speed.[24] In other words he anticipated the fourteenth-century impetus theory of projectile motion. It is also notable that the Christian Tomaeus (he evidently joined the Roman church but, like other Greeks, maintained use of the Greek liturgy) differed with Aristotle on the question of the immortality of the individual versus the world soul, producing a commentary on Alexander of Aphrodisias and writing his own essay, both later utilized by the famous Pomponazzi.[25]

---

italiano nell'umanesimo. Also P. O. Kristeller, "Paduan Averroism and Alexandrinism in Light of Recent Studies," *Renaissance Thought,* vol. 2 (New York, 1965), 111–18.

21. On Tomaeus and the pseudo-*Mechanica* see esp. P. Rose and S. Drake, "The Pseudo-Aristotelian *Questions of Mechanics* in Renaissance Culture," *Studies in the Renaissance* 18 (1971): 78–80. For Tomaeus's interest in both Plato and Aristotle see Legrand, *Bibliographie hellénique,* vol. 3 (1903), 283, where he is referred to by a contemporary professor at Padua as "doctus disciplinae Platonicae et Aristotelicae." Also, Giovio, *Italian Portrait Gallery,* 129: Tomaeus "expounded to his friends the true doctrines of the Peripatetics and the Academicians." See also M. Sicherl, "Platonismus und Textüberlieferung," *Jahrbuch der österreichischen byzantinischen Gesellschaft* 15 (1966): 221. Erasmus, in *Epistolae Erasmi,* ed. P. Allen, vol. 8 (Oxford), 245, calls Tomaeus "vir integer et in platonica philosophia feliciter exercitatus."

22. Besides Averroës, he even used and cited the Latin Scholastic Thomas Aquinas when it suited him. See De Bellis, "Niccolò Leonico Tomeo," 83, 85, citing his use of Michael of Ephesus and other Byzantine commentators on Aristotle's *Parva naturalia.*

23. See *Manoscritti e stampe venete dell'Aristotelismo e Averroismo* (sec. X–XVI), catalog of XII International Congress of Philosophy, Venice, Biblioteca Nazionale Marciana (1958), 26. Cf. De Bellis, "Niccolò Leonico Tomeo," 83 n. 44.

24. On this treatise of Philoponus see M. Cohen and I. Drabkin, *A Source Book in Greek Science* (New York, 1948), 217–21; cf. Geanakoplos, *Byzantium: Church, Society and Civilization Seen Through Contemporary Eyes,* no. 324.

25. See Tomaeus, *Dialogi* (Venice, 1524), where in one part he expounds on the soul. Also see De Bellis, "Niccolò Leonico Tomeo," 83, on his use of Alexander of Aphro-

Tomaeus's use of the ancient Greek commentators on Aristotle was inspired primarily by other Greek scholars in Italy who themselves had learned of their importance as part of their training in the Byzantine philosophical tradition of the late Palaeologan period.[26] Along with Philoponus, several other famous ancient commentators on Aristotle were Themistius, the Byzantine pagan philosopher of Emperor Constantine's time (Theodore Gaza was probably his first Greek translator into Latin), and Simplicius, the last important teacher of pagan philosophy at the academy of Athens (in Justinian's reign). Most important for Padua University, certainly for his views on the immortality of the soul, was the Alexandrist philosopher Alexander of Aphrodisias.[27] As noted earlier, the Venetian Ermolao Barbaro (a pupil of Gaza) was the first Italian to render a work of Themistius into Latin. But it was the great Cretan scholar Marcus Musurus who edited (for the Aldine press) the Greek text of the commentaries of Philoponus (1505) and of Alexander of Aphrodisias (1513). Indeed Musurus participated in the monumental publication in 1525–28 of the very first edition, in the Greek text, of Aristotle's *Opera,* published by his close friend and associate, the Italian Aldus Manutius.[28] There can be little doubt that Tomaeus (as well as many other Italian literary and scientific figures) profited enormously from this Aldine publication, which in fact was appearing during Tomaeus's tenure at Padua. The question arises, however, whether Tomaeus himself contributed anything to this celebrated edition, even indirectly.

I am convinced that the paths of Musurus and Tomaeus must have crossed repeatedly. We know that both Greeks were friends of Aldus, both knew and corresponded with the Venetian humanist Cardinal Pietro Bembo and also with Erasmus;[29] both in addition were apparently

---

disias in general, and De Bellis, "La vita di Tomeo," 42–45, on the theory that Tomaeus left Padua to teach in Venice from 1504 to 1506 and then returned to Padua.

26. Tomaeus probably reflected his teacher Chalcondyles' views (which were typical of the Palaeologan Renaissance) that Aristotle and Plato were not really antithetical and could be reconciled on all important points: see B. Tatakis, *La philosophie byzantine* (Paris, 1949), 294f.; and essay 1 above. Both of these emphasize the Byzantine Palaeologan Renaissance view that the two philosophers were reconcilable on virtually all major views—certainly much more so than was believed by the Italian Renaissance scholars of the quattrocento.

27. For what seems to be Tomaeus's rather frequent citation of Alexander of Aphrodisias see De Bellis, "Niccolò Leonico Tomeo," 89. On Alexander, see article by F. Cranz in *Catalogus Translationum et Commentariorum,* ed. P. O. Kristeller and F. Cranz, vol. 1 (Washington, D.C., 1960), 77–135.

28. On Calliergis's edition of commentaries of Simplicius (1500) and Musurus's editions of Philoponus (1505) and Alexander of Aphrodisias (1514) for the Aldine press, see Geanakoplos, *Greek Scholars in Venice,* 208, 141, 154, 296.

29. Bembo (probably earlier his pupil) wrote the poetic inscription on Tomaeus's

proud of their Byzantine and ancient Hellenic heritage, though Tomaeus, it should be observed, was born not in the old Byzantine territory but in Venice. (Whether Tomaeus had associations with the Greek colony of Venice I have been unable to ascertain definitively, although we know definitely that Musurus did.)[30] Finally, the teaching of both at Padua University overlapped for a time.[31] Nevertheless, they seem at Padua to have held chairs of somewhat different scope, Tomaeus in Aristotelian philosophy, primarily, as noted, for explication of the Aristotelian Greek texts and Greek commentaries, and Musurus as successor to the already famous chair of Greek language and literature first occupied by Demetrius Chalcondyles. But whether a clear-cut line separated the subject matter taught by one from that of the other is hard to establish. Certainly both men possessed literary interests, although Musurus did not share Tomaeus's very strong proclivities toward science. Musurus, as we also know, first edited for the Aldine press many if not all of the works of the great Greek dramatists, Euripides, Aeschylus, and Sophocles as well as Aristophanes—a sphere of learning in which Tomaeus seems to have evinced no strong interest.[32]

Surprisingly, although the two men taught in the same faculty at Padua, I have been able to find no explicit evidence of relations between the two scholars, something which suggests that there may have been hard feelings between them. Interestingly, I cannot even find mention of Tomaeus's membership in the celebrated Aldine Greek Academy, of which Musurus was a leading member and which, we know, attracted to its meetings many learned Northern and other Italian Hellenists then living in or visiting Venice-Padua, Erasmus, for example. (Tomaeus did, however, dedicate his edition of Aristotle's *De animalium incessu* to

---

tomb: see Giovio, *Italian Portrait Gallery,* 130, quoted below, n. 51; cf. Gasquet, *Cardinal Pole,* 102–3. On Erasmus and Tomaeus see nn. 48, 51–52 below.

30. Geanakoplos, *Greek Scholars in Venice,* esp. 178.

31. Musurus taught at Padua from 1503 to 1509 and then at the ducal chancery school in Venice from 1512 to 1516. Tomaeus taught officially at Padua from 1497 probably to 1507 and from 1506 to 1507 also at the school of Venice. (King, *Venetian Humanism,* 432, differs on the years.) Later he also taught in some capacity or other (privately?) probably at Padua and in Venice until sometime before his death. See Venetian document cited in De Bellis, "Niccolò Leonico Tomaeo," 73 n. 7, on his earlier years. Others (e.g., Erasmus) attest to his teaching later in Padua. Sathas, *Neohellēnikē philologia,* 92–94, and Kyrou, *Hoi Hellēnes,* 112–13, simply write that Tomaeus taught about three decades at Padua, from 1497 to his death in 1531, the view often held today but not entirely correct. Erasmus, *Epistolae Erasmi* 5:520–21, says Tomaeus returned to Padua in 1524 from Venice.

32. On Musurus's editions see A. Turyn, *The Manuscript Tradition of the Tragedies of Aeschylus* (New York, 1943), . . . *of Euripides* (Urbana, Ill., 1957), . . . *of Sophocles* (Urbana, Ill., 1952), index to each volume.

Janus Lascaris, the Greek envoy of France to Venice, who was a known friend and associate of Musurus's in the Aldine academy.) I have also found that Aldus published one work by Tomaeus (his translation of the well-known astronomy of Ptolemy).[33] It is possible that Musurus, although generally believed to have possessed a lofty character, may have been jealous of a perceived rival to his endeavors in Greek studies in the environment of Venice. On the other hand, it is possible that Tomaeus may have envied the apparently more renowned Musurus.[34]

A highly respected and admired teacher, Tomaeus enjoyed the longest teaching span at Padua and in Venice of any Greek émigré scholar, apparently instructing there officially or unofficially, and with perhaps a few interruptions, from 1497 until sometime before his death in 1531.[35] It was his tenure, in a sense, that marked the culmination, if not the effective end, at least among the Greeks in Italy (but *not* among the Italians), of the sharp conflict between the adherents of Plato and of Aristotle inaugurated in 1439 in Florence, Italy by Gemistas Pletho, and then continued in Greece and Italy by the émigré Greeks (and also Scholarios).[36] Evidence for the culmination or resolution of this conflict in the work of Tomaeus is seen not only in his deference to both Aristotle and Plato, but especially in his attempt to achieve a reconciliation of the metaphysical systems.[37] In his opinion they were less antagonistic than Italian humanists then generally believed. In this respect Tomaeus was like his Byzantine predecessor Bessarion, who, in his work *In calumniatorem Platonis,* though defending Plato against the impertinent attacks of George of Trebizond, also sought to play down the two philosophers' differences while at the same time affirming Plato's greater affinity to, and easier assimilability with, the dogmas of Christianity than Aristotle's.[38]

Tomaeus was especially fitted for this work of conciliation, being at once philosopher, natural scientist, literatus, philologist, historian, and connoisseur of art. Nevertheless, before an authoritative judgment can be rendered on the degree of his success in trying to reconcile the philos-

33. See Legrand, *Bibliographie hellênique* 3:284, for dedication to Lascaris. See on Lascaris, Geanakoplos, *Greek Scholars in Venice,* 136, 147, 215.

34. See Geanakoplos, "Marcus Musurus: New Information on the Death of a Byzantine Humanist in Italy," in *Interaction of the Sibling Cultures,* 226–30, which seeks to deny the authenticity of the "story" repeated by Giovio that Musurus died of jealousy after being refused a cardinal's hat. This, of course, may or may not be relevant here.

35. See n. 31 above.

36. On this conflict see below, essay 11.

37. See above, n. 26.

38. See Bessarion, "In calumniatorem Platonis," in L. Mohler, *Kardinal Bessarion als Theologe, Humanist und Staatsmann,* 3 vols. (Paderborn, 1923–42), esp. vol. 2, including editions of his works. Cf. above, essay 3 on Gaza, 79.

ophies of Aristotle and Plato, it would be necessary to read all of Tomaeus's many published works, some of which are very obscure and today hardly known. Evidently all are listed in Legrand's *Bibliographie hellénique,* vols. 3–4.[39]

Besides his primarily metaphysical and scientific bent, Tomaeus's special interest in moral philosophy is revealed by his efforts to establish the original text of Plutarch's *Moralia.* His endeavors in this regard are in fact looked upon by modern philologists as of considerable value and significance. (The *editio princeps* was edited by Demetrius Ducas in Aldus's publication of 1509, but whatever connections there may have been with Tomaeus's work have yet to be investigated).[40]

Tomaeus also made a translation of Galen, interspersed in whose medical writings (as Tomaeus himself stressed) were useful comments on Aristotle's *Logic* and even on Plato. Further, Tomaeus also translated certain writings of Hippocrates, as well as rendering into Latin Proclus's *Commentary on Plato's Parmenides.*[41] Probably more important, Tomaeus was the second (after Vettore Fausto) to translate and thus to make known to the West, in the most popular version of the sixteenth century, the text of Pseudo-Aristotle's *Mechanica,* so important for the information it provided on stresses and balances in problems of engineering.[42] Tomaeus's interests, then, were extremely broad. In addition, they included an interest in history, as attested by his *De varia historia,* a virtuosic compendium of myth and history that became perhaps his most popular work.[43]

39. Legrand, *Bibliographie hellénique,* esp. 3:215, 281–84, 296–97, 336–39, 438, etc., for his famous edition of Aristotle's *Parva naturalia,* his famous translations of Ptolemy's astronomy and Aristotle's *De partibus animalium,* additional translations and commentaries, and his own works *De varia historia, Dialogi,* and *Opuscula* (1525). See also De Bellis, "La vita di Tomeo," and De Bellis, "Autokineton e Entelechia. Niccolò Leonico Tomeo: l'Anima nei Dialoghi intitolati al Bembo," *Annali dell'Istituto di filosofia della Facoltà di littere e filosofia dell'Università di Firenze,* vol. 1 (1979) 47–68, for references to his works.

40. Geanakoplos, *Greek Scholars in Venice,* 264–65 and note. For Tomaeus's work on Plutarch's *Moralia* see A. Turyn, *Dated Greek Manuscripts of the Thirteenth and Fourteenth Centuries in the Libraries of Italy,* 2 vols. (Urbana, Ill., 1972), 1:xx, 85–87 (cf. F. Sandback, *Plutarch's Moralia,* vol. 7 [Leipzig, 1967], 1–10, xii–xiii). See also on Tomaeus's work M. Sicherl, "Platonismus und Textüberlieferung," 211; M. Treu, *Zur Geschichte der Überlieferung von Plutarchs Moralia,* vol. 3 (Breslau, 1884), 12.

41. On Galen and Tomaeus see Saitta, *Pensiero italiano nell'umanesimo,* esp. 449. For his work on Parmenides see Sicherl, "Platonismus und Textüberlieferung," 211.

42. On this Latin translation of the Aristotelian pseudo-*Mechanica* (Tomaeus's version became standard in the Renaissance) see Rose and Drake, "The Pseudo-Aristotelian *Questions of Mechanics,* 58–80, esp. 78–80.

43. On *De varia historia,* see Giovio, *Italian Portrait Gallery,* 29. This work, which demonstrates a tremendous range of knowledge, is an elegant compendium of myth and

It seems possible that Tomaeus's remarkable skills as editor and translator of ancient scientific, philosophic, and literary texts proved detrimental in certain ways to the quality of his own original literary treatises. For the latter, such as his *Dialogi* (including essays on divination, immortality of souls, the game of dice, etc.)[44] and his *De varia historia,* both evidently the result of his own reflections, were in large part based on the writings of earlier Greek authors, ancient or Byzantine. Only his poems and verses, often charming, seem to show a certain degree of literary creativity.[45] But this criticism could, with very few exceptions, be levied at almost all of the humanists of this period. Tomaeus probably did reveal some degree of genuine scientific originality in his treatise (or rather commentary) on the immortality of the soul incorporated in his *Dialogi.*[46]

At Padua Tomaeus taught two generations of students, including many Greek youths from the wreckage of the Byzantine East, especially Crete.[47] Of the many Western students he instructed, no few came from northern Europe, especially England, whose youth were attracted to Padua primarily because of the fame of its medical school, its liberal policies, and the cosmopolitanism of the Venetian-Paduan environment. Early in his career Tomaeus was named by the Venetian Senate special tutor for the numerous young English noblemen who came to study at Padua. He particularly oversaw their Greek studies, as we may observe from many of his surviving letters, which are written in flawless Greek.[48]

---

history. Though very popular, it seems to be a work of no great depth. It was printed posthumously in 1531 by Froben in Basel. See Legrand, *Bibliographie hellénique* 2:316. Erasmus may have pilfered Tomaeus's essay on dice for a work of his own: see below n. 51. Tomaeus was also interested in art and moved in a widely cultured circle: De Bellis, "La vita di Tomeo."

44. See list of titles in his twelve *Dialogi,* published in Venice in 1524 and dedicated to Reginald Pole.

45. For his verses, many addressed to close friends such as Bembo, see below, n. 51, and n. 39 above.

46. Essay included in his *Dialogi* in which he argues the soul is immortal. See n. 25 above. He and Bembo especially discussed the question of the soul. Cf. title in n. 39 above.

47. See G. Fabris, "Professori e scolari greci all'Università di Padova," *Archivio veneto* 30 (1942): 121–65. And G. Plumidis, "Gli scolari greci nello studio di Padova," *Quaderni per la storia dell'Università di Padova* 4 (1971): 127–41.

48. On his English students (or friends) who included a brilliant group: Reginald Pole, William Latimer, Thomas Linacre, Thomas Lupset, Cuthbert Tunstall, and Richard Pace, see esp. Gasquet, *Cardinal Pole,* chaps. 4–13. Also W. Zeeveld, *Foundations of Tudor Policy* (Cambridge, Mass., 1948), 43. Also references made by Erasmus to the English students Thomas Pace and Reginald Pole and to Tomaeus, in *Epistolae Erasmi* 1:445n., 6:144.

To cite one example, he wrote to Thomas Latimer, then in England, that he and the youth Reginald Pole (the later-famous Cardinal Pole) were reading together the eight books of Aristotle's *Topics,* four of Aristotle's *De caelo* and *De generatione,* and also the original Greek text of the Byzantine church father John Chrysostom. In several highly informative letters written to his English students (with whom he kept in close contact even after their return to England), he mentioned various editions and translations on which he was engaged. To Thomas More he sent a copy of his edition of Aristotle's *Parva naturalia* and requested in return a copy of More's *Utopia,* which, as we know, was based on or inspired by Plato.[49]

A gentle, modest person who never married, Tomaeus had a special fondness for birds and left behind verses extolling the pleasures of nature. Paolo Giovio, who generally had little good to say about any humanist but who praised Tomaeus's erudition and character, noted his fondness for his pet pelican. Indeed Tomaeus felt that the bird's death would presage his own demise, and he in fact died soon after his pet.[50] Tomaeus's vast erudition and generous character were universally admired, in particular by Cardinal Bembo, his intimate friend (and very probably earlier his student) who penned the verse carved as an epitaph on his tomb.[51] And Erasmus, one also not given to high praise of other humanist scholars, had words of commendation for both his learning and personality. Tomaeus's funeral was attended by a large group of Italian notables, civil as well as ecclesiastical.[52]

To conclude: Tomaeus's tenure at Padua constituted in some ways the culmination of the Byzantine émigré scholars' efforts in Italy to bring to the West the entire corpus of the literature and scientific writings of

49. Gasquet, *Cardinal Pole,* 11ff., 34–35, 66ff. The mention of Chrysostom may possibly be further evidence of Tomaeus's ethnic Greek pride.

50. Giovio, *Italian Portrait Gallery,* 129.

51. For Bembo's verses see ibid., 130: "Naturae si quid rerum te forte latebat, Id legis in magno nunc, Leonice, Deo" ("If by chance something in nature lay hidden from you, You read it now, Leonicus, in great God himself"). On Bembo as his student see De Bellis, "La vita di Tomeo," 47, and for probable reference to Bembo, see *Epistolae Erasmi* 7:477. Erasmus knew Tomaeus between 1506 and 1509, when Erasmus was in Italy, especially in Venice-Padua: see *Epistolae Erasmi* 8:245 and 5:520. Cf. my *Greek Scholars in Venice,* chap. 9. For mention of the secretary of Pope Leo X, Jacopo Sadoleto, and Tomaeus see also *Epistolae Erasmi* 7:161. Erasmus (8:245) describes Padua University's important professors thus: "Habet enim ea scholia . . . Nicolaum Leonicum et Petrum Bembum, duo praecipua huius seculi lumina." Erasmus wrote a colloquy recalling Tomaeus's on dice ("Samnutus sive de ludo talarico"). For other friends of Tomaeus and the possibility that Copernicus studied with him see De Bellis, "La vita di Tomeo," 47 esp. and 67.

52. *Epistolae Erasmi* 3:333, where Erasmus terms Tomaeus "vir optimus, santissimus, atque dictissimus"; Giovio, *Italian Portrait Gallery,* 130.

Greek antiquity and to a great extent of Byzantium as well. Moreover, his appointment at Padua marked the turning point whereby the Greek text of Aristotle, and also of Aristotle's ancient and early Byzantine commentators, was finally officially recognized and began, if not to displace, certainly successfully to challenge and finally to surpass the hitherto dominant influence of Averroës. Tomaeus's emphasis on the metaphysical teachings of Aristotle helped to elucidate the Aristotelian question of the unity of the intellect and to bring to the forefront at Padua the problem of the immortality of the individual soul. In this regard his activities helped prepare the way for the doctrine of Pietro Pomponazzi on the logical impossibility of proving the immortality of the individual soul.[53]

In at least three respects, then, Tomaeus's career had genuine significance for Italian Renaissance thought: besides of course influencing scores of Italian humanists in almost all aspects of Greek learning, he in effect brought a final end in Italy to the Aristotle-Plato controversy among the Greeks (though certainly not among the Latins) by seeking to reconcile their philosophies. Through his Greek exegesis of Aristotelian philosophy, which drew heavily on the ancient Greek and Byzantine commentators, he brought about, if not the complete victory, at least the ascendancy of the "Byzantine" perspective over Averroist philosophy at Padua, Italy's leading medical school. Finally, through his influence on Pomponazzi, who in turn influenced the precursors of Galileo, it may be affirmed that the career of the polymath Tomaeus helped to pave the way for the emergence of modern science in the work of Galileo and Leonardo da Vinci.

53. On Pomponazzi see Randall, *School of Padua;* P. O. Kristeller, *Renaissance Concepts of Man* (New York, 1972), 18–19, 38–41, 48. On Tomaeus's achievement and his connection with Pomponazzi see also Sherrard, *Greek East and Latin West,* 173, who cites Bembo as affirming that Tomaeus's appointment at Padua "opened a new era in philosophy" which led to "Averroism's eclipse at Padua." Also on this point see Randall, 71–73. For another reference to Tomaeus's immense erudition, see M. Gilmore, "Myth and Reality in Venetian Political Theory," in *Renaissance Venice,* ed. Hale (London, 1973), 436, citing a quotation from the *Opera* of the humanist D. Giannotti affirming that Tomaeus was skilled in discussing questions of political theory, especially "on simple or complex republics." Finally, see M. Lowry, *World of Aldus Manutius* (Oxford, 1979), 231, for mention of Tomaeus's borrowing of a MS (probably of Bessarion's) from the Marciana library in Venice, and his holding it for nearly forty years—something perhaps not untypical of the times.

Additional Bibliography for Essay 5

A. Serena, *Appunti letterari* (Rome, 1903) 3–32. G. Pavanello, *Un maestro del Quattrocento (Giovanni Aurelio Augurello)* (Venice, 1905) 115–19. V. Branca, "L'umanesimo veneziano alla fine del quattrocento: Ermolao Barbaro e il suo circolo," in *Storia della cultura veneta,* vol. 3, pt. 1 (Vicenza, 1980), 123–75. A. Poppi, ed., *Scienza e filosofia all'Università di Padova nel quattrocento* (Padua and Trieste, 1983), including the essay of E. Mahoney, "Philosophy and Science in Nicoletto Vernia and Agostino Nifo," 135–202; and especially that of C. Schmitt, "Aristotelian Textual Studies at Padua: The Case of Francesco Cavalli," 287–314, affirming that, though direct documentation is lacking, on the basis of a statement of the later, sixteenth-century scholar Francesco Patrizzi, Francesco Cavalli was the first to teach Aristotle in the Greek interpretation in Italy. (However, as is argued in my essay, according to direct contemporary evidence, Tomaeus was the first to be *officially* appointed by the Venetian Senate to teach Aristotle "in the Greek [text]" at Padua University. Thus, the truly significant step would be the teaching and influence exercised by Tomaeus.) T. Pesenti, *Professori e promotori di medicina nello studio di Padova dal 1405 al 1509* (Padua and Trieste, 1984), a bio-bibliography in which Pesenti affirms Cavalli was the first in Italy to teach the Greek interpretation through recourse to the Greek commentators. (Nor would his statement, however, deny Tomaeus the honor of achieving the ascendancy, if not triumph, of Greco-Byzantine exegesis at Padua University.) See now M. King, *Venetian Humanism in an Age of Patrician Dominance* (Princeton, N.J., 1986), with references to Tomaeus. And D. De Bellis, "La vita e l'ambiente di Niccolò Leonico Tomeo," *Quaderni per la storia dell'Università di Padova* 13 (1980): 37–75, which came to my attention when this book was in press but which I was able to use. Finally see A. Pertusi, "L'umanesimo greco dalla fine del secolo XIV agli inizi del secolo XVI," in *Storia della cultura veneta,* vol. 3, pt. 1 (Venice, 1980), 177–264. In relation to this article, see my new, more accurate transcription of Chalcondyles' inaugural Latin oration at Padua (1463) printed in the new Greek translation, *Byzantio kai dysē* (Athens, 1985), 430–41, of my *Interaction of the Sibling Cultures* (New Haven, Conn., 1976), 296–304.

Part II

The Byzantine and Roman Churches

Six

Edward Gibbon and Byzantine Ecclesiastical History

It is generally acknowledged that Gibbon's *Decline and Fall of the Roman Empire* ranks as one of the supreme masterpieces of historical writing. Yet surprisingly enough, more than a third of his entire narrative, that portion dealing with the later Roman or Byzantine Empire, has been badly neglected by historiographers. Now as a Byzantinist, Gibbon must be an ecclesiastical historian as well, given the nature of Byzantine civilization with its close identification of the religious and the political. But here again, though sharp controversy has long raged over Gibbon's judgment of early Christianity, especially its responsibility for the fall of the Roman Empire in the West, his treatment of medieval Greek Christianity has been almost ignored by critics except for sporadic, general remarks by J. B. Bury, C. Dawson, G. Giarrizzo—remarks which have added little to the traditionally accepted view that Gibbon was contemptuous of Byzantine civilization.[1]

This paper (here revised) was originally read in December 1964 at the joint session of the Church History–American Historical Association. It is dedicated as a small contribution to the furtherance of better understanding between the Roman Catholic and Orthodox churches, so auspiciously begun 7 December 1965 with Pope Paul VI and Patriarch Athenagoras's joint annulment of the historic excommunications of 1054.

1. See J. B. Bury's edition of Edward Gibbon, *History of the Decline and Fall of the Roman Empire* (London, 1896 and later; last ed., New York, 1914). I have used here the 1909 edition; Gibbon's notes and text are the same in all these editions. Various editors have added their own notes to those of Gibbon, such as Bury, Dean Milman (the standard nineteenth-century edition), and the French scholar François Guizot. For

One of the most important, if not the central theme in Byzantine ecclesiastical history from the eighth, certainly from the eleventh, century onward is that of the schism between the Eastern and Western churches. And if Gibbon be the master historian he is acclaimed to be, his treatment of this crucial topic (thrust into the foreground by Vatican Council II and the recent meeting of patriarch and pope in Rome in late 1987) should be examined in any attempt to evaluate his competence as an ecclesiastical historian. I have therefore elected here to deal primarily, though not exclusively, with Gibbon's treatment of the schism between Constantinople and Rome, not only because it involves, in one way or another, almost all aspects of the church—differences in dogma, ecclesiology, monasticism—but also because the schism is an underlying theme running through the political, social, and cultural as well as religious development of Byzantine history. Indeed, to this problem of the schism and its immediate corollary, the attempts to reunite the two churches, Gibbon devotes more pages and a more-continuous narrative

---

Bury's (very few) remarks on Gibbon's treatment of the Byzantine church see vol. 1, esp. Introduction, vii–xxii. Also C. Dawson, "Edward Gibbon and the Fall of Rome," in *The Dynamics of World History* (New York, 1956), 319–45; and G. Giarrizzo, *Edward Gibbon e la cultura europea del settecento* (Naples, 1954), 408–26. Dawson says practically nothing about Byzantine history after the ninth century, and Giarrizzo never gets past Heraclius (seventh century) in his discussion. None of these three historians focuses at all on the question of the schism, Bury's great works (*The Later Roman Empire,* 2 vols. [London, 1923], and *The Eastern Roman Empire* [London, 1912]) concentrating on the period up to the end of the ninth century. Besides the above, the principal works I have used to help me prepare this essay are Per Fuglum, *Edward Gibbon, His View of Life and Conception of History* (Oslo, 1953); E. J. Oliver, *Gibbon and Rome* (London, 1958); S. L. McCloy, *Gibbon's Antagonism to Christianity* (Chapel Hill, N.C., 1933), with almost nothing on Byzantine church history; M. Joyce, *Edward Gibbon* (London, 1953); A. Momigliano, "La formazione della moderna storiografia sull'impero romano," sec. 2, *Rivista storica italiana,* ser. 5, vol. 1 (1936): 35–60, 19–48; W. H. Chamberlain, "On Re-reading Gibbon," *Atlantic Monthly* 174 (1944): 65–70; J. Morison, *Edward Gibbon* (New York, 1901); H. Butterfield, *The Whig Interpretation of History* (New York, 1951); J. B. Bury, s.v. "Gibbon," *Encyclopaedia Britannica,* 14th ed.; G. J. Gruman, "'Balance' and 'Excess' as Gibbon's Explanation of the Decline and Fall," *History and Theory* 1 (1960): 75–85; D. M. Low, *Edward Gibbon* (London, 1937); A. Vasiliev, *History of the Byzantine Empire,* vol. 1 (Madison, Wis., 1952), chap. 1; M. Liutov, *Zhizń i trudy Gibbona* (Life and Work of Gibbon) (St. Petersburg, 1899); D. Zakythinos, *Byzantium* (in Greek) (Athens, 1951); D. D. Hailes, *An Inquiry into the Secondary Causes Gibbon Assigned for the Rapid Growth of Christianity* (Edinburgh, 1786); Edward Gibbon, *Letters,* ed. J. Norton (London, 1956); *Edward Gibbon, the Autobiography,* ed. O. Smeaton (London, 1911); J. B. Black, *The Art of History* (London, 1926); P. Quennell, *Four Portraits* (London, 1946); J. M. Robertson, *Gibbon* (London, 1925); G. M. Young, *Gibbon* (New York, 1933); and E. Cassirer, *Philosophy of the Enlightenment* (Princeton, N.J., 1951), the best work on the philosophy of the period.

than to any other aspect of later Byzantine ecclesiastical history. Finally, as Gibbon himself informs us more than once, for the first six centuries of church history he was heavily indebted to the monumental but today almost forgotten seventeenth-century work of the French church historian Tillemont.[2] By examining the *Decline and Fall,* then, for the period *subsequent* to that covered by Tillemont we are able to evaluate Gibbon as an ecclesiastical historian of more independent judgment.

Before we can pass judgment on the pages of Gibbon devoted to Byzantine ecclesiastical history, we should set forth, briefly, certain major criteria that a competent church historian of that period must meet. Indispensable first would be familiarity with and ability to use the complex ecclesiastical source materials, implying of course linguistic proficiency in Byzantine Greek and Latin. Second would be the ability to extract the essence from or, so to speak, simplify the prolix, often obscure, and frequently unused passages from the Byzantine historians, retaining the accuracy of the facts without distorting their general meaning. With respect to theological questions in particular, the church historian must not only understand the subtle doctrinal points at issue (the *filioque,* for example) but also try to steer a middle course between the intensely biased Greek and Western sources for the period. This raises the even more basic question of the objectivity required of an ecclesiastical historian for that or any age. Indeed, one may fairly ask: Could Gibbon with his pronounced Enlightenment presuppositions—a lack of sympathy for any kind of superstition or excess in religion to the point of disparaging even such an institution as monasticism, and with his emphasis on the rational to the exclusion of an understanding of the specifically religious values in Christianity's development—could Gibbon, given these underlying assumptions, write satisfactory church history?[3]

A final word on my method of investigation: Gibbon's treatment of the history of the schism seems to fall into a pattern of five or six principal

2. Le Nain de Tillemont, *Mémoires pour servir à l'histoire ecclésiastique des six premiers siècles,* 16 vols., 3d ed. (Venice, 1732), and his *Histoire des empereurs . . . durant les six premiers siècles,* 6 vols., 2d ed. (Brussels, 1707). Dawson, "Gibbon and the Fall of Rome," 331, after noting Gibbon followed Tillemont in the earlier section, says he is "left to his own resources" in the later Byzantine portion. But Dawson has not really examined this later part. Smeaton, editor of Gibbon's *Autobiography,* remarks, 175, that Gibbon falls into errors and solecisms, especially in ecclesiastical affairs, after losing the help of Tillemont.

3. See esp. Dawson, "Gibbon and the Fall of Rome," 325. Also A. M. Jones, *Constantine and the Conversion of Europe* (London, 1948), 260: "Gibbon has not so much anti-Christian bias as a temperamental incapacity to understand religion." Also L. Stephen, *History of English Thought in the 18th Century,* 2 vols., 3d ed. (New York, 1902), 1:449. Also see below, n. 41.

episodes, beginning with the Iconoclastic conflict of the eighth century and extending to the Council of Florence in 1439. It is these episodes, from the point of view of the above criteria and insofar as time and Gibbon's material itself permit, that I shall focus on in my discussion. At the end I shall draw certain conclusions and, after placing my analysis in the framework of his Byzantine history as a whole, seek to judge Gibbon's worth as an ecclesiastical historian.

Although Gibbon views the conflict between pope and emperor during the Iconoclast struggle as primarily an "Italian" revolution against Byzantine authority, he realizes its importance for the origins of the schism. Beginning as a theological question over image worship, the conflict between pope and emperor led, for Gibbon, to a "political schism" between East and West which, unlike the temporary Iconoclastic religious schism, was never healed and was crystallized in 800 by the pope's coronation of Charlemagne as Roman emperor. Gibbon's statement of the causes for the imperial policy against the images is admittedly narrow in the light of modern research.[4] But his estimate of the forces at work in the political division of East and West does much to set the stage for his treatment of the subsequent schism between the churches.

Thus in his discussion of the schism proper, beginning with chapter 60, Gibbon's emphasis indicates—and not long ago such perceptive historians as S. Runciman and Y. Congar were adopting this kind of approach[5]—that the schism cannot be treated exclusively from a theological point of view, important as that may be, but must be analyzed in a wide context of political, cultural, even psychological considerations. For Gibbon the *underlying* cause of the schism was the long-developing Greek feeling of aversion for the Latins, which, he wrote with insight, "was originally derived from the [Greek] disdain of servitude [at the time of the Roman conquest] inflamed after the time of Constantine by the pride of equality or dominion, and exasperated by the preference which their rebellious subjects [i.e., the popes] had given to the alliance of the Franks." Drawing out his theme further, Gibbon sees at the roots of the schism the Greek feeling of cultural and hence religious superiority over the Latins. Thus he writes succinctly, *"In every age* the Greeks were proud of their superiority in profane and religious knowledge: they had first received the light of Christianity; they had pronounced the decrees of the

4. See Gibbon, vol. 5, chap. 49, pp. 244–81. Subsequent citations to Gibbon (by volume, chapter, and page number) will appear in the text. Modern research has been done on Iconoclasm by P. Alexander, M. Anastos, V. Grumel, G. Ostrogorsky, K. Schwarzlose, S. Gero, etc.

5. S. Runciman, *The Eastern Schism* (Oxford, 1955); Y. Congar, *After Nine Hundred Years* (New York, 1959).

seven general councils, they alone possessed the language of Scripture and philosophy; nor should barbarians, immersed in the darkness of the West presume to argue on the high and mysterious questions of theological science" (16.60.366–67). Such a clear statement, with its insight into the origins of the schism, is not to be found in the works of J. Mosheim, D. Petavius, Abbé Fleury, and certainly not in the famous cardinal Baronius—seventeenth- and eighteenth-century authorities, all of whom Gibbon, according to his own testimony, used at one time or another as guides.[6] Nor does Gibbon underestimate the Latin antipathy for the Greeks, who in their turn were despised by the Latins "for their restless and subtle levity, the authors of every heresy." Having pointed out these *underlying* cultural and in a sense psychological causes for the schism, Gibbon, with appreciation for the human factor in ecclesiastical disputes, observes that the *immediate* cause of the schism was the jealousy of the prelates of old Rome at seeing their place usurped by the new capital Constantinople, and later, the pride of the Byzantine prelates, who "wished to maintain their position inferior to none in the Christian world" (6.60.367–69).

To exemplify this rivalry, he then enters directly into a discussion or rather sketch of the celebrated affair of Patriarch Photius and Pope Nicholas I (6.60.366–69). In the Catholic medieval tradition regarding the Byzantine church, to which (as is not always realized) the Protestants are heir, Photius is considered to be the archvillain of the drama of the schism.[7] Gibbon, however, seems to be more objective, like Father Dvornik distributing the blame instead between the two prelates. He refers to Photius as "an ambitious layman, promoted by merit and favor to the more desirable office of patriarch," but one who "sacrificed the peace of the world to a short precarious reign." Nicholas he terms "one of the proudest and most aspiring of the Roman pontiffs, who embraced the welcome opportunity of judging and condemning his rival of the East." Remarkably enough, Gibbon makes no mention of the false, but traditionally accepted *"second* Photian schism," a crucial point only recently laid to rest by the important researches of Father Dvornik.[8]

6. John L. Mosheim, *An Ecclesiastical History,* 2 vols. (New York, 1856), trans. A. Maclaine from Latin original, *Institutiones historiae ecclesiasticae* (1726). D. Petavius, *Rationarium temporum editio novissima* (Venice, 1758) (other works of Petavius unavailable to me); Abbé Fleury, *Histoire ecclésiastique,* 36 vols. (Paris, 1713–38), vols. 23–36 written by continuators; Cardinal C. Baronius, *Annales ecclesiastici* (Rome, 1588), continued from vol. 13 on by others, written in 1864 and later. Baronius's vol. 12 ends in 1198.

7. See F. Dvornik, *The Photian Schism, History and Legend* (Cambridge, 1948), 348; cf. Congar, *After Nine Hundred Years,* 70.

8. Dvornik, *Photian Schism,* esp. 202ff., shows that the so-called second papal excommunication of Photius never occurred, and the false tradition of it was due in

The lack of research up to Gibbon's time in the church history of the tenth century is revealed by his brief statement, correct in its wider implications, that "the darkness and corruption of the tenth century suspended the intercourse without reconciling the minds of the two nations" (6.60.370). We know today that some relations, though sporadic, did exist, and as H. Grégoire has recently pointed out, it was in this period of the so-called papal Pornocracy that the Byzantine state and church, now at their apogee, lost a good deal of respect for the papacy.[9]

Skipping the question of the remarkable revival of the papacy, which he discusses elsewhere, Gibbon moves immediately into the episode of Patriarch Michael Cerularius. Brief as his discussion is, it brings out some important points which disclose his intuitive grasp of church affairs. While mentioning as the *casus belli* the patriarchal protest against the papal attempt to substitute the Latin for the Greek rite in southern Italy, Gibbon emphasizes as the basic cause of the schism of 1054 "the rising majesty of Rome [which] could no longer brook the insolence of a rebel, and Michael Cerularius was excommunicated in the heart of Constantinople by the pope's legates. . . . The Greeks have never recanted their errors, the popes have never repealed their sentence and from this thunderbolt," Gibbon concludes, "one may date the consummation of the schism" (6.60.370).

Gibbon had evidently read the text of the papal bull of excommunication with care, for he notes that it was directed against "the guilty teachers and their unhappy sectaries," meaning Cerularius and his followers. Thus he correctly implies—in contrast, for example, to Petavius, the century-earlier Jesuit historian-theologian—that the emperor in particular and the Eastern Christians in general, were exempt. But Gibbon fails to mention (this is a common omission of a number of Western ecclesiastical historians including Petavius and even the usually judicious Congar) that Cerularius at once summoned the Synodos Endemousa of Constantinople and in return excommunicated the papal envoys (ibid.).[10]

Recent scholarship has tended to minimize the overall significance of

---

large part to the influence of Baronius. Hence it is surprising that Gibbon, who used Baronius, did not make much of it. Did Gibbon's historical intuition lead him to suspect the authenticity of this long-accepted tradition of the Roman church? Gibbon, 6.60.369 n. 8, mentions that he also used an account by L. Dupin (probably the *Nouvelle bibliothèque des auteurs ecclésiastiques* [Paris, 1686–1719]).

9. See H. Grégoire, "The Byzantine Church," in *Byzantium: An Introduction to East Roman Civilization,* ed. N. Baynes and H. Moss (Oxford, 1948), 123.

10. Papal bull published in Latin in C. Will, *Acta et scripta quae de controversiis ecclesiae graecae et latinae* (Leipzig, 1861), 153–54, and the Greek version, esp. 162, 165. For English translation of the Latin and Greek excommunications see Geanakoplos,

1054. True, the Greek historians of the period hardly mention the papal excommunication, and, M. Jugie has shown that a religious breach as such should be dated some years earlier when the pope's name was removed from the diptychs of Hagia Sophia.[11] Modern historians tend instead to view 1204, the sack of Constantinople by the Latins in the Fourth Crusade and the beginning of the forced Greek conversion to Catholicism, as the date when the schism became truly definitive. But Gibbon seems already to have anticipated this view and at the same time preserved a better balance. On the one hand, he correctly calls the excommunication of 1054 the *consummation* of the schism—a point he could have made even stronger by noting the Greek excommunication of the papal legates as well. On the other hand, he certainly recognizes the responsibility of the first four crusades for deeply embittering relations between East and West. He shows that Greek hostility became increasingly focused on the Latin faith as the most evident outward symbol of Western culture. As he puts it, "These profane causes of national enmity were fortified and inflamed by the venom of religious zeal" (6.60.371). In his long description, so vivid and faithful to both Latin and Greek sources, of the sack of Constantinople in 1204 with its barbaric treatment of the Greek churches, Gibbon clearly implies that it was this event and the ensuing half century of Latin occupation that made the schism irrevocable. In his words, "The national and religious prejudice of the Orientals was inflamed by persecution, and the reign of the Latins *confirmed* the separation of the two churches" (6.61.443).[12]

In the long-protracted attempts of East and West to reunite their churches after the Greek reconquest of Constantinople in 1261, the reign of the Emperor Michael Palaeologus is noteworthy. And to this reign Gibbon devotes no less than twenty-two pages (in Bury's edition), eleven focusing on what he considers, rightly, its central issue: Michael's efforts to reunite the churches in order to ward off the grave threat to Constantinople of Charles of Anjou.[13] In his analysis Gibbon provides an amaz-

---

Byzantium: Church, Society and Civilization (Chicago, 1984), no. 151A and B. On Petavius see *Rationarium temporum* 1:437. Mosheim, *Ecclesiastical History* 1:445, mentions Cerularius's excommunication of the envoys. For Congar, see *After Nine Hundred Years,* esp. 71–73. Cf. Baronius, *Annales ecclesiastici* 17:100, who does say Cerularius removed the pope's name from the diptychs. Also Runciman, *Eastern Schism,* 50.

11. M. Jugie, *Le schisme byzantin* (Paris, 1941), 166ff., 230. Cf. A. Michel, *Humbert und Kerullarios,* 2 vols. (Paderborn, 1924–30).

12. For Gibbon's vivid account of the Fourth Crusade, drawn from both Latin and Greek historians, see 6.60.377–412.

13. Gibbon, 6.61.439–42, and 6.62.460–79. On Michael's reign see Geanakoplos, *Emperor Michael Palaeologus and the West.*

ing wealth of detail, remarkable in its exactitude and quarried primarily from the Greek historians Pachymeres, Gregoras, and Acropolites. Thus he describes Michael's falsification of certain bishops' signatures in a document sent to the pope before the Council of Lyons and relates that Michael even sent rich ornaments from Hagia Sophia as gifts to St. Peter's (6.62.471–72).[14] Once again appreciating the complex interplay of factors at work in the question of union, Gibbon realizes that Michael, faced with the anti-Latin prejudices of his people and clergy with their only too recent memories of the Latin occupation, had to follow one policy toward his subjects and another toward the papacy. In contrast to the famous nineteenth-century English historian, George Finlay, who views Michael's motives primarily as those of "an in-born liar, vain, meddling, ambitious, cruel, and rapacious,"[15] I am more in accord with Gibbon's judgment that Michael's so-called "hypocrisy" was prompted essentially by political necessity arising from the desperate situation of his empire.

Though it is less directly related to our main theme, we examine here the question of Hesychasm, since it permits us to see something of Gibbon's treatment of the more-internal aspects of the Byzantine church. It is sometimes said that Gibbon lacked appreciation or even understanding of theological considerations. On the contrary, when discussing the question of whether the light seen by the fourteenth-century Hesychast monks of Mt. Athos was the same, as they maintained, as that seen by the apostles on Mt. Tabor, Gibbon accurately sets forth the subtle theological differences between essence and energies in the Godhead. To be sure, as a representative of the Enlightenment, Gibbon is unsympathetic, indeed hostile to the monks. As he puts it with his most mordant wit, "This light [seen by the monks], the production of a distempered fancy, the creature of an empty stomach and an empty brain, was adored . . . as the pure and perfect essence of God Himself" (6.63.506). Although Gibbon holds the views of the Athonite monks up to ridicule, affirming they were deluded in their beliefs, it must be noted that he does not really question the monks' sincerity. Moreover, he comprehends the broader theological issues—among them the difference between the Aristotelian view of Barlaam and the Neoplatonic mysticism of the monk Palamas. Nonetheless,

14. Cf. Geanakoplos, *Emperor Michael,* 258, who shows that Pachymeres says that Michael even stripped off Hagia Sophia's altar cloth to send to St. Peter's. Gibbon also used hitherto unknown or little-used Latin sources, e.g., the Franciscan L. Waddingus's *Annales minorum* (Quarracchi, 1931–34) (see Gibbon, 6.62.472 n. 43). More important, see 6.62.473 n. 45.

15. George Finlay, *A History of Greece from the Conquest by the Romans to the Present Time,* vol. 3 (Oxford, 1877), 372.

it must be admitted that despite Gibbon's intellectual comprehension of the theology involved, the inner, spiritual meaning of Hesychastic mysticism certainly seems to have escaped him (6.63.506–8).[16]

Gibbon devotes fourteen of his most brilliantly written pages to the last and greatest confrontation of the Eastern and Western churches, the Council of Florence in 1438–39 (7.66.101–14). His treatment of the council and of the events leading to it is well delineated, polished in style, and very accurate in its detail. Dawson's view that Gibbon did not usually go to the sources or, if so, merely to check their use by other historians he was using at the moment,[17] is again belied when we observe that for the Council of Florence Gibbon's principal source is the Greek *Memoirs* of the grand ecclesiarch of Hagia Sophia Syropoulos. For centuries, and as recently as several decades ago when it began to be used by myself and Father Gill of the Vatican,[18] this account had been considered by Western scholars as completely biased and therefore to be avoided. And yet we see that Gibbon, already in the eighteenth century, could refer to Syropoulos's work as "a genuine and original narrative [which ranks] with the best of the Byzantine writers for the merit of his narrative and even his style" (7.66.104 n. 53). (I am informed, incidentally, by the present editor of Syropoulos, the eminent Catholic scholar V. Laurent, that he too would rank Syropoulos among the best Byzantine historians.) Though Gibbon viewed Syropoulos's account as "often partial [but] never intemperate" (ibid., n. 52), he apparently considered it, if used with care, the only source able to provide an accurate and complete picture of the mentality of the Greek delegation at the council. One may insist that Gibbon also had available the Latin translation of Syropoulos done by the sharply anti-Catholic, seventeenth-century Anglican bishop Robert Creyghton. But Gibbon's close reading of the original Greek text is evidenced by his criticism at more than one point of Creyghton's translation. Thus in one instance he compares Creyghton's Latin rendering of a certain passage with the corresponding Greek text of Syropoulos and concludes that Creyghton has so corrupted the original text as even to interpolate words and thoughts alien to it.[19]

Despite his close attention to Syropoulos Gibbon does not follow him

16. One may well ask, what is the "inner, spiritual meaning of Hesychasm?" I would say an understanding at least partly on an emotional, nonintellectual level of the monks' desire for union with God (i.e., mysticism). Gibbon was certainly not a mystic and could not, it seems, appreciate specifically religious values. See below n. 41.

17. Dawson, "Gibbon and the Fall of Rome," 331–32.

18. J. Gill, *The Council of Florence* (Cambridge, 1959), passim; and essay 11 below.

19. On R. Creyghton's edition of Syropoulos, *Vera historia unionis non verae . . .* (The Hague, 1660), see Gibbon, 7.66.105 n. 54. The Greek text referred to means, in

servilely. In a footnote, for example, he notes that Syropoulos lists more Greek representatives at the council than were actually present (7.66.102 n. 43). Moreover, he attempts in places to control Syropoulos's statements by reference to the accounts of the unionist or anti-unionist Greek historians Sphrantzes, Chalcondyles, and Ducas.[20]

In his discussion of one of the main questions debated at Florence, that over the *azyma* (unleavened bread), Gibbon reveals his Enlightenment penchant for religious toleration by writing, sarcastically but with no little truth, that "we may bestow some praise on the progress of human reason by saying that the *azyma* was now treated as an immaterial rite varying with the fashion of the age" (7.66.109)—a judgment, we may note, more in keeping with modern mentality on such matters. With reference to the primary theological question at issue, however, the *filioque,* Gibbon seems to support the Greek view. "Perhaps it may not be necessary," he writes as only he could put it, "to boast here of my own *impartial indifference,* but I think the Greeks were strongly supported by the Council of Chalcedon, prohibiting adding any article whatever to the creed of Nicaea-Constantinople" (ibid.). On the other hand, he correctly understood as conducive to misunderstanding the deep Greek ignorance of the character and writings of the Latin Fathers. While he was not taken in by the involved and wearisome theological logomachy at the council, Gibbon affirms with real modernity that the texts cited there on the *filioque* could be "corrupted or entangled by sophistry" (7.66.110). At the same time he sensed that the question of the *filioque* was symptomatic of the mutual Greco-Latin fears and hostility. Cutting through all the argumentation and analyzing the reasons for the intransigence of either side at Florence, he wrote: "We may be sure that neither side could be con-

---

translation, "So that he [the emperor] might be thought by the Italians as a great emperor coming to Italy with pomp. . . ." Creyghton's Latin rendering reads, "Ut pompa circumductus noster imperator Italiae populis aliquis deauratus Jupiter crederetur aut Croesus ex opulenta Lydia." Note that in 7.66.104 n. 51 Gibbon also criticizes Creyghton's rendering of Syropoulos's name as "Sguropulos," a correct observation, as we know today. Gibbon also seems to accept as correct Syropoulos's implication of pressure exerted by the papal withholding of the monthly subsidy promised to the Greeks at Florence, a statement denounced by modern Catholic historians but which has, at least in part, now been corroborated by the researches of Father Gill of the Vatican: "The 'Acta' and the Memoirs of Syropoulos as History," *Orientalia christiana periodica* 14 (1948): esp. 339. There is now a new edition of Syropoulos's memoirs by V. Laurent (Paris, 1971); see essay 11.

20. On Gibbon's use of Ducas to control Syropoulos see 7.66.111 n. 69. For use of Sphrantzes, Chalcondyles, and Ducas see notes to chap. 66. Gibbon also used the Greek "Acts" of the Council of Florence (see essay 11, n. 1), as he tells us in his *Autobiography,* 170.

vinced by the arguments of their opponents; prejudice may be enlightened by reason and a superficial glance may be rectified by a clear and more perfect view of an object adapted to our faculties. But the bishops and monks had been taught from their infancy to repeat a form of mysterious words; their national and personal honor depended on the repetition of the same sounds, and their narrow minds were hardened and inflamed by the acrimony of a public dispute" (ibid.). This remarkable if somewhat cynical passage, as perhaps no other by any modern church historian that I am aware of, gets at once to the heart of the psychological causes for the long stalemate in the Greek and Latin positions at Florence. In contrast to what Father Gill seems to imply in his fine work on the Council of Florence, I think the Greek defeat at Florence, by recourse of the Westerners to the Aristotelian Scholastic syllogism, does not mean (as Gibbon would probably agree) that the Greeks were emotionally convinced of the truth of the Latin position.[21]

Finally, Gibbon also understood, as some modern historians such as Georg Hofmann apparently have not, that certain phrases of the decree of union are not to be taken literally.[22] At certain points the decree was purposely phrased in an ambiguous manner so that, as Gibbon puts it, "to satisfy the Latins without dishonoring the Greeks . . . they weighed the scruples of words and syllables till the theological balance trembled with a slight preponderance in favor of the Vatican" (7.66.111).[23] Irony, consummate irony yes, but again succinctly expressing the situation with perhaps better insight than any parade of facts.

Gibbon's recital of the reception of the union in Constantinople after the council, the refusal of the great majority of the people to accept it and the violent dissension that broke out, to continue to the very day of Constantinople's fall to the Turks, is masterfully set forth. As Gibbon summarizes, significantly and with only slight exaggeration, "By alienating her most useful allies [the West] and provoking her most dangerous enemies [the Turks] the schism of Constantinople has precipitated the Decline and Fall of the Roman Empire in the East" (6.60.366).[24]

21. Gill, *Council of Florence,* 153, 227ff. I think the Latin side used Scholastic syllogisms in argument at Florence less than is generally believed.

22. See on this question essay 11, nn. 87–89, citing G. Hofmann, "Papato, Conciliarismo, Patriarcato (1438–1439)," in *Teologi e deliberazioni del concilio di Firenze* (Rome, 1940), 69–73. Also see B. Stephanides, *Ekklēsiastikē historia* (Athens, 1959), 361–64.

23. Cf. essay 11, text and n. 89. Also T. Frommann, *Kritische Beiträge zur Geschichte der florentiner Kircheneinigung* (Halle, 1872), 19, "a brilliantly indefinite and ambiguous definition."

24. See 7.67.135–37 (cf. 6.60.366) for reception of Greek delegation in Constantinople. Note Gibbon's revealing statement opening chap. 66: "In the last four centuries

Now that we have examined one, if not the most important of the aspects of Gibbon's treatment of the Byzantine church, what conclusions can we draw about him as an ecclesiastical historian? We should note first, however, that in contrast to the more unified nature of the first part of the *Decline and Fall,* Gibbon's treatment of Byzantine history is less well organized, in certain respects overly brief and episodic, digressing frequently with long excursuses on such subjects as the rise of the Arabs and Turks. Second, we must bear in mind that his Byzantine history was not created *ex nihilo.* He had as predecessors several important seventeenth- and eighteenth-century scholars. On the political side he could draw especially on the great Ch. Ducange, who may be said to have written the first scientific Byzantine history.[25] With respect to church history proper, Gibbon, as we have seen, was able for the earlier part of the *Decline and Fall* to raise himself on the shoulders of that fantastic researcher the Jansenist Tillemont, whereas for the later period he had as guides both Protestant and Catholic ecclesiastical historians—the Lutheran minister Mosheim, the Jesuit Petavius, and the Abbé Fleury, not to forget the arch-Catholic Cardinal Baronius, along with one or two others.[26] Nevertheless, it was Gibbon's unique powers of synthesis and analysis and his lofty (sometimes too lofty) and lucid style that gave flesh and bones to the scholarly but dry-as-dust data of Tillemont, the brief annalistic statements of Petavius, the extensive documentary sources quoted in Baronius's *Annales ecclesiastici,* and the somewhat more satisfactory but pedantic and essentially nonanalytical accounts of Fleury and Mosheim.[27] Gibbon, who in contrast to these religious-oriented clerics was a layman, may thus be called a pioneer—one if not the first among modern historians to put ecclesiastical phenomena within the larger historical framework of their time. In his hands the history of the schism in particular becomes a readable analytic narrative, integrated, if sometimes faultily, with other concurrent events.

---

of the Greek Emperors their friendly or hostile aspect towards the Pope and the Latins may be observed as the thermometer of their prosperity or distress."

25. Ch. Ducange, esp. his *Histoire de l'empire de Constantinople sous les empereurs français* (Paris, 1657) and his great medieval Greek and Latin dictionaries. Also see Ch. Lebeau, *Histoire du Bas-Empire* (Paris, 1757–; new ed. Paris, 1824), a very arid work.

26. Gibbon was also indebted to the tremendous researches of the diplomatist Jean Mabillon and the palaeographer Bernard de Montfaucon. The researches of these and several other seventeenth-century French scholars provided a mine of information, the raw materials (including ecclesiastical) for historians like Gibbon to draw upon.

27. R. Porson says (see Morison, *Edward Gibbon,* 146) that "sometimes Gibbon draws out the thread of his verbosity finer than the staple of his argument." See H. L. Bond, *The Literary Art of Edward Gibbon* (Oxford, 1960). Mosheim was probably the most objective of the church historians preceding Gibbon.

Though Gibbon often cites his secondary guides, he provides myriads of details not to be found in their works and that in many cases can have been drawn only from the Byzantine historians. No doubt Gibbon, as accused by Dawson and K. Amantos, made liberal use of Latin translations of the Greek originals, given his greater fluency in Latin than Greek.[28] Available to him was the Latin translation of the famous Louvre collection of Byzantine historians, which was hardly inferior to the Bonn corpus used today, and in both of which the more difficult Greek passages are often merely paraphrased in Latin, or on occasion actually omitted. Gibbon, we see from his notes, even utilized L. Cousin's French translation of the Byzantine historians. In my view there is nothing reprehensible about the use of such aids, provided of course he constantly used the originals as a check. Such indeed seems to have been his method, at least in a number of instances where he takes Cousin to task for a faulty rendering of the Greek text.[29] With respect to other sources such as the historian Cedrenus he notes that certain passages in the original Greek are richer than their Latin translation.[30] We have already noted his pioneer use of Syropoulos. Neither Mosheim nor Petavius even mentions Syropoulos, and though Fleury, or rather his continuator, refers to Syropoulos three times, he draws no material of any consequence from him and therefore cannot be said to have really used his account.[31]

How successful can we say Gibbon was in his treatment of the schism? Was he able to draw the essence from the sources available, to make his

28. See Dawson, "Gibbon and the Fall of Rome," 331; and K. Amantos, *Great Greek Encyclopedia* (in Greek), vol. 8 (Athens, 1926), 358, neither of whom evidently had carefully read the latter part of Gibbon. See Gibbon, 7.66.95 n. 28, commenting on the historian Chalcondyles's use of a Greek verb and its Latin equivalent. Cf. also Bury's ed., vol. 1 (New York, 1914), ix: "His knowledge of Greek was imperfect." And yet Bury in his article on Gibbon in the *Encyclopaedia Britannica* says that "Gibbon was never content with secondhand accounts when primary sources were available." Gibbon himself wrote, "I have always endeavored to draw from the fountainhead" (Preface to vol. 4, 3d ed. [London, 1777]).

29. L. Cousin, *Histoire de Constantinople depuis Justin jusqu'à la fin de l'empire,* 8 vols. (Paris, 1672–74). See Gibbon, 7.68.168 n. 22, who comments on Cousin's translation; in 7.68.181 n. 54 he again criticizes Cousin. See also 7.68.183 n. 60. Joyce, *Edward Gibbon,* 127, quotes Gibbon as saying, "From the entire and diligent perusal of the Greek text I have a right to pronounce that the Latin and French versions of [Hugo] Grotius and Cousin may not be implicitly trusted."

30. See 6.54.120 n. 27, where in discussing the Paulicians Gibbon cites the Greek of the historian Cedrenus and comments, "How elegant is the Greek tongue even in the mouth of Cedrenus." See also 6.60.400 n. 86. On Gibbon's early study of Greek see his *Autobiography,* 70. Gibbon also used a work of Dupin and another of Petavius *(Dogmata theologica)* both unavailable to me (cf. 6.60.367 n. 3, and 369 n. 8).

31. See Abbé Fleury, *Histoire ecclésiastique,* vol. 22 (1726), esp. 231, 246. Nor does Baronius's continuator seem to have used Syropoulos.

way through the complex materials of the Latin and Byzantine historians without distorting their meaning? Given the extreme prejudice of both Greek and Latin accounts,[32] our criteria of his objectivity here would have to be based on two factors: first, on the evidence of his efforts to check one source against another, and, second, on how his interpretations compare with the generally accepted results of modern research. With these points in mind let us very briefly summarize our analysis of the principal phases of the schism:

Gibbon's treatment of Iconoclasm is necessarily inadequate because, as we now realize, the subject in its larger ramifications had not yet begun to be explored. His discussion of the Photian affair, however, despite its brevity, seems reasonably objective and fairly adequate.[33] With respect to "1054 and all that," Gibbon, in contrast to the recent emphasis of Runciman and other scholars including myself, affirms that 1054 was the *consummation* of the schism.[34] And from the technical point of view this may in one important respect be correct, since until the very recent, praiseworthy approaches between Catholicism and Orthodoxy culminating on 7 December 1965 in the lifting of the mutual excommunications of 1054 by Pope Paul VI and Patriarch Athenagoras, the bitter anathematizations had never been revoked.[35] At the same time, in agreement with prevailing modern interpretation, Gibbon clearly recognized the role of the crusades in so exacerbating Greco-Latin relations that 1204, by climaxing the *underlying* considerations making for East-West hostility, marked the point of no return for the schism. And it is this inherited hostility, together with nine centuries of different ecclesiastical development, that today remains the basic obstacle to reunion of the churches.

As for his discussion of the repeated negotiations for union, from the Council of Lyons in 1274 to 1453, Gibbon's treatment seems to be generally very good. In its presentation of the facts, in the balance struck between synthesis and analysis and between the Latin and Greek viewpoints, it constitutes one of the best sections of his entire Byzantine history. With rare skill he interweaves the problems of ecclesiastical polity with the political, social, and psychological-pragmatic considera-

32. They are perhaps the most consistently biased of any group of medieval sources.

33. Cf. Dvornik, *Photian Schism,* passim.

34. Runciman, *Eastern Schism,* Introduction, vi, and 159–70. Also Geanakoplos, "On the Schism of the Greek and Roman Churches" (1954), 17–18.

35. As noted above Cerularius was careful not to excommunicate the pope, only his envoys, but he did not restore the pope's name to the diptychs. Of course, Runciman and other modern scholars do not call 1054 the *definitive* schism. Instead 1204 marks that.

tions that his Enlightenment mentality could perhaps best appreciate. Finally, in showing that the interminable squabbles over union weakened the empire internally, he is able to demonstrate, correctly I believe, the importance of this problem in leading to the fall of the empire in the East.[36]

Gibbon is admittedly much less successful with respect to the more internal aspects of Byzantine Christianity. He does not always understand the nuances in the relationship between the church and state. Like some modern historians he tends to overemphasize the emperor's authority over the church, his so-called Caesaropapism.[37] Nor, more fundamental, is he able to penetrate into the inner life, the spirituality of the Eastern church. He sees the outward significance of it in the actions of the principal actors and, better than some scholars of today, comprehends the psychology of the Greek opposition to union. But because he does not sympathize with the Christian faith as such, he cannot really appreciate or empathize with, for example, the mysticism of the monks on Mt. Athos, as he certainly did not with the spirituality of the early Christian martyrs. Thus in neither case does he convince the reader to take their fanaticism seriously. On the other hand, despite what certain scholars have said, Gibbon usually had a very adequate comprehension of Byzantine theology, understanding well the differences between Eastern and Western doctrine.[38] To be sure, in connection with the Council of Lyons he could have emphasized that no theological discussion took place, while at Florence, though in the long run in vain, the intensive theological

36. See text and n. 24 above. Gibbon, 5.49.256, makes the shrewd observation that the Greeks loved their church more than their country. Actually, they had identified the two.

37. See 5.49.256: "The Greek prelate [patriarch] was a domestic slave under the eye of his master at whose nod he alternately passed from convent to throne and throne to convent." Also 6.60.369–70, on the clergy "submissive" to the emperor. Yet 7.66.104 and n. 50 (based on Syropoulos) notes that the Patriarch Joseph said in private that he had come to Florence, among other things, to find out from the pope how to oppose the emperor. See essay 11, n. 41; and Geanakoplos, "Church and State in the Byzantine Empire," chap. 2 of *Byzantine East and Latin West: Two Worlds of Christendom.* Cf. Gibbon, 7.66.89, where he mentions, regarding John V in Rome in 1369, that the Byzantine emperor, unlike the Western, could not be entitled by the pope to the privilege of chanting the gospel in the rank of deacon.

38. See e.g., Bury's ed., vol. 1, esp. xxxix. Cf. n. 44 below. Also Smeaton's remark in n. 2 above, with which I disagree. Gibbon clearly explains both sides of the theology of the *filioque,* also Hesychasm, and in the earlier volumes the theology of the Incarnation, and has excellent though ironic accounts of Simeon Stylites and other ascetic monks—all this, according to some scholars, in a first-class manner, e.g., Fuglum, *Edward Gibbon,* esp. 125: "Gibbon unravels with supreme mastery and relish the complicated systems of Arians and Agnostics, of Essenes and Nestorians. . . ."

disputes were themselves revealing of a basically different East-West approach to the problems of ecclesiology (e.g., papal authority versus a more conciliar, semidemocratic approach) as well as doctrine. Gibbon is all too often contemptuous of the Greek church, but it is not usually realized by critics that when, in the latter part of his history, he compares its characteristics, such as militancy or moral corruption of the clergy, to those of the Western church he seems, however grudgingly, to give the palm to the Eastern.[39]

In this general context, we may now finally ask the question: Is it necessary that the competent ecclesiastical historian have sympathy or empathy for the spirituality of Christianity? Must he believe a priori that Christian dogma is the truth? To these difficult, controversial questions I think that a good, though not necessarily a truly satisfactory answer can be given by posing an antithetical question: Does one who accepts the supernatural aspects of the Christian faith as truth necessarily write more satisfactory church history than one who does not? Or in more concrete terms: Can one who does not truly sympathize, say with ancient Greek paganism, adequately pass judgment on it?[40] Be that as it may, it must be recalled that it was a standard Enlightenment trait to try to view historical events dispassionately, to preserve a proper detachment from them. Gibbon could perhaps be accused of violating this axiom since, though basically religious albeit in a rationalist almost Deistic sense, he often held the institutions of Christianity, especially monasticism, up to ridicule.[41] Indeed, his epigrammatic, biting remarks to this effect are often

39. See esp. 6.54.123, where he rather briefly compares the Greek and Latin clergy. In noting in several places that the Greek patriarch (cf. the pope in the West) never presumed to set himself over imperial authority Gibbon might have emphasized the great exception, the apparent aspirations of Cerularius to become a kind of Byzantine Hildebrand. On the different ecclesiologies of the two churches see esp. Congar, *After Nine Hundred Years,* 58–59, who stresses the primacy of the pope as the focal point. See also the Orthodox S. Tsankov, *The Eastern Orthodox Church,* trans. D. Lowrie (London, 1929), 84–100; F. Dvornik's *Byzance et la primauté romaine* (Paris, 1964); and Geanakoplos, "Church and State in the Byzantine Empire." On what seems to have been the superior morality of the Greek clergy, at least to the eleventh century, see also Grégoire, "Byzantine Church," 123.

40. L. von Ranke, a good Lutheran, and the Catholic L. von Pastor both wrote fine, objective ecclesiastical histories of the papacy: *History of the Popes,* trans. G. Dennis (London, 1912); and *History of the Popes* (London, 1891–), respectively. Interesting in this respect is the view of Butterfield, *Whig Interpretation of History,* 105: "The historian may be cynical with Gibbon or sentimental with Carlyle; he may have religious ardor or he may be a humorist. . . . It is not sin in a historian to introduce a personal bias that can be recognized and discounted. The sin . . . is bias [that] cannot be recognized."

41. See Fuglum, *Edward Gibbon,* 116: "In most respects Gibbon tends toward a

quoted. But we must note two things here: first, that there is invariably a kernel of truth in his irony which is able to convey a certain feel for the event to the reader more quickly and sometimes even better than a long explanation would; second, that those few readers who have the patience to reach the Byzantine portion of his work are too often tempted to gloss over his more serious writing here in order to look for these pithy gems. The wrong things, I think, are frequently quoted from the Byzantine portion of Gibbon.

In our analysis of Gibbon as a church historian, we must of course be careful not to make generalizations about the whole Byzantine part of his work on the basis of an examination, however detailed, of only a part. Gibbon admittedly has many basic flaws as a Byzantine historian. Most seriously, he fails to see Byzantine civilization as essentially a new creation—growing out of the earlier Greco-Roman to be sure but with an identity of its own. Since he sees the Byzantine state and its culture too much in terms of a degraded continuity or discontinuity of ancient ideals, he fails to realize the true significance of Byzantium's own achievements.[42] And of course, with respect to more recently developed research areas such as internal history, culture, and Byzantine relations with the Slavs, there are great gaps in his work.[43]

Nevertheless, on the basis of our analysis I think we may conclude by essaying the judgment that, at least as regards the portion of his Byzantine history dealing with the schism, he is in general a reasonably com-

moderate form of agnosticism." Also Jones, *Constantine and the Conversion of Europe,* 260: "[Gibbon's weakness is] not so much anti-Christian bias as a temperamental incapacity to understand religion." We should not forget that as a sixteen-year-old boy (see his *Autobiography,* 52–54) Gibbon was converted briefly to Catholicism, and after his reconversion to Protestantism and during his later career he became, it seems, more anti-Catholic than anti-Christian. See 6.54.125–28, where he discusses the Roman and Protestant churches. Also Fuglum, 20–21, on Gibbon's later religious views.

42. Gibbon's famous phrase should be cited here, that Byzantium's history, in the light of ancient Greek and Roman culture, is "a tedious uniform tale of weakness and misery" (5.48.169). On this see esp. comments of Dawson, "Gibbon and the Fall of Rome," 332; also Fuglum, *Edward Gibbon,* 150ff.

43. For his shortcomings as a Byzantine historian see esp. Bury's ed., Introduction, esp. xvi–xxii, which stresses, among other things, the advances of textual criticism as applied to Byzantine texts since Gibbon's time. Cf. Dawson, "Gibbon and the Fall of Rome," 335, who says correctly that Gibbon regarded Byzantium simply as a degraded successor of classical Greece and Rome. Yet despite his love of classicism Gibbon hated the Athenian democracy when it was controlled by "mob" rule. But cf. Giarrizzo, *Edward Gibbon,* 408, 414. Also on Gibbon's faults as a Byzantine historian see Vasiliev, *History of the Byzantine Empire* 1:8–11; and G. Ostrogorsky, *History of the Byzantine State* (Oxford, 1968), 6.

petent, in certain sections even a brilliant ecclesiastical historian.[44] Of course one who considers specifically religious values the most overridingly important aspect of church history in this period will not agree with this judgment. But given the qualification of Gibbon's natural prejudice as a man of the Enlightenment and his lack of knowledge of subsequently discovered source materials, I think that most of the ecclesiastical portions of his Byzantine history still deserve to be read. Whether he is as successful in the first part of his *Decline and Fall,* where his prejudices against the faith of the early Christian martyrs and monasticism in particular come even more into play, is much more questionable.[45] It was Gibbon's many positive qualities, pointed out here, together with his lack of sympathy for the spirituality, the charismatic quality if you will, of Christianity, that John, later Cardinal, Newman must have had in mind when in 1845 he wrote, "It is melancholy to say it but the chief, perhaps the only English writer who has any claim to be considered an ecclesiastical historian, is the unbeliever Gibbon."[46]

44. Fuglum, *Edward Gibbon,* 125: "As a church historian Gibbon has few equals . . . his surveys of the theological controversies reach a high degree of perfection . . . but no attempt is made to explain the development of church doctrine or elaboration of theological disputes." Cf. Bury's ed., vol. 1, xxxix: "Neither the historian nor the man of letters will any longer subscribe without a thousand reserves to the theological chapters of the *Decline and Fall* and no discreet inquirer would go there for his ecclesiastical history." But, as we have seen, Bury as a specialist in earlier Byzantine history has clearly not analyzed Gibbon's treatment of the schism after Photius, nor the history as a whole of Byzantine-Latin ecclesiastical relations in the later centuries. His judgment therefore doubtless refers to the earlier period.

45. See the remarks of Dawson, "Gibbon and the Fall of Rome," 326. Yet he praises his theological knowledge of the Incarnation. See also J. Morison's (*Edward Gibbon,* 146) praise of his theological knowledge. To elaborate a bit more on why Gibbon could be considered a good Byzantine church historian while at the same time an inadequate *general* Byzantine historian: for the later (Byzantine) period he had available most of the important ecclesiastical source materials, while many sources for other aspects of Byzantine history (economic, cultural, etc.) were then still unknown. Moreover, in the development of Christianity itself there was a shift of emphasis. In the earlier section of his work, when discussing the triumph of Christianity over paganism, Gibbon had to deal with the deep faith of the early martyrs. He was unable to sympathize with this spiritual value, however. In the later period (that under discussion in this essay) questions of church polity, ecclesiastical diplomacy, and to some extent theology—considerations themselves to be placed against a larger backdrop of political, ethnic, and cultural differences—are probably more important for the historian than purely spiritual factors. And these more mundane considerations were factors which Gibbon's Enlightenment temperament, skeptical and almost cynical as it was, could very well understand.

46. John Henry Newman, *An Essay on the Development of Christian Doctrine* (London and New York, 1906), 8 (written just before his conversion to Catholicism). In another work *Essays and Sketches,* vol. 1 (new ed., New York, 1948), 270, Newman writes of Gibbon's objectivity in church history: "Gibbon who looked at things with less

of prejudice than heretics [i.e., Protestants] as having no point to maintain." For a discussion of the schism in a broader, political-cultural context, see Geanakoplos, *Byzantine East and Latin West,* and *Interaction of the "Sibling" Byzantine and Western Cultures,* esp. Prologue and Epilogue. Finally, see essays 10–12 below.

Additional Bibliography for Essay 6

See the summer 1976 issue of *Daedalus,* devoted to "Gibbon and the Decline and Fall of the Roman Empire," especially the stimulating essays by S. Runciman, "Gibbon and Byzantium," 103–10, in particular 106–9, stressing Gibbon's views of the role of the Byzantine church in Byzantine culture; P. Brown, "Gibbon's Views on Culture and Society in the Fifth and Sixth Centuries," 73–88; and O. Chadwick, "Gibbon and the Church Historians," 111–23. Also the perceptive essay by S. Vryonis, "Hellas Resurgent," in *The Transformation of the Roman World: Gibbon's Problem after Two Centuries,* ed. L. White, Jr. (Berkeley, 1966), 92–118, stressing the persistence of the Greek language and literature in Byzantium's existence (papers all rather peripheral to this essay).

Seven

The Second Ecumenical Council at Constantinople (381): Proceedings and Theology of the Holy Spirit

In the long annals of the Christian church, it is the First Council of Constantinople held in that capital in 381 that marks the emergence of the see of Constantinople to preeminence over the Eastern sees of Christendom. More important, theologically, it was at this council that the most fundamental of Christian doctrines, that of the Trinity, was completed, with the Holy Spirit declared, at least implicitly, to be divine and *homoousios* with the Father and the Son in the Godhead.[1] Henceforth, all forms of Arianism, which had denied the consubstantiality of the Son with the Father, and in particular the heresy of the Pneumatomachians (or Macedonians), who believed the Holy Spirit to be merely a creature of the Son, were declared anathematized; and the Creed of Nicaea, with certain amplifications relating primarily to the Holy Spirit, became Orthodox dogma. For these reasons, the First Council of Constantinople

1. It is important to note that in the symbol (or creed) of Constantinople, the terms *divine* and *homoousion,* relating to the Holy Spirit, do not explicitly appear. But the divinity of the Holy Spirit is certainly implied in the terms *symproskynoumenon* and *syndoxazomenon* ("worshiped and glorified together with the Father and Son"). Evidently, when they formulated the creed, the Fathers of 381 were trying not to *directly* antagonize their opponents, the Macedonian group. Moreover, the Macedonians, who believed the Holy Spirit to be a creature of the Son, were *explicitly* anathematized in canon 1 of this Council of 381.

in 381, though not recognized as ecumenical until the Fourth Ecumenical Council of Chalcedon in 451, was of profound importance not only for the Christian church as a whole, but also for the future development of the Orthodox patriarchate of Constantinople in particular.

The *praktika* or *acta* of this synod have not survived. Thus, we know even less about its proceedings than we do about the First Ecumenical Council of Nicaea.[2] It is the primary intention of this paper to try to reconstruct, insofar as possible, the proceedings of this council at Constantinople, discussing the reason for its convocation and the nature of the deliberations that took place. In the course of this essay, I will devote time to certain matters somewhat peripheral to the main business of the council, then to the central theological question of the nature of the Holy Spirit and its relationship to the Father and Son in the Trinity, and also to the canons of the council, especially the third, so significant for the future development of the see of Constantinople. Finally, I will consider the question of the council's ecumenicity in the light of its own deliberations as well as those of succeeding councils. In this way I hope to provide not only a reasonably adequate sense of the proceedings and conciliar decisions, but also of the reception and meaning of the council in the Greek East and the Latin West.

The concept of the convocation of a universal or ecumenical council of the bishops of the entire Church, assembling in order to solve questions disturbing the peace of the Church, originated with Emperor Constantine the Great. At the First Ecumenical Council, which he convoked at Nicaea in 325, the pressing and critical theological problem, that of the relationship of the Father and the Son (or *Logos*), was precisely defined. The Son was declared to be of exactly the same substance *(homoousios)* as the Father, not different *(anomoios)* or even similar *(homoiousios),* as the more prominent groups of Arians maintained. The Council of Nicaea marked the triumph, above all, of the views of Saint Athanasius of Alexandria over the Arians. According to Athanasius, identity of substance between Father and Son was an absolute necessity. Since God (in Christ) became man so that man could become God, without precise identification of the substance of Father and Son, man's salvation would be impossible.[3]

2. For information on the council provided by sources other than the *acta,* see notes below.

3. See, e.g., A. McGiffert, *A History of Christian Thought, Early and Eastern* (New York and London, 1947), 1:246–57; also B. Stephanides, *Ekklēsiastikē historia* (Athens, 1959), 151–91.

Strangely enough, up to the time of Nicaea virtually no theologian, except in passing, had considered the corollary fundamental question of the precise relationship of the Holy Spirit to the Father and the Son.[4] When mentioned, in fact, the Holy Spirit was usually considered an inferior being, a creature, usually of the Son. Others conceived the Holy Spirit as a vague sort of spirit not infrequently mentioned in the Old and New Testaments. Indeed, some believed the Holy Spirit of the Old to be different from that of the New Testament.[5] Finally, an extreme view even believed in a kind of descending hierarchy of Father, Son, and Holy Spirit.[6]

In any event, in the half century after the Council of Nicaea sharp disagreements broke out among those fathers of the church who wished to define precisely the nature and function of the Holy Spirit in the Trinity. It is obvious that belief in the Holy Spirit as inferior in any significant way to the other persons of the Trinity would destroy the unity of God, the very monotheism of Christianity.

What I have set forth is, of course, a rather simplified version of the many theological views and disputes of the age. But it serves to provide the background and in some measure the rationale for Emperor Theodosius's decision to convoke a council in 381 at his capital city, Constantinople, in order to bring about concord in the church and public order in the empire. Actually, the fifty-six years between convocation of the councils of Nicaea in 325 and Constantinople in 381 had been marked by constant theological and ecclesiastical turmoil, but much more so in the East.[7] This was owing in part to ecclesiastical rivalry of the various sees,[8] in part to the different emphasis on biblical exegesis of the rival Alexandrian and Antiochene schools. The two basic approaches of these schools gave rise to different views in doctrine on the Trinity, some of

4. See the objective and well-documented study of H. Jedin, *History of the Church, the Imperial Centuries from Constantine to the Early Middle Ages* (New York, 1980), 2:73.

5. McGiffert, *History of Christian Thought,* 1:271–72.

6. A. von Harnack, *History of Dogma* (New York, 1961), 4:119. The one really convincing argument for the divinity of the Spirit and his equality with the Father and the Son, according to St. Basil, *On the Holy Spirit,* vol. 8, 2d ser., of *Nicene and Post-Nicene Fathers* (New York, 1895), 24, is the association of the Spirit with Father and Son in the baptismal formula (cf. McGiffert, *History of Christian Thought,* 1:272).

7. On the various conflicts, almost entirely over Arianism, and the numerous local councils held in the West and especially the East to resolve the problem of Arianism see esp. Jedin, *Imperial Centuries,* 59–67. Also his shorter work, *Ecumenical Councils of the Catholic Church* (Freiburg and London, n.d.), 21–24.

8. On rivalries based on apostolic claims of the various sees see esp. F. Dvornik, *Byzantium and the Roman Primacy* (New York, 1966), 28–32.

which, at least indirectly, may have influenced the various forms of Arianism and certainly later the debates over Christology.[9]

Under Valens, the pro-Arian emperor who ruled in the East just before Theodosius, the Nicene bishops had been expelled and their churches in the East handed over to the various groups of Arians. At the death of Valens in 378 at the battle of Adrianople, Gratian, his Nicene co-emperor in the West of the still theoretically undivided Roman Empire, appointed as emperor in the East his Spanish general Theodosius. A Westerner by birth, Theodosius I, like most of the Latin West including Pope Damasus, was Nicene in belief. In an edict he issued in February of 380, Theodosius ordered the people, especially of Constantinople, to follow the religion the Apostle Peter had handed down to the Romans and was now professed by Pope Damasus and Bishop Peter of Alexandria. Those deviating from this profession, which recognized "the one divinity of the Father, Son, and Holy Spirit in equal majesty and Holy Trinity" were to be considered heretics.[10] When Theodosius made his triumphant entry into Constantinople on 24 November 380—a city he soon became enamored of—he quickly expelled its Arian bishop Demophilos.

Theodosius, intending to enforce his religious and political program, not unilaterally but with the ecclesiastical representatives of the Nicene faith, then quickly moved to convoke a council. Two urgent problems in the East which he wanted settled by a council were first, the ecclesiastical schism in Antioch; and second, doctrinally, the question of the Holy Spirit. The latter question was particularly pressing because of the emergence to prominence of the Pneumatomachian party.

Why Theodosius dispatched invitations to a council to be convoked in 381 in Constantinople only to bishops of the East and not of the West can perhaps best be explained as follows: Technically he was ruler of the East but not yet of the Western half of the empire. Moreover, the problems of doctrine, especially the various ramifications of the Arian heresy, seemed to be concentrated primarily in the East. In any case, the idea of a council was apparently his alone, although he had made known his intent to the bishop of Thessalonica, who had in turn informed Pope Damasus of his plan.[11] The text and exact date of the imperial edict of convocation have not survived, but on the basis of the synodical letter of another synod held in Constantinople one year later, in 382, it may be dated to the end of 380 or beginning of 381. The word "ecumenical" is used in the text of

9. The Antiochene stressed literal interpretation in a historical framework, and the Alexandrian, following Origen, stressed an allegorical, often mystical, exegesis.

10. For this edict, "Cunctos populos," see *The Theodosian Code,* ed. C. Pharr (Princeton, NJ , 1952), 16.1.2. Cf. Jedin, *Imperial Centuries,* 68.

11. Jedin, *Imperial Centuries,* 69.

the synodical letter of 382 referring to the Council of 381. It seems clear, however, that the term as used by the synod of 382 was not intended to refer to the entire church but only to the ecclesiastical areas of the Eastern or Greek-speaking portion of the empire.[12]

In the fashion of Constantine, whose spiritual heir he undoubtedly envisioned himself, Theodosius probably addressed the bishops at their first assembly.[13] The council seems to have opened in the imperial palace, though later sessions apparently took place in the cathedral.[14] In contrast to the Council of Nicaea, where 318 Fathers appeared, only 150 bishops, all from the Eastern dioceses, were in attendance. Included were some famous names, Fathers noted for their doctrinal beliefs and apostolic endeavors. The most eminent were Gregory the Theologian, intimate friend to, and Gregory of Nyssa, brother of, St. Basil (who had died only two years before); Meletius, bishop of Antioch, who arrived early accompanied by seventy bishops from his diocese of the East, who constituted the largest contingent at the council; Cyril, bishop of Jerusalem; Diodoros of Tarsus; and Peter of Sebastia, a younger brother of Basil.[15] Virtually all these Fathers were in essence Nicene in their faith and largely in agreement about the expression of the precise words of dogma since the emergence to prominence of the Cappadocian or Neo-Nicene party. The Cappadocian Fathers based their view of the Trinity on Saint Athanasius, but unlike him they drew a genuine distinction between the terms *ousia* and *hypostasis* as reflected in Basil's phrase, "One *ousia* in three *hypostases*" (one essence in three persons).[16]

Early in the council, Meletius, bishop of Antioch, was elected presiding official of the assembly. This choice was easily accepted by Theodosius, who, according to the historian Theodoretos, recognized in Mele-

12. Text in Mansi, *Sacrorum conciliorum . . . collectio,* vol. 3, cols. 557–60. On this cf. Jedin, *Imperial Centuries,* 76-77, esp. text and n. 89.

13. Jedin, *Imperial Centuries,* 70, who says, "Theodosios neither took part [in the sessions] personally nor was even represented by officials at the Council." But the latter seems unlikely to me. Emperor Constantine at Nicaea, Theodosius II at Ephesus, and Marcian at Chalcedon (451), even if they did not participate, all were represented by civil officials. And certainly all emperors exerted their influence behind the scenes.

14. Whether this was at Hagia Sophia or Church of the Holy Apostles is not entirely clear, although Hagia Sophia (the Great Church) seems more likely. Cf. *Nicene and Post-Nicene Fathers,* vol. 8 (on Saint Basil), introduction, xliv, noting that Gregory the Theologian was enthroned in Hagia Sophia at the beginning of the synod.

15. A list of the participants survives.

16. On St. Basil's important contribution to solving the basic question of the difference between *ousia* and *hypostasis* see his treatises *On the Holy Spirit* and *Against Eunomius,* in *Nicene and Post-Nicene Fathers* 8:1, 23, 33. Also cf. Jedin, *Imperial Centuries,* 64–67, on "the young Nicenes" Basil, Gregory of Nyssa, Gregory the Theologian, and Amphilochius of Iconium, all of whose theological work prepared the decisions on the faith at the Synod of Constantinople in 381.

tius the prelate who had earlier appeared to him in a dream and crowned him emperor.[17] Besides 150 Orthodox Fathers, a number to become famous in history, there were also present, by order of the emperor, thirty-six Pneumatomachian or Macedonian bishops, so-called after their leader Macedonius, former patriarch of Constantinople. They came headed by their leader, Eleusis of Cyzicus, earlier a champion of the *homoousios* as related to the Son.[18]

The first order of business was probably the question of naming a bishop for the see of Constantinople. The chief candidate for the post was the Cappadocian Gregory the Theologian, who was evidently the choice of Meletius of Antioch, which assured him the support of most of the Eastern bishops. Few apparently took seriously the claims of the opportunistic Maximos the Cynic, who was the preferred candidate of Peter, patriarch of Alexandria. As to a possible technical objection against Gregory's nomination—that he had earlier been named bishop of Sasima—the assembly was willing to overlook this on the ground that he had never taken possession of that diocese. President Meletius and the assembly, accordingly, formally installed Gregory as bishop of Constantinople, evidently in the Church of the Holy Apostles.[19]

At this time Meletius died unexpectedly. Theodosius assisted at his last rites, with the funeral eulogy delivered by Gregory of Nyssa.[20] Meletius's death opened a dangerous crisis for the council, for it soon led to the resignation from the see of Constantinople of Gregory the Theologian.

Meletius had been involved in the current schism at Antioch over the rightful occupant of the bishopric there. This schism, involving not only Constantinople but Alexandria and even distant Rome, provides a striking example of the contemporary practice of the interference of leading bishops in affairs of other dioceses.[21] After Meletius's death Gregory made sincere attempts to solve the schism over Antioch, offering even to

17. See Theodoretos in Migne, *Patrologia graeca* (hereafter MPG), vol. 82, col. 1208 (his *Ecclesiastical History*, vol. 7). Cf. Ortiz de Urbina, *Nicée et Constantinople* (Paris, 1963), 172.

18. See Jedin, *Imperial Centuries*, 71, citing the contemporary or near-contemporary historians Socrates and Sozomenus.

19. On Maximos the Cynic and the Alexandrian intrigues, see de Urbina, *Nicée*, 164–65. On the church of Gregory's installation, see ibid., 168. Gregory himself in his farewell address speaks of the Church of the Holy Apostles and in his (short) *Autobiography* says he was installed in the Church of the Holy Apostles (not Hagia Sophia).

20. See de Urbina, *Nicée*, 175.

21. Canon 2 of the Synod of Constantinople, it is generally agreed, was directed against Alexandria and Rome's interference in affairs of other Eastern sees. For text and discussion see H. Schroeder, *Disciplinary Decrees of the General Councils* (St. Louis and London, 1937), 64–65.

accept the opposing party's candidate, Paulinos, for that see. But the Meletian faction, as well as the Egyptians (who arrived later), refused and insisted on reserving action until the delegates' return to Antioch. But worst things were in store for Gregory. Arriving late at the council (evidently in response to a new and urgent summons from Theodosius) were Timothy, the Egyptian bishop of Alexandria, and Ascholius, bishop of Thessalonica.[22] These two bishops now not only opposed Gregory in the matter of the see of Antioch but even proclaimed their opposition to Gregory's own election to the see of Constantinople. They insisted his election was invalid on the grounds it violated canon 15 of Nicaea, prohibiting translation of a bishop from one see to another.[23] This disturbed Theodosius, who was partial to Gregory, since several years earlier Gregory, at great personal sacrifice, had been primarily responsible for the effective reestablishment of the Nicene faith in Constantinople to the detriment of the formerly predominant Arian faction.[24]

After considerable dissension between himself and the supporters of Alexandria and Thessalonica, Gregory, exasperated, weary, and perhaps ill, finally came to the magnanimous decision to abdicate his see and thus open the way to election of a third party. A homily Gregory delivered before the council informs us in vibrant and emotional tones of his decision, while reflecting a sense of discriminating tact as well as disappointment. While presenting in his address a last public declaration of his belief in the full divinity of the three persons in the Trinity, Gregory bade an extremely touching farewell to his flock, his cathedral, and his episcopal throne:

> Farewell ye Apostles, noble settlers here, my masters in the strife [probably referring to the Apostles' relics in the Church of the Holy Apostles]. . . . Farewell mighty Christ-loving City. . . . Farewell, East and West, for whom and against whom I have had to fight. . . . Last of all and most of all, I will cry . . . farewell ye Angels, guardians of this church, and of my presence and pilgrimage, since our affairs are in the hands of God. Farewell, O Trinity, my meditation and my glory. Mayest Thou be preserved by those who are here, and preserve them, my people. . . .[25]

22. For the text of Gregory the Theologian's oration given on the arrival of the Egyptians see vol. 7 of *Nicene and Post-Nicene Fathers* (New York, 1894), 334–37.

23. On canon 15, see Schroeder, *Disciplinary Decrees,* 44–46.

24. See Jedin, *Imperial Centuries,* 62f.; and J. Quasten, *Patrology* (Utrecht, 1966), 3:237–38.

25. See translation of Gregory's oration "The Last Farewell," in *Nicene and Post-Nicene Fathers* 7:385–95, esp. 394.

After this solemn farewell, so full of pathos, Gregory left Constantinople to return to Nazianzus in Asia Minor, where he lived until his death.

The sensational abdication of Gregory and the rejection of Maximos, the Alexandrian candidate for the see of Constantinople, now constrained the council Fathers to look for a person acceptable to all. Finally selected was an unknown, the layman Nectarius, a senator from Tarsus who, despite some slight opposition, was duly consecrated bishop of Constantinople.[26]

The council's attention now turned to the most critical point of business, the theological doctrine of the Holy Spirit. In the Nicene confession of faith, the Holy Spirit had been mentioned only once, and in vague and general terms. Thus after a declaration of belief in the divinity and consubstantiality of the Father and Son, the simple phrase "And in the Holy Spirit," had been included at Nicaea.[27] Theodosius, as seems implied by all three historians who discuss the council at Constantinople, Socrates, Sozomenus, and Theodoretos, worked behind the scenes to win over the Pneumatomachians (literally, the "fighters against the Holy Spirit") to belief in the divinity of the Father, Son, *and* Holy Spirit.[28] But despite imperial efforts and those of the Orthodox majority, all attempts to convert the Pneumatomachians failed and they left the council. As they departed, we are told, they warned the others not to cede to the dogma of the *homoousion* with respect to the Holy Spirit.[29]

As A. von Harnack puts it, "One is surprised to observe the strange obstinacy of those who, after admitting the divinity of the Son, opposed with so much tenacity that of the Holy Spirit."[30] The Macedonians found

26. On Nectarius's election, see Sozomenus, *Ecclesiastical History,* 7.8 in MPG, vol. 67. Cf. Jedin, *Imperial Centuries,* 71; and de Urbina, *Nicée,* 179, who says Nectarius was then a senator from Tarsus.

27. The creed of Nicaea reads: "We believe in one God, the Father Almighty, maker of all things visible and invisible; and in one Lord Jesus Christ, the Son of God, begotten from the Father, only-begotten, that is, from the substance of the Father, God from God, light from light, true God from true God, begotten not made. . . . And in the Holy Spirit. . . ."

28. See Jedin, *Imperial Centuries,* 71, who cites references from the Greek church historians

29. Ibid., 71. It is to be noted that Sozomenus and Socrates place the negotiations with the Macedonians *before* the beginning of the synod. Yet they limit the opposition of the Macedonians (only) to the *homoousios* of Nicaea, though Gregory the Theologian, *Carmen de vita sua,* in MPG, vol. 37, 1739–77, denies this. Cf. J. N. Kelly, *Early Church Creeds* (London, 1972), 327, citing Ritter, who believes the initiative for the negotiations with the Macedonians and for the planning of the line to be followed lay with Theodosius.

30. A. von Harnack, *History of Dogma,* trans. N. Buchanan (New York, 1961), 4:117–20.

it difficult to conceive of a Trinity of persons in the Godhead all of equal dignity, not to speak of the Holy Spirit as of the same substance *(homoousion)* with the Father and Son. To the Macedonians, one might say, the Godhead seemed almost binitarian. Their view of the Holy Spirit, in a sense, paralleled the view of Arius in the earlier period that Christ was a third something, a tertium quid, between God and Man. Thus, analogously, the Pneumatomachians conceived of the Holy Spirit as a creature, a kind of super-angel created in time by the Son.

It was primarily as a result of the insistent hammering of St. Basil in his discourses *On the Holy Spirit* and *Against Eunomius,* and perhaps even more of Gregory the Theologian's celebrated *Five Theological Orations on the Trinity* (composed just before the council in the summer or fall of 380), that the third member of the Trinity was finally recognized as having full divinity and consubstantiality coeternally with the other two members of the Trinity.[31] The key to the solution was in the Cappadocian exegesis (particularly of Patriarch Gregory) which, following St. John, explained the origin of the Holy Spirit in terms of "procession" *(ekporeusis)* or of "sending forth" *(ekpempsis),* rather than in terms of being begotten. This means that the Son and Holy Spirit, though both *homoousioi* with the Father, are related to him in a different way, the first being *begotten* of the Father, the second *proceeding* from him.[32]

After apparently little more than two months, certainly not an excessive time for discussion, the assembly promulgated a dogmatic *tomos,* that is, a creed. In this the Fathers would ratify and complete in greater detail the Symbol of Nicaea. This symbol, according to Greek Orthodox tradition, is the one today called the Nicene- Constantinopolitan Creed. (It should be noted, however, that modern scholarly discussion on the background and the date of the text of this creed has not yet reached full agreement; see discussion below.)[33]

After this the Fathers at Constantinople occupied themselves, it seems, with juridical questions, that is, the drawing up of canons (which I shall discuss shortly). The council ended its deliberations on 9 July 381. Before dismissal, its members wrote a synodical letter to Theodosius,

31. See St. Basil, *On the Holy Spirit,* 2–50; and *Against Eunomius* in MPG, vol. 29, cols. 497–669. Also n. 46 below.

32. Gregory says the distinctive characteristics of the three divine persons are *agennēsia, gennēsis,* and *ekporeusis* (or *ekpempsis*) (*Oration* 25.16; *Oration* 26.19). He also says, "The proper name of the unoriginate is Father; and that of the unoriginately begotten is Son; and that of the unbegottenly proceeding or going forth is the Holy Spirit" (*Oration* 30.19). Gregory is fully aware he contributed the term "procession."

33. On this difficult question see especially the best and most recent summary and explanation in Kelly, *Creeds,* 289ff., and passim. Also Jedin, *Imperial Centuries,* 71–72. The earlier views, especially of Harnack and others, are now not accepted.

thanking God and his instrument the emperor for procuring peace in the church and preserving the integrity of the faith. Then, to quote from the letter, "with a unanimous heart, and confessing the faith of Nicaea and condemning its opponents" they begged the emperor to ratify their deliberations.[34] Subsequently, on 30 July 381, the emperor issued an official decree to the Eastern churches directing that whatever churches remained to the Arians be turned over to the Orthodox. He also specified who were to be considered Orthodox: "Those in communion with Bishop Nectarius of Constantinople, Timothy of Alexandria, Diodoros of Tarsus, Amphilochius of Iconium, Gregory of Nyssa, etc."[35]

Now that we have reconstructed the proceedings of the council in the order in which they seem to have occurred, let us turn more specifically to the creed of Constantinople. At the second session of the Fourth Ecumenical Council at Chalcedon, held seventy years later in 451, and whose acts and deliberations serve to cast a little much-needed light on the Council of Constantinople, the imperial commissioners representing Emperor Marcian insisted that the assembled Fathers compose a formula of faith to combat the growing heresies on Christology, that is, on the relationship of the divine and human natures in Christ. The bishops then read the symbol formulated at the Council of Nicaea. But at the insistence and initiation, it might be noted, of the imperial commissioners, they then read, publicly, another symbol, which they attributed to the council "of the 150 bishops of Constantinople."[36] Later at the fifth session of Chalcedon, the symbol of Constantinople was again read, in order it seems, to give the creed an ecumenical validity. And in fact it was these official readings at the undeniably ecumenical Fourth Council at Chalcedon which served thereafter to grant the rank of ecumenicity to the Council of 381.[37]

But why did the imperial commissioners insist on the reading of the creed of Constantinople, especially in the light of the prescription of the Council of Ephesus held in 431 that nothing could be added to the creed of Nicaea? (Ephesus, incidentally, said nothing about the Council of

34. See Kelly, *Creeds,* 331. Also J. Lebon, "Les anciens symboles dans la définition de Chalcédoine," in *Revue d'histoire ecclésiastique* 32 (1936): 860.

35. See *The Theodosian Code,* 16.1.3.

36. See summary in Kelly, *Creeds,* 313–31, esp. 316 (based on A. M. Ritter, *Das Konzil von Konstantinopel und sein Symbol* (Göttingen, 1965) 322–31. The Fathers at the Council did not see themselves as promulgating a new creed; they simply hoped to *confirm* the Nicene faith. Ritter stresses that, however paradoxical it seems to us, they really adopted a different formula from Nicaea, but we should recall that at that time importance was attached to the Nicene *teaching* rather than to the *literal wording* of Nicaea (Kelly, *Creeds,* 325).

37. See esp. Jedin, *Imperial Centuries,* 76–78. This is the common view.

Constantinople.) The imperial representatives (who apparently had obtained a copy of the creed from the imperial archives) must have realized that, since Nicaea had in the end successfully prevailed over the views of the heretic Arius, and the Council of Constantinople had succeeded in destroying the party of the Macedonians, conciliar acceptance of the Nicene-Constantinopolitan creed would be the most effective way to insure doctrinal unity on the Trinity before moving to consideration of the difficult Christological problem, now the chief point of dogmatic controversy.

Though at Chalcedon the symbol of Constantinople was read twice—and there is no record any of the Fathers present seriously questioned its derivation from the Council of Constantinople—certain modern critics, notably Harnack, G. Bardy, and F. J. Hort have maintained that it does not truly belong to Constantinople.[38] The most recent and persuasive scholarly opinion, however, that of A. Ritter, followed by J. Kelly, now accepts that the symbol was indeed approved at the Council of Constantinople, although it almost certainly did not originate there. The principal reason for this view is, as first shown by Ch. Papadopoulos, that a symbol almost literally identical with what we term that of Constantinople is quoted at the end of the treatise *Ankoratos* of St. Epiphanius of Cyprus, dated 374, that is seven years *before* the Council of Constantinople.[39] Epiphanius was not at the Council of Constantinople, but his fellow bishops from Cyprus could easily have brought his creed with them.[40] Moreover, a close examination of the symbol of Constantinople shows it also to be the baptismal symbol of the Church of Jerusalem, which St. Cyril of Jerusalem, who was at the council, had been employing as the basis for his *catecheseis* or manuals for religious instruction.[41]

There are, in addition, certain repeated references, if only hints, in the sources before 451 to the existence of the symbol of Constantinople and especially to the amplifications it made to the creed of Nicaea, for example, in Gregory the Theologian's famous autobiographical poem *Carmen de vita sua,* written after his abdication.[42] Clearer is a passage from the *Tenth Catechetical Homily* of Theodore of Mopsuestia (d. 428), a pupil of Bishop Diodoros of Tarsus, who was present at the Council of

38. See, e.g., A. von Harnack in *Revue ecclésiastique,* 3d. ed , vol. 11, pp. 12–28; also F. J. Hort, *Two Dissertations* (Cambridge, 1876), 54–72. On all these see Kelly, *Creeds,* esp. 313–22.

39. Ch. Papadopoulos, *Das Symbol der 2. ökumenischen Synode* (Athens, 1924).

40. Jedin, *Imperial Centuries,* 72; de Urbina, *Nicée,* 187.

41. Jedin, *Imperial Centuries,* 73–74; and Kelly, *Creeds,* 304f.

42. Gregory the Theologian, *Carmen de vita sua* (in Greek), MPG, vol. 37, cols. 1148ff.

Constantinople. This passage states that at Nicaea the bishops were content to provide a symbol that dealt with the first two persons of the Trinity, but that "the Fathers who came after them [meaning of the Council of Constantinople] transmitted a *complete* doctrine of the third person, the Holy Spirit" (emphasis added). Theodore in fact enumerates certain additions to the Nicene symbol made at Constantinople: the phrase "which [the Holy Spirit] proceeds from the Father," mention of "one holy catholic Church" and "remission of sins," and the phrase "resurrection of the dead and the life of the world to come."[43]

An analysis of the text of the symbol of Constantinople reveals that the symbol of Nicaea was left intact but that amplifications were made in the first, second, and, above all, the third article. The additions to the first and second articles, such as "maker of heaven and earth," "eternally begotten," and "by the power of the Holy Spirit he was born of the Virgin Mary and became man," are found in other formulas and texts and are therefore not new creations of the Council of Constantinople.[44] What makes the creed of Constantinople so important, however, are the new statements—merely amplifications, the Fathers considered them—included in the third article, where the simple phrase in the Nicene symbol "And [we believe] in the Holy Spirit" in the symbol of Constantinople is elaborated to read, "The Lord and giver of life, who proceeds from the Father, who with the Father and the Son spoke through the prophets."[45]

The question of the divinity of the third person, the Holy Spirit in the Trinity, had very early been raised by Origen. But it was saints Basil and Gregory the Theologian who wrote most authoritatively on the Holy Spirit, in order above all to show its divinity and consubstantiality with the Father and the Son. Basil showed that certain passages in the New Testament using the term "Lord" *(Kyrios)* refer specifically to the Holy Spirit.[46] And Gregory of Constantinople, in his *Fifth Theological Oration,* systematically listed all the various divine names applied in the New Testament to the Holy Spirit, concluding that the Holy Spirit must be divine. As he put it, "He is not a creature nor an angel." To answer the

43. Theodore of Mopsuestia, *Homélies catéchetiques 9 et 10,* ed. Tonneau R. Devreese (Rome, 1949), 215ff. Also see Jedin, *Imperial Centuries,* 72; and Kelly, *Creeds,* 321.

44. See de Urbina, *Nicée,* 214–17; also Kelly, *Creeds,* 323ff.

45. Kelly, *Creeds,* 298ff.

46. See St. Basil, *On the Holy Spirit,* chap. 21. Basil refers to Paul's Letter to the Thessalonians (2 Thess. 3.5): "May the Lord direct your hearts to the love of God and the steadfastness of Christ." See also Corinthians 3.17. Also John 15.26: "But when the counselor comes, whom I shall send to you from the Father, even the Spirit of truth who proceeds from the Father, he will bear witness to me." Also John 14.26: "But the counselor, the Holy Spirit whom the Father will send in my name."

Macedonian view that the Holy Spirit is a creature made by the Son, the symbol of Constantinople quoted from St. John (15.26) affirming that the Holy Spirit, "proceeds from the Father." The Father, of course, is divine.

Gregory's opponents (in order to oppose the divinity and *homoousion* of the Holy Spirit) had proposed the following syllogism:

> Either the Holy Spirit is altogether unbegotten, or else it is begotten. If it is unbegotten, there are two unoriginates. If it is begotten, you must make a further subdivision. It is so either by the Father or by the Son. And if by the Father, there are two sons, and they are brothers. And you may make them twins if you like. . . . But if by the Son, then such a one will say we get a glimpse of a grandson God, than which nothing could be more absurd.

Combating the view that there is no mean between begotten and unbegotten, Gregory adduces a key term to identify the distinctive property of the Holy Spirit, namely, procession or sending forth. And this he bases on the New Testament, John 15.26, the passage just cited, affirming that the Holy Spirit "proceeds from the Father." As Gregory asked his opponents: "Tell me what position will you assign to that which proceeds? . . . Or perhaps you have taken that word out of your Gospels for the sake of your third Testament, the Holy Ghost, which proceeds from the Father; who, inasmuch as he proceeds from that source, is no creature."[47]

Gregory also employs the term *agennēsia* (unbegottenness or innascibility) to refer to a basic property of the Father in the Trinity. Saying that if his interlocutor can explain the mystery of the *agennēsia* of the Father,

> I [Gregory] will explain to you the physiology of the generation of the Son and the procession of the Spirit. And we shall, both of us, be frenzy-stricken for prying into the mystery of God. And who are we to do these things, we who cannot even see what lies at our feet, or number the sand of the sea, or the drops of rain, or the days of eternity, much less enter into the depths of God and supply an account of that nature which is so unspeakable and transcending all words.[48]

Here, I believe, is one of the supreme expressions of the ineffability and incomprehensibility of God the Father, the Son, and the Holy Spirit in all of Christian literature.

47. See Gregory's *Oration* no. 2 in *Nicene and Post-Nicene Fathers* 7:319–20.
48. Ibid., 320.

In the same *Fifth Oration* Gregory totally rejects the Pneumatomachian view that the Holy Spirit, to be God, should have been the Son. According to the Macedonians, "If he is not [the Son], how can he be consubstantial with the Father?" Gregory cites here the example of Adam, Eve, and Seth. Eve was a fragment of Adam, and Seth was begotten of both Adam and Eve, but all three are of the very same substance.[49] This, I believe, is less-convincing proof, since it argues from the analogy of the human to the divine.

From several other phrases or words incorporated in 381 into the creed of Nicaea we may determine still other points of discussion at the council on the divinity and consubstantiality of the Holy Spirit with Father and Son. The most decisive statement of all on the divinity of the Holy Spirit is probably the use of the Greek terms *symproskynoumenon* and *syndoxazomenon,* the first acknowledging that the Holy Spirit should be *worshipped,* or adored, along with the Father and Son; the second acknowledging that the same *doxa* (glory) should be rendered to Father, Son, *and* Holy Spirit.[50] As Basil put it, "Glory to the Father with the Son and the Holy Spirit."[51] Basil thus disputes those who deny to the Holy Spirit the worship and the glory, urging that in the adoration the Holy Spirit is inseparable from the Father and Son.

Since the time of Cyril of Jerusalem, Orthodox theology had fought for inclusion of the Holy Spirit in the doxology (the glorification) as a ritual liturgical formula. The approval and inclusion of the Holy Spirit in the adoration and glorification equally with the Father and Son would be in effect equivalent to profession of the consubstantiality of the Holy Spirit with the Father and Son.[52] The defenders of adoration equally for the Holy Spirit were supported by certain early baptismal formulas and by New Testament texts which justified liturgical usage glorifying the three members of the Trinity in the same doxology.[53] Gregory the Theologian, in still another passage of his *On the Holy Spirit,* wrote: "The Old Testament proclaimed the Father openly and the Son more obscurely. The New manifested the Son and suggested the deity of the Spirit. Now the Spirit himself dwells among us and supplies us with a clearer demonstration of himself."[54]

Still another phrase incorporated into the Creed of Constantinople

49. Ibid., 321.

50. On these terms and their use see discussion in Kelly, *Creeds,* 322–23; Jedin, *Imperial Centuries,* 73–74; and de Urbina, *Nicée,* 199–203.

51. St. Basil, *On the Holy Spirit,* chap. 24, pp. 35–36.

52. Jedin, *Imperial Centuries,* 74.

53. Ibid.

54. Gregory the Theologian, *On the Holy Spirit,* 326.

was one derived from the Old Testament: "The Holy Spirit spoke through the prophets."[55] Already St. Athanasius, in his third letter to Serapion, affirmed (and this text was doubtless quoted at the synod): "The Spirit is so inseparable from the Son that what we have said before does not permit us to doubt it. . . . The Father himself makes and gives all through the Son in the Spirit."[56]

Why was the term *homoousion* not explicitly adopted for the Holy Spirit in the symbol of 381? One modern critic surmises that the Orthodox majority at Constantinople hoped thereby to render the Macedonians better disposed to union by means of an argument closer to Scripture.[57] This theory, of course, would imply discussion of the symbol *before* the departure of the Macedonian faction from the council. Even more important, why did the doctrine on the divinity and also the consubstantiality of the Holy Spirit with Father and Son, even if not explicitly stated in the symbol, nevertheless prevail at the council, as is clearly implied by the council's first canon anathematizing the Macedonians, and also by the unequivocal phrase of the subsequent synod of 382 in Constantinople, "one divinity, power, and substance of the Father, Son *and* Holy Spirit"?[58]

We now come to the question of the canons of the Council of 381: How many were actually promulgated? The Greek tradition, the canonists Balsamon and Zonaras in particular, usually attribute seven to the council.[59] Western canonists, on the other hand, include only four, affirming that canons 5 and 6 came from the synod of Constantinople of 382 and canon 7 from the mid fifth century.[60] Here I shall discuss only the more important first four canons.

The first canon states that the confession of faith of the 318 Fathers assembled at Nicaea should not be abolished but is to remain in force, and that every heresy is to be anathematized, especially that of the Eunomaeans or Anomaeans, the Arians or Eudoxians, and the Semi-Arians, a term which then seems to have embraced all those who, without necessarily being Arian, at bottom were not in accord with Nicaea.[61] The

55. Jedin, *Imperial Centuries,* 74; and esp. de Urbina, *Nicée,* 203.

56. Athanasius, *Epistle to Serapion,* 1.31, in MPG, vol. 26. Cf. de Urbina, *Nicée,* 203.

57. See Jedin, *Imperial Centuries,* 74.

58. Cited ibid. See above, n. 29, on whether the creed was discussed before the Macedonians' departure from the synod.

59. I. Karmires, *Ta dogmatika kai symbolika mnēmeia,* vol. 1 (Athens, 1960), 132–33. Cf. de Urbina, *Nicée,* 206; Stephanides, *Ekklēsiastikē historia,* 182.

60. Jedin, *Imperial Centuries,* 75–76; also Schroeder, *Disciplinary Decrees,* 63–68.

61. Canon cited in Schroeder, *Disciplinary Decrees,* 63. For all four canons quoted see Ch. Hefele, *History of the Councils of the Church,* trans. H. Oxenham (Edinburgh, 1876),

Pneumatomachians, who denied the divinity of the Holy Spirit while admitting that of the Son, had from 360 onward left the ranks of Semi-Arians. In these anathematizations we see vividly, though briefly, the many types of Trinitarian heresies derived largely from Arianism that had emerged between the time of the Nicene Creed and the Council of Constantinople, along with mention of the first Christological heresy, Apollinarianism. The belief of Apollinarius of Laodicea, originally an ardent defender of Nicaea, that in the Incarnation the Logos did not assume the principal part of man, the rational soul, scandalized the Antiochenes and in a real sense paved the way for Monophysitism.[62]

Canon 2 has to do with ecclesiastical organization in the Eastern part of the empire and decrees that the affairs of each ecclesiastical province are to be dealt with by its provincial synod. In other words, bishops should not leave their dioceses to interfere in the affairs of other churches. Note that the term "dioceses" as used here means an administrative group of various provinces following the civil organization of the empire introduced earlier by Diocletian. This canon enumerates the civil dioceses in the East, with the ecclesiastical diocese closely following the civil: Thrace with its capital at Heraclea, now displaced by Constantinople; Asia with its capital at Ephesus; Pontus with capital at Caesarea of Cappadocia; the Orient with capital at Antioch; and Egypt centered in Alexandria.[63] Clearly, in this canon the council intended to censure the conduct of Alexandria, which, long considering itself first in the East, was continually interfering in the affairs of other Eastern dioceses. The belief that this canon was not directed at Rome is probably correct, although it cannot be said with certainty that this canon does not reflect Eastern objection to interference by Rome in affairs of the Eastern churches.[64]

Canon 3 is without doubt the most important decree of the council, certainly regarding the church of Constantinople. Its text states simply that "the Bishop of Constantinople shall have the primacy of honor *[presveia timēs]* after the Bishop of Rome, for their city is the New Rome." This canon may well reflect, not only the attitude of Constantinople's clergy,[65] but above all the attitude of Emperor Theodosius, who,

2:353–69. Note there that a distinction is made between Arians and Eunomaeans, and between Semi-Arians and the Pneumatomachians. Marcellus of Ancyra, originally a strong supporter of the Nicene creed, now believed God was of one *person* (one *hypostasis*) only.

62. On Apollinarius, see Stephanides, *Ekklēsiastikē historia,* 191–92.

63. Quoted in Schroeder, *Disciplinary Decrees,* 64; and Jedin, *Imperial Centuries,* 75.

64. Cf. Schroeder, *Disciplinary Decrees,* 64–65.

65. Ibid., 65–67.

full of admiration for his new capital and again in imitation of Constantine, had definitely fixed the seat of his government in Constantinople, in contrast to his immediate predecessors, who were absent for long periods in Antioch.[66] Theodosius must have seen the advantages accruing to an emperor resident in Constantinople of having a Constantinoplitan ecclesiastical primacy in the East, even if only of honor. Such a development could avoid seeing Constantinople fall again into the hands of heretics like the Arians and also lessen the disorders that plagued relations between Alexandria and Antioch.

Constantinople had now truly become a second Rome, with splendid buildings, a senate, and the imperial court in residence. Echoes of such considerations are found in the farewell sermon of Gregory of Constantinople delivered just before his abdication. He calls Constantinople the "eye of the universe *[oikoumenē]*, a city very powerful on sea and land, which is, as it were, the link between the Eastern and Western shores, in which the extremities of the world from every side meet together, and from which, as the common mart of the faith, they take their rise."[67]

Instead of reflecting primarily, as some historians affirm, the ambition of Constantinople's bishop to surpass Alexandria (and Antioch), would it not seem more accurate to affirm that the naming of Constantinople as first in honor after Rome because it is the second Rome was basically to recognize the realities of the political situation and to transfer them to the ecclesiastical sphere—that is, in accordance with the old so-called theory of accommodation?[68] One may cite as a precedent for thinking of this kind, besides canon 4 of Nicaea, canon 9 of the synod of Antioch of 341, a largely Semi-Arian conciliabulum, to be sure, but at which it was specified that "the dignity of an episcopal see is according to the political rank of a city."[69]

Canon 4, of less importance, asserted the invalidity of the consecration of Maximos, the candidate supported by Alexandria to the see of Constantinople.[70] To be noted is that both Alexandria and Rome soon repudiated Maximos and accepted Nectarius as legitimate bishop of

66. See Jedin, *Imperial Centuries,* 75–76.

67. Gregory the Theologian, "The Last Farewell," 394–95.

68. On *accomodatio,* see esp. Dvornik, *Byzantium and the Roman Primacy,* 29–31. Dvornik, 31, stresses that Rome itself had previously accepted canon 4 of Nicaea, that ecclesiastical organization be modeled on political organization. See also Jedin, *Imperial Centuries,* 74: "In this canon one can hardly discover any anti-Roman spite."

69. Karmires, *Mnēmeia* 1:113.

70. See Schroeder, *Disciplinary Decrees,* esp. 67–68. Cf. Lübeck, *Die Weihe d. Cynikers Maximus zum Bischof von Konstantinopel in ihrer Veranlassung dargestellt* (Fulda, 1907); and C. Ullmann, *Gregorius von Nazianz der Theologe* (Gotha, 1866), 137–42.

Constantinople. Nevertheless, this canon clearly served as a rebuke to Alexandria and, though certainly to a lesser extent, Rome.[71]

The ecumenical character of the Council of Constantinople, as noted, was not officially recognized by the entire Church, West and East, until the Council of Chalcedon in 451. To be sure, the Fathers of the synod convoked in Constantinople in 382 (at which virtually the same Fathers assembled as in 381),[72] in the letter they sent to Pope Damasus communicating the results of the Council of 381, refer explicitly to "the creed promulgated for greater clarity one year before at Constantinople by the ecumenical council."[73] But, as noted earlier, the term ecumenical as used here is to be taken in the restricted sense of the eastern, Greek *ecumenē.* As for the Third Ecumenical Council at Ephesus in 431, it made no reference whatsoever to the Council of 381. It was, then, the public reading of the symbol of Constantinople at Chalcedon that served primarily to render the Council of Constantinople ecumenical. The final seal of ecumenicity for both East and West, however, was placed on the council by Emperor Justinian's prominent mention of Constantinople in his edict as one of "the Four Ecumenical Councils."[74]

True, Pope Damasus, on the grounds he was not officially informed of the canons of the Council of Constantinople, refused at first to ratify the acts of the council. But after Chalcedon, Constantinople's symbol was accepted by Rome as well as the East, though the West continued for centuries to refuse to ratify the canons. Thus, Pope Gregory the Great, at the end of the sixth century, while refusing to acknowledge the canons, did accept the symbol of Constantinople and the council itself as one of the "Four Ecumenical Councils," comparing them to the four Gospels of the Church.[75] Only in 1215 did Rome finally accept the validity of the third canon of Constantinople, but by that time Constantinople had been conquered by the West and a Latin patriarch presided over the see of Constantinople.[76]

71. Catholic historians do not view it as a rebuke to Rome: see Schroeder, *Disciplinary Decrees,* 65–67.

72. Obviously the 36 Macedonian Fathers were absent, as were a few others. The synod of 382 was evidently called primarily to resolve the schism of Antioch. Rome, immediately after the Council of 381 (and before 382), called for a synod to meet, but the East rejected this.

73. Jedin, *Imperial Centuries,* 77, citing Theodoretos, *Historia ecclesiastica,* 5.9, 13, 15.

74. Edict (Novel 132, 1) cited in Jedin, *Imperial Centuries,* 77 n. 91. Cf. Harnack, *History of Dogma,* 217.

75. Jedin, *Imperial Centuries,* 77 (Ep. 4.25).

76. Mansi, vol. 22, cols. 989–92 (de Urbina, *Nicée,* 237). On Latin Constantinople see Geanakoplos, *Byzantium: Church, Society and Civilization,* nos. 154–55.

The famous canon 28 of the Council of Chalcedon was undoubtedly a restatement and further development of the third canon of Constantinople. But canon 28, besides again affirming the place of honor to Constantinople after Rome, secured to Constantinople also the right to consecrate the exarchs (chief bishops) of the diocesan capitals of Ephesus in Asia, of Caesarea of Cappadocia in Pontus, and of Thrace, of which Constantinople was now the primatial see, a circumstance which gave Constantinople jurisdiction over Thrace and most of Asia Minor.[77] Canon 28 of Chalcedon, then, reflected even further the theory of accommodation of the ecclesiastical structure of the church to the political organization of the empire. It should be stressed that accommodation did not begin in 381. As Father Dvornik has convincingly and temperately shown in his *Byzantium and the Roman Primacy,* "accomodatio" as distinguished from the concept of "apostolicity" began earlier at the time of the apostles themselves and continued under Constantine the Great. Therefore, at the councils of Constantinople and Chalcedon, it was simply a recognition that, politically, Constantinople had become the capital, at least in the East, of the Roman Empire.[78]

To conclude: the Council of Constantinople thus ratified and completed the Creed of Nicaea by defining the precise relationship of the Holy Spirit to the Father and Son in the Trinity. Though the creed itself did not explicitly employ the term *homoousion,* it implicitly rejected the view of the Macedonians, who refused to admit the divinity and consubstantiality of the Holy Spirit with Father and Son. Moreover, the Macedonians were categorically anathematized as heretics by the first canon of that council. Why were the 150 Fathers of Constantinople able to succeed so well in their work of elaborating on the Nicene Creed and condemning Macedonianism? Besides the importance of the role of the Nicene emperor Theodosius, the council's success, in contrast to the turmoil of Nicaea and especially that of the many post-Nicene local synods, was, I think, in

77. For canon 28 see Schroeder, *Disciplinary Decrees* p. 25: "And [we decree] therefore that in the dioceses of Pontos, Asia, Thrace, the metropolitans only . . . shall be ordained by the aforesaid most holy see of the most holy church at Constantinople . . . but the metropolitans of the aforesaid dioceses, as has been said, shall be ordained by the archbishop of Constantinople after the proper elections have been held according to custom and reported to him."

78. See the Catholic writer Dvornik, *Byzantium and the Roman Primacy,* 47–51: "Canon 3 merely brings conformity to a practice *(accomodatio)* all had accepted as regular." "The Pope was angered at canon 28 of Chalcedon because in it no mention was made of the Apostolicity or the Petrine character of Rome." Canon 28 text in Karmires, *Mnēmeia,* 176. Cf. Schroeder, *Disciplinary Decrees,* 126 esp., which says (as the Roman church believes) that by canon 28 Constantinople "was granted the rights and privileges of a patriarch in violation of canonical prescriptions."

large measure owing to the more homogeneous theology and the commonly understood terminology of the assembled Fathers. They perceived not only a clear distinction between the terms *ousia* (essence) and *hypostasis* (person) but also, now especially, a clear distinction between the generation of the Son and the procession of the Holy Spirit from the Father. The great Cappadocian Fathers Basil, Gregory the Theologian, and Gregory of Nyssa had done their work well.

It should be noted that the East, with its emphasis on the monarchy of the Father as the root of the Trinity, accepted this definition as meaning the Holy Spirit proceeds from the Father *alone* (a word, however, not expressed in the creed). Indeed, Basil and Gregory of Nyssa, in order evidently to stress the intratrinitarian unity of the Trinity even further, seemed sometimes to prefer the formula "from the Father *through* the Son." Athanasius implies something similar, it seems, in his third letter to Serapion, which had said, "The Father himself makes and gives all *through* the Son in the Spirit."[79] And at the famous Council of Florence in 1439 over a millennium later, both Greeks and Latins accepted that the Holy Spirit proceeds from the Father through the Son.[80] The West, on the other hand, at least some Fathers at Constantinople in 381 and especially later, by placing the emphasis rather on the equality of the three persons in the Trinity, each partaking of the same divine essence, drew the implication that the Holy Spirit proceeds from the Father *and* the Son *(filioque).* This term was first added to the creed and recited in the Mozarabic liturgy of late sixth-century Spain.[81] But addition of this term, according to the Greek church, would imply two *archai* or root sources for the Trinity.

Thus, the Second Ecumenical Council at Constantinople had the honor of ratifying and completing the creed of Nicaea, which, after the Council of Chalcedon and under the name of the Nicene-Constantinopolitan symbol, henceforth became the standard creed for all of Christendom. At the same time, the Council of Constantinople, by raising Constantinople to a position second to Rome in honor, exalted it above the other Eastern sees, especially Alexandria, and thus constituted the first important step in the emergence and development of the patriarchate of Constantinople, whose patriarch, in the late sixth century, adopted the title "ecumenical."[82] In retrospect, the Council of Constan-

79. See St. Basil, *On the Spirit,* 1–3; Gregory, *Oration* 5.12, 28; and St. Athanasius, *Epistle to Serapion* 1.31 (cf. de Urbina, *Nicée,* 202).

80. See J. Gill, *The Council of Florence* (Cambridge, 1959), 258ff.; and essay 11 below.

81. Stephanides, *Ekklēsiastikē historia,* 244; Harnack, *History of Dogma,* 447.

82. On the title ecumenical (but referring essentially only to the Byzantine East) see Dvornik, *Byzantium and the Roman Primacy,* 80.

tinople, by elevating Constantinople to second place immediately behind Rome in the Church, may be said to have sowed the seed, if unwittingly, for the later rivalry between Rome and Constantinople, which, little by little, developed into the "Great Schism," so tragic for the relations between Eastern and Western Christendom.

Additional Bibliography for Essay 7

K. Bonis, *Gregorios ho theologos patriarchēs Konstantinoupoleōs (329–25 January 390/1)* (Athens, 1982). W. Eborowicz, "La procession du St. Esprit d'après de IIe concile oecuménique de 381, dans le cadre du magistère et de la théologie de l'époque," *Lateranum* 47 (1981): 380–412. P. L'Huillier, "Faits et fiction à propos du deuxième concile oecuménique," *Eglise et théologie* 13 (1982): 135–56. D. Constantelos, "Toward the Convocation of the Second Ecumenical Council," *Greek Orthodox Theological Review* 27 (1983): 395–405, surveying conditions immediately preceding the council. G. Ettlinger, "The Holy Spirit in the Theology of the Second Ecumenical Council and in the Undivided Church," *Greek Orthodox Theological Review* 27 (1983): 431–40. The last two articles were read at the Union Theological Seminary together with the present essay. T. Zisis, "He B' Oikoumenikē Synodos kai hē Trias tōn proedrōn autēs (Meletios Antiocheias, Grēgorios Theologos, Nektarios Konstantinoupoleōs)," *Epistēmonikē epetērida theologikēs scholēs* 26 (1984): 447–60.

Eight

The Byzantine Recovery of Constantinople from the Latins in 1261: A Chrysobull of Michael VIII Palaeologus in Favor of Hagia Sophia

In 1261, after fifty-seven years of Latin occupation, the Byzantine capital of Constantinople was reconquered from the Latins by Emperor Michael VIII Palaeologus. Among the many pressing political and administrative tasks facing the emperor after return of the seat of empire and church from Nicaea to the Bosporus was the restoration or grant to the church of revenues and lands for its subsistence and support. The document with which this study is concerned is a chrysobull (imperial edict) issued by Michael VIII in favor of the Great Church of Hagia Sophia. The document's significance lies in part in its explicit, detailed enumeration of properties and privileges granted to Hagia Sophia and to the patriarch Joseph.[1] The section of the document which provides this particular information has already been analyzed by H. Ahrweiler in an essay

1. Document printed first (in Greek) by J. Sakellion, "Hison Khrysoboullou Mikhaēl H' Palaiologou gegonotos tēi megalēi tou Theou Ekklēsiāi epi tois dōrētheisin autēi Ktēmasin (1272)," *Pandora* 15 (1864): 27–32; rpt. in J. Zepos and P. Zepos, *Jus graecoromanum,* vol. 1 (Athens, 1931), 659–66. Not mentioned in V. Grumel, *Les regestes des actes du patriarcat de Constantinople, 1208–1309* (Paris, 1972). Dated 1272 by Sakellion and Zepos. All references to the original text are to page and column number as in Sakellion.

discussing the geographical importance of areas in western Asia Minor, especially around Smyrna and Nicaea.[2] The remaining material, however, has been almost completely ignored by scholars—important material which describes how Michael restored churches, city walls, and buildings and, no less significant, which reflects the exultant mood in Constantinople at the restoration of the Queen City to the Greeks. Accordingly, this essay, while making some reference to the section of the chrysobull assigning privileges to the Great Church, will focus primarily on the neglected portions of the document which reflect not only Michael VIII's attitude to the Latin expulsion and the Greek restoration but also the feelings evoked among the Greek population as a whole.

Let me quote first from the *proemium,* which, I believe, reflects better than any other source the mood in the capital at the Greek restoration (the translation is mine):

> "Hail, hail indeed Daughter of Zion, rejoice daughter of Jerusalem. The Lord has redeemed you from your sins. He has released you from the hands of your enemies and you will suffer no more misfortunes. The Lord God will bring you joy and will renew *[kainizei]* you as on a feast day." These are the words of the admirable prophet Sophonius which of old he was joyously singing for the renewal of Zion when he foresaw the return of the Hebrews from Babylon and the release of Israel from the hands of its enemies, and announced that no further trials were any longer to be expected.

Especially meaningful here is the analogy drawn by Michael (an analogy used by other Byzantine sources of the period) between the Byzantines of 1261 and the Jews of the Babylonian exile. As Michael clearly implies, the period of the Byzantine exile in Nicaea was for the Greeks their Babylon, and like the Jews, after a period of atonement and renewal of the purity of their faith, they were now being led back in triumph from Nicaea to their Zion, Constantinople. The text continues:

> Our majesty, responding to these words and relating them to our own circumstances, will now appropriately set these forth as a *proemium* to this chrysobull. For it is now opportune that my reign chant joyfully the "rejoice" [*khaire,* of the liturgy] and the "exult"

2. H. Ahrweiler, "L'histoire et la géographie de la région de Smyrne entre les deux occupations turques (1081–1317) particulièrement du XIII siècle," *Travaux et mémoires* 1:57–58, esp. For summary of contents relating specifically to properties of Hagia Sophia see F. Dölger, *Regesten der Kaiserurkunden des oströmischen Reiches,* pt. 3 (Munich, 1932), 52, no. 1956.

> *[euphrainou]* to the Great Church of God, which takes precedence over other churches and is honored as the metropolis of the metropolises. . . . This discourse will refer to her [Constantinople] as the new Zion and the New Jerusalem, and will say appropriately about her . . . the Lord of all, the God of wonders has released her [Constantinople] from her sins and from the hands of her enemies. But now the sweet fragrance of the sacrifice of lambs and of the blood of calves, does not, as of old in the Temple of Old Zion, reach the Lord's nostrils, but, rather, through the true sacrifice of the lifegiving blood from the side of the spiritual calf [Christ], the only begotten Son of God. . . . This city has been delivered, not as were the Jews long ago from the hands of the Babylonians, but from the contemptible Italians, whose "nation" *[ethnos]* is worse than the Babylonian serpent *[drakōn]* because it [the Latin army] a long time ago crept against it [Constantinople] stealthily with the "windings" of their ships and, penetrating into the interior of its habitations [and] spreading itself through the dark places *[katadyseis]* of the city's quarters *[epauleōn],* it rendered desolate and destroyed everything it found which adorned the city.[3]

Note the striking image of the Latin forces Michael projects here—that of a serpent gradually uncoiling itself and spreading throughout all parts of Constantinople.

> Others have tragically lamented the extent and magnitude of the destruction. But today is a holiday and a festival because the city is again coming to life and being revived. And as God in his goodness has until now many times bestowed his favor on my reign in many matters, He now has proclaimed my reign to be the instrument of this restoration and renewal *[tou kainismou toutou kai tēs ananeōseōs tautēs].* Our Majesty has decided to spur on this renewal and restore not only the buildings of this New Zion, not only His church [Hagia Sophia] and the sacred vessels and holy objects *[epiplōn]* but also the estates and properties from which the yearly revenue is drawn for the sake of the things of God. Thus we have decided to issue this chrysobull in behalf of this church as a kind of renovation and renewal. For these rights, which it had previously

3. For these passages see text, p. 27, col. 1. The sentence referring to the sacrifice in the Temple of Jerusalem and the "life-giving blood of Christ" in Hagia Sophia and also that comparing the Latin army to the Babylonian serpent draw on the Book of Revelation.

been granted by emperors through edicts and chrysobulls, were lost to her through the things that happened during the Latin dynasty.[4]

The reference here at the end is of course to seizure of the patriarchal properties in 1204 by the Latin church. We know that the Latins made considerable changes in the Byzantine ecclesiastical structure, for example, substituting Latin prelates for recalcitrant Greeks and reducing the total number of Byzantine episcopal sees by combining two or more bishoprics in order to produce increased revenues for each newly installed Catholic prelate.[5] Moreover, owing to differences in the Greek and Latin ecclesiastical rites, certain changes must inevitably have been made by the Western clergy in the internal decoration of Hagia Sophia and also in the composition of the clerical staff of the cathedral.[6] Such

4. See text, p. 27, col. 2. This passage on the revivification of Constantinople may be compared to Michael's own description in his "Typikon for the Monastery of St. Michael" published in A. Dmitrievskii, *Opisanie liturgiceskih rukopisej,* vol. 1, pt. 1, *Typika* (Kiev, 1895), 771, where Michael implies that the most immediately visible sign of the Greek restoration was that "in Constantinople there is no longer heard the confused tongue [broken Greek] spoken by a half-barbarian people [the Latins] but that of the Greek population now spoken correctly by all." For other examples of the explosion of popular Greek jubilation at the capital's recovery see George Acropolites, *Historia* (Teubner ed., 1903), 1:87–89; S. G. Mercati, "Giambi di ringraziamento per la reconquista di Costantinopoli," *Byzantinische Zeitschrift* 36 (1936): 289–90, written by a certain Nicetas, who calls Michael VIII the "New David" (founder of the Hebrew dynasty in Jerusalem). Also on the Greek elation see the encomia written by Michael's official panegyrist, Manuel Holobolos, *Orationes,* ed. M. Treu (Potsdam, 1906–7), 58ff.; Gregory of Cyprus, "Laudatio," in Migne, *Patrologia graeca* (hereafter MPG), 142, cols. 346–86; and finally, the very important L. Previale, ed., "Un panegyrico inedito per Michele VIII Paleologo," *Byzantinische Zeitschrift* 41 (1942): 1–27, which uses some of the same epithets for Michael as in the present document.

5. On the reduction of the number of Byzantine episcopal sees as compared to those in 1198, see R. L. Wolff, "The Organization of the Latin Patriarchate of Constantinople, 1204–1261: Social and Administrative Consequences of the Latin Conquest," *Traditio* 6 (1948): 56–57.

6. See esp. R. Janin, "Les sanctuaires de Byzance sous la domination latine," *Etudes byzantines* 2 (1944): 134ff. Also E. Swift, "The Latins at Hagia Sophia," *American Journal of Archaeology* 39 (1935): 458–74. Janin affirms that in Constantinople twenty churches and fourteen monasteries were occupied by the Latins (some Greek sanctuaries were deserted by Greeks who fled). Most Greek ecclesiastics and monks refused to submit to the pope. Janin (150–51) says we do not know of Latin changes in decoration of Hagia Sophia (to conform to the Western ritual) though we do know that Thomas Morosini, the new Venetian patriarch, put up marble columns to ornament the altar, and that in 1261 the Latin emperor Baldwin II removed from Hagia Sophia a great number of plaques of marble. The Venetian doge Enrico Dandolo was interred in Hagia Sophia. Swift, 464, 473, shows the Latins believed they strengthened the building, the dome especially, by erecting a number of flying buttresses in the current Western style!

considerations (as well as the looting and destruction) would of course have subsequently made it difficult for Michael to restore to their original condition the church buildings and the clerical staff of Hagia Sophia and other Constantinopolitan churches.

A similar state of disorganization also obtained in the civil affairs of restored Byzantium. Thus we know that in 1261 when many Greeks returned to their capital from exile, it was difficult in many instances to recall even the names of previous owners of properties in the city. In a document published by S. Kougeas, the case is cited of the grand logothete George Acropolites, who in 1261 took over the house of an Anconitan, since it could not be recalled to which Greek it had previously belonged. Since it was a difficult task to divide up equitably the houses and residences among the Byzantine nobles and people, Michael VIII declared all land and houses of the city to belong to the emperor pending appropriate distribution.[7] Reading again from our document:

> Our Majesty therefore issues this chrysobull on behalf of the most holy Great Church of God as a beginning, as another foundation for the increase of ecclesiastical revenues which Our Majesty has inaugurated and toward which, with God's help, my reign is disposed and eager to build upon. Our reign is determined that it [Hagia Sophia and its revenues] will be extended and increased in beauty and greatness by our successors in authority and government.

This last statement is probably a less than veiled allusion to Michael's aim of establishing his own dynasty on the throne. In fact only a short time after Constantinople's recapture by his troops, Michael had himself *and* his son Andronicus (together with the latter's Hungarian wife) crowned for a second time in August 1261 (the previous coronation taking place on Christmas day of 1258 in Nicaea). At this time, it seems Andronicus was granted the title Autokrator.[8]

7. See S. Kougeas, "Ho Georgios Akropolitēs ktētor tou parisinou kodikōs tou Souida," *Byzantina metabyzantina* 1 (1949): 61ff. On Michael's arrogation of all property to the imperial government for disposition see George Pachymeres, *De Michaele et Andronico Palaeologis,* 2 vols., ed. I. Bekker (Bonn, 1835), 1:391 (cf. Geanakoplos, *Emperor Michael Palaeologus and the West,* 124). Michael assigned special lands to the *thelēmatarioi,* who had helped him take the city from the Latins.

8. See text, p. 27, col. 2. On the coronations see F. Dölger, "Die dynastische Familienpolitik des Kaisers Michael Palaiologos (1258–1282)," in *Festschrift E. Eichmann* (Paderborn, 1940), 179ff.; and A. Heisenberg, "Aus der Geschichte und Literatur der Palaiologenzeit," *Sitzungsberichte der bayerischen Akademie der Wissenschaften zu München* 10 (1920): 1–44. Dölger shows that Andronicus was crowned basileus in August of 1261 when Michael was recrowned; P. Wirth, "Die Begründung der Kaiser-

After a long section on the desirability of granting additional revenues and properties to Hagia Sophia, the text continues:

> And so that it may be clear how everything pertaining to the church has been arranged—since God, because of his great favor toward me *[peri eme eleous]* has entrusted to my reign the *epistēmonarkhian* [lit., supervision or disciplinary authority over the church—a more accurate expression, I suggest, for imperial authority over the church than the term Caesaropapism].[9] [Since God has done this and] so that it may be known how affairs were conducted before our reestablishment and recall [by God] to this Queen of Cities *[tēn basileuousan],* and to ascertain how matters were arranged and have fared since our divinely arranged return *[epi tēide theosygkrotēton hēmeteran epanodon]* to this city, Our Majesty has decided to dispose of all these matters one by one through this chrysobull.

What should be noted here above all is Michael's constant repetition of what he clearly wishes to be the central theme of this document: God's divine plan for Byzantium using Michael as his divinely chosen instrument.[10] My translation continues:

> We note the small size of the ecclesiastical estates in former times and their division later, and [we state] this not in order that we be considered conscientious—because what can anyone offer of worth in comparison to that which he has received from God? For we have been taught that no one can honor God deservedly but only rightfully.

Observe Michael's indirect disclaimer here of any responsibility for the events of 1261, presumably in order the more to stress God's freely bestowed gift to him and the Greeks of their capital. Then the document affirms:

---

macht Michaels VIII. Palaiologos," *Jahrbuch der österreichischen byzantinischen Gesellschaft* 10 (1961): 85–91, says there were three coronations of Michael.

9. See G. Lampe, *A Patristic Greek Lexicon* (Oxford, 1961), 535, s.v. "epistēmonarkhēs," defined as "a disciplinary office in a monastery," hence supervisor or "regulator" of the church.

10. Text, p. 27, col. 2; p. 28, col. 1. In his *Orationes,* 68, Holobolos, Michael's official encomiast, refers to Michael as *theokybernēte basileu* (God-directed emperor). Dölger, *"Die dynastische Familienpolitik,"* 45, notes that through the use of this term Michael sought to give the impression of acting under divine guidance and providence.

> We mention all this in order to describe the former weakness of things and to reveal the fullness of mercy which God has shown in our behalf. . . . The inhabitants of Constantinople fled from their fatherland *[patris]* into exile, and the cup *[kondy]* which was alloted them to drink was overflowing as a penalty for their sins, and the bitterness was emptied like water into their entrails.[11]

This latter, striking metaphor refers of course to the idea prevalent among the Byzantines—and the Latins as well—that Constantinople fell to the Latins in 1204 because of the many sins of the Greeks, and would be restored to them only when their sins were fully expiated.[12] To continue with the text:

> And the ecumenical patriarch resided away from Constantinople and the metropolises and archbishoprics took refuge abroad. The metropolitan city of Nicaea was established as the patriarchal see and residence for all of the patriarchal clergy. And the formerly wealthy estates and rich properties of this church were together at once swept away by the [Latin] dynasty of the time and were lost to [Byzantine] authority and no revenues any longer remained to the patriarch and his clergy except for the income from the metropolis [of Nicaea]. And the God of mercy who punishes justly and heals benevolently *[philanthrōpōs]*, who rehabilitates ruins and releases from suffering and from our bonds, through much sweat and effort of the late blessed Lord Theodore [I] Lascaris and through the great struggles and labor of John [Vatatzes] Ducas who, after him took up the reins of government—God [then] looked with favor so that the church's affairs, with respect to its revenues and expenses, could have a new beginning.[13]

There follows a bit later a passage vivid in its reflection of the Greek feeling toward their reconquest:

> Then by the will of the Almighty, Our Majesty entered Constantinople from which the Romans had been expelled because of their sins, and to which the mercy of God brought them back. And Our

11. Text, p. 28, col. 1.

12. See next page of document: "Then by the will of Almighty God our Majesty entered Constantinople from which the Romans were expelled because of their sins." Evidently only Gregory of Cyprus, among the Byzantines, attributed the Byzantine loss of their capital rather to fate.

13. Text, pp. 28, 29, col. 1.

> Majesty took care, first and above all else, to render to God on this occasion of the restoration *[apokatastasis]* of the Romans, the first fruits *[aparkhas]* of the return of the Romans to their ancestral lands, which happened during our reign.[14] Our Majesty had the aim of restoring to the sons and grandsons of the Romans who had been expelled from Constantinople, those things the loss of which their fathers and grandfathers had suffered two generations before at the hands of the barbarian dynasty *[barbarikē dynasteia]*. And I sought to renew our rightful patrimony which was cut off by the sword of the unlawful hand. Because if, according to Solomon, it is wise to know who partakes of God's grace, how otherwise could Our Majesty, after our restoration, begin the apportionment of property? For Our Majesty received the grace of God and so Our Majesty bestows land first on the church of God which was left neglected during the long period of exile. This is the area of Hagiosophitika [lit., "the Hagia Sophian property"] which until now has preserved its name as a clear sign of its previous owner with all its rights on land and sea.[15]

It is at this point that the chrysobull begins its detailed, precise delineation of the various properties being awarded to Hagia Sophia—material which F. Dölger has summarized cogently in his *Regesten* and which H. Ahrweiler has studied carefully. I note in passing the importance of this enumeration of properties for the study of the development in Byzantium of such protofeudal institutions as the *pronoia* and *kharistikion.* It would be useful if other technical terms employed in this section, such as *paroikoi, kommerkion, ennomion, topiatikon,* etc., could be analyzed for possible importance for Byzantine social and institutional history.[16]

To continue quoting from our document, Michael mentions as now awarded (or reawarded to Hagia Sophia)

> also the buildings located [in Constantinople] around the district of the famous church of the Wisdom of God [Hagia Sophia] and those which are within and outside the courtyard of the Augusteion and the area of the Milion,[17] just as, concerning these, is more fully

14. Text, p. 28, col. 1. The Jews gave the first fruits of their crops to the Temple. Michael and his people were imbued with the fixed idea that good acts would bring back God's favor and avert punishment, a view consistent with the Orthodox faith.

15. Ahrweiler, "L'histoire de Smyrne," 57f., has dealt in great detail with the Hagiosophitika (the property, as noted, belonging traditionally to Hagia Sophia around Smyrna).

16. Text, p. 29, col. 2.

17. See R. Janin, *La géographie ecclésiastique de l'empire byzantin,* vol. 1, pt. 1 (Paris,

> described in the promulgated *horismos* [edict] of Our Majesty, along with the area adjoining the old patriarchate of [Hagia] Irene, the Word of God.[18]

These two churches referred to, Hagia Sophia and Hagia Irene, did in fact constitute the two poles of the district of the patriarchate.[19] In this same section Michael informs us how the revenues from the areas mentioned should be allotted—one-third to the patriarch's household *(patriarkhikon kellion),* one-third *(to de dimoiron)* to his "officialion," his staff of presbyters, deacons, and cantors (we may recall that in Justinian's time the clerical staff of Hagia Sophia consisted of over four hundred persons), and, finally, among other things, a small part to be set aside for lighting, that is, candles to be used in Hagia Sophia *(lykhokaia).*[20]

After more material on Hagia Sophia's properties in Constantinople being awarded (or reawarded) to the church comes a passage mentioning in strikingly laudatory terms the incumbent patriarch Joseph, who is referred to as

> conducting himself during these years . . . honorably, freely offering aid to those who needed it, pouring out his mercy like a river to the poor, offering in abundance whatever the prelates, clerics, and monks needed, providing sustenance to those who in everything took care of the patriarch [and] showing the same care as before for those who abandoned the clerical state, fostering abundant support to the monks who could not be nourished from the monasteries *[koinobia],* offering assistance to poor girls so that they could marry legally and be spared a life of sin, looking out for the lives of widows, and in all he did evoking gratitude.[21]

1953). In front of the open area of the Augusteon (named for the Augusta Helen, Constantine's mother), was the Milion, from which all distances were measured. It was originally a column, later a square building on pillars with a platform on top: D. Rice, *Constantinople: From Byzantium to Istanbul* (New York, 1965), 18.

18. Text, p. 29, col. 2; p. 30, col. 1. Evidently, soon after entering the capital, in 1261 or 1262 Michael had previously issued another edict relating to properties granted to Hagia Sophia. Note text: "as are more fully described in the [already] promulgated *horismos.*" Hagia Irene was the cathedral church before Hagia Sophia's erection (hence called here "the old patriarchate"). Both churches together were referred to as "the Great Church": see A. Van Millingen, *Byzantine Churches in Constantinople* (London, 1912), 84–85.

19. See Janin, *La géographie ecclésiastique,* vol. 1, pt. 1.

20. Text, p. 30, cols. 1–2. See G. Downey, *Constantinople in the Age of Justinian* (Norman, Okla., 1960), 113, on Justinian's time.

21. Text, p. 30, col. 2.

Several of these references may be to those Greek clerics and monks who, displaced by the Latin clergy, suffered from want or who, from religious conviction, refused to continue in their functions while subject to Latin ecclesiastical authorities.

The real reasons for the rich gifts and emoluments so ostentatiously presented to Patriarch Joseph by Michael in this document are not mentioned here. But significant in my view is the timing of the issuance of this chrysobull. For Patriarch Joseph's attitude to Michael had recently begun to change. Joseph had earlier in Nicaea earned Michael's thanks by removing the ecclesiastical excommunication levied against Michael by his predecessor, Patriarch Arsenius, after Michael's usurpation of the throne at Nicaea and his callous blinding of the legitimate boy-emperor, John Lascaris. But Joseph now had turned openly against Michael's policy of religious union with Rome, a course of action necessitated, Michael believed, by the pressing need to avert the threat of a second Latin occupation of Constantinople by Charles of Anjou, King of Sicily.[22] J. Sakellion, who first printed this document in 1864, and J. Zepos and P. Zepos, who reprinted it, date the chrysobull to 1272. I would agree, though Dölger more cautiously placed it in the period from 1261 to 1271.[23] In the latter year there broke out into the open clerical and monastic opposition to Michael's growing attempts to coerce the Greek clergy and people into acceptance of the *filioque* and other Latin doctrinal and liturgical concessions for religious union demanded by the papacy. In this bitter struggle, the support of Patriarch Joseph and the higher clergy of Hagia Sophia obviously could be of great value to Michael. Thus, through the more than generous grants made by this chrysobull, Michael may well have been seeking to placate Joseph and his prelates, a group already commonly referred to as the faction of "Josephites."

22. On Patriarch Joseph I, who was in office from 1268 to 1274 (and later again from 1282 to 1283), see G. Ostrogorsky, *History of the Byzantine State* (New Brunswick, NJ, 1969), 462–86. Also Geanakoplos, *Emperor Michael,* 262; V. Laurent, "Le serment anti-Latin du Patriarch Joseph I[e]," *Echos d'Orient* 27 (1927): 396ff.; a letter from the emperor to Patriarch Joseph in F. Miklosich and J. Müller, *Acta et diplomata res graecas italasque illustrantia* 5 (Vienna, 1860–), 247 (where the term *epistēmonarkhēs* is used to refer to the emperor's authority over the church); and, finally, documents from Joseph's patriarchate in V. Grumel, *Les regestes des actes du patriarcat de Constantinople,* 180–210.

23. On date, 1272, see Sakellion, "Hison Khrysoboullou," 32, note a; Zepos, *Jus graecoromanum,* 659; and Dölger, *Regesten,* no. 1956, pp. 52–53. It is possible that this document of 1272 may have been a formalization or extension of privileges granted earlier (perhaps in 1261 or 1262) by Michael to the church. See above, at n. 18, where the document reads: "as are fully described in the [already] promulgated *horismos* of Our Majesty." Cf. also Pachymeres, *De Michaele Palaeologis* 1:172, 173, stating that Michael presented lavish treasures to Hagia Sophia soon after entering the city. On Charles of Anjou see Geanakoplos, *Emperor Michael,* 189–371.

The next passage is very similar to parts of Michael's two *typika* (monastic charters) issued in favor of the monasteries of saints Demetrius and Michael, in which, as a kind of apologia, he enumerated the principal steps of his career, presumably thus demonstrating or seeking to justify God's election of him as his chosen instrument.[24] As our chrysobull continues:

> Our Majesty has been crowned by God with the imperial rank, a gift not only extraordinary but superior to anything on earth and more exalted and renowned than any worldly office. We were created . . . were nourished by Him who controls life, who provides sustenance. We grew up . . . became a man, and were trained in military exercises. We achieved glory through our military virtue; we were honored with senatorial rank; we have with God's help carried out our duties well *[kalōs diethēkamen to hēmeteran]* and, militarily, we have punished our enemies. We became emperor, something shared by no other of our people *[homophylōn],* a rank in which God in his grace has placed us.[25]

Of course Michael does not here mention, nor does he anywhere in his two *typika,* his usurpation of the throne or his earlier excommunication by Patriarch Arsenius (from which Patriarch Joseph had finally absolved him). But he knew only too well the stigma with which these two acts had branded him and the necessity of attempting to erase their memory from Greek minds.

Then, after noting "the shortcomings of my own eagerness," Michael inserts a curious statement about his successors, that is, members of his own house:

> And you descendants who will follow—you should not in any way be jealous of my reward from the community *[oude hymeis . . . misthou moi phthonēsete]* for which you may also prepare yourselves if God shall look with favor in your time on your increase of holy votive offerings. . . . For, if the favor *[elaios]* of God returned us to Constantinople, we did not spare any human effort and treasure in taking care of everything that was necessary and in disposing of affairs, as it seemed to us, in the best military manner. All that we

24. See J. Troitskii, ed., *Imperatoris Michaelis Palaeologi de vita sua opusculum necnon regulae quam ipse monasterio S. Demetrii praescripsit fragmentum* (St. Petersburg, 1884); and in Dmitrievskii ed., *Opisanie liturgiceskih rukopisej,* vol. 1, pt. 1, pp. 769–94. Both are also cited in Geanakoplos, *Emperor Michael,* 16 n. 1.

25. Text, p. 31, col. 1.

did after our return here could uphold us since acts are more persuasive as evidence than easy words.[26]

In a subsequent passage Michael enumerates one by one his acts after his entering the city. (By the way, before 1261 Michael had evidently never set foot in Constantinople, though Pachymeres relates that from childhood onward he had fantasies about himself retaking the glorious city.)[27] Michael affirms here that "[first] we repaired the walls all around the city, most of which we found completely ruined and which we reerected from their very foundations *[krēpidōn],* in some other places extending the restored parts for a considerable stretch." This attention to the walls was an act of critical importance if the Venetian fleet, the Latin Empire's chief defense, were (as did in fact happen) to return from Daphnusia, the isle in the Black Sea to which it had been lured, possibly by Michael himself.[28] "In addition," the chrysobull continues, "we restored parts of other sections of the walls, so that no part of the wall of the city remained bereft of care *[amoiron],* left, that is, either partly or completely unrebuilt." Michael stresses, secondly, that "at my orders there was begun the restoration of the holy churches everywhere in the city, the beauty and buildings of which had suffered from the work of destruction by the Latin plot *[latinikēs epiboulēs]."* Then, Michael refers, thirdly, to his "reestablishment and rebuilding of the monasteries." And, finally, to "the new luster *[hai . . . neai phaidrotētes]* of the palace, which we found a remnant of its former glory and which we took care to renew and make more splendid than before."[29]

All these works of restoration on the part of Michael are corroborated in detail by contemporary Greek sources; by the histories of Pachymeres, Acropolites, and the later Gregoras; and by the official encomia of Holobolos and that of the later patriarch Gregory of Cyprus.[30] Regarding the monasteries, one of Michael's own two *typika* relates in particular how he rebuilt the monastery of St. Demetrius, founded earlier by his ancestor George Palaeologus.[31] As for churches, we know from the studies of R.

26. Text, p. 31, cols. 1–2.

27. Pachymeres, *Historia* 1:128 (cf. Geanakoplos, *Emperor Michael,* 19).

28. See Geanakoplos, *Emperor Michael,* 99–102.

29. For this entire paragraph see text, p. 31, col. 2. This agrees with Pachymeres, *De Michaele Palaeologis* 1:161, and Nicephorus Gregoras, *Byzantina historia,* ed. L. Schopen, 3 vols. (Bonn, 1829–55), 1:87, who affirm that he moved into the Great Palace because the Latins had made the Blachernae unfit for habitation. See n. 33 below.

30. For all these sources and exact citations see Geanakoplos, *Emperor Michael,* 122–37 and also works cited above in n. 4.

31. Ibid., 16 n. 1; and see above, n. 4.

Western (above) and Byzantine (below) portraits of Michael VIII Palaeologus, Restorer of Constantinople to the Greeks. From D. Geanakoplos, *Emperor Michael Palaeologus and the West, 1258–1282: A Study in Byzantine-Latin Relations* (Cambridge, Mass., 1959), p. 194.

Janin that twenty Greek churches and monasteries, the latter including the Pantokrator and Studius, had been taken over by the Latin clergy during the occupation and that under the tutelage of the Cistercian order gold decoration had been placed in Hagia Sophia.[32]

In connection with Michael's repair of the imperial palace, Pachymeres recounts that he chose to restore the Great Palace overlooking the Golden Horn rather than the more recently built Blachernae Palace, which was deemed uninhabitable because of the smoke and debris of the Latins. As Pachymeres scornfully puts it, "It was filled with thick smoke and Italian fire, which the servants of the uncouth Baldwin had allowed to permeate the palace."[33] Holobolos, Michael's officially appointed panegyrist, refers to this Latin emperor even more derisively as a "manling" *(andrarion).*[34]

In the light of these various examples of repair and reconstruction one can well image how vast must have been the task facing Michael to restore Constantinople to even a semblance of its former condition. Gregoras, perhaps only somewhat exaggeratedly, wrote: "After 1204 Constantinople was then an enormous, desolate city, full of ruins and stones, of houses razed to the ground, and of the few remains of the great fire. Enslaved, it had received no care from the Latins except destruction of every kind day and night."[35]

Our document continues with Michael's lavish praise for the Great Church of Hagia Sophia, termed here the "common metropolitan church of the faithful, the holy sanctuary, the holy abode, the truly divine palace, and Your abode, though we have not learned to make God dwell in houses built of human hands."[36]

At this point there follows a passage of some theological subtlety:

> . . . the enhypostatic Wisdom of God *[enypostaton Sophian Theou],* the self-existent *[authyparkton]* power of Him who emptied Himself for us and so humbled Himself as to take on the form of a slave and received the whole man so that we could share in the first glory [referring to Adam's life before the fall] and in the more divine life and participate in the divinity *[kai theōi tēi metousiāi genoimetha].* . . . For what can one add about the essence *[ousia]* which created

32. Janin, "Les sanctuaires de byzance," 134, 172. On the Cistercians in general see E. Brown, "The Cistercians in the Latin Empire of Constantinople and Greece, 1204–76," *Traditio* 14 (1958): 63–120.

33. Pachymeres, *Historia* 1:161 (cf. Geanakoplos, *Emperor Michael,* 122).

34. Holobolos, *Orationes,* 68 *(andrarion ti brakhytaton).*

35. Gregoras, *Byzantina historia* 1:87–88.

36. Text, p. 31, end of page.

> everything through the *logos* which controls and rules over all . . . so that the Roman possessions *[skhoinismata]* would continue to increase forever *[eis apeiron]* and the boundaries [of the empire] would be immeasurably extended.

This last phrase is consonant with the idea expressed by Michael immediately after his entrance into the capital when he called an assembly together and announced it would be his primary aim to recover the lost territory of his empire.[37] The document concludes with the following fervent prayer, a desire shared by the entire Greek populace: "May the affairs of the Very Great Church return to their previous prosperity and may [the Empire] with your [God's] consent recover its previous possessions and its former good order *[eukosmia]* and splendor."[38]

In the concluding sentence, a kind of signature to the chrysobull, the dates of the month and indiction are obliterated. Literally, the text reads: "This [document] has been drawn up in the month of ______in the ______indiction of the year 1272 [6700], in which year our pious and 'God-impelled' *[theoproblētos]* power has signed it." Note the use here of *theoproblētos,* a term which was then and today still is applied to a bishop, and which probably was used here by Michael purposely in order to point up once again his selection as the chosen instrument of God's will.[39]

To conclude my remarks: this chrysobull, then, from which I have quoted the more important passages, besides enumerating the specific properties and privileges accorded to the Great Church after the Greek return and expressing Greek emotion over restoration of Constantinople to Byzantine hands, constitutes, from the author's, that is, Michael's, point of view—and herein lies its real importance for us—a subtle piece of political-ecclesiastical propaganda. For through issuance of this document Michael hoped, as we can clearly see from other of his public pronouncements, to make Constantinople's recovery redound in Greek minds to his own benefit.

By repeatedly referring to himself as the instrument employed by God to restore Constantinople and its greatest treasure, Hagia Sophia, to the Greeks, and in addition, by according or re-according properties to Patriarch Joseph and his church, Michael sought, on the one hand, to make his people forget his criminal usurpation of the throne and, on the other, to

37. Text, p. 32, col. 1. On Michael's oration to the people in 1261 see Pachymeres, p. 153, line 9, up to p. 155, line 12 (cf. Geanakoplos, *Emperor Michael,* 120).

38. Text, p. 32, cols. 1–2.

39. For *theoproblētos,* see Lampe, *Patristic Greek Lexicon,* 632.

win over Joseph and the Josephite party to his unionist policy. This interpretation of Michael's aim in issuing the document—in effect to legitimize his reign through emphasis on God's selection of him as the instrument of God's will—seems pointed up even further in the use made by Michael's chancery (as by other contemporary official Greek sources inspired by Michael) of various titles that were applied to Michael. Such Old Testament titles as the "New David," the "New Moses," even the "New Zerubbabel" (who restored the Jewish Temple as Michael did Hagia Sophia)[40]—all express a sense of revivification or renewal as in the work of the Jewish prophets and rulers of old. Even more meaningful, however, is the Christian title the "New Constantine," which Michael naturally preferred above all.[41] For like Constantine the Great of the fourth century, Michael did not see himself as the founder of a new empire but, as he repeatedly puts it in this document, as a "restorer" and "reestablisher" of the Roman Empire. In Michael's case, however, the empire was restored and revived not because of a pagan barbarian threat as in Constantine's time. Ironically, it was freed from the pollution of other Christians, the Latins and their "heresy," and the purity of the Orthodox faith thereby restored.

40. On these titles see esp. text in Previale, "Un panegyrico inedito," 20; also Geanakoplos, *Emperor Michael,* 121 n. 8.

41. Pachymeres, *Historia* 1:300, attributes to Germanos, the future patriarch, the invention of the title the "New Constantine." Cf. Acropolites, *Historia* 1:183–84; and Gregoras, *Byzantina historia* 1:86.

Additional Bibliography for Essay 8

R. Makrides, "The New Constantine and the New Constantinople, 1261," *Byzantine and Modern Greek Studies* 6 (1980): 13–41, the sole work corresponding in some ways to this essay. J. Darrouzès, *Recherches sur les "Offikia" de l'église byzantine* (Paris, 1970), on Byzantine ecclesiastical titles and offices. My *Emperor Michael Palaeologus and the West* has now appeared in Italian, *L'Imperatore Michele Paleologo,* with an updated bibliography. See also my "Byzantium and the Crusades, 1261–1354," chap. 2 in *A History of the Crusades,* ed. K. Setton, vol. 3 (Madison, Wis., 1975), 29–33. On Hagia Sophia and its ecclesiastical officials and organization see now J. Hussey, *The Orthodox Church in the Byzantine Empire* (Oxford, 1986), 297–368.

Nine

The Greek Population of South Italy and Sicily and Its Attitudes toward Charles of Anjou and Michael Palaeologus before and during the Early Phase of the Sicilian Vespers (1282)

Virtually every conceivable aspect of the famous Sicilian Vespers has been analyzed by historians. One aspect, however, though mentioned sporadically in the sources, has not yet been focused upon: the attitudes of the Greek-speaking population of the Regno, that is, of southern Italy and Sicily. It is impossible to provide accurate figures on the size of the Greek-speaking population of the Regno in the thirteenth century, though from inscriptions, legal documents, and specimens of poetry and prose, it is clear that throughout that century a very vigorous Greek culture still existed, especially in the area of Messina around the Monastery of San Salvatore, in Calabria centering on Rossano and the Monastery of St. Mary Paterion, and in the area of Otranto in Apulia, around the Monastery of San Niccolò of Casole. Ever since the Norman conquest of Byzantine southern Italy and, to a lesser degree, of Sicily, the Greek-speaking population continued to constitute an identifiable social unit and to maintain its cultural identity. Indeed, it has been shown that during the thirteenth century the Greek communities of Calabria and Apulia became even more fervently attached not only to their liturgy, as distinguished from the Latin, but also to the Orthodox patriarch of

Constantinople, whom they considered, rather than the pope, the real head of their church and numerous monasteries. Besides preserving intact the Greek language and liturgy, they maintained close cultural and economic relations with the "motherland" of Greece. It is their special allegiance to the patriarch of Constantinople that caused Roberto Weiss to term these Greeks "virtually a fifth column of the patriarchate of Constantinople in an alien Latin land."[1]

During the eleventh and twelfth centuries the Norman rulers of Sicily had looked with genuine favor on the Greek population with its generally superior culture, sponsoring the building of important Greek monasteries, such as St. Mary Paterion in Rossano. The attitude of the Normans' Hohenstaufen successors, Frederick and his son Manfred, was equally favorable to the Greek element. The Greek population therefore gave unstinting support to these rulers in their struggles against the pope, whom they came to look upon as an oppressor and virtually a foreign overlord. True they still accepted, in theory, the ecclesiastical jurisdiction of the papacy imposed upon them at the Council of Bari in 1098. But in practice they sought to preserve the Byzantine ecclesiastical rite and Greek language in the face of increasingly oppressive attempts to force them to submit completely to Rome and to make their liturgy conform to Rome's. It was precisely during the reign of the tyrannical Charles of Anjou that the animosity of the Greek populace reached its climax not only toward the Angevin displacers of their cherished Hohenstaufen rulers but also toward the papacy, which, since even before 1098, had been seeking to Latinize them.[2]

After this brief introduction, let us examine passages from the sources relating to these Greek communities to see if they reveal any meaningful role played by the Greek population in the events leading up to the Vespers. I quote first certain passages from the Venetian historian Marino Sanudo Torsello, a generally objective and knowledgeable writer. In one passage he states that "sonovi anco molti Greci in Calabria e in Terra d'Otranto, che ubbidiscono alla Santa Chiesa Romana, ma forse non così devotamente come farianno se l'imperator Sior Michael Paleologo e il Patriarca Costantinopolitano ed il Figlio del detto imperator Sior Andronico, fossero fermi e ubbidienti alla Chiesa Romana. . . ."[3] This

1. R. Weiss, "The Greek Culture of South Italy in the Later Middle Ages," *Proceedings of the British Academy* 37 (1951): 25ff., esp. 29. M. Scaduto, *Il monachismo basiliano nella Sicilia medievale* (Rome, 1947), 29.

2. F. Giunta, *Bizantini e Bizantinismo nella Sicilia normanna* (Palermo, 1950), 109–16.

3. Marino Sanudo Torsello, *Istoria del regno di Romania,* ed. C. Hopf, *Chroniques gréco-romanes* (Berlin, 1873), 143.

passage indicates, above all, the influence over this south Italian Greek population on the part of Michael Palaeologus and his patriarch, suggesting that he was at least in part responsible for their recalcitrance toward papal jurisdiction, then and after. True, Michael tried to force religious union with the papacy upon the Byzantines of his own empire, but this would probably not have antagonized the Regno Greeks, who had nominally already accepted papal jurisdiction and who traditionally had much closer ties to the papacy than their Byzantine brethren.

In another passage Sanudo writes, "L'isola di Scicilia ribellò al Rè Carlo, come hò detto, e fu per trattato dell'imperator Sior Michiel e suoi seguaci."[4] Who exactly the term *seguaci* refers to here is not clear. It may refer to Michael's agents in Italy or to those Greeks who sympathized with him in south Italy and Sicily. We know from the Byzantine historian Pachymeres that Michael Palaeologus utilized Italian monks, *frerioi* the Byzantines called them, as his agents in Italy. But who better could he have employed than Italian-speaking *Greek* monks? Pachymeres states in fact that "Michael was in the habit of warmly receiving at his court Italian *frerioi,* including Greeks of Italy, whom he used to associate with Byzantine clergy at Hagia Sophia to show the Byzantines they had little to fear from religious union with Rome." (Among these was the Greek bishop Nicholas of Croton in south Italy—also known as Nicholas of Durazzo—to whom Michael even gave a diocese in the Greek East.)[5]

Later, Sanudo speaks of the city of Messina, which had been exempted by Charles from certain of the severe imposts he had imposed for the Greek war: "Il terzo giorno il Popolo di Messina, sollevatosi con furor ed arme, ito alli Navilij, li amazzò, tutti: e ebbero il Castello di Matta Griffon e il Monasterio di S. Salvatore, si chè per tutta la Schicilia la gente di Rè Carlo rimase morta."[6] Mention here of the Monastery of San Salvatore di Messina is of special interest because it was the chief Greek monastery on the island. Strategically situated on the promontory or tongue (*lingua Phari,* from *pharos* meaning lighthouse in Greek), it dominated in a sense the area around Messina. San Salvatore of course contained numerous Basilian Greek monks and may well have been a focus of Greek disaffection with the Angevin regime.

The main contemporary source for the Vespers, the Sicilian Bartolomeo di Neocastro (who was probably an eyewitness), declares that one of the principal Sicilian grievances was that "Charles assumed a robber's

4. Ibid., 147.

5. George Pachymeres, *De Michaele et Andronico Palaeologis,* 2 vols., ed. I. Bekker (Bonn, 1835), 1:371–72. On Nicholas see Geanakoplos, *Emperor Michael Palaeologus and the West,* 177ff., with documentation.

6. Torsello, *Istoria,* 148.

cross against our friends the Greeks," "amicos nostros Danaos," an ancient term for the Greeks but referring here clearly to the Byzantines. After discussing Charles's wrath at hearing of the initial revolt in Palermo (that is, after the French molestation of a Sicilian woman), Bartolomeo notes that Charles became more infuriated to hear that Messina had joined the rebellion. "Biting his scepter in wrath" ("iracundia fervidus dentibus frendet rodens robur"), Charles then "ordered all the entire armament that had been prepared against the Greeks diverted in order to besiege Messina." Strikingly, Bartolomeo then writes that the people of Messina—he specifically speaks of "populus Pharius," which may well refer to the Greeks of the lighthouse *(pharos)* area—at once took care to inform the emperor Michael of their actions ("oportebat populum Pharium in principio guerrae hujus ad notitiam Paleologi Romaeorum imperatoris notos facere motus suos, etc.").[7] From this statement we may infer that the Greeks surrounding the area of San Salvatore on lingua Phari may have already been engaged in negotiations against Charles with agents of Michael or, already predisposed in Michael's favor, might have realized that, in this moment of his supreme crisis, he would be the one most likely to aid them. Bartolomeo continues that the Messinesi selected a Genoese named Alafrancus Cassanus to send to Michael. A Greek or Sicilian would doubtless have been stopped by the Regno authorities, whereas a Genoese, if not exactly neutral, would be more likely to get through.

We know that Michael himself utilized Genoese citizens as intermediaries, most notably the famous Benedetto Zaccaria, his chief agent in his conspiratorial negotiations with the pro-Hohenstaufen Sicilian nobles and, very possibly, with Peter of Aragon. (To his friend Zaccaria, Michael had granted as a gift the enormously valuable alum mines of Phocaea in Asia Minor,[8] possession of which would surely not have remained long in Zaccaria's hands if Charles were to take Constantinople from Michael.)

Meantime, as Bartolomeo di Neocastro relates further, seventy Angevin ships lying in the arsenal of Messina were burned. In this incident, it is very possible that members of the Greek colony of Messina, along with any Byzantine agents of Michael who were present, may have had a hand.

Another possible, though indirect, evidence of connections between the south Italian anti-Angevin Greeks and Byzantium—hitherto almost completely ignored—are documents apparently issued by Charles of Anjou himself, according to which Charles tried to draw to his court the

7. Bartolomeo di Neocastro, *Historia sicula,* ed. G. Paladino, Rerum italicarum scriptores, vol. 13, pt. 3 (Bologna, 1921), 10, 22, 42; cf. Geanakoplos, *Emperor Michael,* 360, 365.

8. Geanakoplos, *Emperor Michael,* 357–58, 251f.

dethroned, legitimate Byzantine emperor, the blinded boy John Lascaris. According to these documents, young John actually arrived at the Angevin court in Naples and was granted a pension by Charles. But these documents are directly contradicted by the two principal Byzantine historians, Pachymeres and Gregoras, who affirm that, many years later, Michael's son Andronicus visited John in a fortress at Dacibiza in Asia Minor where he was still imprisoned.[9]

The significance of what I believe to be the fraudulence of these Angevin documents lies in the idea that Charles, by presenting in Naples a pretender posing as the legitimate Byzantine ruler and enemy of the usurper Michael, may have thus been hoping to secure the adhesion to his cause of some of the Greek population of south Italy, especially the monks, clergy, and leading laymen. At least he might thus hope somewhat to diminish the anti-Angevin sentiment of the Greeks of south Italy. True, Charles had already allied with two renegade Greek princes, both enemies of Palaeologus, Nicephorus, the Despot of Epirus, and his brother John the Bastard of Thessaly.[10] But they were too close to the actual events transpiring in the East to have been affected by documents drawn up in Latin in the distant kingdom of Sicily.

To conclude: On the basis of these admittedly very fragmentary pieces of evidence, it is not possible to affirm that the south Italian Greeks, especially the abbots, monks, clergy, and the leading laymen, played any clearly delineated role in the Vespers. Nevertheless, the evidence does prove conclusively that the sentiment of this important Greek segment of the Regno population was to a remarkable degree anti-Angevin and evidently very pro-Byzantine. That Michael Palaeologus, often termed the most astute diplomat of all Byzantine emperors, did not try to make use of this virtual "fifth column" in the Regno, especially in view of his truly desperate position vis-à-vis Charles's formidable coalition organized against him, seems very difficult to believe.

What is lacking in the sources to prove a pattern of action or of plans for action is some concrete evidence describing specific negotiations between Michael and the chiefs of the Greek monasteries or communities in the Regno. But then of course such negotiations would necessarily have had to be kept secret. It is important to stress that, while virtually all classes of Sicilian society had grievances against Angevin rule, the Greeks of the Regno had probably the strongest reasons for hostility toward Charles. In addition to the oppressive taxes levied by him on all citizens

9. *Archivio storico italiano* 22:32. For Pachymeres and Gregoras see Geanakoplos, *Emperor Michael,* 217–18, with documentation.

10. Geanakoplos, *Emperor Michael,* 231, 309, 323.

of the Regno, certainly including the Greeks, for his expedition against their kinsmen the Byzantines of Constantinople, the Regno Greeks under Charles, now for the first time to such an onerous degree, suffered widespread suppression of their religious rite and their language—in other words, they were experiencing a concerted attack on their cultural and, in effect, ethnic, tradition, which was so dear to them.[11]

11. On taxation and suppression of the Greek rite see Geanakoplos, *Emperor Michael,* 360–61; S. Runciman, *The Sicilian Vespers* (Cambridge, 1958), 127–28; and Weiss, "Greek Culture of South Italy," 28–29.

Additional Bibliography for Essay 9

Geanakoplos, *L'Imperatore Michele Paleologo e l'Occidente 1258–82,* Italian translation of *Emperor Michael Palaeologus and the West* with updated bibliography. F. Giunta, *Alcune narrazioni sul Vespro* (Palermo, 1969). Geanakoplos, "Byzantium and the Crusades, 1261–1453," chaps. 2 and 3 in *A History of the Crusades,* ed. K. Setton, vol. 3 (Madison, Wis., 1975), esp. 27–34. A. Franchi, *I Vespri siciliani e le relazioni tra Roma e Bisanzio* (Palermo, 1984), an extremely detailed, technical study in the sources with no new historical facts. K. Setton, *The Papacy and the Levant,* vol. 1 (Philadelphia, 1976), 140–42, summary on the Vespers.

Ten

Bonaventura, the Two Mendicant Orders, and the Greeks at the Council of Lyons (1274)

For centuries it has been believed that at the famous Council of Lyons, held in 1274 to reunite the Latin and Greek churches, the leading role defending Latin theological views in the debates that presumably took place was played by the great Franciscan theologian Bonaventura.[1] Recently, however, this view has been seriously called into question,[2] and a re-evaluation of his role and that of other leading protagonists seems to be in order. Far from being the "soul of the union," and the man who "crushed the Greeks in theological debate," as has been generally believed,[3] Bonaventura seems to have played a very limited part in the

1. Several works have been written relatively recently in connection with the problem of religious union at the Council of Lyons: see Geanakoplos, *Emperor Michael Palaeologus and the West,* chaps. 11 and 12; B. Roberg, *Die Union zwischen der griechischen und der lateinischen Kirche auf dem II. Konzil von Lyon* (Bonn, 1964); A. Franchi, *Il Concilio II di Lione secondo la ordinatio concilii generalis lugdunensis* (Rome, 1965); and H. Wolter and H. Holstein, *Lyon I et Lyon II* (Paris, 1965). Pertinent articles on the council, or specific aspects of it, are cited below. I note here one of the more recent, that of J. Gill, "The Church Union of Lyons (1274) Portrayed in Greek Documents," *Orientalia christiana periodica* 40 (1974), 5–45, containing some unpublished Greek texts relating to the union. See also works in additional bibliography (at end), which have been used throughout this essay.

2. Esp. by Franchi, *Concilio II di Lione,* 158–72. Roberg, *Union auf dem Konzil* (see esp. 136 n. 9), it seems, had suspected this.

3. See, e.g., R. Menindez, "Saint Bonaventure, les frères-mineurs et l'unité de l'église

union It is the purpose of this essay not only to put in clearer light and in its true context the work of Bonaventura with regard to the Greeks at the council, but also to indicate, if only rather briefly, the parts taken by other mendicants, the Franciscans John Parastron and Jerome of Ascoli and the Dominicans Albertus Magnus, William of Moerbeke, and their minister-general, Peter of Tarentaise. Our aim, then, is to ascertain the relative importance of their respective roles in the preparations for, and the proclamation of, religious union.

This essay will be divided into two sections, the first part dealing with the preparations made by Pope Gregory X for two years before convocation of the council, together with the parallel, preconciliar events in the Byzantine East; and the second part discussing the activities at the actual conciliar proceedings of the various Franciscan and Dominican, as well as Greek, participants.

No formal acts as such of the conciliar proceedings remain in either Latin or Greek, and the sometimes exaggerated, encomiastic statements of the Franciscan and Dominican sources must be examined with care. But we do have available a precise, if rather brief, account in Latin of the proceedings, a kind of minutes or diary of the council and its liturgical ceremonies. This was formerly entitled, in Mansi and elsewhere, the *Notitia brevis.* But in the new edition recently prepared by A. Franchi from a more accurate, anonymous Vatican manuscript, it is more correctly entitled *Ordinatio concilii generalis lugdunensis (The Order* [or agenda] *of the General Council of Lyons).*[4] The famous work of the Dominican Thomas Aquinas, the *Contra errores Graecorum,* written some years before but not for the use of this council, will not concern us.[5]

On the Greek side, while we have no Syropoulos as at the Council of Florence to illuminate the innermost thoughts of the Greek envoys,[6] the lengthy and detailed account of the contemporary historian George Pachymeres tells us much about events in Constantinople before and

---

au concile de Lyon de 1274," *La France franciscaine,* vol. 5, no. 18 (1935): 363–92; also L. Wegemer, *St. Bonaventure the Seraphic Doctor* (New York, 1924), 1ff.; L. De Simone, "S. Bonaventura al concilio di Lione II e l'unione con i Greci," *Asprenas* 9 (1962): esp. 125.

4. Franchi, *Concilio II di Lione,* 67–100, for new edition of the Latin text. Cf. S. Kuttner, *L'édition romaine des conciles généraux et les actes du premier concile de Lyon* (Rome, 1949).

5. See P. Glorieux's new edition of *Contra errores Graecorum* (Tournai and Paris, 1957); and A. Dondaine, "*Contra Graecos,* premiers écrits polémiques des Dominicains d'Orient," *Archivum fratrum praedicatorum* 21 (1951): 320ff.

6. See excellent new edition of Syropoulos by V. Laurent, *Les mémoires du grand ecclésiarche de l'église de Constantinople Sylvestre Syropoulos sur le concile de Florence (1438–39)* (Paris, 1971). Also on Syropoulos see essay 11, below, with bibliography cited.

after the union, though very little about the council itself.[7] Indeed, Pachymeres seems to believe that it was held in Rome. We have, in addition, a short but little-used account on Lyons written by Archdeacon George Metochites, a pro-unionist Greek envoy sent to the Roman Curia almost immediately after the council in order to help implement its decisions.[8]

In order to understand the context of events in which the Council of Lyons took place, we must go back to the early thirteenth century. The destruction of the Byzantine state in 1204 as a result of the Fourth Crusade and the subsequent erection of a Latin empire in its place, with the forced conversion of the Greek clergy and people to Catholicism, had created in Greek minds such hostility that, even after Constantinople's recovery by the Byzantine emperor Michael VIII Palaeologus in 1261, most Greeks would hear nothing of religious union of the churches. By this time, in fact, fear of the West had created in Greek minds almost a paranoia regarding any future Latin aggression.[9] Thus the principal differences between the two churches, doctrinally the *filioque* (procession of the Holy Spirit from both Father and Son) and liturgically use of the *azyma* (unleavened bread) in the Holy Eucharist, came, after the Latin occupation of Constantinople in 1204, to assume not only religious but ethnic significance as well. Were a Byzantine even to suggest consideration of the *filioque* or *azyma,* he was at once branded by his compatriots with the abusive epithet *Latinophron.* As one imperial Greek envoy, George Metochites, bitterly but meaningfully complained after returning from the Council at Lyons, "Instead of a conflict of words, instead of refutative proof, instead of arguments from the scriptures we [envoys] constantly hear [from the Greek populace] *'Frangos kathestēkas'* ['You have become a Frank']." "Should we pro-unionists," he continues with acute insight, "simply because we favor union, be subjected to being called supporters of another nation and not Byzantine patriots *[alloethneis hemeis all'ou philorōmaioi]*? "[10]

After 1261 the principal enemy of the Byzantine empire was the newly enthroned, highly ambitious king of Sicily, Charles of Anjou. To the

7. G. Pachymeres, *De Michaele et Andronico Palaeologis,* 2 vols., ed. I. Bekker (Bonn, 1835), vol. 1. Cf. Geanakoplos, *Emperor Michael,* esp. 248ff.

8. For Metochites' text, see C. Giannelli, "Le récit d'une mission diplomatique de Georges Le Métochite et le Vat. Gr. 1716," in H. Laurent, *Le Bienheureux Innocent V (Pierre de Tarentaise) et son temps* (Vatican, 1947), esp. 419–43.

9. On this "paranoiac" fear of the Greeks see, e.g., Geanakoplos, "Byzantium and the Crusades, 1261–1453," chaps. 2 and 3 in *A History of the Crusades,* ed. K. Setton, vol. 3 (Madison, Wis., 1975), 30, 55, 103; and esp. Geanakoplos, *Interaction of the "Sibling" Byzantine and Western Cultures in the Middle Ages and Italian Renaissance (330–1600),* Prologue and Epilogue.

10. For Greek text see Laurent, *Le Bienheureux Innocent V,* esp. 424ff.

Greek emperor Michael Palaeologus the only power able to restrain this grave military threat to Constantinople was Charles's feudal lord for Sicily, the pope. But the papal price for aid was religious union with Rome, meaning in most Greek minds dogmatic and jurisdictional subordination, once again, of the Greek church to Rome. Nevertheless, despite the intense popular opposition to union, Michael was convinced of the political necessity of union with the Roman church.[11] Michael's desire for union was shared, though on other grounds of course, by the new pope, Gregory X. Gregory, who had lived long in the Holy Land, had considerable knowledge of the Greek East. It was in fact his aim, publicly announced soon after his elevation, to convoke a general council not only to bring about much-needed reform in the Latin church, but also to effect religious reunion with the Greeks and then, with Greek aid, to launch a crusade to recover Jerusalem.[12] Writing to Emperor Michael, therefore, Pope Gregory stated that, if the latter were truly receptive, the pope would send nuncios to Constantinople to discuss religious union and a joint crusade.[13]

But even before dispatching formal ambassadors to Constantinople, the pope, upon receiving a positive reply from the emperor, sent to Constantinople the Franciscan friar John Parastron in order to instruct Michael in the theological beliefs of the Roman church.[14] His choice of a mendicant for this mission in preference to a member of the secular clergy reflects the long history of Franciscan and Dominican connections with the Greek East. Almost from their foundation, in fact, both orders had turned their attention to missionary work in the East in the dual aim of recovering the Holy Land and bringing about the *reductionem* (return, or perhaps more precisely, "reduction") of the "schismatic" Greeks to the Roman church.[15] The choice of John Parastron, a Constantinople- born,

11. On the relations between Charles and Michael see Geanakoplos, *Emperor Michael;* S. Runciman, *The Sicilian Vespers* (Cambridge, 1958); and Geanakoplos, "Byzantium and the Crusades," 33–42. On March 1272 Gregory publicly announced his plans for a general council.

12. See esp. V. Laurent, "La croisade et la question d'Orient sous le pontificat de Grégoire X," *Revue historique du Sud-Est européen* 22 (1945): 105–37.

13. See papal letter in J. Guiraud, *Les registres de Grégoire X* (Paris, 1892–96), no. 194, 68b. Cf. Geanakoplos, *Emperor Michael,* 239.

14. Parastron had earlier been sent to Gregory by Michael. Indeed, already in 1270 Michael had included Parastron in an embassy he had sent to St. Louis of France, in order to restrain Charles of Anjou, at which time Parastron presented Louis with a precious illuminated Greek New Testament. See Geanakoplos, *Emperor Michael,* 224 n. 133, and p. 239. On Parastron, see esp. G. Golubovich, "Cenni storici su Fra Giovanni Parastron," *Bessarione* 10 (1906): 295ff.

15. On both orders' work in the East, see M. Roncaglia, *Les frères mineurs et l'église grecque orthodoxe au XIIIe siècle (1221–74)* (Cairo, 1954); more important, G. Golu-

Greek Franciscan, to perform the delicate task of instructing Michael proved to be a wise one. For Parastron soon came to be greatly esteemed not only by Michael but by the Greek populace as well, despite his being a Latinophile and zealous advocate of union. For, unlike the usual convert, he was still favorable to the Greek rites. Viewing the bitter arguments over the question of the procession of the Holy Spirit as excessive, indeed unnecessary (an attitude remarkable for the time), Parastron, Pachymeres informs us, "was in the habit of entering into the sanctuaries of the Constantinopolitan churches and, standing at the side of the Greek celebrants, would join in the reading of the offices."[16] Moreover, at the end of the service, he and other friars (*frerioi,* as Pachymeres puts it) would join in partaking of the *antidōron* (unconsecrated bread).[17] Significantly, they did not participate in the sacrament of Holy Communion—doubtless because of the difference in the Greek usage of leavened instead of unleavened bread *(azyma)* in the Eucharist.

Parastron became popular even among the Greek clergy, who, if we may believe the later Franciscan chronicler Nicholas Glassberger, at Parastron's death shortly after Lyons, even sought his canonization from the pope.[18] Parastron's Greek birth, tolerance, and above all empathy with the Greek mentality, in particular with that of the lesser clergy and common people, made it easier for him to stress that union should be considered more a reversion to the original unity of the church than an acceptance of any new dogmatic beliefs or rites.

The pope's reliance on the Franciscan order was not limited to his use of Parastron's talents. For in the crucial matter of choosing nuncios to send to Michael for discussion of the union, Gregory now turned to his friend and former teacher at the University of Paris, Bonaventura, the minister-general of the Franciscans (he had been instrumental in Gregory's election as pope), and directed him to send four members of his order to Constantinople. Bonaventura thereupon selected the Franciscan friars Jerome of Ascoli, Bonaventura da Mugello, Bonagratia, and Raymond Berengar, who on 24 October 1272 set forth for the Bosporus.[19] Of

---

bovich, *Biblioteca bio-bibliografica della Terra Santa e dell'Oriente francescano,* vol. 2 (Quarracchi, 1913); J. Moorman, *A History of the Franciscan Order* (Oxford, 1968), 226ff., 298–99; also R. Loenertz, "Les établissements dominicains de Pera-Constantinople," *Echos d'Orient* 34 (1935): 332–49; and Dondaine, "Ecrits polémiques."

16. Pachymeres, *De Michaele Palaeologis* 1:371–72.

17. Ibid., 360–61, 368 (cf. Geanakoplos, *Emperor Michael,* 267).

18. Nicholas Glassberger, *Chronica,* Analecta franciscana, vol. 2 (Quarracchi, 1887), 88: "Pro eius canonizatione Imperator Graecorum et Praelati Graeciae instanter apud dominum papam laborabant."

19. See Roberg, *Union auf dem Konzil,* 102ff. and sources cited. Also for date see

these four envoys it is certain only that the chief legate, Jerome of Ascoli, knew Greek. To judge, however, as we shall see, by certain somewhat inaccurate remarks he made about Greek religious practices in a later report to the pope, Ascoli's Greek must have been considerably less than perfect.[20]

As for the minister-general, Bonaventura, he seems to have known no Greek except perhaps for a few theological phrases. His *Opera omnia,* to be sure, reveal familiarity with basic Greek theological views, especially of the fourth- and fifth-century Greek Fathers. Of the Greek Fathers the names of Chrysostom, the Pseudo-Dionysius, and the later John of Damascus appear most frequently in his writings. But they belong, in large part, to the common Christian heritage of both East and West. Nevertheless, several other passages in Bonaventura's *Opera omnia* indicate more than passing familiarity with current Greek views on the disputed *filioque* and *azyma* questions.[21]

Regarding the *azyma* (use of unleavened bread in communion), after discussing the views of both Latins and Greeks, Bonaventura affirms that, though both had originally received the practice from the Lord, the Greeks had altered the tradition. Therefore, he concludes, "either the apostles erred or the Greeks invented this" *(finxerunt).*[22] Elsewhere he implies that for the Greeks, the Latin *azyma* was an example of Judaizing practices,[23] something that they found particularly reprehensible. Regarding the *filioque,* it seems that Bonaventura reflects the common Western view that the Greeks were wrong in considering the phrase an unlawful addition to the creed instead of, as the Latins held, a necessary clarification of dogma.[24] His emphasis on prayer and contemplation leading to a kind of mystical union with God (recall the important Byzantine concept of *theosis*),[25] his essentially antipathetic attitude to the Scholastic,

Geanakoplos, *Emperor Michael,* 239; and the sometimes inaccurate Roncaglia, *Les frères mineurs,* 125 (cf. Pachymeres, *De Michaele Palaeologis* 1:3–68). On Bonaventura's selection of the envoys see Roberg, 103 n. 6, citing a Franciscan source.

20. See below text and nn. 31–34. Also Wolter and Holstein, *Lyon I et II,* 159, who believe Jerome (the future Pope Nicholas IV) knew Greek "badly."

21. On his knowledge of the Greek Fathers see L. Wegemer, *St. Bonaventure the Seraphic Doctor,* 9.

22. Bonaventura, *Opera omnia,* vol. 4 (Quarracchi, 1889), *Sententiarum,* 260–61: "Iuxta hoc quaeritur de controversia Graecorum et Latinorum, unde venerit; et videtur, quod non poterit esse; quia ipsi acceperunt ab Apostolis, et Apostoli ab uno Domino: ergo vel Apostoli erraverunt, vel Graeci finxerunt."

23. Bonaventura, *Opera* 4:261, no. 5, and 4:262, *Conclusio,* no. 5.

24. On the *filioque* see, e.g., Bonaventura, *Opera,* vol. 1 (1882), 211–23, mentioning the views of the Greeks John of Damascus, Dionysius, and Gregory among others; see also Geanakoplos, *Byzantine East and Latin West,* 99–102.

25. On "theosis" see recently J. Meyendorff, *Byzantine Theology* (New York, 1974), 163–64. Cf. Bonaventura's famous mystical work, *Itinerarium mentis ad Deum* on the

Aristotelian approach of the Dominicans,[26] the Franciscan emphasis on Mariology (despite Bonaventura's own denial of the immaculate conception of the Virgin),[27] and the possible Franciscan use of the so-called "Jesus prayer"—the latter of which apparently had its genesis in the Byzantine East[28]—seem to indicate far greater affinity between his Franciscan type of spirituality and that of the Greeks than between the Dominican and the Greek. Thus, if any formal dialogue did in fact take place at Lyons, it is reasonable to assume that Bonaventura and the Greek envoys got along rather well together. Indeed, one later apostolic notary at the papal court wrote—but this is not corroborated by the original, contemporary sources—that the Greeks called Bonaventura "Eutychios" (the "well-fated" or "fortunate one").[29] Besides being a literal translation of his name, this appellation might also have carried the implication of a person of affable personality and sympathetic beliefs.

To return to the Franciscan embassy to Constantinople under Jerome of Ascoli, it seems that Bonaventura, as the immediate superior who had selected the nuncios in the first place, should deserve some credit for its success, however ephemeral. Bonaventura probably had some communication with his envoys during their one and a quarter year sojourn in Constantinople, and on their return to Lyons it is likely that they made a report to him personally as well as to the new Franciscan minister-general, as they did, of course, to the pope.[30] Sometime during their stay in Constantinople, Jerome and his colleagues sent a communication to

---

ascent of the soul to God through faith, reason, and contemplation (*Dizionario biografico degli Italiani,* s.v. "Bonaventura," 2:618–19). The treatise *Teologia mystica* is now generally believed to be not by Bonaventura but by Hugh of Balma, a late thirteenth-century Carthusian.

26. See *Dizionario biografico degli Italiani,* vol. 2, esp. pp. 618–19, 623. Also see E. Gilson, *History of Christian Philosophy in the Middle Ages* (New York, 1955), 331–40, who says Bonaventura tried to combine Aristotle and Plato; elsewhere, however, he says that Bonaventura made little concession to Aristotle.

27. *Oxford Dictionary of the Christian Church* (hereafter *ODCC*) (Oxford, 1963), s.v. "Bonaventure."

28. See esp. article on the "Jesus prayer" by F. X. Murphy, in *The New Catholic Encyclopedia* (New York, 1967), 971; and *On the Prayer of Jesus* by Bishop Ignatius Brianchaninov (London, 1965) (with little on this point).

29. Petrus Galesinus, *Sancti Bonaventurae vita,* in Bonaventura, *Opera* 1:1–20. On Galesinus see A. Potthast, *Bibliotheca historica medii aevi* (Berlin, 1896), 486. Passage quoted by Franchi, *Concilio II di Lione,* 164, and by Roberg, *Union auf dem Konzil,* 136 n. 9: "Hic doctrinae Bonaventurae nomen magnum hic Eutychii, sic enim Graeci ilum vocabant. . . ."

30. Franchi, *Concilio II di Lione,* 81 n. 25, cites a Vatican source cited by Giannelli in Laurent, *Le Bienheureux Innocent V,* 442, on a papal audience then granted to Ascoli, during which Ascoli probably gave Gregory a letter from Joseph, patriarch of Constantinople.

Pope Gregory X. This is especially interesting because it constitutes an illuminating source for contemporary Latin views of Greek religious practices.[31] Thus Ascoli affirms that the Greeks believe all Latins are excommunicated for rejecting the symbol of faith adopted at Nicaea as the Greeks confess it and for adding the *filioque* to the creed. Ascoli also states that the Greeks recognize no jurisdiction on the part of the pope over the entire Christian church without consent of the other four patriarchs, that the Greeks do not consider fornication a mortal sin,[32] that they do not believe in purgatory, that for them the Latin sacraments have no efficacy, and that they do not admit that the Holy Spirit proceeds from the Son. Differences of rite, Ascoli states, lead the Greeks in fact to rebaptize Latin converts. Ascoli is inaccurate with reference to Greek ecclesiastical practices, however, in saying that the Greeks do not know the four minor orders. (Actually, though the actual titles and functions differed at this time, the Greeks did not lack their own minor orders.)[33] Erroneous, too, is his statement that the Greeks do not practice extreme unction and that they lack the sacrament of confirmation.[34] (Here the Greek practice of confirmation at the same time as baptism may have escaped his notice.)

But the most important result of Ascoli's fifteen-month embassy in Constantinople was to prevail upon Michael and his sixteen-year-old son, Andronicus, to accept the papal confession of faith sent earlier to the emperor by the pope and which Parastron explained to Michael.[35] Ascoli obtained the imperial acceptance of the Roman confession at a meeting held in the presence of a pro-unionist group of Greek clergy at the imperial Blachernae Palace in February 1274, that is, shortly before the Franciscan legates' departure with the Greek envoys to attend the council at Lyons.[36]

31. For text of report (which is incomplete) see Roberg, *Union auf dem Konzil,* 229–31, and for discussion, 130–34. Cf. Geanakoplos, *Interaction of the Sibling Cultures,* 169.

32. The Greeks in fact do not consider fornication a very serious sin.

33. *ODCC,* s.v. "Minor Orders," listing those for the Latin and for the Greek church.

34. Latin text in Roberg, *Union auf dem Konzil,* 230–31.

35. For analysis of this confession of faith (based on Pope Clement's letter sent earlier, in 1267, to Michael and the points of which Michael now repeated in his letter to Gregory) see J. Karmires, "Hē apodidomenē eis ton Michaēl VIII Palaiologon latinikē homologia pisteōs tou 1274," *Archeion ecclesiatikou kai kanonikou dikaiou* 2 (1947): 127ff., who believes it entirely Latin (as I do). Interestingly, Michael's confession of faith sent to Pope Gregory contains the first formal enumeration by the Greek church (or emperor) of *seven* sacraments. This seems to be the sole remaining legacy of Lyons in the Orthodox church, see N. Patrinakos, *The Individual and His Orthodox Church* (New York, 1970), 23–24.

36. Several studies include a discussion of this episode. Besides Roberg, *Union auf dem Konzil,* 113ff., see D. Nicol, "The Greeks and the Union of the Churches: Prelim-

In this confession, which Michael now sent back to Lyons with his own ambassadors, the emperor explicitly accepted the *filioque, azyma,* and Roman primacy of ecclesiastical jurisdiction, even the seven sacraments as prescribed and enumerated by Rome—everything to the letter demanded of him by the papacy.[37] At the end of his long letter, however, Michael begged that "the Greek church be permitted to recite the creed as it had been before the schism up to our time, and that we remain in observance of the rites we had before the schism—these rites not being contrary to the faith declared above. This is not crucial for your holiness," Michael wrote, "but for us it is a matter of vital importance because of the immense multitude of our people."[38] This latter point attests to the extreme attachment which the mass of the Greek clergy and people felt for their traditional doctrine and especially ritual, in particular the leavened bread of the Holy Eucharist. To the Greeks their liturgy had by now perhaps come to mean more than any other aspect of their religious life, and, as noted above, they had since 1204 (whether they realized it consciously or not) come more and more to identify the Byzantine ritual with their ethnic feelings as a people distinct from the Latins.

The letter of Andronicus, the son and heir of Michael, merely repeated what the father had already affirmed. The letter drawn up by the Greek clergy, however, was another matter. What Pope Gregory essentially requested of the Byzantine clergy was a profession of faith in the form he prescribed, including explicit acceptance of the *filioque* and *azyma,* along with recognition of Roman primacy of both honor and jurisdiction, that is, the right of appeal to Rome. What evoked the greatest protest in Constantinople, according to the Greek historian Pachymeres, was Michael's insistence on the proclamation of the pope's name in the diptychs, the tablets from which the names of those commemorated at the Eucharist were publicly read aloud in the liturgy.[39] Mention of the pope's

---

inaries to the Second Council of Lyons," in *Medieval Studies Presented to A. Gwynn* (Dublin, 1961), 463–80.

37. For Latin translation of Michael's profession see Roberg, *Union auf dem Konzil,* 239–43. French translation of Michael's profession in Wolter and Holstein, *Lyon I et II,* 276–80.

38. See French translation of text in Wolter and Holstein, *Lyon I et II,* 279–80. See also Roberg, *Union auf dem Konzil,* 227–28, for quotation of Michae's request, which appears also in Ascoli's letter. Cf. below, n. 105, citing Beck's view on this matter of Greek rites.

39. See Pachymeres, *De Michaele Palaeologis* 1:386, 395. Also Nicephorus Gregoras, *Byzantina historia,* ed. L. Schopen, 3 vols. (Bonn, 1829–55), 1:125–26. This demand of Michael about the diptychs was made, possibly, in response to Gregory's instructions to Ascoli. See Geanakoplos, *Emperor Michael,* 240–41, for English translation from the papal letter regarding three possible "verbal" ways submission to Roman primacy could

name in the diptychs would signify to the Byzantine clergy that they were already in communion with Rome and therefore that they approved, at least tacitly, of what they considered such Western *kainotomias* ("innovations," in effect "heresies") as the *filioque* and the *azyma,* that is, the sacrament of the Holy Eucharist with unleavened bread.

The letter drawn up by the Greek clergy was, for the most part, vaguely composed and fell far short of constituting a profession of faith in the manner required by Rome.[40] In fact it lacked the endorsement of most of the Greek clergy, being signed by some forty-odd prelates out of a possible total of one hundred and forty-four bishops in the empire.[41] In consequence, though Ascoli had skillfully guided the negotiations with the emperor and his son, he now had to be content with this very weak epistle from the Greek prelates, one which at best indicated only partial submission to Rome.

The Greek clergy did not even mention the crucial theological issues, and the exact forms of papal privilege were left conveniently vague, being referred to only as "those the pope had enjoyed before the schism." What the Greek clerics apparently envisaged by this phrase was restoration of the kind of relationship that had existed between the two churches before the schism, presumably meaning 1054—a view which would probably imply deletion of the *filioque* from the creed and repudiation or annulment of the many papal claims which had burgeoned after that date.[42] Thus the Greek prelates, while leaving it to Michael and his son explicitly to accept everything the pope demanded, submitted on their part only an incomplete and ambiguously phrased letter.

Shortly after Michael's acceptance of the papal invitation to send

---

be expressed by the Greeks, text in Guiraud, *Registres de Grégoire X,* no. 194, 67–73. Also, Geanakoplos, *Emperor Michael,* 264.

40. For a Latin edition of the bishops' letter see Roberg, *Union auf dem Konzil,* 235–39. Cf. Greek text in Gill, "Church Union of Lyons," 28–33. The letter was dated February 1274.

41. Nicol, "Greeks and Union," 476, calculates 35 or 38 bishops, which he changes to "40 odd bishops" in his "The Byzantine Reaction to the Council of Lyons," *Studies in Church History* 7 (1971): 122. More recently, Gill, "Church Union of Lyons," 6, speaks of 41 signatures. H. Beck, chap. 16 of *From the High Middle Ages to the Eve of the Reformation,* Handbook of Church History, ed. H. Jedin and J. Dolan, vol. 4 (New York, 1970), 126, writes of "44 bishops," which number seems correct, to judge by the episcopal letter quoted verbatim in Roberg, *Union auf dem Konzil,* 235–39. (See also Roberg's views on the MS tradition of this text, 255–63.) On the context for this episode, besides the studies mentioned, see the several articles of H. Evert-Kapessova, esp. "Une page des relations byzantino-latines: Byzance et le St.-Siège à l'époque de l'union de Lyon," *Byzantinoslavica* 16 (1955): 297–314.

42. This would show, contrary to some modern views, that the Greeks themselves considered 1054 rather definitive for the schism.

envoys to the forthcoming council, the emperor selected as the Greek representatives three men: as his personal ambassador, the grand logothete ("prime minister") George Acropolites, and to represent the Byzantine clergy, the ex-patriarch Germanos III and the archbishop of Nicaea, Theophanes.[43] Let us look closely for a moment at the leader of the Greek delegation, Acropolites, whose career has not been sufficiently scrutinized with respect to his involvement in this council. Though a civilian official, he was something of a theologian as well.[44] Above all, however, he was a faithful civil servant who understood the necessity of the imperial policy of *economia*—that is, elasticity or flexibility in the administration of ecclesiastical affairs when vital interests of the state were endangered.[45] An extremely learned man, Acropolites taught the philosophy of Aristotle and Plato (note this—a Greek with a good knowledge of Plato in the West two centuries before the famous Renaissance figures Chrysoloras and Pletho)[46] as well as the mathematics of Euclid and Nicomachus at the Academy (higher school) of Constantinople, then situated near the Church of St. Paul.[47] The modern editor of Acropolites' writings, A. Heisenberg, believes that Acropolites, on his arrival at Capua in southern Italy on his way to Lyons, wrote, at the request of a certain Archbishop Marinos of Eboli (who, if not a Calabrian Greek, may at least have been Byzantine oriented), a work entitled "On Saints Peter and Paul"—something that would undoubtedly please the pope and which, according to Heisenberg, is still worth reading for theological and rhetorical reasons.[48] In this treatise on Peter and Paul and their importance for the Byzantine church, Acropolites terms them the *koryphaioi* (chiefs or highest) of the

43. The metropolitan of Philippi was also selected, but he died before departure of the embassy on 11 March 1274.

44. On Acropolites see esp. A. Heisenberg's "Prolegomena" to his *Georgii Acropolitae, Opera,* vol. 2 (Leipzig, 1903), iii–xxvi. Also see Beck, in *Middle Ages to Reformation,* 126: "Acropolites lacked theological depth."

45. On *economia* see, e.g., Geanakoplos, *Emperor Michael,* 265, 270; *Byzantine East and Latin West,* 77; and *Byzantium: Church, Society and Civilization,* no. 98A, B, C.

46. It is interesting that in 1271 William of Moerbeke translated from the Greek Proclus's commentary on the *Parmenides* of Plato (see Minio-Paluello, 46, cited n. 58 below). On Chrysoloras and Pletho see Geanakoplos, *Greek Scholars in Venice,* 24–28, 85–86, and above, essay 1.

47. See Heisenberg, "Prolegomena," *Acropolitae Opera,* 2:xi; cf. S. Runciman, *The Last Byzantine Renaissance* (Cambridge, 1970), 57–58.

48. See Heisenberg, "Prolegomena," *Acropolitae Opera,* 2:xxi. On Marinos of Eboli (apparently archbishop of Capua to 1261) see C. Eubel, *Hierarchia catholica medii aevi* (Regensburg, 1898), 170; and G. Tafuri, *Istoria degli scrittori noti del regno di Napoli* (Naples, 1748), vol. 2, pt. 1, pp. 449–52. Also see Franchi, *Concilio II di Lione,* 138 n. 27; and F. Schillman's mention of Marino's "Formulario," in his "Zur byzantinischen Politik Alexanders IV," *Römische Quartalschrift* 22 (1908): 108–31.

apostles. But this did not at the same time mean that he (like other Byzantines) accepted Roman claims to jurisdictional primacy. (His was an attitude common enough in Byzantium but which, according to the Greek historian Syropoulos, at least with respect to St. Peter, was to be a subject of argument on the part of Greeks later at the Council of Florence.)[49] It is possible that, if indeed George did find time to write the treatise on his arrival in Italy (something highly unlikely), he did so perhaps as a tribute to the pope, or to convince the papal Curia of Michael's sincerity, which for years had been suspect in Western eyes. Another possibility is that Acropolites wrote the work after his return to Constantinople, in the aim of supporting Michael's unionist policy among the Greeks by showing that, from patristic times onward, the Greek church itself had venerated saints Peter and Paul as the *koryphaioi* of the apostles.[50]

In still another work, written by Acropolites before Lyons and in which he opposed the *filioque* doctrine, he reveals himself, nevertheless, fairly tolerant of the Latins. He stresses, among other things, that in order to achieve religious union the churches should return to the common views shared in the patristic period—the implication being not only that there were common beliefs but also that the *filioque* should be deleted from the creed.[51] This, then, was the able diplomat and erudite scholar whom Michael had judiciously chosen as his chief lay ambassador, who, no doubt, had discussions with the pope over political questions and who at Lyons took a public, oral oath of allegiance to the pope in the name of Michael and his son.

As for the Byzantine ecclesiastical representatives, ex-patriarch Ger-

49. On Syropoulos see Geanakoplos, *Byzantine East and Latin West,* 95–96, relating the disputes over the matter of the Greek clergy's objection to the kissing of the pope's foot, and on the question of the primary rank of St. Peter among the apostles. Also chap. 11 below.

50. See esp. J. Meyendorff et al., *The Primacy of Peter in the Orthodox Church* (London, 1963); and Meyendorff, *Byzantine Theology* (New York, 1974), 96. *Primacy of Peter,* esp. 9, 12, 15, etc., shows that the Byzantine attitude toward the primacy and succession of Peter was determined by an "ecclesiology" different from that of the West. The title *koryphaios,* e.g., was often given not only to Peter but also to other apostles, esp. Paul and John. The term did not mean to Byzantines that Peter, and therefore Rome, had jurisdiction over the other apostles or sees. In other words the apostolic and the episcopal functions of Peter were not identical and the Byzantines did not consider a single bishop as the successor of one apostle, as the West did. For the Greeks, all bishops are successors of all apostles. Thus the East accepted Peter as chief of the apostles without accepting other Roman claims. (Incidentally, in Acropolites' work there is no mention of the city Lyons.)

51. See A. Heisenberg, "Prolegomena," to *Acropolitae Opera,* "Logos Deuteros peri tēs ek patros tou hagiou pneumatos ekporeuseōs," 45–66."

manos and Archbishop Theophanes, neither could lay claim to any particular distinction, theologically or intellectually. Indeed, Germanos had been removed from office by Michael some years before for ineptitude, and Theophanes was apparently not as yet a fully convinced pro-unionist.[52] These three Greek ambassadors, together with the chief imperial interpreter, George Berroiotes, and the *Prokathemenos tou Vestiariou* (grand chamberlain) Nicholas Panaretos, together with the Franciscans Ascoli, Bonagratia, and Parastron, now on 11 March 1274 embarked in two ships for the council in the West.[53] One ship, according to Pachymeres, who, besides Ascoli, alone mentions the specific Greek personalities, carried the three principal imperial envoys, as well as Parastron, Ascoli, and Bonagratia, along, of course, with sufficient crewmen to navigate the boat. The second ship, apparently functioning as a supply vessel, carried gifts for the pope and, presumably, servants to minister to the needs of the ambassadors, Greek and Latin. None of those aboard the second ship, except for Berroiotes the interpreter and Panaretos, were significant enough to merit mention in Pachymeres' detailed account.[54] Though other names are not mentioned, it is possible, nevertheless, that the ship may also have carried passengers attending to personal business in the West. Off the dangerous coast of Malea (southern Peloponnesus), the latter vessel was lost in a storm, with the interpreter Berroiotes, Panaretos, and two hundred and eleven other Greeks aboard, as well as all the lavish gifts for the pope, including golden icons, censers, and the very altar cloth Michael had stripped from the Cathedral of Hagia Sophia.[55]

Gregory's preparations for the council were not limited to sending ambassadors to Constantinople. Already as early as 11 March 1273, he

52. See Pachymeres, *De Michaele Palaeologis* 1:384. Cf. Nicol, "Greeks and Union," 477, esp. n. 70.

53. Pachymeres, *De Michaele Palaeologis* 1:385–86. For specific date see Gill, "Church Union of Lyons," 10.

54. On the embassy as a whole see esp. Pachymeres, *De Michaele Palaeologis* 1:384–85 (cf. Geanakoplos, *Emperor Michael,* 258–59).

55. Pachymeres, *De Michaele Palaeologis* 1:396–97; cf. Roberg, *Union auf dem Konzil,* 126–27; and Nicol, "Greeks and Union," 477. Pachymeres, 1:396, mentions 213 men *(in toto)* as does the report of Ascoli (all civilians, says Franchi, *Concilio II di Lione,* 76). See also the late fifteenth-century chroniclers, Peter of Prussia, *Vita B. Alberti,* 279, and Rudolf of Nijmegen, *Legenda Beati Alberti* (both discussed in Franchi, 136 n. 24), who mention 120 persons composing the Greek delegation. But no original source is indicated for their statement. Ascoli's letter to Gregory from Cape Leucas also mentions the Greek envoys—the same persons as in Pachymeres, but adding the archbishop of Philippi, who died before departure of the embassy: see Ascoli's letter in Roberg, 227–29; see also Franchi, 76 n. 22. Ascoli mentions that the lost ship was sunk off Negropont! (Roberg, 227–29). On the gifts, esp. the altar cloth, see Pachymeres, *De Michaele Palaeologis* 1:384–85.

had asked for the writing of reports or position papers from Western scholars with experience of the East.[56] Especially important was the treatise *Opus tripartitum,* written by the former Dominican minister-general Humbert of Romans. His report is in many ways unique, for it avoids the usual polemics and propagandistic approach to the problem of union. Comprehending the need to understand what we would now call the psychology of the Greeks, the dynamics of their hostility, Humbert stresses political as well as dogmatic matters, affirming that the chief political difference stemmed from Greek anger at the re-creation, in 800, of the Roman Empire in the West by the pope and Charlemagne despite the already existing Roman (Byzantine) Empire in the East. Moreover, with subtlety of understanding, Humbert stressed that no true union could come about unless the Latins and Greeks familiarized themselves with each other's ecclesiastical writings and canons. He even maintained that the pope should not insist on complete obedience *at once* and that the Greeks should be permitted to retain their own ritual—all views that for a Latin were far ahead of his time. To quote from this remarkable work: "Above all, to further union it is important to study Greek, as was the case in the time of Jerome and Augustine. At the present time knowledge of Greek is so rare in the Roman Curia that almost no one can read the language. Indeed, it would be precious for union if Latins could read the theologically important Greek works, the acts of the Greek councils, and diverse canonists [note the mention of Greek canon law, which rarely ever interested the West], and their ecclesiastical history. There is too little interest in these writings and too much in philosophy." (Particularly striking is the latter remark, made by a Dominican at the very height of the Western Scholastic achievement!) Humbert concludes, equally perceptively, "It is essential that the Latin fathers be translated into Greek and that they be sent to the Greek East."[57] Note the emphasis here on the importance of a mutual knowledge of each other's theology and religious practices. Despite his rare perception of Greek attitudes, however, Humbert still regarded the Greeks as "schismatics" from the Roman church.

Besides the Franciscans mentioned—Jerome of Ascoli, Parastron, and Bonaventura—several Dominicans also played roles in the preparation for the council at Lyons. Among these is the famous translator of Aristotle and Archimedes, William of Moerbeke.[58] As a youth William had

56. See Guiraud, *Registres de Grégoire X,* no. 220, 11 March 1273.

57. For French translation of important extracts from Humbert's work, see Wolter and Holstein, *Lyon I et II,* 268–76; original Latin text in Mansi, vol. 24, cols. 125b–32d; also Roberg, *Union auf dem Konzil,* 83–95.

58. On William's translations see esp. M. Grabmann, *Guglielmo di Moerbeke il tradutorre delle opere di Aristotele,* Miscellanea historiae pontificiae (Rome, 1946), 36–

been sent to the Greek East, where he had learned Greek exceptionally well at the Dominican convent in Pera (Constantinople) and later at that of Thebes in Greece.[59] The Dominican minister-general at the time was none other than Humbert of Romans, who, as just noted, attached special importance to the Latin learning of Greek. In view of Humbert's strong recommendations to the pope on the value of Greek and of Moerbeke's long residence in the East, it seems likely that Gregory summoned the latter to Lyons precisely because of his Greek knowledge and, possibly, in order to further other suggestions of Humbert. Indeed, at the council Moerbeke served in the capacity of interpreter, probably for both sides, since, as we have seen, the official Greek interpreter, Berroiotes, had drowned on the way to the council

Another Dominican whose presence at the council and whose relations with the Greeks are generally mentioned by modern authorities but about whom the primary sources seem strangely silent—the *Ordinatio,* for example does not even cite his name—is the famous but now aged theologian Albertus Magnus. Though it appears that he actually was present at the conciliar proceedings, he does not seem to have attended as an official delegate either of the pope or of his own Dominican order. Evidently, Albert was sent to Lyons as a representative of Rudolf of Hapsburg, the new Holy Roman Emperor, whose candidacy was then in dispute in the Curia.[60] Moreover, it is plausible that in the face of strong attacks on the rapidly proliferating mendicant orders, Albert raised his voice primarily on behalf of his own Dominican order, which, with the Franciscan, some of the lay clergy even wished to abolish.

Regarding Albertus's possible connections with the Greek delegation at Lyons, a passage in his *Opera omnia* contains a curious remark that might seem to link him with the Byzantine delegation: "And at the council of Lyons the Greeks were forced to admit that fornication, as they

51. It has been shown by Grabmann and by L. Minio-Paluello, *Opuscula, the Latin Aristotle* (Amsterdam, 1972, rpt. of earlier articles), 40–56, that Moerbeke translated works of Aristotle much before 1274, and specifically (56) that he completed his translation of Aristotle's *Poetics* in 1278 in Viterbo, Italy. (Evidently he remained in Italy after the Lyons council.) We know, moreover, that William translated Proclus's *Elementatio theologica* at the papal court, so he probably went to Lyons from Italy, not from the Byzantine East; cf. Minio-Paluello, 36, affirming that "we do not know exactly when William went to and left Greece," also noting that every year the Dominicans sent monks to Greece for missionary work. Besides Aristotle's *Politics* and *Poetics,* William translated a good part of Archimedes' works (Geanakoplos, *Byzantine East and Latin West,* 23).

59. On William's education see esp. Grabmann, *Guglielmo di Moerbeke,* 36.

60. On Albertus at Lyons see Franchi, *Concilio II di Lione,* 129 n. 14; and Roberg, *Union auf dem Konzil,* 143 n. 41, and esp. 169–70.

do not accept, is a cardinal sin"—the same point, it should be observed, made by Ascoli in his report to the pope.[61] That Albertus was well aware of the Greek view of the *filioque* question is indicated by several long passages in his writings defending the Latin view against the Greek.[62] Nevertheless, that he actually engaged in formal debate with the Greeks seems, on the basis of the primary sources, as yet undemonstrated, though exchanges on an informal basis certainly cannot be ruled out. Nevertheless, the late fifteenth-century Dominican chronicler Peter of Prussia records that "in hoc concilio venerabilis frater Albertus plures errores destruxit praecipue Grecorum."[63] This passage, imprecise as it is, should perhaps rather be taken to refer to *private* or *informal* discussions engaged in by Albertus with one or another of the Greek envoys. Other than this, there seems to be no specific reference to Albertus's involvement at Lyons in the question of religious union.

Having sketched the roles of the leading protagonists, the pope, the Byzantine emperor and his envoys, and the various Franciscan and Dominican intermediaries, let us now focus on the actual conciliar proceedings at Lyons, as set forth especially in the *Ordinatio*.

The council opened on 4 May 1274 at the Cathedral of St. John in Lyons. But the Greeks did not appear until seven weeks later. About 20 May, when a letter of the pope's ambassador to Constantinople, the Franciscan Jerome of Ascoli, was received from Cape Leucas (near Brindisi in Italy)[64] announcing his imminent arrival with the Greek ambas-

61. See Albertus's *Opera omnia,* ed. A. Borgnet (Paris, 1890–99), 18:60: "Graeci qui dicebant quod fornicatio non esset mortale peccatum, in concilio Lugdunensi coacti sunt hoc revocare." Cf. M. Albert, *Albert the Great* (Oxford, 1948), 103: "Thomas set out for Lyons but the old man [Albertus] arrived there and played a leading part in the proceedings"; also J. Sighart, *Albert the Great of the Order of Friar Preachers* (London, 1876), 372; and W. Hinnebusch, *History of the Dominican Order,* vol. 2 (New York, 1973), 26.

62. See esp. article on Albertus by A. Stohr, "Der Hl. Albertus über den Ausgang des Heiligen Geistes," in *Albertus Magnus Festschrift* (Freiburg, 1932).

63. Passage (dated 1487) quoted in Franchi, *Concilio II di Lione,* 171. The Dominican Rudolf of Nijmegen in 1490 printed his *Legenda Beati Alberti,* which copied Peter of Prussia's biography printed in 1487. For modern biographies of Albertus, which repeat errors regarding his participation in formal theological debates with the Greeks, see P. von Loé, "Albert der Grosse auf dem Konzil von Lyon (1274)," *Kölnische Volkszeitung* 55 (1914): 225–26; D. Lathoud, "Saint Albert le Grand et l'union des grecs au second concile de Lyon," *L'unité de l'église* 8–10 (1929–32): 461–62 (based on erroneous statements of Peter of Prussia); and A. Garreau, *Albert le Grand* (Paris, 1932), 170: "Lyons was a triumph for the pope *and the Dominicans*" (emphasis added).

64. And not from the Greek island of Leucas, as scholars have wrongly believed (cf. Franchi, *Concilio II di Lione,* 76 n. 11; and Roberg, *Union auf dem Konzil,* 136).

sadors, the pope appointed Bonaventura to deliver a sermon.[65] Bonaventura selected a most appropriate text for the occasion, from the apocryphal Old Testament book Baruch, as he drew an analogy between the Greeks and the Israelites who had long been in captivity in Babylon. From the Latin point of view, the Greeks too—in a symbolic sense captives of heresy—were now, finally, in general council, returning from the East to the "true wisdom of the church" in the West. As the text from Baruch reads, "Arise *[Exsurge]* O Jerusalem [meaning here the entire church] and stand on high and look about toward the east and behold thy children gathered together from the rising to the setting sun."[66]

On the actual arrival, on 24 June, of the Greek representatives together with Ascoli and Parastron, the *Ordinatio* relates, the entire community of cardinals, bishops, and abbots with their households went forth to meet the Greeks in order to lead them to the pope, who, with his retinue, was standing awaiting them in the *aula* (hall) of the papal palace. On their arrival, the pope gave the Greek envoys the "kiss of peace."[67] Then, according to the *Ordinatio,* the Greeks, travel-weary and no doubt still deeply disturbed over the deaths of so many of their fellow travelers off Cape Malea, after being formally received by the pope and presenting their credentials—letters with the imperial gold seal—were escorted to their quarters.[68] Evidently no formal discussion of any kind took place at this time.

Meanwhile, the pope, as we learn from another source, summoned in private session (to which Bonaventura may also have been invited) his envoy Jerome of Ascoli and his companion Bonagratia.[69] (The other two

65. See text in Roberg, *Union auf dem Konzil,* 227–29; cf. Franchi, *Concilio II di Lione,* 75–76.

66. Text of Baruch (a major Old Testament prophet) reads: "Exsurge Jerusalem et sta in excelso, et circumspice ad orientem, et vide electos filios tuos ab oriente sole usque ad occidentem in illo sancti gaudentes Dei memoria."

67. Franchi, *Concilio II di Lione,* 79–80, esp.: "ad pacis osculum honorifice sunt recepti." Evidently, unlike at Florence later, the Greeks were not required to kiss the foot of the pope (see Geanakoplos, *Byzantine East and Latin West,* 64–65, and essay 11 below). Gregory also was standing, not seated, when he received the Greeks.

68. The Greek envoys brought several letters to the pope, among them one each from Michael and his son, and the letter from the Greek bishops: see *Acta Urbani IV, Clementis IV, Gregorii X,* ed. A. Tautu (Vatican, 1953), nos. 43, 45; Roberg, *Union auf dem Konzil,* 228. According to Franchi, *Concilio II di Lione,* 81 n. 25, "The Byzantine legates had two other documents with them but we are not certain they were presented in this public audience: Andronicus' letter, read later at the Fourth Session of the Council, a letter from Michael to Gregory accrediting Germanos and Acropolites to treat of 'mundane negotiations'" (doubtless on the restraint of Charles' ambitions and on the future crusade).

69. On Ascoli's papal audience see Franchi, *Concilio II di Lione,* 81 n. 25, referring to

of the original four Franciscan envoys sent to Constantinople had long before returned to the West, dispatched by Palaeologus in order to report to the pope.) Ascoli and Bonagratia now, it seems, presented to Pope Gregory special letters from the Greek emperor and his son. Among the letters brought to the pope by the Greek envoys was included, it might be noted, a special imperial communication to the pope's nephew. In this letter Michael stressed (recall that Gregory himself had lived for years in the Holy Land) that one of his envoys, his relative the ex-patriarch Germanos, had from childhood spent many years in Jerusalem living in Greek monasteries.[70] This remark was no doubt intended as a way of creating a bond between Germanos and Gregory and his nephew.

Inasmuch as Emperor Michael sent no form of oath, questions were apparently rather quickly raised at the council about the official authority of the logothete George Acropolites to swear in the emperor's name. For he presented, it seems, no document specifically authorizing him to sign any binding agreement on the emperor's behalf. When queried about this lack, Acropolites claimed that, before he left Constantinople, the emperor had given him authority viva voce.[71] And indeed a passage quoting the words of Michael (as repeated in Ascoli's report) would seem to support this contention: "It is not the habit of the Greeks to take an oath, rather a subscription has the same authority as an oath" (a rather dubious statement, to say the least).[72] In view of this omission and also of several others in connection with the letter from the Greek clergy, serious doubts should have arisen in Western minds about flaws and loopholes in the Greek manner of participation in, and acceptance of, religious union. Even the aforementioned letter of the Greek bishops, most fundamental of all, since the implementation of union depended primarily upon the

---

the report of Metochites (published by Giannelli in Laurent, *Le Bienheureux Innocent V,* 442). According to Roberg, *Union auf dem Konzil,* 138, at this time Ascoli probably consigned to Pope Gregory another document, a personal letter from Patriarch Joseph of Constantinople.

70. See text in Roberg, 232. Cf. above, n. 30.

71. Franchi, *Concilio II di Lione,* 89, noting that the Greek legates had full powers conferred by Michael, but that one of these powers, that of taking an oath, was based only on oral authorization from Michael. Cf. Tautu, *Acta,* no. 47.

72. Quoted in Franchi, *Concilio II di Lione,* 90 n. 40: "asserens [Michael] hoc non esse consuetudinis apud eos et subscriptio habetur pro firmitate etiam juramenti." A Latin document printed in Tautu indicates that, in order to assuage the suspicions of the Latin canonists at Lyons, Acropolites and the other legates signed a document indicating their acceptance of the papal terms in the name of the emperor. But see now Geanakoplos, *Emperor Michael,* 262 n. 18, citing a Paris MS quoting what seems to be a Latin translation of Emperor Michael's written authorization to Acropolites to take an oath in his behalf. This has been largely overlooked.

Eastern clergy, was but a copy, though it had been signed by the grand chartophylax of Hagia Sophia, John Bekkos, the later pro-unionist patriarch. The original letter bearing the signatures of the bishops, was retained in the imperial chancery at Constantinople (*in munimine imperatoris,* as Ascoli put it).[73] Perhaps Michael thought these signatures too precious to risk losing. Or, more probably, he thought the sparse number of signatures would look dubious to the pope. Whatever the reason, it seems clear, contrary to the view of some modern historians,[74] that Gregory must have been aware of the shortcomings of the Greek clergy's letter and the lack of unity it reflected. It should be noted here that all medieval popes, and to a certain extent perhaps even Gregory himself, were imbued with the belief that the emperor, because of what they believed to be his "Caesaropapistic" powers, could with no great difficulty bend the church to his will.[75] That it was always the emperor, not the patriarch, who initiated negotiations for union certainly strengthened this view.

To continue the calendar of events according to the *Ordinatio:* on 29 June, five days after the Greek arrival, the pope, surrounded by all his cardinals, bishops, and other clerics, celebrated mass in the presence of the Byzantine ambassadors. The epistle was read in Latin and Greek, and the gospel chanted, first in Latin by the pope's relative, Cardinal Ottobono, then in Greek by a Greek deacon dressed in the habit of his own rite.[76] Bonaventura then delivered a sermon, after which the creed was intoned, first in Latin by the archbishop Erard d'Auxerre and other Latins, and then repeated in Greek by the ex-patriarch Germanos and the Byzantines, along with the Greek bishops of Calabria and the Dominican William of Moerbeke and the Franciscan John [Parastron] of Constantinople, both referred to here as "penitentiaries" (that is, "confessors") of the pope. Three times *(ter)* the phrase *ex patre filioque procedit* was chanted.[77] Contrary to what used to be believed by historians, the famous story of Theophanes at this moment keeping his mouth shut has recently been shown to be false.[78]

73. For Latin text see Roberg, *Union auf dem Konzil,* 229; cf. Franchi, *Concilio II di Lione,* 80 n. 24, on the phrase from Ascoli's letter: [the letter with the bishops' signatures had remained] *in munimine* (a safe place = chancery) *imperatoris.*

74. See, e.g., W. Norden, *Das Papsttum und Byzanz* (Berlin, 1903), 548–62. Cf. Geanakoplos, *Emperor Michael,* 265–66, on Michael's "dual policy" to the pope and his own clergy.

75. Cf. H. Beck, "From the Second Council of Lyons to the Council of Ferrara-Florence," chap. 51 of *From the High Middle Ages to the Eve of the Reformation,* 488; and Geanakoplos, *Byzantine East and Latin West,* 94.

76. Franchi, *Concilio II di Lione,* 82, cf. 110.

77. Ibid., 83, cf. 111.

78. See Nicol, "The Byzantine Reaction," 114 n. 12, listing authors who have

When recitation of the creed was finished, ex-patriarch Germanos, Archbishop Theophanes, and Logothete Acropolites together chanted *laudes (enkomia)* in Greek in honor of the pope. Thus the mass, with the Greeks standing near the altar *(iuxta altarem)* was completed.[79] There is no mention in the sources that the Greeks then participated in Holy Communion, which is understandable since the union, though already negotiated in Constantinople, had not yet been formally proclaimed.[80] Subsequently, during the five-day interval between 24 and 29 June, some private conversations in all probability did take place between Greeks and Latins. But no formal public debates of any kind on the matter of reunion seem to have transpired. Nor is there any reliable document or other primary source that I can find to contradict this view. There may be one slight exception, however: a little-known source that mentions, if obscurely, that in a letter written after the council by Pope Innocent V (formerly the Dominican minister-general Peter of Tarentaise) to Emperor Michael, he made allusion to certain (theological?) exchanges at Lyons "between Latins and Greeks."[81] Whether these were formal or private exchanges, or merely conversations, is not clear. It would seem likely, in any event, that Bonaventura and perhaps his envoy Jerome (as happened later with Greek envoys at the Council of Florence) may well have been invited to dine with the pope and the three Greek envoys, at which time they surely would have engaged, informally, in some kind of theological or other discussions of opinion, at least off the record. We know that Acropolites was explicitly charged by the emperor to discuss with the pope the political aspects of union, that is, the restraining of Charles militarily. And Pope Gregory, it appears, usually sought to tie such considerations closely to ecclesiastical concessions on the part of the Greeks.

To return to the account of events at the council as recorded in the *Ordinatio,* on the fourth day of July a reception was held by Pope Gregory for the ambassadors of the great khan of the Tatars (Persians) Abaqa il-Khan, whom the pope hoped to convert to Catholicism.[82] This was an

---

repeated the story about Theophanes. See Franchi, *Concilio II di Lione,* 91, ll. 296ff., where he corrects the corrupt text of earlier editions of the *Ordinatio.*

79. Franchi, *Concilio II di Lione,* 83.

80. Receiving the sacrament of communion would be the main test, if at this time it were a true concelebration of mass. Evidently it was instead a "pontifical mass" held in the presence of the Greek envoys, who were probably at this time not yet considered "Catholics."

81. See Franchi, *Concilio II di Lione,* 46 n. 37, citing a Dominican source referring to Innocent's letter.

82. Ibid., 84.

extraordinary event which apparently absorbed the attention of all present at Lyons.

Only two days later, on 6 July, during the fourth session of the council, on the feast day of saints Peter and Paul, the actual ceremony proclaiming religious union of the churches took place. After the seating of the Greek envoys, to the right but *behind* the cardinals (cardinal deacons),[83] the Dominican minister-general, Peter of Tarentaise, rose to deliver a sermon, which, however, like that of Bonaventura, has not survived. Thereupon, the pope delivered an allocution, the original text of which has also been lost. After restating the three aims for his calling of the council—regarding (1) the crusade, (2) union with the Greeks, and (3) correction of abuses in the church—he expressed his jubilation at the conclusion of union between the two churches. As Gregory pointedly emphasized (not without exaggeration), Michael had returned to obedience of the papacy, "voluntarily and with no other motive than the religious." (Here the *Ordinatio* steps out of character, as it were, and records "which was strongly doubted").[84] In George Metochites' account there is a passage that seems pertinent here: describing the pope for whose sincerity, lack of personal ambition, and ability he had genuine admiration, he wrote, "Gregory even pronounced a public discourse glorifying our Greek nation before an enormous crowd of ecclesiastical dignitaries." Metochites also speaks of Gregory's great love for the ancient Greek Fathers and, strikingly enough, for the necessity to recover Asia Minor for the Byzantines in the coming joint crusade. Praising Gregory's love of union, Metochites compares him to his successor pope (Innocent V), then Peter of Tarentaise, who "was a dialectician of note and had a profound knowledge of Scripture and who desired union but less profoundly than Gregory." Metochites' report, interestingly, affirms that, in his great zeal for the crusade, Gregory even made plans to meet personally with Michael in the Italian city of Brindisi, or, if the danger from Charles seemed too threatening, in Avlona in the Balkans.[85]

At this point the letters of Michael and his son were read aloud (in Latin translation) in which, in precise and unmistakable language, Michael declared his adherence to the Roman faith, including acceptance of the *filioque, azyma,* and primacy of papal jurisdiction. Afterward, the letter of the Greek prelates was in turn publicly read. Whereupon in the name of the emperor and his son, the layman George Acropolites solemnly and publicly abjured the schism.[86] So far as I can determine from

83. Ibid., 85 (cf. 87): "a latere dextro *post cardinales* (diaconi)."

84. Ibid., 86, 112. The *Ordinatio* here reads, "de quo multum dubitabatur."

85. See Laurent, *Le Bienheureux Innocent V,* 439–40.

86. Franchi, *Concilio II di Lione,* 81–91. See discussion of Acropolites' oath taking

the sources, Acropolites had no authority to do the same on behalf of the Greek clergy. Nor, apparently, did the ex-patriarch Germanos or Archbishop Theophanes at any time explicitly and publicly make any such declaration, apart from the vague letter they brought from the Greek clergy.

After the proclamation of union, the Greek clergy were reseated in the cathedral, but in a place probably again little to their satisfaction, for they were placed to the left, but this time behind the cardinal-presbyters.[87] After this, the symbol of the faith was chanted by the pope in Latin, together with the entire body of Latins. And, finally, ex-patriarch Germanos and Archbishop Theophanes, along with the Greek bishops and abbots of the kingdom of Sicily, again chanted the creed in Greek, during which, according to the *Ordinatio,* the *filioque* was this time chanted (only) twice *(bis).*[88]

The next day, on 7 July, the council considered the important question of reform in the (Western) church, especially the method of papal election and the abuses in the mendicant orders. These discussions, it appears, continued among the Latins alone until 17 July.

Meantime, during the night between 14 and 15 July, Bonaventura suddenly died.[89] One Franciscan chronicler, seeking to explain the suddenness of his demise, declared that contributory to his death were his intensive negotiations with the Greeks over union.[90] But no corroboration seems to exist for this statement, it apparently having been made for the first time about a century after the fact. A more likely cause would have been Bonaventura's intense preoccupation with the new constitutions of the church, in particular those dealing with the fate of his own beloved Franciscan order.

In the promulgation of these constitutions, which, besides involving the future of the mendicants, concerned, among other matters, a new method of papal election and the doctrine of the procession of the Holy Spirit, the Greeks should have shown keen interest, to say the least. After all, they were now, presumably, an integral part of the "one united Christian church." But the Greek envoys, evidently in accordance with in-

---

(and text of the oath translated into English) in Geanakoplos, *Emperor Michael,* 262 n. 18 (cf. above, n. 72). Also see text in Tautu, *Acta,* no. 48. Acropolites' oath had apparently not been prescribed by Michael in the form he took it.

87. Franchi, *Concilio II di Lione,* 91: "in loco in quo sedebant presbyteri cardinales, post eos." Cf. p. 238 at Florence, n. 52.

88. Ibid., 92. At the conclusion, it is to be noted, on the order of Gregory "some words were read aloud from the ancient councils."

89. Ibid., 95.

90. See, e.g., Roncaglia, *Les frères mineurs,* 176 n. 8; and esp. Franchi, *Concilio II di Lione,* 159, 156, attributing this to Paolino of Venice, a Franciscan bishop of Pozzuoli, 324–44: see G. Sbaralea, *Supp. script. Francisc.* (Rome, 1806), 574.

structions given them by Michael himself, took care to avoid presenting any dissenting opinions. And this despite the quite different Greek method of choosing the chief hierarch, and in the light of Byzantine religio-political theory, according to which the emperor, not the pope, was vicar of Christ on earth—not to speak, finally, of the polemical Greek attitude toward the vexing *filioque* question. But, again, I find no record in any primary source—Greek, Franciscan, Dominican, or in the *Ordinatio*—of Greek participation in any of these public discussions despite what one would normally expect.[91]

On 16 July, after baptism of the Tatar ambassador, the new constitutions were read aloud and a eulogy preached over the body of Bonaventura by Peter of Tarentaise, the Dominican minister-general, at which time the Greeks must also have expressed their lament at Bonaventura's demise. Peter's text, a moving one, was taken from David's psalm lamenting the death of "my brother Jonathan," certainly another testimonial to the affection felt by the clerics, high and low, for Bonaventura.[92]

On 17 July, at the sixth and final session of the council, two more constitutions were promulgated, only one, however, the *Cum sacrosancta,* concerning the Greek union. After this the council adjourned. Only a few days later, at the end of July, the Greek delegation departed for home accompanied by envoys of the pope. During the last few days, whatever discussions may have taken place with the Greeks very probably concerned how the newly proclaimed union was to be implemented in Constantinople among the Greek clergy and people. For, as noted earlier, Ascoli and Parastron, and probably even Acropolites, must have informed the pope about the still strong opposition to union of many, if not most, of the Greek people and clerics.

We take note here of only the one constitution which, besides *Ubi periculum* on the method of papal election,[93] must have been of special interest to the Greeks, *Cum sacrosancta.* This was read out on 17 July in the council in the presence of the Greeks.[94] In this constitution it is stated, unquestionably for the benefit of the Greeks, that the Holy Spirit

91. Even if the legitimate Byzantine patriarch, Joseph, had gone to Lyons, he alone could not have abjured the schism. Byzantine canon law required the presence and assent of all five patriarchs at an ecumenical council.

92. Franchi, *Concilio II di Lione,* 95–97. On Peter of Tarentaise (later Innocent V), see H. Laurent, *Le Bienheureux Innocent V (Pierre de Tarentaise), Studia et documenta* (Rome, 1943).

93. On this constitution see B. Roberg, "Der konziliare Wortlaut des Konklave-Dekrets 'Ubi periculum' vom 1274," *Annuarium historiae conciliorum* 2 (1970): 231–62, which lists the names of bishops who signed. No Byzantine is included, however.

94. See Gill, "Church Union of Lyons," 10–11. Franchi, *Concilio II di Lione,* 137, believes, I think correctly, that Theophanes and Germanos must have approved the text of *Cum sacrosancta.* This occurred probably outside the formal sessions.

proceeds "not as from two principles but as from one, not by two spirations but by one unique spiration." (This, by the way, is a definition in traditional Latin, Augustinian terms.) And it was presumably couched in these terms to answer the perennial Greek accusation of Latin belief in two archic sources, Father and Son, for the Holy Spirit. The constitution concludes: "This is what the holy Roman church . . . has always professed. It is what comprises the immutable, true doctrine of the Fathers and orthodox doctors, Greek and Latin."[95]

If exchanges did indeed take place at the council between Greeks and Latins, they must have occurred, with few exceptions, through interpreters—through John Parastron and William of Moerbeke, who, apparently alone, had a complete and facile knowledge of *spoken* Greek and Latin. As we have seen, Bonaventura had virtually no knowledge of Greek, and the Greek of Albertus Magnus was faulty and doubtlessly limited to knowledge of the ancient language. To be sure, we should not overlook the still bilingual Greek bishops from southern Italy. (Recall the passages in the *Ordinatio* that they joined the Greek envoys in chanting the *filioque* in Greek.)[96]

To return once again to the *Ordinatio,* if one examines carefully the events and ceremonies it lists, one wonders where sufficient time could have been found in the interval from the time of the Greek arrival on 24 June to the public ceremony of union (6 July) for any substantive theological exchanges or formal debates between Greeks and Latins to have taken place. Moreover, the problem of religious union, however important, was frequently not even the primary issue. The council spent long hours discussing the question closest to the pope's heart—the launching of a crusade to Jerusalem. Let us not forget that this involved the heavy taxation of all the usually reluctant Western clergy.[97] Even more atten-

95. *Cum sacrosancta* is the same constitution as *Fideli ac devota* (text in Roberg, *Union auf dem Konzil,* 247; French translation in Wolter and Holstein, *Lyon I et II,* 286). It was not known for some time that these two canons were the same; see Franchi, *Concilio II di Lione,* 124.

96. Franchi, *Concilio II di Lione,* 91; cf. a remark of the fourteenth-century Marino Sanudo Torsello, *Istoria del regno di Romania,* ed. C. Hopf, *Chroniques gréco-romanes* (Berlin, 1873), 143, that "more Greeks of Calabria and Terra d'Otranto would have been more faithful to Rome if Michael and his patriarch had been more obedient to the pope." The south Italian Greeks had been united to Rome since the Council of Bari in 1098.

97. See Franchi, *Concilio II di Lione,* 98–99, mentioning the pope's pleasure at discussions for a crusade. Indeed, Franchi, 122, lists the crusade as the "primary" theme of the council. See also the contemporary Venetian Martino da Canale, "La cronique des Veniciens," *Archivio storico italiano* 8 (1845): 670–71 (cf. Franchi, 124): "Io so apertamente che grande parlamento sara tenuto colà [Lyons] della Santa Terra." Plans

tion was devoted to the drawing up of new constitutions to correct abuses in the church, notably on the procedure for electing a pope (a method, by the way, still in effect today), and on the excessive proliferation of the many new mendicant orders with their irregularities. It was undoubtedly Bonaventura and Peter of Tarentaise who had to bear the brunt of the attack from the secular clergy, who felt strongly that, on account of the growing abuses of the mendicants, their orders should be curtailed or even abolished.[98] Bonaventura, now a cardinal but still high in Franciscan councils, was always at the side of the pope, as was the Dominican minister-general Peter of Tarentaise. And both were deeply involved in the day-to-day business of the council.

In the light of these various considerations, one may justifiably argue that inadequate opportunity existed even to discuss, much less formally to debate in any extensive, detailed fashion, the burning questions for centuries separating the churches—the *filioque, azyma,* purgatory, and the overriding matter of papal supremacy.[99] Such an argument would, of course, as stressed earlier, not preclude the possibility of informal talks or conversations, for instance at dinner or between formal conciliar sessions. Indeed, we know that ex-patriarch Germanos and George Acropolites were empowered by the emperor to engage in negotiations with Pope Gregory over political matters having to do with Charles of Anjou.[100]

But another view is at the same time plausible and even probable—that neither pope nor emperor even desired any formal discussion on religious union to take place at Lyons. On the papal side, earlier documents reveal that for decades it had been papal policy that the emperor first accept the Roman confession of faith proposed by the pope, and only then would the pope agree to convoke an ecumenical council and grant military aid to the Greeks. As an earlier pope, Clement IV, had intransigently written to Michael, "The truth of divine dogma can never be put in jeopardy by discussion."[101] It seems, therefore, that what Pope Gre-

---

were presented to the pope for a crusade by, among others, Fidenzio of Padua, then a leading crusader propagandist. On the crusade see also Tautu, *Acta,* no. 49.

98. *Dizionario biografico degli Italiani,* s.v. "Bonaventura," 2:617–18, says (correctly) that Bonaventura's principal work at the Council of Lyons was in defense of the Franciscan order.

99. One may recall the interminable discussions, lasting longer than an entire year, at the later Council of Florence (1438–39) almost exclusively on the question of the *filioque* (see Geanakoplos, *Byzantine East and Latin West,* 99–103. See below, essay 11.

100. See Geanakoplos, *Emperor Michael,* 237–45; and Tautu, *Acta,* nos. 63–64, where proposals are made by the Greeks to Gregory regarding "peace with the Latins" (meaning Charles).

101. Quoted in Geanakoplos, *Emperor Michael,* 203.

gory really wanted at Lyons was not formal theological exchanges but simply ratification of the union which, in his mind, had already been negotiated at Constantinople—to put the seal, so to say, of an ecumenical council on that which had previously been accepted by Michael, his son, and a segment of unionist-minded clergy in Constantinople in the negotiations with Jerome of Ascoli.

From Michael's side, the argument against formal debate seems even more persuasive. For as Michael was clearly aware, in the face of serious rebellion in his capital against his unionist policy not only on the part of virtually all the common people and monks and of many leading prelates, but even of his own family—not to speak of the pro-Lascarid party—discussion of such sensitive issues would probably provoke bitter debate at the council and jeopardize what, above all, he expected as recompense for the union—papal cooperation to force the papal vassal Charles of Anjou to desist from his projected attack on Constantinople. In support of this view, we may cite the document that Jerome of Ascoli had sent to the pope from Byzantium stating that papal primacy and dogma had already been recognized and agreed to in writing by Michael and his son at a meeting with the Greek clergy and Ascoli in Constantinople.[102] In further support of this theory, let us recall that Michael sent to Lyons not the incumbent patriarch Joseph, but rather a sympathetic ex-patriarch and relative of his who was willing for the sake of political expediency, or, as Michael put it in ecclesiastical terms, of *economia,* to reestablish religious union with Rome in order to safeguard the Byzantine capital. As Michael in effect said to his prelates, "For the salvation of the ship of state [that is, the *Basileia*] it is often necessary [in matters of the church] to cast overboard all extraneous cargo."[103]

Contrary to generally held modern scholarly opinion, Pope Gregory probably comprehended more or less accurately the ecclesiastical situation in Constantinople. For in their letter the Greek clergy had informed him that the incumbent Greek patriarch, the anti-unionist Joseph, had been forced to withdraw from his post, to be re-installed only if Michael's embassy returned unsuccessfully from Lyons.[104] Moreover, to reiterate once again, Gregory must surely have heard from Ascoli, Parastron, and probably Acropolites of the tremendous pressures against union faced by Michael. (It was in fact in Michael's own interest to have this point emphasized by Acropolites.) This could serve to explain Gregory's ap-

102. See Franchi, *Concilio II di Lione,* text on 229.

103. On Michael's speeches stressing *economia* (the concept expressed here) see Geanakoplos, *Emperor Michael,* 265, esp. n. 28. Now also on Michael and *economia* see Geanakoplos, *Byzantium,* no. 98. Dogma was supposed to be excluded from *economia.*

104. See Geanakoplos, *Emperor Michael,* 262 nn. 15–16.

parent leniency, especially his willingness to overlook the Greek clergy's ambiguous acceptance of his directives and the rather serious omissions in their episcopal letter brought to Lyons.

In view of Pope Gregory's sincerity, which is praised even by the Greeks Pachymeres and Metochites, his apparent lack of objection—probably even agreement—to Michael's plea for retention of the Byzantine ritual,[105] and his toleration even for the Greek clergy's imperfect letter, it seems that Humbert of Romans's advice to Gregory in his *Opus tripartitum*—to advance cautiously but surely[106]—may not have been in vain. Like Humbert, and unlike his papal predecessors Urban and Clement (who had expected immediate and total capitulation of the Greek clergy to everything they demanded, both confessionally and jurisdictionally), Gregory probably believed that, with patience and a certain tolerance on both sides, the union already realized (if imperfectly) in Constantinople would in time become a lasting reality.

It seems likely, then, that from the viewpoints of both Pope Gregory and Emperor Michael the council of Lyons was intended merely to *ratify officially* what had *already been negotiated* in the East by the Franciscan delegation headed by Jerome of Ascoli. This hypothesis seems to be corroborated by the almost total lack of material in the contemporary sources of the time relating to theological exchanges, particularly in the principal record of the council's activities, the *Ordinatio.*

In the light of our discussion, we may therefore conclude that, despite the Franciscan Bonaventura's attractive personality, profound learning, and, as we have described, presumably sympathetic attitude toward some Greek theological and mystical beliefs, the traditional Western opinion as to the key role played by him (and, to a lesser degree, by the Dominican Albertus Magnus) at the council with regard to theological debates with the Greeks has been a gross exaggeration and even misrepresentation. The question, of course arises: why this exaggeration and why for so many centuries? It is to be attributed, it appears, not only to contemporary Franciscan writers, but especially to later Franciscan adherents of Bonaventura who, at the time of his canonization in 1483 and still more in 1588, when he was officially pronounced a "Doctor of the Church," wanted to exalt him even more by terming him "the soul of the Greek union" and even "the president of the Council of Lyons."[107] Despite the

105. Beck, in *From the High Middle Ages to the Eve of the Reformation,* 126, observes (correctly) that the question of the *filioque* and of rites "was presumably arranged, orally but successfully, between the pope and the Greek legates."

106. Translation in Wolter and Holstein, *Lyon I et II,* 272.

107. On this exaggeration see esp. Franchi, *Concilio II di Lione,* 158ff. In *Bullarium franciscanum Sixti IV,* n.s., vol. 3, ed. J. Pou y Marti (1949), no. 1562 (cf. Franchi, 160),

undeniable magnitude of Bonaventura's contribution to many aspects of the Council of Lyons, his greatness seems to lie in areas other than theological victories over the Greeks.

The real protagonists who deserve credit for the success, however ephemeral, of the religious union proclaimed at Lyons—despite the presence of such brilliant Western theologians as Bonaventura and Albertus Magnus, and even, so to speak, of the spirit of the dead Thomas Aquinas, and, on the Greek side, of the able diplomat-scholar Acropolites and bishops Germanos and Theophanes—are the two rather obscure Franciscan friars, John Parastron and Jerome of Ascoli. Through his personal instruction of Michael in the theology of the Latin faith, and more particularly through his sympathetic participation in liturgical ceremonies with an initially almost totally hostile Greek clergy,[108] Parastron, it may be said, prepared the climate for union among at least some bishops in Constantinople, in the process helping them to come to the realization that religious union with the Latins was perhaps not so reprehensible after all. Even more significant, perhaps, was the role of the Italian Franciscan Jerome of Ascoli, later Pope Nicholas IV. Although to be sure, Ascoli achieved something less than complete success with the Greek hierarchy regarding their letter of submission to the pope, it was certainly his conclusion of negotiations with the emperor and his son, as well as with at least a part of the Greek episcopacy, that permitted union, untenable as it later proved, to be at last formally and publicly proclaimed at Lyons.

A word about the significance of the council in East and West: for the West, with its emphasis on papal authority, Lyons has always been considered a true ecumenical council. For the Greek East, on the other hand, the council has been linked with that of Ephesus II (449) as a "robber council" *(lēstrikē synodos).*[109] In explanation of this Byzantine view, two

---

Bonaventura is termed "Concilio Lugdunensi Praesidens"—manifestly false, unless it refers to his chairmanship of certain committees for matters other than union.

108. Beck, in *From the High Middle Ages to the Eve of the Reformation,* 125: "A first inventory of the higher clergy yielded only a half-dozen partisans of union."

109. See Geanakoplos, *Emperor Michael,* esp. 263 n. 20. Also Geanakoplos, "Byzantium and the Crusades," 55–56, quoting a letter of the south Italian Greek Barlaam to the pope affirming the Greek view of Lyons as a "robber council," because only the emperor and not the four eastern patriarchs had been represented. See also Geanakoplos, *Byzantium,* no. 159; and M. Calecas, *Adversus Graecos* (MPG, vol. 152, col. 211), who says the Greeks call Lyons a "tyrannical council." See Beck, "From the Second Council of Lyons," 488: "Lyons was rejected in the East mainly because it was attended by imperial legates, not by any of the Orthodox church." And cf. his p. 125: "Gregory had . . . an unfailing sympathy for the difficult situation of Michael."

considerations, repeatedly affirmed by subsequent Greek theologians and historians, must be emphasized, both of which, incidentally, have been demonstrated or implied in this paper: first, the lack of any formal theological debate—recall that, unlike later at Florence, the Greek emperor and clergy sent to Lyons no prominent theologian to defend Byzantine doctrinal views[110]—and, second, and of even greater import, the absence of legates representing all four of the Orthodox patriarchs. It is these two criteria, fundamental for Byzantine "ecclesiology," that still in the mind of Eastern Christendom serve to negate the "ecumenicity" and validity of the Council of Lyons.

110. The leading Greek theologians at that time were probably Gregory of Cyprus, Manuel Holobolos, Job Iasites, and perhaps John Bekkos, but none of these was sent to Lyons.

Additional Bibliography for Essay 10

See my "A Greek Libellus against Religious Union with Rome after the Council of Lyons (1274)," in *Interaction of the Sibling Cultures,* 156–70, a contemporary anti-unionist Greek pamphlet reflecting many popular Greek and some Latin beliefs and prejudices making religious union so difficult. V. Laurent and J. Darrouzès, "Dossier grec de l'union de Lyon (1273–77)," *Archives de l'Orient chrêtien* 16 (1976). C. Capizzi, "Il II° Concilio di Lione e l'unione del 1274: Saggio bibliografico," *Orientalia christiana periodica* 51 (1985): 87–122. J. Hussey, *The Orthodox Church in the Byzantine Empire* (Oxford, 1986), 229–35, a short summary. J. Gill, "John Beccus, Patriarch of Constantinople 1275–82," *Byzantina* 7 (1975): 251–66. E. Brett, *Humbert of Romans: His Life and Views of Thirteenth-Century Society* (Toronto, 1984). K. Setton, *The Papacy and the Levant,* vol. 1, *The Thirteenth and Fourteenth Centuries* (Philadelphia, 1976), 110–20. A. Failler, ed., *Pachymeres, Romaikē historia* (Paris, 1984). And my *Byzantium: Church, Society, and Civilization Seen through Contemporary Eyes,* 217–20, for translation of documents relevant to the council.

Eleven

The Council of Florence (1438–39) and the Problem of Union between the Byzantine and Latin Churches

I

For the medieval world the Council of Florence, held only fifteen years before the end of the Byzantine Empire, offered the last great opportunity to close the gap separating Eastern from Western Christendom. Not only was it the most brilliant convocation of Greeks and Latins in the entire Middle Ages, but it marked the first occasion in centuries that East and West assembled in ecumenical council to debate the differences separating their two churches.[1]

For almost four hundred years before the Council of Florence, from the schism of Patriarch Michael Cerularius and Pope Leo IX in 1054 to the convening of this council in 1438, it had been a primary aim of popes and emperors to restore ecclesiastical communion. Negotiations with this object in view had, in fact, been conducted on approximately thirty different occasions.[2] Strong forces motivated the desire for union. To the

1. On this council's ecumenicity see the official decree of union in the so-called *Acta graeca (Quae supersunt actorum Graecorum concilii florentini necnon descriptionis cuiusdam eiusdem)*, ed. J. Gill (Rome, 1953), 461 (hereafter referred to as *Acta*). Also in Mansi, *Sacrorum conciliorum . . . collectio,* vol. 31A, cols. 1027–28. At Florence, in contrast to the Council of Lyons in 1274, formal debate over ecclesiastical differences took place for the first time in centuries.

2. Thus calculates L. Bréhier, "Attempts at Reunion of the Greek and Latin Churches," *Cambridge Medieval History* 4 (1936): 594ff.

papacy union was the most effective way to extend its ecclesiastical authority over East as well as West, while for the Byzantine emperors of the fourteenth and fifteenth centuries, union with the Latin church seemed the sole means to insure papal aid against the peril of either a Latin crusade or Turkish attack against Constantinople.[3] Of lesser importance but worthy of note was the rare idealism of such thirteenth-century figures as Pope Gregory X and Patriarch John Bekkos, or the Western publicist Humbert of Romans and the Greek Franciscan John Parastron, to whom Greco-Latin religious accord was the supreme remedy for the problems of Eastern and Western Christendom.[4]

As a result of these considerations, union was actually declared at three separate times: first, following the Fourth Crusade of 1204 with enforced Greek conversion to Catholicism, then at the Council of Lyons in 1274 by personal agreement between Pope Gregory and Emperor Michael Palaeologus, and, finally, at Florence itself through the convocation of a general council.[5] But although union thus seemed to have been achieved, it was in reality each time only ephemeral and without lasting effect. In view of the various forces conducing toward union, how can these repeated failures be explained? Why in particular did the Greek population, for whom the existence of the empire itself was often at stake, always repudiate union?

The answers to these questions lie partly in the nature of the motivations themselves. For to emperors and popes union was less a matter of merging two spiritual bodies than a means for the satisfaction of political ends. Religious sincerity, indispensable for permanent union, was too

3. For bibliography on the complex problem of unionist negotiations in the period from 1054 to 1453 see Geanakoplos, *Byzantine East and Latin West,* 196–98, and the bibliographical note at the end of this essay.

4. For works on Gregory X and Bekkos (who at first opposed union) see V. Laurent, "La croisade et la question d'Orient sous le pontificat de Grégoire X," *Revue historique du Sud-est européen* 22 (1945): 105–37; and Laurent, "Grégoire X et le projet d'une ligue antiturque," *Echos d'Orient* 37 (1938): 257–73; G. Hofmann, "Patriarch Johann Bekkos und die lateinische Kultur," *Orientalia christiana periodica* 11 (1945): 141ff.; and Geanakoplos, "Michael VIII Palaeologus and the Union of Lyons" (1953), 78–89. Also Geanakoplos, *Emperor Michael Palaeologus and the West,* 237–45, 307–8. On the Dominican Humbert, who acutely foresaw durable union only through pacific rapprochement and mutual education of both churches, see extracts from his *Opus tripartitum* in Mansi, vol. 24, pt. 2, cols. 120–30; and cf. K. Michel, *Das Opus tripartitum des Humbertus de Romans O. P.* (Graz, 1926). On Parastron, a Constantinople-born Greek of Latin faith who declared he would gladly give his life for the success of union, see M. Viller, "La question de l'union des églises entre grecs et latins depuis le concile de Lyon jusqu'à celui de Florence (1274–1438)," pt. 1, *Revue d'histoire ecclésiastique* 16 (1921): 265 n. 4; and Geanakoplos, "Michael Palaeologus and the Union of Lyons," 84. Also see Geanakoplos, *Emperor Michael,* 267–68 and above essay 10.

5. On these specific episodes see above, n. 3 and essay 10.

often lacking, and if the objectives of the papacy remained generally constant, the enthusiasm of the emperors for union fluctuated in accordance with their need for Western aid.[6]

From the viewpoint of ecclesiastical government, a more fundamental reason for the failure of union was the conflict between two basic conceptions of the church. To the monarchical claims of the papacy was opposed the Byzantine concept of the pentarchy, what might be termed a kind of "collegial" authority. In accordance with this theory the Eastern patriarchs, while acknowledging the honorary primacy of Rome, rejected papal assertions of universal disciplinary jurisdiction which would have permitted the papacy, on appeal, to intervene directly in affairs of the Greek church, in effect rendering the Eastern bishops mere satellites of the Holy See.[7] Whereas for the West, in accordance with medieval canonistic development, supreme ecclesiastical jurisdiction came to be vested in the pope alone, for the Eastern church the highest religious authority was believed to reside in the ecumenical councils in which all five patriarchs of East and West had to be represented. It was this emphasis on the authority and canons of the first seven ecumenical councils, transmitted inviolate through the centuries, which constituted for Byzantium the essence of Orthodoxy.[8]

Complicating the difference in ecclesiastical polity from the Byzantine side, of course, was the traditional authority of the emperor over the Greek church—the so-called Caesaropapism. Whether the term is justifiable or not, it is clear that many emperors in times of political stress did use their authority in an attempt, successful or otherwise, to accommodate the Greek church to the needs of the state.[9]

6. See Viller, "La question de l'union," pt. 1, p. 280: "negotiations were more political than religious [and] between two governments than two heads of churches"; Bréhier, "Attempts at Reunion," 596. For a convenient summary of the shifts in Greek imperial policy in accordance with the degree of external danger to Byzantium, see esp. Bréhier, 695–96. For translation of documents on some unionist attempts between the churches of Constantinople and Rome from 1054 to 1453 see Geanakoplos, *Byzantium,* nos. 151–63.

7. On recognition of Roman primacy of honor see the treatise of the famous fourteenth-century Greek theologian Nilos Cabasilas, "De causis dissensionum in ecclesia," in Migne, *Patrologia graeca* (hereafter MPG), vol. 149, col. 685B. Cf. F. Heiler, *Urkirche und Ostkirche* (Munich, 1937), 141. Also on papal primacy F. Dvornik, *Byzance et la primauté romaine* (Paris, 1964); and J. Meyendorff et al., *The Primacy of Peter in the Orthodox Church* (London, 1963). On pentarchic theory see esp. F. Dvornik, *The Photian Schism* (Cambridge, 1948), 150 and n. 2; M. Jugie, *Le schisme byzantin* (Paris, 1941), 37–38, 222–23, 232; and J. Karmires, "The Schism of the Roman Church" (in Greek), *Theologia* 21 (1950): 30–31, 49, 56, and esp. 65–66.

8. See Dvornik, *Byzance et la primauté romaine,* 420, 423; and cf. Karmires, "Schism of the Roman Church," 29.

9. The role of Caesaropapism has been the cause of much controversy. According to

These politico-ecclesiastical considerations, however, were not the only obstacles to union There was another factor, more difficult to define but of at least equal importance—the deep-rooted antagonism for the Latins felt by the Greek population of Constantinople, on whom, in the last analysis, the success of union depended.[10] This popular antipathy for the Latins was more than religious in scope, but it tended, in the spirit of the age, to find expression in the church. For in that institution were reflected not only the basic difference of language, but the development of theories and practices characteristic of the mentality of each people.[11] It is therefore in the broad context of East-West antagonism that a full solution for the problem of union must ultimately be sought. Only thus can the endless and seemingly unproductive deliberations over such questions as the *filioque,* purgatory, *azyma* (the use of unleavened bread in the Eucharist), or even the shaving of clerical beards acquire genuine significance. For apart of course from any dogmatic importance, these questions were symptomatic of the more-underlying issues separating East from West, and it is this fact which made the problem of union so difficult.

It is not my purpose here to analyze the successive attempts at union. Rather it is my aim to focus on the disputations at the Council of Florence, which brought to a climax four hundred years of unionist efforts. Through an examination, necessarily brief, of certain aspects of the proceedings of the council as well as of the circumstances which brought it about, I hope to provide some insight into the complexities of union and especially into the forces which prevented its successful conclusion. While I shall deal with some of the more generally known events of the council, I shall at the same time touch upon several incidents relatively

---

the Catholic historian M. Jugie, *Le schisme byzantin,* 3–9, and esp. 10, Caesaropapism "incontestably should bear the chief responsibility for the preparation of the schism." Cf. the typically Greek attitude of Ch. Papadopoulos, *The Primacy of the Bishop of Rome* (in Greek) (Athens, 1930), esp. 207ff., who attributes the basic cause of the schism to papal attempts to impose primacy of jurisdiction over the Greek church. On the accommodation of the church to the state, the Byzantine theory of *economia,* see Geanakoplos, *Byzantium,* 133–35.

10. The Emperor Manuel II (d. 1425) realized this well when he warned his son John VIII that the pride of the Latins and the obstinacy of the Greeks would never agree, and attempts at union would only widen the schism (Sphrantzes, *Chronicon* [Bonn, 1838], 178–79). Cf. Syropoulos, 448.

11. On identification of the Greek language with Orthodoxy, and the unfavorable Byzantine attitude to Latin see S. Runciman, "Byzantine Linguists," *Prosphora eis S. Kyriakeden,* ed. J. Kakrides (Thessalonica, 1953), 596–602. For widespread Western prejudices against Greeks and their language, see Viller, "La question de l'union," pt. 1, pp. 284–305. On reciprocal ignorance of Latin and Greek see Jugie, *Le schisme byzantin,* 39–42; and Geanakoplos, *Interaction of the Sibling Cultures.*

unimportant in themselves, but revealing basic attitudes indicative of the underlying tensions between the two peoples and their churches.

II

As no official acts as such survive for the Council of Florence, our information must in the main be drawn from three accounts of participants: first, the so-called *Acta graeca,* written in Greek most probably by the pro-unionist Latinophile bishop Dorotheos of Mytilene;[12] second, the Latin account in dialogue form by the papal advocate Andrea of Santacroce;[13] and, finally, the Greek history or memoirs of Sylvester Syropoulos, grand ecclesiarch of Hagia Sophia in Constantinople. While the *Acta graeca* has been considered most authoritative by Western scholars, the work of Syropoulos, well known in the East, has long been neglected, indeed generally rejected, by the West. This neglect was in part attributable to the adverse influence of an early editor, the Anglican bishop Robert Creyghton, who in 1660 published the Greek text together with a frequently inaccurate, sharply antipapal translation into Latin.[14] More important, however, was the attitude of leading Catholic historians, such as Ch. Hefele, E. Cecconi, and L. Allatius in particular, who violently

12. The best edition is now that of J. Gill (see above, n. 1). On Dorotheos of Mytilene as author of the *Acta graeca* (in this essay generally referred to simply as *Acta*), see *Acta,* lxiii–lxix; and J. Gill, "Sources of the 'Acta' of the Council of Florence," *Orientalia christiana periodica* 14 (1948): 43ff. Supporting Dorotheos's authorship are V. Laurent, "Apropos de Dorothée métropolite de Mytilène, *Revue des études byzantines* 9 (1951): 163–69, a biographical sketch of Dorotheos; G. Hofmann, "Die Konzilsarbeit in Ferrara," pt. 1, *Orientalia christiana periodica* 3 (1937): 110; T. Frommann, *Kritische Beiträge zur Geschichte der florentiner Kircheneinigung* (Halle, 1872) 63–79; A. Vogt's article on the Council of Florence in *Dictionnaire de théologie catholique,* vol. 6, col. 28 (cf. col. 49) (hereafter cited as *Dic. Théol Cath.*); and D. Balanos, *The Byzantine Ecclesiastical Writers* (in Greek) (Athens, 1951), 172 n. 1. See, however, the older work of H. Vast, *Le Cardinal Bessarion* (Paris, 1878), 436–49; and Ch. Hefele and H. Leclercq, *Histoire des conciles,* vol. 7, pt. 2 (Paris, 1916), 957, who ascribe authorship of the *Acta* to Bessarion.

13. In Mansi, vol. 31B, cols. 1431ff. (Also printed in *Andreas de Santacroce Advocatus Consistorialis Acta Latina Concilii Florentini,* ed. G. Hofmann [Rome, 1955]. Referred to hereafter as Andrea of Santacroce.

14. The full title assigned by Creyghton is S. Sgouropoulos [sic], *Vera historia unionis non verae inter Graecos et Latinos, sive Concilii Florentini exactissima narratio, etc.* (Hague, 1660) (but see new ed. by V. Laurent, cited next note). S. G. Mercati's article in *Enciclopedia italiana* 21:910 says that Syropoulos's anti-unionist tendencies are accentuated by Creyghton, whose inexact translation in turn provoked the confutation of the Greek Catholic L. Allatius, *In Robert Creygtoni apparatum, versionem . . . scriptam a*

attacked the work of Syropoulos for its anti-unionist views, considering the author to be a kind of Sarpi of the Council of Florence.[15]

For these reasons, not to mention the relative unavailability of Creyghton's edition, comparatively few Western scholars have even been aware of the remarkable store of information Syropoulos provides. Yet his work is practically the sole record of what went on behind the scenes among the Greek delegation. Beginning with the diplomatic preliminaries to the council, Syropoulos describes in detail the dangerous journey of the Greeks from beleaguered Constantinople to Venice; their day-by-day activities at the council; their hopes, frustrations, and petty quarrels; and, above all, their private discussions both among themselves and with the Latins. In short, Syropoulos draws a remarkably complete picture of the Greek mentality, especially of the deep conflict between the unionist Latinophiles and the anti-unionist Orthodox during this critical period of Byzantium's dying days. (In this book I shall use the excellent recent edition of Syropoulos by V. Laurent.)[16]

Recently Joseph Gill, professor at the Pontifical Institute in Rome (who has published a valuable edition of the *Acta graeca* and the most detailed book on the Council of Florence) has demonstrated the accuracy of some (but not all) of Syropoulos's statements hitherto considered false or grossly exaggerated.[17] Based on examination of some papal and

---

Silvestro Syropulo . . . exercitationes (1665; Rome, 1674). See further the article of J. Gill, "The 'Acta' and the Memoirs of Syropoulos as History," *Orientalia christiana periodica* 14 (1948): 300–41, rpt. in Gill, *Personalities of the Council of Florence* (New York, 1964), 144–77. For a Greek point of view on Syropoulos see A. Diamantopoulos, "Silvestros Syropoulos and his *Memoirs* at the Florence Synod" (in Greek), *Nea Sion* 18 (1923): 241ff. and later issues.

15. On this see Frommann, *Kritische Beiträge,* 37–58. Also E. Cecconi, *Studi storici sul concilio di Firenze* (Florence, 1869), who in his long, 224-page introduction generally impugns Syropoulos's accuracy esp. 14–15, 32, 36, 45, 50. Cf. Hefele and Leclercq, *Histoire des conciles,* vol. 7, pt. 2, pp. 958–59; and, on Allatius, see preceding note. See finally the harsh invective of Ph. Labbé, in J. Hardouin, *Concilia generalia,* 9, 1079, who places Syropoulos in the company of such notorious heretics as Arius, Nestorius, and the Albigensians: But see the more objective judgment of the now standard, authoritative edition of Syropoulos by V. Laurent, *Les "Mémoires" du grand ecclésiarche de l'église de Constantinople Sylvestre Syropoulos sur le concile de Florence (1438–39)* (Paris, 1971), esp. 21–35, where he calls Syropoulos's work "a source of the first rank for the historian of the Council of Florence." He admits the account contains errors but that they are "not so continuous and so ordered as to permit us to suspect the author of desiring systematically to alter the facts."

16. Some years ago, the only available printed copies of Creyghton's edition in America to my knowledge were at Harvard University and the Library of Congress. I have now used the new edition by Laurent, cited above.

17. See above nn. 1, 12, and below, n. 18; also J. Gill, *The Council of Florence* (Cambridge, 1959); and Gill, *Personalities of the Council of Florence.*

Medici documents, Gill analyzed, for example, the correctness of Syropoulos's numerous figures regarding the daily subsistence promised by the papacy to the Greek delegates at Florence.[18] Some use of Syropoulos had also been made by other notable Catholic scholars, such as G. Hofmann, V. Laurent, and R. Loenertz, while several modern Greek historians have found corroboration for statements of Syropoulos in passages of contemporary Byzantine writers.[19] Syropoulos's remarks are, to be sure, often partisan, but is it not necessary for the historian to understand the anti-unionist as well as unionist views at the council? It is indeed these very attitudes which may best explain the failure of lasting union. Provided Syropoulos's statements can be controlled by other Byzantine writings or, whenever possible, by contemporary Latin accounts, there is no justifiable reason to reject his history as an important and basic source for certain aspects of the council.[20]

Seven years of diplomatic negotiation preceded the assembling of the council at Florence,[21] during which the papacy, after centuries of refusal, finally accepted the conditions of the Greek people and clergy for the

18. Gill, "The Acta and the Memoirs of Syropoulos," 330–41, esp. 339: "[The Acta camerae apostolicae] reveal that Syropoulos' dates of payments and sums recorded as paid are often exact and that the Greeks had real grounds for complaint." Also Gill, *Council of Florence.* Cf. Cecconi, *Concilio di Firenze,* 478–86; and also Syropoulos, who makes numerous references to papal subsistence or payments (see 244–45, 378ff., 404, and also esp. 246, where he records that no money or subsistence was ever given to the Greeks without ulterior motives). The *Acta* says almost nothing about the penury of the Greeks except that the pope's financial embarrassment was the main cause of the council's transfer from Ferrara to Florence (220; Mansi, col. 696). Cf. n. 81, below.

19. Hofmann, "Die Konzilsarbeit in Ferrara"; Laurent, "Apropos de Dorothée," 163–66; and R. Loenertz, "Les dominicains byzantins Théodore et André Chrysobergès et les négociations pour l'union des églises de 1415 à 1430," *Archivum fratrum praedicatorum* 9 (1939): 5–61, esp. 32, 46. Also Gill, *Council of Florence.* Cf. also M. Jugie, "Note sur l'histoire du concile de Florence de Sylvestre Syropoulos," *Echos d'Orient* 38 (1939): 70ff.; and J. Décarreaux, "L'arrivée des grecs en Italie pour le concile de l'union d'après les Mémoires de Syropoulos," *Revue des études italiennes* 7 (1960): 27–58. Among modern Greek historians see esp. Diamantopoulos, "Silvestros Syropoulos," 265ff.; P. Kalligas, *Studies and Speeches* (in Greek) (Athens, 1882), 1–186; see now also C. Woodhouse, *George Gemistos Plethon. The Last of the Hellenes* (Oxford, 1986) chaps. 8, 10, for use of Synopoulos (but not the *Acta graeca* or Andrea of Santa Croce).

20. F. Dölger, review in *Byzantinische Zeitschrift* 47 (1954): 154, and Frommann, *Kritische Beiträge,* 6, n. 1, consider Syropoulos the second important source for the Florentine council after the *Acta graeca.*

21. Unionist pourparlers had been going on intermittently since long before this, but the Turkish conquest of Thessalonica in 1430 and the accession of Pope Eugenius IV in 1431 marked a new stage in the negotiations. See Loenertz, "Les dominicains byzantins," 5; and C. Diehl and R. Guilland, *L'Europe orientale de 1081 à 1453* (Paris, 1945), 359.

establishment of valid union—namely, the convocation of an ecumenical council.[22] This stipulation is perhaps nowhere more clearly defined than by the Italo-Greek monk Barlaam of Calabria, who in 1339, exactly a century before Florence, had been secretly sent by the Emperor Andronicus III to the papal court at Avignon to plead the cause of union.[23] Inasmuch as Barlaam's discourse reflects the sentiment prevailing among the Greek people also later during the period of the Council of Florence,[24] it is worth quoting. Barlaam said to the pope:

> That which separates the Greeks from you is not so much a difference in dogma as the hatred of the Greeks for the Latins provoked by the wrongs they have suffered. It will be necessary to confer some great boon on them to change their feeling. . . . There is only one effective means to bring about union: through the convocation of a general council to be held in the East. For to the Greeks

22. This Greek attitude was expressed only a short time after 1054, the date usually considered as marking the definite schism (see Geanakoplos, "On the Schism of the Greek and Roman Churches," *Greek Orthodox Theological Review* 1 [1954], 17–18, and bibliography), when the emperor wrote to the pope that union could be realized only through the convocation of the general council (see W. Norden, *Das Papsttum und Byzanz* [Berlin, 1903], 48). The popes of the fourteenth century themselves seemed to favor a council but never gave their full support until the Western conciliar movement forced their hand (M. Viller, "La question de l'union," pt. 2, *Revue d'histoire ecclésiastique* 18 [1922]: 20–35) and see below, text and n. 30. See also D. Nicol, "Byzantine Requests for an Oecumenical Council in the Fourteenth Century," *Annuarium historiae conciliorum* 1 (1969): 69–95.

23. Barlaam's discourse is printed in MPG, vol. 151, col. 1332. On Barlaam's mission see C. Giannelli, "Un projetto di Barlaam Calabro per l'unione delle chiese," *Miscellanea Giovanni Mercati,* vol. 3 (Vatican, 1946), 171 and n. 22; and Viller, "La question de l'union," pt. 2, pp. 21–24. See further on Barlaam, M. Jugie's article in *Dic. His. Géog. Ecc.,* vol. 6, cols. 817–34.

24. The idea of an ecumenical council to end the schism was expressed by many Greeks between the period of Barlaam and the Council of Florence: Nicephorus Gregoras, *Byzantina historia,* ed. L. Schopen, 3 vols. (Bonn, 1829–55), 10.8; John Cantacuzenos, *Historiarum libri IV,* ed. L. Schopen, 3 vols. (Bonn, 1828–32), 4.9; Cabasilas, "De causis dissensionum," MPG, vol. 149, cols. 684ff. (for a related article touching on Cabasilas see M. Paulová, "L'empire byzantin et les Tchèques avant la chute de Constantinople," *Byzantinoslavica* 14 [1953]: 164); and Joseph Bryennios (who died just before the convocation at Florence), *On the Union of the Churches* (in Greek), ed. Bulgaris, vol. 1 (Leipzig, 1768). Noteworthy, on the Western side, is the attitude of the Dominican Humbert of Romans, who just before 1274 had favored the convocation of a council but in the East (Mansi, vol. 24, col. 128). Cf. Viller, "La question de l'union," pt. 2, p. 23 n. 1, and pp. 20–35, for mention of representatives of the University of Paris like Jean Gerson in the early fifteenth century who demanded a council to treat of the Greek union. Finally see Loenertz, "Les dominicains byzantins," 42–43; and Nicol, "Byzantine Requests for an Oecumenical Council."

> anything determined by a general council has the authority of law. You may object and say that a council has already met at Lyons to treat of union. But no Greek recognizes the ecumenicity of the Council of Lyons, since no subsequent council has declared it so. The Greek legates at Lyons were, in fact, sent there neither by the four patriarchs who govern the Eastern church, nor by the Greek people, but by the emperor alone, who, without trying to gain the support of his people, sought only by force to realize the union.[25] To the four patriarchs therefore send legates, and under their presidency a general council will convene which will achieve union. Then all of us present at the council will say to the Greek people: Here is what the Holy Ecumenical Council has decreed: It is your duty to obey its decisions, and all will submit.[26]

Barlaam's appeal was ignored at the time, for the Avignonese papacy had no intention of compromising its absolute authority by assembling a council to debate differences with the "schismatic" Greeks.[27] But the subsequent decline of papal prestige in the West as a result of the Great Schism and the increasing Western emphasis on conciliar supremacy eventually induced the Holy See to view the Greek demands in a more favorable light.[28] This change of attitude coincided with an even more pressing need of the Greek emperors for Western aid in order to salvage their last remaining territories of Constantinople and the Morea from the Turks, now practically at the gates of the capital.[29]

The situation became three sided, however. For besides the Holy See, its bitter rivals, the Western conciliarists sitting at Basel, also looked

25. As Jugie, *Le schisme byzantin,* 259, justifiably emphasizes, there were only two Greek bishops at the council, and the union was concluded "without psychological preparation and theological discussion on the disputed points." In fact, the concessions mentioned in letters borne by the imperial envoys had been extorted from the Greek clergy. See above, essay 10.

26. This passage follows the quotations conveniently cited in Viller, "La question de l'union," pt. 2, pp. 22–23. For Greek text see MPG, vol. 151, cols. 1332ff. Cf. Geanakoplos, *Byzantium,* no. 159.

27. For Pope Benedict XII's refusal of Barlaam's proposal see MPG, vol. 151, cols. 1255ff. The chief point at issue was the *filioque* (on which see below, text and n. 64) .The pope and Curia did not want to question an article of the faith already defined (see Viller, "La question de l'union," pt. 2, p. 23; and Jugie, *Le schisme byzantin,* 251).

28. On this see Paulová, "L'empire byzantin," 164–67; Loenertz, "Les dominicains byzantins," 42–43; Viller, "La question de l'union," pt. 2, pp. 20–35; and Jugie, *Le schisme byzantin,* 251. On the Great Schism see also O. Halecki, "Rome et Byzanz au temps du grand schisme d'Occident," *Collectanea theologica* 18 (1937): 476–532.

29. Bréhier, "Attempts at Reunion," 617ff.; A. Vasiliev, *History of the Byzantine Empire* (Madison, Wis., 1952), 640, 672, etc.

upon a Greek union as the best means of establishing ecclesiastical superiority in the West. Thus the Byzantine emperor and patriarch were courted by both Pope Eugenius IV and the assembly of Basel, each promising military aid for Constantinople together with the payment of all expenses for the journey of a Greek delegation to a general council to be held in the West.[30]

The contest for Byzantine favor grew increasingly severe. Indeed, the account of Syropoulos, corroborated by a report of the legate of Basel, John of Ragusa, and by papal documents, describes the rival Western delegations at Constantinople competing with such intensity as to be restrained from blows only by imperial intervention.[31] Previous to this, an even more violent scene had occurred at Basel itself, where the papal and conciliar adherents created so great a tumult in disputing the question of the Greek union that in the revealing phrase of Aeneas Silvius (later Pope Pius II), "You would have found the drunkards of a tavern better behaved."[32]

Why in the end did the Greeks prefer the offers of the papacy to those of the Basel fathers, when Byzantine tradition itself, at least from the standpoint of the pentarchy, would seem to be conciliar in emphasis? Would it not have been more advantageous, as several modern Greek scholars question, to have preferred the Basel assembly?[33] This problem has not yet been fully elucidated by historians,[34] but we may suggest several reasons for the selection of the papacy. Not only did both emperor and patriarch stipulate the personal presence of Pope Eugenius at the

30. See Syropoulos, 130ff.; Cecconi, *Concilio di Firenze,* 478–86. For the papal-Basel rivalry over Byzantine favor see Frommann, *Kritische Beiträge,* 7ff.; Paulová, "L'empire byzantin," 164–67; W. Waugh, "Councils of Constance and Basel," *Cambridge Medieval History* 8 (1936): 35ff.; and the work of J. Haller, *Concilium basiliense,* vols. 1–5 (Basel, 1896–1905), passim. Also see next essay, 12.

31. See Syropoulos, 176ff. For the report of the Basel envoy John of Ragusa see Cecconi, *Concilio di Firenze,* 487ff., and esp. dxi, dxii. On John of Ragusa's account see Diamantopoulos, "Silvestros Syropoulos," 274–75. On John also see F. Dölger, "Ein byzantinisches Staatsdokument in der Universitätsbibliothek Basel: Ein Fragment des Tomos des Jahres 1351," *Historisches Jahrbuch* (1953): 218–220; and cf. Gill, *Council of Florence,* 63–66, 74–83. As for the papal embassy's account, see Cecconi, esp. dlxxvii: "ad vitandum quondam motionem galiotarum nostrorum [!] contra gentes illarum galearum. Imperator fecit dictas galeas transire ad portum ante palatium suum."

32. See *Der Briefwechsel des Eneas Silvius Piccolomini,* ed. R. Wolkan, pt. 1, vol. 1, *Briefe aus der Laienzeit* (Vienna, 1909), letter 24, pp. 58ff., dated 21 May 1437. (English translation in W. Boulting, *Aeneas Silvius* [London, 1908], 82.) Cf. Mansi, vol. 31, cols. 223ff.

33. See esp. Diamantopoulos, "Silvester Syropoulos," 265ff.; and Kalligas, *Studies and Speeches,* 11–32.

34. See Paulová, "L'empire byzantin," 167ff.

council[35]—a condition uncertain of attainment at Basel[36]—but the Greeks naturally preferred as a site for the council the papal choice of Ferrara in Italy as opposed to more distant Basel, Avignon, or Savoy, places insisted upon by the Basel conciliarists.[37] Added to this, probably, was the Greek familiarity with the traditional prestige of the papacy in contrast to the relatively recent emergence of Western conciliarism. Not to be overlooked, finally, is the role of the Greek emperor. In line with Byzantine autocratic ideas, he may well have preferred to negotiate with a single absolute authority instead of the notoriously factious assembly at Basel.[38] We must be careful in this connection, however, not to overstress the concept of an all-pervasive Caesaropapism on the part of the emperor during this period, inasmuch as the very failures of the many unionist attempts initiated by the emperors themselves militate against such a theory.[39]

On the 24th of November 1437, in ships provided by the pope, a huge Byzantine delegation of seven hundred ecclesiastics and laymen, headed

35. See documents published by G. Hofmann, in *Orientalium documenta minora,* vol. 3, fasc. 3 (Rome, 1953), nos. 9–10, pp. 13–15, dated 11 and 26 Nov. 1435, letters of Patriarch John II and Emperor John VIII to Pope Eugenius IV: "cognoscimus, quod presentia vestre beatitudinis multum necessaria est in futura synodo" (also in Cecconi, *Concilio di Firenze,* 154-55 and 166–67). Cf. Paulová, "L'empire byzantin," 167.

36. Just before the convocation of the council at Ferrara-Florence, the Basel fathers had suspended the pope from his functions. See also Hofmann, *Orientalium documenta minora,* vol. 3, fasc. 3, p. 29, letter of John Palaeologus to the Basel synod declaring himself free of obligation because Basel had not carried out its promises.

37. On these sites see the reports of the papal embassy in Cecconi, *Concilio di Firenze,* no. 188, esp. pp. dlxxvii–dlxxx, and of the Basel envoy John of Ragusa, p. dxvii. Cf. Syropoulos, 130. Acceptance of the cities specified by Basel would have permitted exercise of great influence by the conciliarists.

38. Syropoulos, 220–27, reports that as late as his arrival in Venice the emperor was still undecided whether to go to Basel or to Ferrara, the site fixed by the pope. According to Syropoulos, he was advised by the doge to select the site most advantageous to himself. (Cf. Gill, *Personalities of the Council of Florence,* 178–85, who questions the truth of this.) But news of the death of the Western emperor Sigismund, a supporter of Basel from whom the Greek emperor expected aid, probably helped to induce the Greeks to go directly to Ferrara. On the accuracy of this report see Frommann, *Kritische Beiträge,* 9; and B. Stephanides, "The Last Stage of the Development of the Relations between the Byzantine Church and State" (in Greek), *Epetēris hetaireias byzantinōn spoudōn* 16 (1953): 27–40, both of whom seem to accept its authenticity. Cf. Hefele and Leclercq, *Histoire des conciles,* vol. 7, pt. 2, p. 961, which denies its accuracy. However, Laurent, Syropoulos, 210, 212 n. 1, does not.

39. The popes tended to overemphasize the power of the emperor over the Greek church and therefore often wrongly attributed Greek popular hostility toward union to imperial perfidy. See Viller, "La question de l'union," pt. 1, p. 264 n. 4, and pt. 2, pp. 20–21. Also A. Fliche, "Le problème oriental au second concile oecuménique de Lyon," *Orientalia christiana periodica* 13 (1947): 4.

by the Emperor John VIII Palaeologus, the Patriarch Joseph of Constantinople, and representatives of the three other patriarchs, finally set out for Italy. After a long, hazardous voyage of three months the Greeks reached Venice.[40] But almost immediately after their arrival, the council was threatened with disruption over a question of protocol. On the entrance of the patriarch Joseph into Ferrara, he absolutely refused, despite his growing pro-unionist tendencies and the demands of the papal representatives, to salute the pope in the Western manner of genuflecting and kissing his foot.[41] According to Syropoulos, the patriarch exclaimed indignantly to the papal legates:

> Whence has the pope this right? Which synod gave it to him? Show me from what source he derives this privilege and where it is written? The pope claims that he is the successor of St. Peter. But if he is the successor of Peter, then we too are the successors of the rest of the Apostles. Did they kiss the foot of St. Peter?[42]

To these remarks the Latin bishops replied that it was an ancient custom for all to kiss the pope's foot—"bishops, kings, and even the emperor of the Germans and the cardinals who are holy and superior to the emperor." The response of the patriarch is significant: "This is an innovation and I will not follow it. . . . If the pope wants a brotherly embrace in accordance with ancient ecclesiastical custom, I will be happy to embrace him, but if he refuses, I will abandon everything and return to Constantinople."[43] (It is interesting to observe that at the first meeting of pope and patriarch since the Council of Florence—the historic one of

40. On the preparations for departure and the voyage itself see Syropoulos, 182–212. Little important information is added by other Greek historians. But see the report of the bishop of Digne (who participated in the papal embassy escorting the Greeks to Venice) in Cecconi, *Concilio di Firenze,* no. 188, esp. p. dlxxxi. For the arrival at Venice see Syropoulos, 212ff. Note his moving account (222–24) of Greek emotion at seeing the former treasures of Hagia Sophia exhibited at San Marco. On the reception at Venice see *Acta,* 1–5 (Mansi, cols. 466–67); and Ducas, *Istoria Turco-bizantina,* ed. Grecu, 265–67.

41. On his unionism see even Syropoulos, 230–32, who reports that the patriarch confided to one of his intimates his hope the pope's cooperation would permit him to cast aside the Greek church's servitude to the emperor and "to recover the authority proper to me." On this curious passage see Stephanides, "Last Stage of Relations," 38ff.; and Diamantopoulos, "Silvester Syropoulos," 275–76. But the patriarch was disillusioned, says Syropoulos, 230, when he heard of Eugenius's demand that he kiss the pope's foot. It seems unnoted by some scholars that the *Acta graeca,* 467, reports that when the union was proclaimed, the Greek bishops kissed the pope's knee and hand, though the *Acta* did not mention the patriarch's refusal, on arrival, to kiss the pope's foot.

42. Syropoulos, 232–34.

43. Ibid., 234.

Pope Paul VI and the Patriarch Athenagoras in Jerusalem in 1964—each prelate embraced the other, giving him the kiss of peace. The lesson of the meeting at fifteenth-century Florence had evidently been well learned!)

In the end the patriarch's inflexibility prevailed. Yet the victory was not entirely his, for Pope Eugenius, instead of welcoming the patriarch and his prelates in public ceremony, received them in his private quarters, where few Western eyes could witness the omission of this traditional mark of subordination.[44]

This initial difficulty, suggested obliquely by the *Acta graeca,*[45] vividly symbolizes Greek insistence on the essential equality of the bishops of Constantinople and Rome, a fundamental principle of pentarchic theory as opposed to the claims of the pope to be the vicar of Christ and successor to Peter, *first* among the apostles.[46] Moreover, in the word "innovation" as used by the patriarch, there is expressed a difference in concept, the significance of which lies at the heart of the conflict between

44. Ibid., 234–36. Also see Andrea of Santacroce, 28 (Mansi, vol. 31B, col. 1435): "in secretam cameram"; and *Acta,* 9: "in palatium papae."

45. The *Acta graeca,* 9–10, pointedly omits mention of the foot kiss, but for evidence that similar practice was current at this time see elsewhere in the *Acta,* 467 (Mansi, col 1040), where immediately after the reading of the decree of union at Florence, Greeks as well as Latins "kissed the knee and hand of the Pope." (Cf. Andrea of Santacroce, col. 1702). Andrea, col. 1435, does not explicitly mention the foot kiss on the patriarch's arrival in Ferrara, but see Hofmann, "Die Konzilsarbeit in Ferrara," pt. 2, *Orientalia christiana periodica* 3 (1937): 410, who seems to accept Syropoulos's statement that it was demanded, as does Hefele and Leclercq, *Histoire des conciles,* vol. 7, pt. 2, p. 962. See also B. Stephanides, *Ecclēsiastikē historia* (Athens, 1959), 359; and Gill, *Personalities of the Council of Florence,* 33–34.

The form of salutation is prescribed in papal pontificals. See M. Andrieu, *Le pontifical romain au moyen age,* vol. 2, *Le pontifical de la curie romaine au XIIIe siècle* (Vatican, 1940), 386, stating that during certain ceremonies king, archbishop, and bishop "osculetur pedem ipsius." Also see 357, par. 16. It is of interest that, while the Dictatus Papae of Gregory VII required the emperor to kiss the foot of the pope and that, according to Western custom, the emperor should hold the bridle and lead the mule of the seated pope, none of the sources of the Council of Florence allude to such a performance on the part of the Greek emperor, recording instead that he rode into the papal palace. See *Acta,* 7 (Mansi, cols. 470–71). Such a practice was the object of acute criticism in the East, being considered highly degrading to the imperial dignity. See esp. G. Ostrogorsky, "Zum Stratordienst der Herrschers in der Byzantinischen-slavischen Welt," *Seminarium kondakovianum* 7 (1935): 189–92; and Geanakoplos, chap. 2 of *Emperor Michael,* 44 n. 61.

46. See F. Dölger, "Rom in der Gedankenwelt der Byzantiner," in *Byzanz und die europäische Staatenwelt* (1953), 105, who emphasizes that the Greeks (esp. of the later period, after 1204) considered Christ himself, not the pope, as head of the church—obviously to denigrate papal claims to primacy. Also Dvornik, *Byzance et la primauté romaine,* 142f. Gill, in his *Council of Florence,* 105, n. 3, minimizes the importance of the incident of the foot-kiss. (But cf. now Gill, *Personalities of the Council of Florence,*

the churches. To the medieval Latin mind, what the Greeks might term innovation in rite and even in dogma—for example, the doctrine of the *filioque*—was not necessarily *change* in ecclesiastical truth but rather a logical *development* and was permissible particularly if sanctioned by the papacy. For the Greeks, on the other hand, anything other than undeviating adherence to the doctrines and traditions as established by the first seven ecumenical councils (apart of course from Holy Scripture) was to be considered innovation and hence reprehensible.[47]

This contrast between what we might term Greek conservatism and the more flexible Western attitude toward ecclesiastical development first becomes clear in the conflict between Patriarch Photius and Pope Nicholas I in the late ninth century, and even more distinct after the pontificates of Leo IX and Gregory VII in the latter part of the eleventh, when papal claims to universal jurisdiction underwent their great expansion at canon law.[48] It is important to observe, therefore, that when, subsequently, representatives of the two churches confronted each other to discuss union, they argued from basically different premises. The Greeks expected the papacy to conform to conditions *before* the schism of 1054. The Holy See, on its part, insisted upon all the prerogatives of papal power developed since that period—in other words, subordination of the Greek church to Rome virtually in the manner of the Latin churches of the West.[49]

Of greater significance at the Council of Florence than the conflict over patriarchal salutation of the pope was the dispute between emperor and pope over the problem of seating in the cathedral at Ferrara where the council was first to convene. In his desire to assume the role of arbiter, Pope Eugenius insisted that his throne be placed in the middle of the

237.) But it is, I believe, symptomatic of an important difference of tradition and mentality in the two churches.

47. Note typical statement of patriarch Joseph at Florence (*Acta,* 438; Andrea, Mansi, col. 1001) that he would never change the dogmas handed down from the fathers. On Greek retention of traditional practices and Latin innovations see also Barlaam's second Greek discourse, in Gianelli, "Un projetto di Barlaam," 165 and text 202.

48. See a Greek discourse of Barlaam, also dated 1339, in which he maintains that to achieve union the pope should return to the traditional form of the creed as it existed before the schism, that is, without the *filioque.* In Giannelli, "Un projetto di Barlaam," 167, 187. On Photius and Nicholas see Dvornik, *Photian Schism,* passim. Also Heiler, *Urkirche und Ostkirche,* esp. 141.

49. See Geanakoplos, "On the Schism of the Greek and Roman Churches," 23. Also not to be overlooked here are the imperfect contacts between Rome and Constantinople which kept each side at least partially ignorant of the precise course of events in the other. It is probably true, nevertheless, that more frequent contacts existed than is generally believed.

church, with the Greek representatives at his left and the Latins on his right. The emperor John Palaeologus, however, considered this an infringement of imperial rights, for in accord with Byzantine tradition reverting to Constantine the Great, he believed it the prerogative of the emperor, as vice-gerent of God, to preside over ecumenical councils.[50]

After prolonged argument a solution was achieved whereby, as the Greeks insisted, the papal throne was placed on the side of the Latins. But it was, at the same time, elevated above all others including that of the emperor. Moreover, another throne, corresponding in every respect to that of the Greek *basileus,* was set up on the Latin side for the emperor of the West, despite the vacancy of the throne caused by the recent death of the Western emperor Sigismund.[51] The poor patriarch of Constantinople, his protests overruled, was in the meantime relegated to a place below both pope and emperors, a position, according to Andrea of Santacroce, corresponding to that of the highest ranking cardinal.[52] Thus, contrary to traditional Byzantine theories, not to mention of course Greek ethnic pride, the Greeks at least symbolically were forced to recognize the supremacy of papal theocratic theory over both their emperor and patriarch. As for the equality indicated between Western and Eastern emperors, it touched upon even more-sensitive feelings of the Byzantines, whose rulers had never really become reconciled to the existence of a rival imperial title in the West.[53]

It is worthy of note that in the heated debates which followed, papal champions apparently made no use of the famous Donation of Constantine to support papal claims of supremacy. One wonders, had he been there, what may have been the role of Nicholas of Cusa, who already in

50. On the seating, see *Acta,* 11 (Mansi, col. 474E); Syropoulos, 240–42; and Andrea of Santacroce, cols. 1435ff. On the imperial presidency over ecumenical councils see Dvornik, "Emperors, Popes, and General Councils," *Dumbarton Oaks Papers,* no. 6 (1951): 1–23.

51. *Acta,* 11 (Mansi, col. 474E); Syropoulos, 242; and Andrea, col. 1436.

52. Andrea, col. 1436: "In oppositum primis cardinalis sedes patriarchae fuerat constituta." The *Acta* does not specify the exact position.

53. Cf. Humbert of Romans (Mansi, vol. 24, pt. 2, col. 124), who says that the chief cause of the schism was rivalry over the claims to the empire. On the beginnings of this problem see W. Ohnsorge, *Das Zweikaiserproblem im früheren Mittelalter* (Hildesheim, 1947). A very curious passage is contained in another MS recension of Syropoulos, indicating that the emperor John VIII had hopes of cooperating to achieve union with the Western emperor Sigismund in the aim eventually of succeeding him on the Western throne. (It is certain at any rate that the two emperors were on cordial terms and that John had at one time even visited Sigismund's court.) See Syropoulos, 584; *Regesta imperii: Die Urkunden Kaiser Sigismunds,* ed. W. Altmann (Innsbruck, 1896), vol. 2, nos. 12226, 11367; and cf. Kalligas, *Studies and Speeches,* 8.

The Byzantine Emperor John VIII Palaeologus and his Patriarch Joseph at the Council of Florence, attributed to an anonymous painter from Urbino. From D. Geanakoplos, *Interaction of the "Sibling" Byzantine and Western Cultures in the Middle Ages and Italian Renaissance (330–1600)* (New Haven, 1976). Painting is in the Galleria Nazionale dell'Umbria.

1431, some years before Lorenzo Valla, had attacked the authenticity of the donation.[54] Cusanus was one of the legates who escorted the Greek delegation from their capital to Venice, and while in the East (where we know that he searched for manuscripts), he probably learned that a Greek translation of the Donation was in circulation at Byzantium.[55] Since the Greeks, or at least a strong body of Byzantine opinion, in the aim of diminishing papal authority, interpreted the document to mean that Constantine had transferred to Constantinople not only the entire Roman government but also ecclesiastical primacy,[56] Cusanus may possibly have seen the danger of trying to support claims through an appeal to such a double-edged weapon as the Donation of Constantine.[57]

When the negotiations at the council at last got under way, as in the past a great part of the discussions centered on such perennial dogmatic and liturgical questions as the nature of the pains of purgatory, the use of leavened or unleavened bread in the Eucharist, the precise moment at which the Eucharistic miracle occurs, and most important, the question of the procession of the Holy Spirit, which has for centuries been the greatest doctrinal stumbling block between the two churches.

The Latins believed that the third person of the Trinity, the Holy Spirit, proceeds from the Father *and the Son (filioque)*—a double procession as it were. The Greeks maintained, on the other hand, that the Holy

54. See E. Vansteenberghe, *Le Cardinal Nicolas de Cues* (Paris, 1920), 27–28. It should be noted that at the time of Cusanus's attack on the Donation he was a supporter of the Western conciliar movement. Now see P. Watts, *Nicolaus Cusanus: A Fifteenth Century Vision of Man* (Leiden, 1982). Cusanus was at Ferrara but not Florence.

55. This Greek translation is evidently referred to in Gill, *Council of Florence,* 280. On this embassy see the reports of the Basel and papal ambassadors in Cecconi, *Concilio di Firenze,* dix ff., dixxvi ff.; cf. Syropoulos, 174–78; and see also Gill, *Council of Florence,* 73, 77. On the manuscripts see M. Honecker, "Nikolaus von Cues und die griechische Sprache," *Sitzungsberichte der Heidelberger Akademie der Wissenschaften: Philosophisch-historische Klasse* 28 (1938): 13.

56. On this significant Greek attitude see esp. Dölger, "Rom in der Gedankenwelt der Byzantiner," 109–10, who shows that the twelfth-century Byzantine canonist Theodore Balsamon and the historians Cinnamos and Anna Comnena (among others) reveal a good knowledge of the Donation, but that they turn this against the papacy. Surprisingly, as Dölger notes, Pope Nicholas I did not use the Donation against the Greeks, although Cardinal Humbert subsequently employed it against Cerularius in the events of 1054.

57. It may be true, on the other hand, as Stephen Kuttner pointed out to me, that by the early fifteenth century the Donation had lost much of its potency even in the West. See the recent work of W. Ullmann, *The Growth of Papal Government in the Middle Ages* (London, 1955), 416–20; and S. Williams, "The Pseudo-Isidorean Problem Today," *Speculum* 29 (1954): 703. Cusanus himself was not at the Council in Florence, having at the time been sent on a papal mission. See also P. Alexander, "The Donation of Constantine at Byzantium and Its Earliest Use against the Western Empire," *Mélanges G. Ostrogorsky,* vol. 1 (Belgrade, 1963), 11–26.

Ghost proceeds from the Father (alone). These two views were the result of basically different approaches to the concept of the Trinity. Of course both were in complete agreement on the fundamental question of identity of substance in the three persons. To the Greek mind, however, most important was the theological truth of one principle or source *(archē)* in the Godhead—that is, in the person of the Father. The Latin view instead took as the point of departure the unitary nature of the "trinity" of persons in the one Godhead. Very simply put, one side tended to emphasize what might be referred to as the "three in one," the other the "one in three." Thus for the Latins the Greek view, which stressed the "monarchy" of the Father, seemed to subordinate the Son to the Father. And to the Greeks, the Latin view, which placed the source of the Holy Spirit in the common nature of the Father and the Son, seemed to indicate the existence in the Trinity of two first principles, or, crassly put, of two gods.[58]

Preliminary proposals for the debate of this problem disclosed the basically different Greek and Latin attitudes toward the church. The Orthodox, led by Mark, fiery metropolitan of Ephesus and exarch of the patriarch of Antioch,[59] tried to cut the ground out from under the Latin position by insisting that the dogmatic aspect of the *filioque* was here irrelevant and that the question for debate should be simply the legality of adding anything at all to the creed as originally established at the ecumenical councils of Nicaea and Constantinople.[60] The Latins, especially their spokesmen Cardinal Giuliano Cesarini and the Greek-born Dominican Andrea of Rhodes,[61] maintained, on the other hand, that the

58. See *Acta,* 413 (Mansi, col. 973), where the Latins remark of the Greeks, "They suspect . . . that we affirm two sources, and two causes for . . . the Trinity . . . but we believe in one source [archic principle]." On the *filioque* in general see esp. A. Palmieri's article in *Dic. théol. cath.,* vol. 5, col. 2309ff.; and on the Greek and Latin positions at the end of the eleventh century, B. Leib, *Rome, Kiev, et Byzance* (Paris, 1924), 331–44. Also Gill, *Personalities of the Council,* 254–63. On ritual differences mentioned above, see 245, 248 below.

59. According to the *Acta,* 12 (but cf. Syropoulos, 164, 194) both Mark and Isidore of Russia represented the patriarch of Antioch. Cf. Andrea of Santacroce, col. 1436. On Mark's significant role see the full-length work of A. Diamantopoulos, *Mark of Ephesus and the Council of Florence* (in Greek) (Athens, 1899) and L. Petit's article in *Dic. théol. cath.,* vol. 9, pt. 2, cols. 1968ff. Also Gill, *Personalities of the Council of Florence,* chap. 5, on Mark of Ephesus.

60. See Syropoulos, 316ff.; *Acta,* 56, 47 and 215–16, 218 where Mark repeatedly says that the true cause of the schism is the illegal addition of the *filioque.* Elsewhere in the *Acta,* 67 (Mansi, col. 529), Mark emphasizes the decree of the Council of Ephesus in 431 which forbade any change whatever in the creed.

61. On Cesarini see Gill, *Personalities of the Council of Florence,* chap. 8. On the soon-to-be pro-unionist Bessarion, later cardinal of the Roman church and protagonist at

The Byzantine anti-unionist monk Mark of Ephesus. From D. Geanakoplos, *Interaction of the "Sibling" Byzantine and Western Cultures in the Middle Ages and Italian Renaissance (330–1600)* (New Haven, 1976). Portrait is in the Benaki Museum, Athens.

argument should focus directly on the question of the truth or falseness of the dogma itself, since, as they insisted, the addition of the term *filioque* merely made explicit what was already implicit in the writings of important fathers of the early church.[62]

Both sides appealed for support to old manuscript texts of the Greek church fathers—a method of striking modernity. Most scrutinized were codices dating from *before* the schism of 1054 (especially one of St. Basil brought from Constantinople by Cusanus), to see if in the statement of the creed were contained the words "through the Son" or "and from the Son."[63] Heated exchanges took place when it was suspected that in certain Greek MSS. such phrases may have been purposely altered or expunged. The debate over the *filioque,* an endless labyrinth of arguments and counterarguments, continued for more than eight fruitless months, until a formula was approved equating the Latin *filioque* ("from the son") with the Greek phrase *dia tou hyiou* ("through the son"), a phrase already used in the fourth century by St. Basil and St. Gregory of Nazianzus.[64] This solution was finally accepted by almost all of the Greeks, either as a result of personal conviction, imperial and patriarchal pressure, or even

---

Florence, see H. Vast, *Le Cardinal Bessarion* (Paris, 1878); and L. Mohler, *Kardinal Bessarion als Theologe, Humanist, und Staatsmann,* 3 vols. (Paderborn, 1923). On his role at Florence see E. Candal, "Bessarion Nicaenus in concilio florentino," *Orientalia christiana periodica* 6 (1940): 416ff.; and E. Udalcova, "The Struggle of Parties in Fifteenth-Century Byzantium and the Role of Bessarion of Nicaea" (in Russian), pts. 1 and 2, *Vizantiysky Vremennik* 2 (1949): 294–307, and 3 (1950); cf. R. Coulon's article in *Dic. His. Géog. Ecc.,* vol. 2, col. 1696ff.; and cf. Loenertz, "Les dominicains byzantins," 5–61.

62. See *Acta,* 446–7 (Mansi, col. 556) where the Latin term *filioque* is accepted by the Greeks (except Mark) as an "explanation . . . not . . . addition." The Greeks at the end accepted the *filioque* as equivalent to their doctrine "through the Son" (see below). Also Andrea of Santacroce, cols. 1459, and esp. 1463ff., 1475ff.

63. *Acta,* 297 (Mansi, col. 769); and Andrea of Santacroce, esp. cols. 155ff., and cf. Syropoulos, 440, 468 on MSS. On the long, involved conflict over MSS and their interpretations in which texts of St. Basil played an important part, see *Acta,* 250–390 (Mansi, cols. 720–876). On the problem of corruption of texts in particular see esp. *Acta,* 296–98, 308, 326ff., 354, 401 (Mansi, cols. 769–72, 783, 840ff., 836, 888). Also letter of Bessarion in MPG, vol. 161, cols. 325ff. Cf. Vast, *Cardinal Bessarion,* 81–82; Vogt, *Dic. Théol. Cath.,* vol. 6, col. 36; and M. Creyghton, *History of the Papacy,* vol. 2 (London, 1892), 184.

64. See decree of union in *Acta,* 461 (Mansi, col. 1029); Andrea of Santa Croce, col. 1696; Mark of Ephesus, MPG, vol. 159, col. 1076. Cf. Stephanides, *Ecclēsiastikē historia,* 362. This identification of terms at Florence was largely the work of Bessarion and Isidore of Russia. On St. Basil's and St. Gregory Nazianzus's earlier use of "through the Son" see above, essay 7, text and n. 79.

sheer weariness. Mark of Ephesus, the hard core of the Orthodox, however, persisted in his intransigence.[65]

Why was the *filioque* such a formidable obstacle to union? What fear motivated the fanatic Orthodox so that they would not yield before entreaties from all sides to accept a solution which could insure aid for their city, now almost the sole remnant of Byzantine territory unconquered by the Turks. The answer to this question is fundamental for understanding the failure of unionist efforts in the entire period of the later Middle Ages.

The position of the Latins is of course clear. They firmly believed that the "addition" to the creed, despite its absence from the original formulation at Nicaea-Constantinople and adoption for the first time at the local Council of Toledo in 589, was a valid clarification of dogma made in order to preclude Arian errors with regard to the full divinity of the Son. And the Latins could not accept it as unauthorized doctrinal innovation without of course implying that for centuries they had been reciting heresy.[66] What the pro-Orthodox on the other hand seemed most to have feared in accepting the *filioque* was not merely alteration of the traditional Orthodox dogma, of what in their view had been established as inviolate by the first seven ecumenical councils, but, by extension, loss of their ethnic identity—in other words the beginnings of a Latinization of the Greek church and people.[67] They could not erase from their memories the experiences of fifty-seven years of oppressive Latin occupation in Constantinople and the continuing Western domination of their islands and other Byzantine areas.

After the Fourth Crusade of 1204 many of the Greek clergy had been

65. Mark insisted to the end that "through the Son" attributed to St. Basil in Cusanus's particular MS had been tampered with. Particularly useful here is Syropoulos's knowledge of behind-the-scenes activities. See Syropoulos, 342ff., 362, 394, 371; and *Acta,* 393, 402, 416, 450 (Mansi, cols. 879, 888, 976, 1016). Gill, "The Acta and the Memoirs of Syropoulos," 303–55; Geanakoplos, *Byzantium,* no. 162; and Gill, *Council of Florence,* passim. See also essay 12, 269–70.

66. For a good example of Latin inability to accept invalidity of the *filioque,* see Giannelli, "Un projetto di Barlaam," 172, and esp. 176.

67. See in *Acta,* 400 (Mansi, col. 885), the revealing remark of a Greek bishop at Florence: "I will not give up our dogma and become Latinized" (cf. Geanakoplos, *Byzantium,* no. 161). It is to be noted that certain Western theorists, especially of the fourteenth century, had proposed elaborate schemes for forcibly Latinizing the Greeks. That set forth in the *Directorium,* written by Brocardus or more probably by the Dominican Guillaume d'Adam, planned to convert the Greek churches into Latin, suppress the fanatically Orthodox Greek monks, burn the heretical Greek books, and, perhaps most important, force certain male Greek children to learn Latin letters. The plan would even have abolished the Greek language (they said) had it not been used at Christ's crucifixion! See Geanakoplos, *Byzantium,* 376–77.

dispossessed of their ecclesiastical properties and the people forced to accept the supremacy of the Roman church. In principle at least it was required that the creed be recited with the *filioque* and the liturgy celebrated with unleavened bread.[68] In addition, certain feudal practices characteristic of the Latin church had been imposed upon the Greek clergy, such as the taking of a compulsory personal oath recognizing papal authority through the clasping of one's hands within those of a Latin superior. The Greek inhabitants of Constantinople had even requested papal selection of a Greek (along with the existing Latin) patriarch for Constantinople, since "it is not proper to confess your secrets through an interpreter to a patriarch of another language." Finally, a papal legate had even been dispatched to Constantinople to dictate ecclesiastical, and in effect influence political, decisions.[69] Eloquent testimony of the deep Greek resentment toward their Latin conquerors is provided by a canon of the Fourth Lateran Council (1215) according to which the Greeks were accustomed to purify their altars following each use by the Latins, and to rebaptize their children after performance of the equivalent Latin rite.[70]

These experiences of a dominated people had remained vivid in the minds of the Greek laity as well as the clergy, and the possible restoration of similar conditions through submission to the pope was a great fear of the vast majority of Greeks. Not all the people shared this feeling, it is true.[71] Some, primarily among the higher ecclesiastics, the intellectuals

68. On Greek experiences under Latin domination in Constantinople see R. L. Wolff, "The Organization of the Latin Patriarchate of Constantinople (1204–61): Social and Administrative Consequences of the Latin Conquest," *Traditio* 6 (1948): 33–34, and 42. At the start of the conquest Innocent III had directed that the Greeks be permitted to retain their rites (MPL, vol. 215, cols. 959ff.), but this was generally not observed. In Cyprus during the fourteenth century, e.g., the Greeks were not permitted to retain their liturgical usages (Raynaldi, *Annales ecclesiastici,* ad. ann. 1338, no. 72; ad ann. 1368, no. 20; ad ann. 1370, no. 4). See now M. Efthimiou, *Greeks and Latins on Cyprus in the Thirteenth Century* (Brookline, Mass., 1987). The Greeks of southern Italy, in 1284, were enjoined by Pope Martin IV to chant the creed with the *filioque* under pain of excommunication (Viller, "La question de l'union," pt. 1, p. 265 and n. 2).

69. On the practice of an ecclesiastical feudal oath see Bréhier, "Attempts at Reunion," 606. On the "dual" patriarchate see Geanakoplos, *Byzantium,* no. 155. On the significance to the Greeks of a Latin legate in Constantinople, see Geanakoplos, "On the Schism of the Greek and Roman Churches," 19–23.

70. Hefele and Leclercq, *Histoire des conciles,* vol. 5, pt. 2, p. 1333. Cf. the remark of Petrarch (in 1366): "These tricksters call the Roman church their mother, but they treat our Latin rites as foolishness, and purify their basilicas after one of our people has entered them": "Rerum sinilium," in *Opera omnia* (Basel, 1554), bk. 7, ep. 1. Also *Lettere senili di F. Petrarcha,* ed. G. Fracassetti, vol. 1 (Florence, 1869), 422–24. Cf. Geanakoplos, *Byzantium,* no. 154.

71. Jugie, *Le schisme byzantin,* 263, believes (correctly) that the increasing number of

and the bureaucracy, as a result especially of their exposure to Latin theological works, were ready to accept the Latin union, either from sincere conviction or, probably much more often, through recourse to the ecclesiastical concept of *economia,* in order to save Constantinople from conquest by the Turks.[72]

It was the view of the majority of the Orthodox that the danger of Latinization threatened not only their religion but their political, social, and economic life as well. For gradually, since even before the First Crusade, Byzantium, more perhaps than is generally realized, had been penetrated by Latin influences. Latin officials participated in the administration, Latin commanders and mercenaries fought in its armies, and everywhere were the Gasmules, children of mixed Greco-Latin marriages. Even more important was the virtual stranglehold exercised by the Venetians and Genoese over almost the entire economic life of the capital.[73]

Some anti-unionists became so extreme in their fear of Latin influence that they openly declared their preference for "the turban of the sultan to the tiara of the pope."[74] This was no idle talk, since it was observed that in

---

Greek translations of Latin theological works (of Thomas Aquinas, etc.) explains the development of pro-unionism among certain of the Greek clergy.

72. On *economia,* in effect accommodation of the church to the needs of the state in time of crisis—but only in administrative and liturgical, *not* doctrinal matters—see essay 12 below, 272, and n. 55. Cf. Geanakoplos, *Byzantium; Church, Society and Civilization,* no. 98A, B, C. On the fear of Latinization and particularly that union would restore Latin domination, see N. Kalogeras, *Mark of Ephesus and Cardinal Bessarion* (in Greek) (Athens, 1893), 57–102; the oration of Barlaam in MPG, vol. 151, col. 133; and the *Directorium* of Brocardus (or more probably Guillaume d'Adam). Cf. Viller, "La question de l'union," pt. 1, p. 274; and Geanakoplos, "Michael VIII Palaeologus and the Union of Lyons," 86–87. On the preference of some Greeks for the Turks see Kalogeras; H. Evert-Kapessova, "Le tiare ou le turbain," *Byzantinoslavica* 14 (1953): 245–55; and finally, Udalcova, "The Struggle of Parties in Byzantium," pt. 2, pp. 106–32, who analyzes the views toward union of the various classes in Byzantium. Regarding Latin military aid for Byzantium see the treatise of Demetrius Cydones (late fourteenth century), *De admittendo latinorum subsidio,* in MPG, vol. 154, cols. 1028D, urging the acceptance of Latin aid against the Turks. For discussion of this see D. Zakythinos, *La Grèce et les Balkans* (Athens, 1947), 46–56. Cf. Geanakoplos, *Byzantium,* 222–23, 376–77.

73. On Latin economic penetration see N. Oikonomides, *Hommes des affaires Grecs et Latins à Constantinople* (Paris, 1979). Geanakoplos, *Emperor Michael;* and Geanakoplos, *Interaction of the Sibling Cultures,* index, under "Latinization." On the importance of the Gasmules see the Byzantine historians Gregoras, *Byzantina historia,* 98; and G. Pachymeres, *De Michaele et Andronico Palaeologis,* ed. I. Bekker, vol. 1 (Bonn, 1835), 188–309. W. Heyd, *Histoire du commerce du Levant au moyen-âge,* 2 vols. (Leipzig, 1885–86; new ed. Leipzig, 1936), 1:427–527, 2:257–313; and G. Ostrogorsky, *History of the Byzantine State,* trans. J. Hussey (New Brunswick, 1969), chap. 8.

74. Statement attributed to the grand duke Lukas Notaras not long before Con-

Asia Minor, the Turks, in accordance with Islamic precepts, had generally permitted the conquered Byzantines the exercise of their religion and retention of their ecclesiastical hierarchy.[75]

It may be too much to speak of a genuine Byzantine "nationalism" in this period, though to be sure, with the loss of the eastern areas to the Arabs and later to the Turks, it seems to have become much more evident than in earlier centuries in the now more homogeneous "Greek" areas of the empire. But it cannot be denied that the Greeks regarded themselves as a people very distinct from the Latins. The crusades and especially the years of subjugation had greatly sharpened this awareness, turning it into overt hostility. It is no wonder, then, that a Greek supporter of the union came to be looked upon as a traitor. Striking confirmation for this statement exists already from the year 1274, when one of the imperial envoys, returning to Constantinople after espousing the religious union at Lyons, was taunted by the rabble with the words, "You have become a Frank" (that is, by accepting religious union you have become a Latin).[76] To the Orthodox party, religious union thus came to mean not only ecclesiastical apostasy but also a betrayal of the Greek heritage and sense of national pride.

In the light of this explanation it appears that the question of the *filioque,* so bitterly debated at Florence, masked the vital, underlying problem of the hostility between Greeks and Latins. To the anti-unionist Orthodox, union, with submission to papal authority, was, in brief, the prelude to assimilation by the Latins.[77] In the words of a leading Ortho-

---

stantinople's fall (in Ducas, 264). Evert-Kapessova, "La tiare ou le turbain," 245–57, shows that this sentiment, usually cited as the expression of a blind hatred, constituted a political program. Cf. the qualifying remarks of I. Ševčenko, "Intellectual Repercussions of the Council of Florence," *Church History* 24 (1955), 315 n. 47. Also S. Runciman, "Byzantine and Hellene in the Fourteenth Century," *Tomos K. Harmenopoulos* (Thessalonica, 1952): 30–31. Cf. the statement of Jean Gerson, chancellor of the University of Paris, in his discourse to the king of France after the Council of Pisa (1409) that the Greeks prefer the Turks to the Latins (in A. Galitzin, *Sermon inédit de Jean Gerson sur le retour des Grecs à l'unité* (Paris, 1859), 29; and cf. Manuel Calecas, MPG, vol. 152, col 239.

75. The Koran prescribed toleration of Christianity. See L. Bréhier, *Vie et mort de Byzance* (Paris, 1947), 498.

76. Quoted in Geanakoplos, *Emperor Michael,* 271. Cf. Geanakoplos, *Byzantium,* 219.

77. On the Greek fear of Latinization see further *Acta,* 400 (Mansi, col. 885), where a Greek bishop, objecting to acceptance of the *filioque,* says pointedly, "I prefer to die than ever to become Latinized." George Scholarios, subsequently an archfoe of union, refers to the union as "Latinism" and warns the Greeks that by accepting it "all of you and this assembly will become Latins" (cited in Demetrakopoulos, *Historia schismatis,* 168). See now Geanakoplos, *Byzantium,* nos. 161, 285. Also a curious letter of Bessarion's, written after the Turkish conquest to the tutor of the children of the last representative of the Byzantine imperial family. He instructs them to live in all respects as Latins, wearing

dox polemist of the fifteenth century, Joseph Bryennios: "Let no one be deceived by delusive hopes that the Italian allied troops will come to save us. If they pretend to rise to defend us, they will take arms only to destroy our city, our race, and our name."[78] And yet, at the end, virtually all of the Greek prelates, led by Bessarion, Isidore of Russia, Dorotheos, and Gregory the Pneumatikos, seemed able to accept religious union with Rome on the simple but incontestible grounds that the saints of each church were inspired by the same Holy Spirit and therefore could not err in spiritual matters. Thus the doctrine of each side on the Procession, however differently expressed, had to be perfectly equivalent in meaning. Some less theologically educated Greek clerics, however, must have been extremely surprised, on hearing that several highly-revered Greek Church Fathers (Sts. Basil, Gregory of Nazianzus, Maximos the Confessor, and the later Nilus Cavasilas) in their use of "through the son" seemed much closer to the Latin *filioque* doctrine than they had realized.[79]

Discussions also took place over the doctrine of the fire of purgatory and such liturgical differences as the use of leavened or unleavened bread in the Eucharist, and the precise moment the Eucharistic miracle occurs.[80] At length, after eighteen months of wearisome theological dissension, resolution seemed to be at hand. Urged on by the Greek Latinophiles, under pressure from the pope, who, owing to policy, financial difficulties, or both, did not pay the Greek subsistence for five months[81]—pushed by the emperor (many of whose delegation were at

---

Latin clothing, attending Latin churches, even praying in the Latin manner (Sphrantzes, 418ff.). But then the situation was different.

78. Quoted in Kalogeras, *Mark and Bessarion,* 70. On Bryennios, who died just before the Council of Florence and who was in attendance at the Council of Constance, see N. Tomadakes, *Ho Iōsēf Byennios* (Athens, 1947); Bréhier's article in *Dic. His. Géog. Ecc.,* vol. 10, cols. 993–96; and Ph. Meyer, "Des Joseph Bryennios Schriften, Leben und Bildung," *Byzantinische Zeitschrift* 5 (1896): 74–111.

79. On this significant point see esp. Gill, *Council of Florence,* 23, citing Greek and Latin sources on the "harmony of the saints." For more on the *filioque* see essay 12, esp. 270–71. See text and n. 64 above.

80. For more on ritual differences see essay 12, 256–57. It is significant that when Pope Eugenius asked the Greeks at Florence to abandon the use of leavened bread (with yeast) the Greeks, according to the *Acta,* 446 (Mansi, col. 1012), responded that the practice was handed down from their ancestors *(patroparadoton)* and should not be altered. On the fire of purgatory see Syropoulos, 282–86, 292.

81. On this see Syropoulos, 379, 492, and see above, n. 18. In justice to the pope it should be noted that his financial difficulties were doubtless aggravated by attacks in the area (especially when the council was in Ferrara) by the condottiere Niccolò Piccinino (Syropoulos, 278, 376), and also because the Council of Basel had deprived him of many ecclesiastical revenues (Boulting, *Aeneas Silvius,* 69). He himself constantly had to borrow funds. See esp. Gill, "The Cost of the Council of Florence," in *Personalities of the*

times living almost in penury), and goaded even by reports of an imminent Turkish attack on Constantinople, the last of the Orthodox finally yielded.[82] With their surrender and Greek concessions on the most important questions at issue, preparations were begun to draw up the decree of union.[83] But as was perhaps inevitable, a conflict arose even over the signing of the document itself, for pope and emperor each claimed the honor of having his name inscribed at the beginning of the text. In true Western theocratic fashion, Eugenius affirmed the superiority of his rank to that of the emperor, while John Palaeologus, in a last assertion of traditional authority, maintained that, as from the time of Constantine the Great it had been an imperial right to convoke synods, his name should take precedence.[84]

Before the desperate need of his capital for aid, however, the emperor gave way, and the signing of the *horos* (decree) began. But one Greek prelate did not sign. The patriarch Joseph had died only a short time before, and another bishop had fled from Florence,[85] but Mark of Ephesus alone resolutely refused to affix his signature. According to Syropoulos, the pope demanded that since Mark refused to accept the decision of the council, he be tried by the council, but the emperor refused the demand. As Pope Eugenius indicated at the time, Mark's failure to sign would prove fatal for the success of the union.[86] It was a prophetic

---

Council of Florence, 166–67, 194–203, 12. Gill believes that the withholding of papal funds from the Greeks was not the pope's fault.

82. *Acta,* 393ff. (Mansi, cols. 880ff.); cf. Vast, *Cardinal Bessarion,* 85, 87–90; Syropoulos, 490–92: the emperor insists that his ecclesiastics sign the union. Syropoulos, 336, affirms Bessarion imposed silence on him (Syropoulos). But cf. a letter of Bessarion's in MPG, vol. 161, col. 424CD, stating that at Florence union was agreed to "absque quocumque violentia sponte et voluntarie." It would certainly seem that, as Gill stresses, some Greek representatives were persuaded by Latin theological arguments.

83. On the final definition of the *filioque* and other disputed points see the discussion and official decree of union in both Greek and Latin versions as printed in the *Acta,* 438–72, 453 (Mansi, cols. 1004–45). It may be noted that each church retained its own rites and usages, esp. the azymes and "enzymes" (unleavened and leavened bread), while the Latin views of purgatory seemed to prevail. On the settlement of the specific points at issue cf. the various opinions of Jugie, *Le schisme byzantin,* 267; Frommann, *Kritische Beiträge,* 18; Stephanides, *Ecclēsiastikē historia,* 326–63; and Gill, *Council of Florence,* 270–97. For the crucial problem of papal supremacy see below, nn. 88–89. Also cf. Syropoulos, 512–14. On the question of purgatory see essay 12, 272.

84. Syropoulos, 478. The primary *Latin* source, Andrea of Santacroce, 257, reports the pope saying after signing of the union: "I do not know what more to ask of the Greeks, for what we have asked for and sought we have." (See ed. Hoffmann, 257).

85. *Acta,* 444–45 (Mansi, cols. 1008–9). The *Acta* does not mention the flight of Isaias, bishop of Stravropol, but his signature is missing from the *tomos* and Syropoulos, 494–95, explicitly mentions his secret departure before the signing of union.

86. Syropoulos, 482–84, 496; esp. *Acta,* 460–71 (Mansi, cols. 1041–45); Syropoulos, 502; cf. Frommann, *Kritische Beiträge,* 26ff.

remark, as on the return of the Greek delegation to Constantinople, Mark became the soul of the rising Orthodox opposition to union.[87]

The most significant aspect of the unionist decree (along with validation of the *filioque* doctrine) was its emphasis on the crucial problem of papal supremacy, acceptance of which would, in effect, mean surrender of the independence of the Greek church.[88] In the document the authority of the pope as universal head of the churches of both East and West was clearly affirmed, although it was stated in the passage immediately following that "all the rights and privileges of the patriarchs of the East are excepted."[89] Despite the lack of precise information in the sources, it seems likely that the curious latter phrase was interpolated to assuage Orthodox feeling by at least the appearance of limiting papal absolutism. As Edward Gibbon put it so well, ironically but accurately, in his famous *Decline and Fall,* "To satisfy the Latins without dishonoring the Greeks . . . they weighed the scruples of words and syllables till the theological balance trembled with a slight preponderance in favor of the Vatican."[90]

87. Gill, *Council,* 355ff. At Mark's death George Scholarios (later as a monk named Gennadios) became the leading anti-unionist (Ducas, ed. Grecu, 315–17).

88. See *Acta,* 451ff. (Mansi, cols. 1016ff.); and Syropoulos, 474ff. The key point was the right of appeal to the pope against the patriarchs.

89. The decree reads that the pope possesses the "primacy over the whole world," and is "successor to the blessed Peter first of the Apostles, true vicar of Christ, head of the entire church, and father and teacher of all Christians, with complete power received from our Lord Jesus Christ via Peter to teach, rule, and govern the universal church, . . ." etc. See *Acta,* 464 (Mansi, cols. 1032); Syropoulos, 496–500; and Andrea of Santacroce, cols. 1697–98. For various opinions regarding papal jurisdiction as expressed in the decree see Frommann, *Kritische Beiträge,* 18; Hefele and Leclercq, *Histoire des conciles,* vol 7, pt. 2, pp. 1049–51; Stephanides, *Ecclēsiastikē historia,* 361–64; G. Hofmann, "Papato, conciliarismo, patriarcato (1438–1439)," in *Teologi e deliberazioni del concilio di Firenze* (Rome, 1940), 69–73. The Latin text of the *Acta,* 464 (Mansi, col. 1032) continues, quoting the decree: "salvis videlicet privilegiis omnibus et iuribus eorum [patriarcharum]." The Greek: "reserving that is, both all their [patriarchal] rights and privileges." Cf. Gill, *Council of Florence,* 286ff.; Gill, *Eugenius IV Pope of Christian Union* (Westminster, 1961), 125f.; and Gill, "The Definition of the Primacy of the Pope," in *Personalities of the Council of Florence,* 281–86.

90. E. Gibbon, *Decline and Fall of the Roman Empire,* ed. J. Bury (London, 1909), vol. 7, chap. 66, p. 111. The appearance of the same clause in a canon of the Fourth Lateran Council of 1215 (at which time the Greek church was forcibly united to Rome) may indicate that no great importance should be attached to the phrase. Indeed at Florence the same words doubtless conveyed different meanings to each side (see Frommann, *Kritische Beiträge,* 18; Stephanides, *Ecclēsiastikē historia,* 363; and Gill, *Personalities of the Council of Florence,* 281.) A severe argument, of course, developed over the addition of this clause. See *Acta,* 457 (Mansi, col. 1025). Cf. the attitude of Hofmann, "Papato, conciliarismo, patriarcato," 69–73. Also on the decree of union itself note esp. the opinion of Frommann, 19: "There took place no union, in fact not even a compromise but a silencing of the differences by means of a brilliantly indefinite and

On the 6th of July 1439, in the cathedral of Florence under the recently completed dome of Brunelleschi, the solemn ceremony of union took place, with Cardinal Cesarini reading the decree in Latin and Bessarion in Greek. Almost immediately afterward, Pope Eugenius, mindful of the recent death at the council of the patriarch Joseph, urged the election of a new patriarch for Constantinople while the Greek clergy was still at Florence. This fact, mentioned by the principal sources, is recorded by Syropoulos with the additional statement that Eugenius proposed the enthronement of the titular *Latin* patriarch of Constantinople, already appointed by the pope.[91] If Syropoulos's remark is correct and the suggestion of Eugenius had actually been carried out, a certain Latinization of the Greek church would thus have already begun at the very top of the Greek hierarchy.[92]

The story of the return of the emperor and his clergy to Constantinople and the repudiation of the union by the great majority of the people is well told by the Byzantine theologians and historians as well as by Syropoulos.[93] The popular opposition was based not only on the underlying attitudes already described, but, more immediately, on the belief (accurate or not) that union had been obtained under duress; that the military aid agreed to by the Holy See would, like previous papal promises, be ineffectual;[94] and, finally, that the Byzantine people themselves would suffer the judgment of God if the purity of the faith were altered.[95]

---

ambiguous definition." See also T. Frommann, *Zur Kritik des florentiner Unionsdecrets* (Halle, 1870); also see above, essay 6, p. 143 and essay 12.

91. Syropoulos, 510, and *Acta,* 468–71 (Mansi, cols. 1041–44). The titular Latin patriarch of Constantinople was then Pope Eugenius's nephew, Francesco Condulmaro. See L. de Mas Latrie, "Patriarches latins de Constantinople," *Revue de l'Orient latin* 3 (1895): 444; cf. Frommann, *Zur Kritik,* 187.

92. That this appointment was at least under discussion may be inferred from a statement of the pope cited in *Acta,* 471 (Mansi, col. 1044) that he wanted selection of the best man, *neither relative nor friend,* as the new patriarch. (Another papal nephew Condulmaro is mentioned in Syropoulos, 176, as having commanded the papal fleet in Constantinople just before the convocation of the council.)

93. Syropoulos, 568–72 (who wrote some years later), lists seven factors for the failure of the union later in Constantinople. See also Ducas, 215, 252ff.; and Mark of Ephesus, MPG, vols. 160–61, passim.

94. This is an argument of Joseph Bryennios in his *Concerning the Union of the Churches,* 1:469 (also cited in Viller, "La question de l'union," pt. 1, p. 283). See esp the speech of George Scholarios quoted in Demetrakopoulos, *Historia schismatis,* 161ff. On Scholarios, who became the first Greek patriarch after the Turkish conquest, see his *Oeuvres complètes,* ed. L. Petit, Ch. Siderides, and M. Jugie (Paris, 1928–). For a sketch of Scholarios's life see Paulová, "L'empire byzantine," 192–203; C. Turner, "The Career of George-Gennadius Scholarios," *Byzantion* 39 (1969): 420–55. Esp. Zisis (see bibl.)

95. On the judgment of God see Ducas, 254ff., and for similar disturbances over the Union of Lyons in 1274, see Geanakoplos, *Emperor Michael,* 264–76. Cf. essay 12, 274–75, on the "conscience of the [Greek] people" as rejecting the Florence union.

So strong was the Orthodox opposition to the union that it persisted to the very capture of the capital by the Turks in 1453. Indeed, even the Turkish conquest did not destroy the ethnic Greek feeling, for it was the church, significantly, which preserved this spirit throughout the long centuries of Ottoman domination.[96]

III

One wonders, in retrospect, what the course of Byzantine history might have been had the Greek and Latin churches been able successfully to consummate union at Florence.[97] Is it possible that the deepening chasm between East and West might have been bridged and the conquest of Byzantium averted?[98]

Probably the only way to have achieved union at this time with even remote chance of success would have been to adopt the kind of policy suggested by Barlaam: in essence, recognition of pentarchic equality by the papacy and the holding of a council in Constantinople itself, so that the Greek populace, by following the discussions at first hand, could allay its deep suspicions of the Latins and especially of its own Latinophiles.[99] On the other hand, a convocation in Constantinople might well have

96. Paparregopoulos, *History of the Greek People* (in Greek), vol. 5 (Athens, 1903), 497ff.; and A. Vacalopoulos, *The Greek Nation, 1453–1669,* trans. I. Moles (New Brunswick, N.J, 1976), chaps. 5–6.

97. It should be pointed out that although the Greek church as a whole repudiated union, it is on the basis of the act of union at Florence that certain Eastern Christians termed Uniates are today in communion with Rome.

98. On the inevitability of Byzantium's fall see Runciman, "Byzantine and Hellene," 29–30; and Runciman, *The Fall of Constantinople* (Cambridge, 1965), xii–xiii

99. See Giannelli, "Un projetto di Barlaam," 175–76. On his return from Avignon Barlaam wrote a treatise against papal primacy of jurisdiction. Nevertheless, he subsequently became closely identified with the Roman church. (On Barlaam see text above and nn. 23–27.) The clause on the patriarchs in the union decree (n. 88) seems to refer to the pentarchy.

The suggestion of a Constantinopolitan council is mentioned several times by Syropoulos. He notes, 120, that the patriarch Joseph favored this proposal because in the West the Greeks would be at the mercy of the Latins for their subsistence. He also records, 312, that in 1426 the famous philosopher Gemistos Pletho had advised the emperor not to go to the West and to insist on Constantinople as the site for a council (see essay 12). Cf. on this Demetrakopoulos, *Historia schismatis,* 103. Though the Latins were in general unwilling to go to Constantinople, it is noteworthy that Humbert of Romans (thirteenth century), who understood the Greek mentality well, had already suggested that "papa in Graeciam debere descendere, si spes esset probabilis, quod propter hoc reuniretur ovile" (Mansi, vol. 24, col. 128).

provoked immediate retaliation from the Turks.[100] But even more important, the papacy could hardly have accepted terms which would have been contrary to the entire monarchical tradition of the Western church and which at the same time would have deprived the Holy See of a decisive victory over the Greeks, so necessary for its triumph over the conciliarists of Basel.

Even had the Greek people accepted the Florentine union, there seems little likelihood that the Latin princes would have responded effectively to papal appeals for a crusade against the Turks. For the West, always doubtful in any case of the sincerity of Greek conversion, was now deeply engrossed in its own problems and therefore in general almost indifferent to the fate of the East.[101] Thus in 1453 when Constantinople finally succumbed to the Turks, only a few humanists, their passion for Hellenism inflamed by their contacts with Greek intellectuals at Florence, lamented the fall of the capital. Significantly, however, they mourned more what they termed "the second death of Homer and Plato" than the passing of medieval Byzantium.[102]

100. Ducas, ed. Grecu, 269, says that the emperor had stressed to the sultan the religious aims of the Council of Florence, but the sultan no doubt realized the political considerations involved. According to Sphrantzes, 178–80, the first and greatest cause of the Turkish attack and slavery of the Greeks after 1453 was the council of Florence.

101. How, cried some of the Greeks, could the Latin princes help them in view of their inability to aid even the Latin states in the East? The great Western states were not yet seriously menaced by the Turks and felt no compulsion to help. Most threatened were Hungary, Albania, Venice, and Genoa with territory in the East. France and England, still involved in the Hundred Years' War, did not respond effectively to papal appeals, not participating in the unfortunate Crusade of Varna (1444), which seemed to seal the fate of the Greek Empire: see D. Nicol, *The Last Centuries of Byzantium* (New York, 1972), 379–81. No secular prince, in fact, except the duke of Burgundy had sent representatives to the Council at Florence. (For the insulting attitude of the Burgundian envoys to the Greek emperor, see Syropoulos, 340–42; cf. *Acta,* 212–13). The absence of Western princes at Florence was a profound disillusionment for the Greek emperor.

102. See especially the eloquent letter of Aeneas Silvius (the later Pope Pius II), in *Opera omnia* (Basel, 1571), 712 (cf. Vansteenberghe, *Cardinal Nicolas de Cues,* 228): "Secunda mors ista Homero est, secundus Platonis obitus!" On Western disinterest in Constantinople's fall and rhetorical laments of the humanists see R. Cessi, "La Caduta di Costantinopli nel 1453," *Atti del Reale istituto veneto di scienze lettere ed arti* (1937–38): 565; M. Gilmore, *The World of Humanism, 1453–1517* (New York, 1952), 15–21; and also Runciman, *The Fall of Constantinople,* 166–67.

For more material on the Council of Florence see next essay.

Additional Bibliography for Essay 11

J. Gill, *Personalities of the Council of Florence and Other Essays* (New York, 1964), careful essays, utilized here. A. Leidl, *Die Einheit der Kirchen auf den spätmittelalterlichen Konzilien: Von Konstanz bis Florenz* (Paderborn, 1966). J. Gill, *Constance et Bâle-Florence,*

Histoire des conciles oecuméniques, vol. 9 (Paris, 1965), 118ff. J. Hussey, *The Orthodox Church in the Byzantine Empire* (Oxford, 1986), 271–86, a narrative account utilizing previous works. S. Mösl, *Das theologische Problem des 17. ökumenischen Konzils von Ferrara-Florenz-Rome (1438–45)* (Innsbruck, 1974). I. Ostroumoff, *The History of the Council of Florence,* trans. B. Popoff (Boston, 1971), a very biased work with nothing new. H. G. Beck, *Geschichte der orthodoxen Kirche im byzantinischen Reich* (Göttingen, 1980), 240–53, with bibliography. C. Patrinelis, *Ho Theodōros Agallianos* (Athens, 1966). T. Zisis, *Gennadios Scholarios: Bios, Syggramata, Didaskalia* (Thessalonica, 1980). A. Failler, ed., *Pachymeres Rōmaikē historia* (Paris, 1984) new ed.

Twelve

An Orthodox View of the Councils of Basel (1431–49) and of Florence (1438–39) as Paradigm for the Study of Modern Ecumenical Councils

The Council of Basel, with its accompanying Council of Florence, which is counted as an ecumenical council by the Roman though not by the Orthodox church, was one of the most extraordinary councils in all of Christian history. Not only did Basel mark the high point of Western conciliar claims to supremacy over papal authority, but during its eighteen-year duration it enabled the beleaguered pope, through his deft diplomacy in achieving religious union with the Greeks at Florence, to administer the decisive coup de grace to his rival conciliarists sitting at Basel and thus to revive papal absolutism once again in the Western church. In the course of Basel and its subsidiary council Florence, opportunity was afforded for the expression of diverse kinds of ecclesiological, doctrinal, and administrative phenomena pertaining to general councils. Even more important, especially from the Greek viewpoint, the Council of Florence marked the first time since before the so-called schism of 1054 that the two churches had met, in an officially sanctioned general council, in order to engage in protracted discussion over the major problems separating the two institutions. Basel and especially its corollary Florence, then, provide an almost ideal paradigm for the study of com-

This essay should be read in conjection with essay 11.

parative Byzantine and Roman conciliar ideas in action during the late medieval and Renaissance period. Indeed, the record of the inner workings of these two councils, especially Florence, presents us with a very useful blueprint, so to say, for the kind of preparation and discussion that must take place before the convocation of a great universal council of Christendom, to meet, I hope, in the not too distant future, though probably not in our lifetime.

The situation of the Roman church is today of course not the same as it was at the end of the Council of Basel under Pope Nicholas V, several reforms including the vernacularization of liturgy having taken place as the result of Vatican Council II. But the general ecclesiastical, monolithic structure of the Roman church is the same, in fact even strengthened by the pronouncement of 1870 on papal infallibility. The Orthodox church, or more accurately, the Orthodox churches, have in general remained the same, though of course the chief protector of the Greek Orthodox church, the Byzantine emperor, has long gone and the ecumenical patriarch of Constantinople now resides amid a religiously alien nation. Yet many theologians of all Orthodox churches believe, as do I, that the best way to restore unity in the church, especially with Rome, is to return to the situation prevailing *before* 1054 when, despite certain largely political, disciplinary, and psychological differences, the two churches were still in full communion. Actually, at Florence in 1438–39, as even earlier at the unionist Council of Lyons in 1274, the Orthodox, who had always prided themselves on being and remaining the church par excellence of the seven ecumenical synods, kept insisting precisely on a return to the situation obtaining before the churches' separation in 1054 as the simplest, most impartial way of recovering their ancient unity.[1] Of course, to the papacy, this proposal was untenable, because it would at one stroke annul the enormous growth of papal authority and claims to jurisdiction over all churches, including the Greek, begun under Gregory VII and continued through 1870 to the present.

To return to the Western conciliar movement: it is very striking that, after almost two centuries of papal refusal to accept Byzantine requests for convocation of a general council to solve their doctrinal and liturgical differences over the *filioque,* use of the *azyma* (unleavened bread), the question of the *epiklēsis* (that is, the exact moment at which the miracle of *metabolē* [transubstantiation] occurs), and the question of celibacy or marriage of clergy, the popes finally relented and in 1431 accepted the

1. On Lyons, see Geanakoplos, *Emperor Michael Palaeologus and the West,* 258–76. On Florence, see J. Gill, *The Council of Florence* (Cambridge, 1959); and essay 11 above. On Greek insistence to return to the situation before 1054, see Geanakoplos, *Emperor Michael,* 261–62; and essay 10 above.

Greek proposal for calling a general council, that is, for a convocation of the bishops of the church in something at least of the manner of the early church councils. What a reversal from the position of popes Urban IV and Clement IV of the thirteenth century that "it would be absolutely improper, indeed a Council cannot be permitted to meet, since the purity of the faith cannot be cast into doubt by discussion with the Greeks."[2] Rome, as always hitherto, insisted on religious union first and then a general council could meet, presumably simply to ratify the decisions. At the Council of Lyons in 1274, Eastern and Western representatives had, to be sure, already met. But there, except for some *private* conversations presumably engaged in by Pope Gregory, the legate, Cardinal Bonaventura, and the chief Greek lay representative, George Acropolites, no public debate or discussion whatever had been permitted by Rome to take place.[3] Indeed, some decades later in the fourteenth century, Barlaam, the Byzantine humanist from south Italy, in explaining the failure of Lyons to achieve union, told the pope categorically that "the Byzantine people will never accept Lyons as an ecumenical council because *all five* patriarchs were not present and no public discussion had taken place."[4] In fact, Emperor Michael could not even induce the incumbent Greek patriarch to go to Lyons and instead had to send an ex-patriarch, so strong was the opposition of the people and clergy. Actually, Michael had sought union not out of sincere conviction of the need for religious rapprochement, but out of sheer desperation and need—in order to secure papal aid against his mortal enemy, the papal vassal Charles of Anjou, king of Sicily, who was threatening Constantinople. The same situation was in a sense now being repeated at Basel and then Florence, but now with the Turks threatening Constantinople. Nevertheless, this time, with the development of greater interest in each other's cultures and religions in the period of the early Renaissance, a number of Greek clergy and intellectuals (Demetrius Cydones and Bessarion, for example) were ready, for the sake of a higher ideal, the unity of Christendom, to sacrifice some of their doubts. And of course the papacy too, finding itself in dire straits, needed a trump card to play against its increasingly powerful opponents, the Western conciliarist movement.

Before the convocation at Lyons in 1274 Pope Gregory X had com-

2. Geanakoplos, *Emperor Michael,* 203, translation of papal document from E. Jordan, *Les registres de Clément IV* (Paris, 1893), 1:199, no. 585; A. Tautu, ed., *Acta . . . Clementis IV . . .* (Vatican, 1953), no. 23, esp. p. 67.

3. See essay 10.

4. See translation of Barlaam's discourse in Geanakoplos, *Byzantium: Church, Society and Civilization,* no. 159 (emphasis added) (text in Migne, *Patrologia graeca* [hereafter MPG], vol. 151, cols. 1332f.).

missioned a position paper from the Latin scholar Humbert of Romans, who had lived long in the East. Humbert, with rare psychological insight, had insisted that the difficulty of Greek and Latin theologians in understanding each other's position could be alleviated, at least partly, if Greeks and Latins would do what he said no one ever did, namely, read through each other's canon law. In his plea for greater understanding, Humbert also stated that the most basic reason for animosity between the two churches was originally not religious at all but political, arising from the re-creation of the Roman Empire in the West in 800 by Charlemagne, an act which served to deny the validity of Byzantine claims to be the true successors of Augustus and Constantine the Great.[5] The lesson to be drawn from this emphasis on differences in Greek and Latin mental and psychological attitudes and the remedies proposed to alleviate them should not be lost on today's theologians interested in the conception of religious union of the ecumene.

The Council of Basel was convened for 1431 by the recalcitrant Pope Martin V at the insistence of the still powerful conciliarist party of the West, which was pressing for reform of the church in head and members, especially in its head, the papacy. To be sure, as a result of the two earlier Western concilarist synods held at Pisa in 1409 and Constance beginning in 1414, the conciliarist party had finally managed to impose on the Western church its theory that a general council is superior to the pope, and that therefore papal sanction in convoking such a council could, contrary to medieval Western canon law, be contravened. Several reasons had led to this conviction: the belief that Christ rather than the pope, successor of St. Peter, was the true head of the church; that in time of extreme emergency for the well-being of the entire church and community—church and community were here considered coterminous—canon law could be dispensed with and emergency measures adopted for the benefit of all. Conciliar theory was finally translated into action not by the two rival popes but by scholars and cardinals of both curias, one residing in Rome, the other in Avignon. At the Council of Constance, in 1417, the revolutionary conciliar edict *Frequens* was adopted, declaring that a council should be convened regularly, first after five years (later seven, then ten) to take care of pressing church problems such as clerical abuses and the regulation of papal affairs.[6] It is important to note that in

5. See Humbert of Romans, *Opus tripartitum,* in Mansi, *Sacrorum conciliorum . . . collectio,* vol. 24, cols. 106–36; cf. essay 10, 208; and E. Brett, *Humbert of Romans His Life and Views of Thirteenth Century Society* (Toronto, 1984).

6. On conciliar theory and its development and the councils of Constance and Basel, see, among others, E. Jacob, *Essays in the Conciliar Epoch* (Manchester, 1953); and A. Flick, *The Decline and Fall of the Medieval Church,* vol. 2 (New York, 1920), chaps. 12–

the formulation of such theories, laymen for the first time took a major role.

Such views sound in certain ways similar to the traditional ones of Byzantines.[7] At least they seem consonant with Byzantine emphasis on councils as the ultimate authority in doctrinal and jurisdictional questions of the church. That is, the superiority of the collective wisdom of the Fathers gathered in council under the guidance of the Holy Spirit is recognized over that of one individual, the pope. For the Byzantines, all the apostles were believed to be equal in authority, though they almost never denied St. Peter primacy of honor.[8] More significant, however, is the Greek interpretation of the statement made by Christ as found in Matthew: "Thou art Peter and on this rock *[petra]* I will found my Church." For the Greeks this *did* refer to Peter, although some Protestants, wrongly I believe, deny it. But Peter's faith according to Orthodox tradition was the same as that held by all the apostles. The rock referred to as Peter, then, means the *common faith* of all the apostles to be disseminated to all Christians.[9] The Orthodox understanding of this locus classicus, it seems to me, has a much more ecumenical ring to it than the Roman view. And of course the meaning of Matthew's passage was much discussed at Florence.

In the Western discussions at the Council of Basel and certainly in the preliminaries to Florence, we know that the fundamental question came up as to who had the authority to call the universal council. Should the old Byzantine tradition prevail of the emperor as the one to do so, or should the pope do so, as formulated by Latin canon law by the time of the twelfth century? In any case, we know that the conciliarists at Basel,

---

19, esp. pp. 107, 135–37 (on Cusanus's ideas); J. Haller, *Concilium basiliense,* 8 vols. (Basel, 1896–1936); F. Oakley, *Council over Pope?* (New York, 1969); O. de la Brosse, *Le pape et le concile* (Paris, 1965).

7. Cf., e.g., Aemilianos, Bishop of Meloa, "The Nature and Character of Ecumenical Councils according to the Orthodox Church," in *The Councils of the Church: History and Analysis,* ed. H. J. Margull (Philadelphia, 1966), 338–69, esp. 348: "The Church (to the East) embraces all humanity and creation to participate in divine life. . . . The human race equals the Body of Christ."

8. See esp. J. Meyendorff, "St. Peter in Byzantine Theology," in *The Primacy of Peter,* by J. Meyendorff et al. (London, 1963), esp. 9–15. Also George Acropolites, "On Sts. Peter and Paul," in his *Opera* (Teubner ed., 1903), 2:45–66. Cf. Bishop of Meloa, "Ecumenical Councils," 354: "The East always accorded primacy of honor to Rome, though not in matters of dogma or jurisdiction."

9. See, e.g., *Thrēskeutikē kai ēthikē egkyklopaideia,* vol. 10, cols. 347f. Also Bishop of Meloa, "Ecumenical Councils," 338–69, esp. 363. "Christ gave authority to all the Apostles collectively, not to one," and "Christ gave power to bind and loose to all bishops, not just to the pope." Cf. Gill, *Council of Florence,* 259.

certainly aware of the implications of this question, tried hard to get the Western emperor, Sigismund, to come to Basel and demonstrate his support for the Basel council, which in fact he did.[10] I shall touch later on the problem of who should convoke a unionist Latin-Greek council today.

A point of interest paralleling that which occurred at early ecumenical synods of the church was that the Body of Christ included—as the Western conciliarists as well as the Greeks maintained—all Christians, laymen as well as ecclesiastics.[11] In the Roman church, the existence of lay theologians was virtually unknown, while in Byzantium the existence of lay theologians was a long-standing tradition. Several of them, such as Scholarius and Pletho, in fact came along to Florence.

The question now naturally arises: to what degree, if any, were Western conciliar theorists, the German Dietrich of Niem, the French Pierre d'Ailly and Jean Gerson, or the German Nicholas of Cusa, influenced, consciously or otherwise, by the Byzantine conciliar example? After all, Western intellectuals were not unaware of the early Byzantine conciliar tradition, which was also common to them.[12] And Cusanus, to mention only the greatest, had been a convinced conciliarist until the pope succeeded in attracting the Greeks to Ferrara instead of Basel or Avignon as the conciliarists wished.[13]

There exists a speech delivered by Gerson before the French king and court in honor of the election at Pisa in 1409 of the Cretan pope Alexander V. As Gerson stresses, Alexander was a Greek Franciscan, one without family (something that would presumably minimize any tendencies to nepotism), and so, as Gerson puts it, "We, therefore, look forward now, finally, to reunion with the Eastern Church."[14] On the other hand, of course, we should not overlook the direct or indirect influence of such earlier lay Western political theorists as Marsilio of Padua and Wycliffe of England.[15] I pose this question of influence because it seems to me likely that some kind of influence, at least by example, would have emanated from the tradition of the Christian East, through whose areas

10. See Flick, *Decline of the Medieval Church,* 136f. and notes.

11. See, e.g., Cusanus's views, ibid., 147. Cf. n. 7 above, view of Bishop Aemilianos.

12. Dietrich's treatises certainly seem to reveal knowledge of the ancient church's ecclesiology, which in the ancient period was common to East and West and largely formulated in the East. See G. Erler, *Dietrich von Nieheim sein Leben und seine Schriften* (rpt. Leipzig, 1977).

13. On the Western conciliar theorists, see Flick, *Decline of the Medieval Church,* vol. 2, esp. chaps. 12–15. On the Council of Basel, esp. Haller, *Concilium basiliense.* Also see n. 6 above.

14. See A. Galitzin, *Sermon inédite de Jean Gerson sur le retour des Grecs à l'unité* (Paris, 1859), 29f.

15. Cf. W. Ullmann, *Origins of the Great Schism* (London, 1948).

so many thousands of Western crusaders, merchants, and, later, Franciscan and Dominican missionaries had passed since the end of the eleventh century.

It should be noted that, according to Byzantine canon law, it was the emperor's duty to convoke general councils. He was often present at sessions; he ratified and finally published the decisions of the council, doctrinal and canonistic. But he could not vote.[16] This to F. Dvornik is convincing proof that the independence of the bishops was preserved from imperial interference. To be sure the emperors, who also paid the expenses of the bishops whom they had invited to attend, might sometimes withhold funds and thereby, so to speak, "pack" the assembly with those they favored. According to the Byzantine ecclesiastic and historian Syropoulos, who, though knowledgeable, is admittedly prejudiced, Pope Eugenius IV seems at Florence to have withheld subsistence funds from the Greeks just before critical votes were to be taken.[17]

Dvornik also believes, following Battifol, that the procedures of the first seven ecumenical synods were modeled after those of the Roman Senate.[18] This opinion, however, is not shared by the modern Orthodox Bishop Aemilianos of Meloa.[19] Since the schism between the two churches in 1054, Rome had, however, in accord with its canon law, asserted the right of the pope to convoke ecumenical councils, which, despite the absence of the Greeks, were and are considered ecumenical by the Catholic West. All this of course evokes a disturbing question for Orthodox scholars, "Who can and will convoke a modern ecumenical council to include both churches?" Not the pope alone, whose canon law development is alien to the Eastern spirit; certainly not the king of the Greeks, who is no longer even functioning. Most probably it will be on the initiative of the pope and the *primus inter pares* of the Orthodox bishops, the ecumenical patriarch of Constantinople. Modern Orthodox scholars, Bishop Aemilianos, Father Georges Florovsky, and others (including myself) point, I believe, to a way out of this seeming insuperable impasse. In their writings they have shown that the emperor was essentially only the protector of the church, not its "Caesaropapist" master,[20]

16. F. Dvornik, "Emperors, Popes, and General Councils," *Dumbarton Oaks Papers,* no. 6 (1951): 1–23.

17. For Syropoulos, see V. Laurent, ed., *Les mémoires du grand ecclésiarche de l'église de Constantinople Sylvestre Syropoulos sur le concile de Florence (1438–39)* (Paris, 1971), 290, 378, 384, 436, etc.; cf. essay 11, at n. 20. But cf. also Gill, *Council of Florence,* 170, 174, 252, 290, who does not accept this view generally. But cf. his *Personalities of the Council of Florence* (New York, 1964), 12 and 188.

18. Dvornik, "Emperors, Popes, and General Councils," 19–23.

19. See Bishop of Meloa, "Ecumenical Councils," esp. 363.

20. See, e.g., Geanakoplos, "Church and State in the Byzantine Empire," in *Byzantine East and Latin West,* esp. 73; and Bishop of Meloa, "Ecumenical Councils," 363: "The

and as such his function in this connection can therefore be dispensed with. Recall Dvornik's views that he had no actual vote in a general council although he could certainly make his opinions felt otherwise. The ecclesiastical assembly was free to vote as it wished and each bishop, though not titular bishops, had a vote. Meeting as a synod the bishops of the first seven synods always strove for unanimity, a consensus which they believed the Holy Spirit helped them to arrive at.[21]

It is true that during councils they convoked, the Iconoclast emperors of the seventh to the ninth centuries *did* impose changes in doctrine. But these Caesaropapistic changes did not endure. The Seventh Ecumenical Synod of 787 and, then, the proclamation of the Feast of Orthodoxy in 843, which definitively restored the icons, completely annulled and indeed forever condemned the work of the Iconoclast rulers. It was, however, as a result of the Iconoclast struggle that the Byzantine patriarch became much more of a full partner with the emperor in the *Basileia* (or empire on earth), as Patriarch Photius's law code, the *Epanagoge,* shows, with the patriarch to deal primarily with souls and the emperor with the body, that is, temporal affairs. D. Obolensky has felicitously termed this cooperation a *symphonia.*[22]

The defeat of the Iconoclast emperors did not mean that the emperor, if he so desired, could not in practice name or even depose a patriarch. But there were limits to his power, as is seen also from the thirteenth century onward by the failure of the emperor's unionist efforts with Rome. The popes of Rome (except perhaps for the understanding Gregory X) always seemed to overstress the power of the Byzantine emperor over his high clergy, not only because of his admittedly complete control over ecclesiastical polity (that is, church administration) but also, I think, in part because of his sacerdotal privileges. The emperor alone, besides the clergy, had the right to enter the sanctuary and to cross before the altar, to take communion with his own hand (though, notably, a cleric had first to consecrate the bread and wine), to cense the people, and to preach in church. All these so-called sacerdotal powers have led some

---

role of the Byzantine emperor in calling councils and his conduct there is widely overestimated. In external matters he orders, organizes, pays, transports, but he could not interfere with doctrine. It is wrong to say ecclesiastical councils were patterned after the Roman Senate in procedures." Synopoulos, 411, notes the emperor called himself *Defensor* of the church (using the Latin term).

21. See Bishop of Meloa, "Ecumenical Councils," 344.

22. See "Epanagoge" in E. Barker, *Social and Political thought in Byzantium* (Oxford, 1957), 92. On this kind of *symphonia* between church and state, see Geanakoplos, "Church and State in the Byzantine Empire," esp. 56–67; now Geanakoplos, *Byzantium,* no. 99.

persons in the West to believe, incorrectly, that he possessed Caesaro-papistic powers and was a true emperor-priest. As I have put it in one of my works, though he could completely control ecclesiastical appointments in what I term the "exoteric" side of the church, he could not enter into the "esoteric" (or inner) life of the church.[23] Specifically, as Maximos the Confessor points out, no emperor could perform the miracle of *metabolē* (transubstantiation), or unilaterally change accepted doctrine.[24]

It is interesting that at Florence (according to the Greek ecclesiastical historian Sylvester Syropoulos, who has left us a very valuable account of what transpired among the Greek legation behind the scenes) the patriarch Joseph, despite the remarkable increase during the last two centuries of Byzantium's life in the patriarch's ecclesiastical authority over the huge territory of what Obolensky calls the "Byzantine Commonwealth," privately intimated in effect to a fellow Greek bishop, "I hope that through the instrumentality of the pope it will be possible to free the church from the servitude the emperor with his privileges has imposed on it."[25]

A remarkable example of personal cooperation between a modern pope and patriarch already exists. In 1965 Patriarch Athenagoras of Constantinople and Pope Paul VI, meeting in Jerusalem and acting alone, annulled the mutual anathematizations of 1054, which, the Latin document makes clear, had excommunicated only Patriarch Michael Cerularius *and all his followers* ("et omnes sequaces"). I do not think that the latter term refers to all Byzantines who came thereafter, for in the same document of excommunication, Humbert and the two other Roman legates to Constantinople actually praised the "orthodoxy" of the emperor and his people. Patriarch Michael and his Synodos Endemousa (permanent standing synod), on their side, had anathematized *only* the three papal legates, not the pope.[26] Thus it seems that, contrary to the

23. Cf. Geanakoplos, "Church and State in the Byzantine Empire," 65–80.

24. In MPG, vol. 10, col. 117: "The emperor is not a priest for neither does he participate in the sanctuary and after the consecration of the bread he does not elevate it and say, 'The holy things belong to the holy.'" See also Geanakoplos, *Byzantium,* no. 100.

25. Syropoulos, 342; cf. B. Stephanides, "The Last Stage of the Development of Relations between Byzantine Church and State" (in Greek), *Epetēris hetaireias byzantinōn spoudōn* 16 (1953): 38f. For D. Obolensky, see his *The Byzantine Commonwealth* (New York, 1971), 75–76. The term "commonwealth" here refers primarily to the Orthodox Slavic areas not technically part of the Byzantine Empire but constituting an integral part of the Byzantine church, being under the patriarch's jurisdiction. On Maximos, see also Bishop of Meloa, "Ecumenical Councils," 363.

26. For Latin documents of excommunication, see C. Will, *Acta et scripta quae de controversiis ecclesiae graecae et latinae* (Leipzig, 1861), 153–54, and 155–56 for the Greek text of excommunication. For English translation of the much neglected Greek anathema of the Synodos Endemousa, see Geanakoplos, *Byzantium,* no. 151B.

belief of later centuries, there really was no schism, canonically, in 1054. In the East, in fact, the pope's name had not been read in the diptychs since 1009, as Martin Jugie has shown—an omission which in itself could indicate not only lack of communication but also cessation of religious communion.[27]

What *did* produce the final, destructive schism were the predatory Latin crusading attacks against the East, above all the Western conquest of Constantinople in 1204, as a result of which a Latin patriarch was named in conquered Greek Constantinople. Of course, Jerusalem and Antioch had had Latin patriarchs since after the First Crusade.

A point vital to an understanding of the problem of modern ecclesiastical reunion is the development of different Latin and Orthodox ecclesiologies, that is, theories of the church. These were vividly exemplified, even dramatized, in several incidents which occurred at Florence. Joseph Gill in his authoritative book on the Council of Florence disparages these as of minor importance involving only matters of protocol.[28] For me, however, these admittedly rather minor encounters between Greeks and Latins symbolize, more vividly and succinctly perhaps than anything else, the differences in mental attitudes and principles underlying the growth of the two similar but in some ways very different ecclesiastical traditions. For example, when the patriarch of Constantinople first arrived in Ferrara, it was demanded that he kiss the foot of the pope. Refusing sharply, he said (as the Greek source Syropoulos alone tells us, though his remark is corroborated by a papal ceremonial book): "Why should I kiss the foot of the pope? What synod gave him this right?" To which the Latins replied, "All bishops, kings, and even the Western emperor perform this act to the pope as Peter's successor." Patriarch Joseph then responded, "Show me where it is written that the other Apostles did this to Peter and we, as representing the other Apostles, shall do the same for the pope. Otherwise I shall leave and go home to Constantinople." Another conflict arose later regarding the seating in the Cathedral of Ferrara of the two bodies of representatives, the pope wishing to seat himself in the middle of the church with the Greeks at his left and the Latins at his right. But the Greeks, insisting on their age-old tradition of the emperor as the vice-gerent of God, affirmed that that was the emperor's prerogative. Finally, the pope prevailed, having himself seated on the Latin side but on a throne higher than the Greek emperor's.

The poor patriarch was assigned a position corresponding to that of

27. M. Jugie, *Le schisme byzantin* (Paris, 1941), 166–67, based on documents found by W. Holzmann, "Die Unionsverhandlungen zwischen Alexios I und Papst Urban II in 1089," *Byzantinische Zeitschrift* 28 (1928): 38–67.

28. Gill, *Council of Florence,* esp. 105 n. 3.

the highest-ranking Western cardinals. A seat was even reserved for the Holy Roman Emperor on a level equal to that of the Byzantine emperor. (It is notable that, since the pope was denied a position in the center of the church, ancient conciliar protocol was followed, and the Bible, as in the first seven ecumenical synods, was placed there.) Finally, at the very end of the council, a dispute arose as to who would first sign the *tomos* (document) of union, the pope or the emperor, the latter in accord with ancient conciliar practice.[29] As before, the pope again prevailed but with the text of union reading that he signed first "with imperial participation." It seems to me that all of these various differences were more than mere matters of protocol.[30] Rather, they reflect basic tendencies or principles of belief of the two churches not only in disciplinary matters but also in conciliar procedure.

Most important of all, of course, is the question of the development of papal authority from the original primacy of honor accorded Peter's successor by the ecumenical councils of Ephesus and Chalcedon to the universal and complete jurisdiction, that is, *plenitudo potestatis* over the entire Christian church including the Greek East, later arrogated to themselves by the popes. The extraordinary development of papal authority from at least the eleventh century onward has led some Protestant and Orthodox canonists and theologians, correctly I believe, to ask, "What is the point of an ecumenical council if the pope persists in his claims that he alone has the right to convoke that council, to ratify it, to interpret it, and to implement it or not, as he chooses?"

In this respect the emergence of so-called collegiality of the episcopate with the pope in Vatican Council II was, from the view of many Christians, a step in the right direction. But, unfortunately, it has proved under the present pope, John Paul II, to be a hollow development. The Byzantine and modern Orthodox views of the functions of bishops and even laymen at the early ecumenical councils seem to reflect a similar sense of "collegiality." Even more so is the sense of collegiality reflected in the ancient Byzantine theory (often objected to by the popes) of the so-called pentarchy of the patriarchs.[31] It is hoped that the apparently abortive

29. On these three episodes, reported fully by Syropoulos (and referred to by other sources), see discussion and references in essay 11, 235–36, 237 with bibliography. Papal ceremonial books of the time mention kissing the pope's foot (rather than the knee).

30. E.g., Bishop of Meloa, "Ecumenical Councils," passim. Also L. Ševčenko, "Intellectual Repercussions of the Council of Florence," *Church History* 24 (1955): 298, who objects to these kinds of incidents being called "trifles."

31. On theory of pentarchy (which was first emphasized by the East in Justinian's reign), see F. Dvornik, *Byzantium and the Roman Primacy* (New York, 1966), 75–76; and cf. Dvornik, *The Photian Schism* (Cambridge, 1948), 150; also Geanakoplos,

appearance of collegiality in the Roman church at Vatican II will once again reemerge at a future universal council which so many churchmen desire.

Had the seven hundred Greeks who went to the papal conclave at Ferrara-Florence appeared instead at Basel, still another factor might well have arisen to injure their sensibilities—their possible relegation, as at Constance, to representing merely another "nation" along with the four Latin "nations" already designated there: the French, English, German, and Italian. (Spain was soon added.) At Constance the voting was done by nations, not individuals.[32] An imperial Greek ambassador had been in the West negotiating with Western authorities at least as early as 1431, and he doubtless reported this fact to his master. Moreover, Emperor John VIII had had many occasions to discuss the situation with members of the rival papal and conciliar delegations sent to Constantinople just before 1438, the latter headed by the Greek-speaking "Roman Catholic" John of Ragusa, in some ways a very sympathetic but today insufficiently known figure, and the former by the more-famous Nicholas of Cusa, the philosopher who searched so hard in Byzantium to find manuscripts of Plato.[33] The Byzantines may well have recalled, in this connection, their relegation at the earlier Council of Lyons (1274) to being seated *behind all* of the Roman cardinals, though ahead of the rest of the Western clergy and monks.[34] At Basel the Greeks would certainly have protested had they been considered merely one among five "nations," in accordance with the growing emergence in the West of the feeling of "nationality." But, as it actually happened, though some attention was indeed paid to the consideration of nationality, the voting procedure at the council was according to interlocking "commissions,"

Byzantine East and Latin West, 86. Pentarchic theory, that is, equality of all five patriarchs, is of course not exactly the same as collegiality.

32. See, e.g., Flick, *Decline of the Medieval Church,* 134–35; and C. Crowder, *Unity, Heresy, and Reform 1378–1468* (London, 1977), 150–52.

33. John of Ragusa was sent in 1431 by the then-occupied Cardinal Cesarini to preside over the opening session of the Basel council: see Flick, *Decline of the Medieval Church,* 136f. Also F. Dölger, "Ein byzantinisches Staatsdokument in der Universitätsbibliothek Basel," *Historisches Jahrbuch* (1953): 218–20; and E. Cecconi, *Studi storici sul concilio di Firenze* (Florence, 1869), 478–86. John's records of the Basel council and esp. those of John of Segovia are the most important sources for that council; many are still unpublished. John of Ragusa knew Greek and was well liked by the Greeks. (On Cusanus, see essay 11, 238–40 and bibliography.) For Segovia's history, see his unpublished *Historia gestarum generalis synodi basiliensis;* and U. Fromherz, *Johannes von Segovia* (Basel, 1960).

34. See A. Franchi, *Il Concilio II di Lione* (Rome, 1965), 84–85. Cf. discussion in Geanakoplos, *Emperor Michael,* 261, and quotation from source. Also see essay 10.

which made for extreme complexity in securing the passage of any proposal. The rivalry of the various national delegations made it virtually impossible for any business to be transacted, and the end result was a dismal failure.[35]

The Byzantines still considered themselves "Romans" (a term implying universality), even though their empire was now gone except for Constantinople, the Peloponnesus, and one or two islands. But in contrast to this diminution of territory the jurisdiction of the patriarch of Constantinople had become more expanded than ever before—to extend over many of the northern Orthodox Slavic lands, over the Slavs in the Balkans, and over Orthodox lands further east.[36] Thus in effect the Byzantines represented the entire eastern half of Christendom, if not more. Yet, despite this fact there was no a priori assurance that at Basel they would have counted as much more than one nation against four for the Latins. Indeed, to quote Syropoulos, the chief source of information on the Byzantine mentality, before the Greeks left Constantinople for Italy, Gemistos Pletho, the great Byzantine philosopher (who, though hardly Christian, was certainly a Greek "patriot"), warned both emperor and patriarch to beware of the majority method of voting at the coming general council, for the Latins would vastly outnumber the Greeks in their own territory.[37]

At the previous Council of Constance and to a lesser extent at Basel, the Western conciliarists had committed a major diplomatic blunder. They had sent a letter to the Greek emperor and patriarch stressing their natural alliance, as it were, against the monarchical-acting papacy. So far so good. But at the same time, and evidently without any real intention to do so, they demeaned the Greeks by speaking of them in the same context in which they wrote of their attempts to win over the "heretic" Hussites.[38] Being lumped together, so to say, with the heterodox Hussites deeply wounded the sensibilities of the Greeks, who considered theirs the most *Orthodox* of churches in the original sense of the word.

Why then did the Byzantines, in view of their own indisputably conciliar emphasis, elect to accept the papal invitation to go to Ferrara-Florence rather than to Avignon or even Basel as the Basel conciliarists

35. For English translation of Segovia's account of the voting, see Crowder, *Unity, Heresy, and Reform,* 150.

36. See Obolensky, *Byzantine Commonwealth,* 264f.; also J. Meyendorff, *Byzantium and the Rise of Russia* (Cambridge, 1981), esp. chaps. 2, 7, 8.

37. See *Mémoires de Syropoulos,* p. 312, 11.9–13, for passage. Pletho was at Florence.

38. On the Hussites, the Greeks, and Basel, see Geanakoplos, essay 11 and its bibliography. Also M. Paulová, "L'empire byzantine et les Tcheques avant la chute de Constantinople," *Byzantinoslavica* 14 (1953).

requested. The then-pope Eugenius IV was by now on bad terms with Basel. They even mutually excommunicated each other at various times. But Pope Eugenius was more astute than the conciliarists with whom the Greeks were also in contact. For he quickly used the Greek request for an ecumenical council as a means not only to bring the Greeks back ("reductio" is the double-edged term used always by the popes) to the Roman church but thereby to weaken and defeat the Western conciliarist movement.

In my view the Greek decision to go to Ferrara-Florence rather than Basel was for the following reasons: First, Basel and Avignon were too distant from Constantinople, and a new and more serious Turkish siege of Constantinople seemed imminent. Second, and much more important, the Byzantines, a few of whom now knew Latin well, evidently believed that the conciliar phenomenon in the West would be short-lived and that in the long run the papacy, with its lengthy tradition rivaling their own, would triumph, as actually happened. Moreover, the Basel conciliarists were divided, as Aeneas Silvius, the later Pope Pius II, relates, even coming to blows in Basel over the question of the Greek union and how to treat the Byzantines. And certainly there was a real danger that the pope would not appear personally in Basel, though he promised to do so at Ferrara-Florence. Of course for the Greeks, as Barlaam had clearly shown, it was absolutely indispensable that all five patriarchs including the pope, or their representatives, be present. Then, too, many secular princes, especially Italian, and the prince of Burgundy (whose military aid the emperor particularly wanted) promised to come to Italy, not to Basel.[39] There is, as noted, also the crucial point of what the voting procedures would be at Basel. And, finally, the papacy, aided by its Medici bankers, was able to promise more financial assistance to the Greeks for the long, difficult journey to the West and for their support while there. Interestingly enough, when the Byzantines reached Venice, the doge asked them where they would go (for they were still hesitant). He himself advised them to go where it was to their advantage.[40]

The Byzantines of course would have no truck at all with people like

39. On these considerations regarding the Greek decision, see essay 11, 233–34. On John's expectations from the duke of Burgundy, see ibid., n. 100; also *Acta graeca,* ed. J. Gill (Rome, 1953), 212–13, for text.

40. *Mêmoires de Syropoulos,* p. 220, 11.5–13, for text. See L. von Pastor, *History of the Popes,* vol. 1 (London, 1891), 312, who indicates the Greeks had selected Ferrara as site of the (papal) council instead of Savona (which could not raise the monetary guarantee) or Basel itself. On papal bankers (lacking to Basel), see Crowder, *Unity, Heresy, and Reform,* 33. Also see Gill, "The Cost of the Council of Florence," in *Personalities of the Council of Florence,* 186–204, 178–85.

the Hussites who seemed, in effect, to deny the importance of holy tradition. This view brings to mind the similar reaction of the Greek patriarch Jeremiah II, later, during the Reformation, after the German humanist Melanchthon, with the best of intentions and confidence, had sent to Constantinople a copy of the Augsburg Confession, perhaps assuming (as some Protestants still do), that the Orthodox church was a kind of tertium quid between Catholics and Protestants and could thus serve as an ally against the Catholic church. But Jeremiah sent back a censuring letter, considering dogmatic points of the Augsburg Confession heterodox.[41]

Despite the major problem of papal jurisdictional primacy, the church closest to the Orthodox is doubtless the Roman Catholic. It is the only one with a claim equal to the Orthodox in apostolicity, catholicity, and ecumenicity. And this despite its convocation after the Seventh Ecumenical Synod of 787 of a great many councils which it has unilaterally pronounced ecumenical but which are not recognized as such by the Orthodox. Both churches still preserve essentially the same basic doctrinal beliefs and sacraments. The *filioque,* for so long the chief dogmatic difference, in my view will no longer be a major block (as will be indicated below). Moreover, it was as a result of the negotiations between Rome and Constantinople before and during the councils of Lyons and Florence that the Orthodox church first enumerated the sacraments as seven. Earlier the Orthodox church had not distinguished, or rather singled out, exactly which were sacraments *(mysteria)* and which were *sacramentalia* (*mysteriakai teletai*).[42] Both churches have the same respect for holy tradition as they have for the sacred Scriptures. Moreover, East and West both participated in the decisions of the first seven ecumenical councils, which all took place in the East and whose conciliar decisions all began with the traditional statement, "According to the example of the Holy Fathers of the Church." In view of all these similarities, it would be a far less arduous task for Orthodox and Latins to come together in union than for Orthodox and most Protestants, or for Catholics and most Protestants. (On the other hand, it should be stressed that Orthodoxy certainly has its own unique characteristics, among them especially the concept of *theosis* [divinization, already to some degree in this life], which is not typical of other Christian faiths.)

One of the problems of the Orthodox in dealing with Rome is that there still lurk in the Greek psyche memories, fading to be sure, of the

41. On Patriarch Jeremiah, see S. Runciman, *The Great Church in Captivity* (Cambridge, 1968), 248–56. Jeremiah, despite his deep disapproval, tried not to seem censorious of the Lutherans.

42. See text in Geanakoplos, "Church and State in the Byzantine Empire," 70f.

hated Latin occupation and the destruction wrought in Constantinople after 1204. At that time the Byzantines were forced to submit to Roman ecclesiastical jurisdiction with Latin patriarchs installed on the patriarchal throne in Constantinople and in the other Eastern patriarchates. We know from a letter of Pope Innocent III himself that in Constantinople, after a Latin priest had baptized a Greek child, a Byzantine priest would rebaptize him, and that after the performance of the Latin rite in Hagia Sophia, old women would rush up and scrub the altar as if it had been polluted.[43] In this connection I might quote from a letter written by the Greek citizens of Constantinople to Pope Innocent III asking for the appointment of a Greek patriarch in Constantinople (along with the Latin), "since," as the Greek citizens put it, "it is impossible for us in confession to tell our secrets to an 'alien,' that is, to a Latin, bishop."[44]

But these kinds of emotional feelings, fortunately, have greatly diminished in intensity and many Orthodox do not remember, or even care to remember, these events any longer. Even the *filioque,* so formidable an obstacle at Florence, should prove far less intractable today. For Florence has provided us with a working through of this vexing question which can still constitute a comprehensive basis for discussion. After an absolutely exhaustive examination (lasting in all almost one and one half years) of patristic texts, Latin as well as Greek, in which both sides piled up catenae of authorities to support their respective positions, the eminently sensible solution was reached that both sides could accept that the Holy Spirit proceeds from the Father *through* the Son. For the Greeks this meant that they could continue to recite the original symbol (the Holy Spirit proceeds "from the Father"), so necessary for them to preserve their belief in the monarchy of the Father, while the Latins in their view could with impunity affirm that the Holy Spirit proceeds also from the Son *(filioque).*[45] Each side was then in effect free to interpret that point of dogma as it wished, since both agreed there was only *one ultimate source* for the Godhead. The difference really was at bottom conceptual, in that the Latins in effect stressed unity in the Trinity and the Orthodox tended to emphasize the threeness.

But even before the examination at Ferrara-Florence of the theology of the *filioque,* the Greeks had objected on the grounds that it was useless to bring up theology since no addition whatever to the creed was permis-

43. Cf. Hefele, *Histoire des conciles,* vol. 8 (Paris, 1872), 124, quoting papal document.

44. See Geanakoplos, *Byzantium,* no. 155.

45. See Gill, *Council of Florence,* 259–61. Also essay 7 above, which discusses this doctrine ("through the Son"), already held much earlier in the age of the Greek Fathers by St. Basil and St. Gregory. See also above essay 11, 240–44.

sible, in accordance with the express prohibitions of the ecumenical councils of both Ephesus and Chalcedon. With this rather simple but ingenious approach, the Greeks meant to cut the ground from under the Latins before theological debate could begin.[46] This points up again the sanctity, the absolute inviolability, of the ecumenical councils and their decisions for the Orthodox. Not one letter of the conciliar decrees should be altered, they insisted.[47]

Before arriving at a final solution of the *filioque,* some of the Greeks (but not Bessarion, Isidore of Kiev, Andrea of Rhodes, and Dorotheos of Mytilene, in particular) were still sharply against acceptance of the *filioque* but gave another reason for rejection of it. One Greek bishop kept repeating: "I will not accept the *filioque* and become Latinized."[48] This touches once more on a deeper psychological motive, for he, like many of the Greeks of the age, especially monks and lower clergy, were fearful that acceptance of the *filioque* would constitute the first step toward Latinization. In other words, they feared loss, or some loss, of their identity as a people. And that apprehension may well have had some basis. For Eugenius's first act after signing the union was to see to the election in Florence of a new Greek patriarch in place of the recently deceased Joseph. He suggested as nominee the Latin patriarch of Constantinople, his own nephew.[49] In the same vein of Greek fear of cultural or even "ethnic" absorption was the statement made not long before this by Joseph Bryennios, a Byzantine monk. He said, "If the Latins come to save us, they will come only to destroy our city, our race and our name."[50] Such manifestations of ethnicity or "nationalism," important for the Greeks at the Council of Florence, should also be taken into account in any future council, especially in view of the even closer identification of church and state in many modern Orthodox countries.

Most serious, of course, was the question of Greek acceptance of the *tomos* of union, which stated or reaffirmed papal jurisdiction and in which the pope was said to "possess the primacy over the whole world" as "successor to Saint Peter," as "first among the Apostles, true Vicar of

46. Essay 11; and Gill, *Council of Florence,* 147. G. Every, *Misunderstandings between East and West* (London, 1965), 43–47.

47. In accord, as noted, with canonical prescriptions of the councils of Ephesus and Chalcedon.

48. See text in Gill, *Acta graeca,* 400. Cf. *Mémoires de Syropoulos,* 546–56, etc.; and Geanakoplos, *Byzantium,* no. 161.

49. Mentioned by principal sources, esp. Syropoulos and *Acta graeca* (see essay 11, 251 and n. 91).

50. See Geanakoplos, *Interaction of the "Sibling" Byzantine and Western Cultures in the Middle Ages and Italian Renaissance,* p. 16 and n. 30; cf. N. Kalogeras, *Mark of Ephesus and Cardinal Bessarion* (Athens, 1893), 70.

Christ, head of the entire Church." But as if the council purposely intended to weaken these affirmations and to pacify the Greeks, after that clause was added the phrase, "All the traditional rights and privileges of the Eastern patriarchs shall be excepted."[51] As strange as that may sound, why could that kind of precedent not be followed today? Let each church have control in its own sphere of jurisdiction and there will be, I suspect, few if any serious collisions. The ecumenical patriarch, before and especially since 1453, has been considered *primus inter pares* in the Orthodox church.[52] Let him exercise his authority, a primacy of honor, in the East and let the pope exert the jurisdiction he is accustomed to in the West. After all, when Pope Gregory the Great in the sixth century complained of Patriarch John the Faster's assumption of the title of "ecumenical," meaning "universal," patriarch, he was apparently finally satisfied by the explanation that it referred only to the churches in the Eastern *ecumenē* (though there is some evidence the title actually meant more than that to the Eastern patriarch).[53] The wording of the *tomos* of union at Florence was such as to permit each church to retain its own ritual, language, and disciplinary practices (marriage of priests or celibacy, for example). True, the Orthodox it seems had to accept the Latin belief in purgatory. But for some Orthodox a reconciliation of the two views may not have been too difficult, since in some quarters of Orthodoxy a kind of inchoate view of purgatory already seemed to exist.[54]

In any present encounter between East and West, if the Orthodox find themselves in a position that seems insoluble, administratively, at least they can always have recourse to their concept of *economia*. *Economia* was (and is) the application of a certain elasticity in ecclesiastical administrative and disciplinary matters (though it is never applied to dogma) whenever the *Basileia,* the Byzantine Empire—that is, the "state"—was

51. Gill, *Council of Florence,* 285f. for text; essay 11, 249–50. For Latin view, M. Schmidt, "The Problem of Papal Primacy at the Council of Florence," *Church History* 30 (1961): 35–49; also Gill, "The Definition of the Primacy of the Pope in the Council of Florence," in *Personalities of the Council of Florence,* 264–85.

52. By decree of the Second Ecumenical Council of 381 at Constantinople, the latter was raised to the position of first in honor (after Rome) over the other Eastern patriarchs.

53. S. Vailhé, "Le titre de patriarche oecuménique avant saint Grégoire le Grand," and "Saint Grégoire le Grand et le titre de patriarche oecuménique," *Echos d'Orient* 11 (1908): 65–69, 161–71.

54. *Tomos* of union quoted in full in Gill, *Acta graeca,* 461. English translation also in Crowder, *Unity, Heresy, and Reform,* 169–72. On purgatory, s.v. "Middle state of souls," in *Thrēseutikē kai ēthikē egkyklopaideia,* vol. 8, cols. 1013–18; and F. Gavin, *Some Aspects of Contemporary Greek Orthodox Thought* (London, 1932), 411, referring esp. to the seventeenth-century Dositheos's views resembling the Catholic view of purgatory.

in mortal danger.[55] Thus in the seventh century, Emperor Heraclius was permitted by the church to overlook the usually stringent canonical strictures on the alienation of church property before the grave Persian danger to the empire, and, with reluctant ecclesiastical approval, Emperor Alexius Comnenus melted down church treasures in order to secure gold and silver coins with which to raise effective armies.[56] The Roman church has long contravened its canon law by granting dispensations for such things as divorce or annulment of marriage. The Orthodox church in a time of crisis or need can invoke its own *economia*. Here surely are two important devices for solution of seemingly intractable problems in the spheres of discipline and ecclesiastical administration, especially for the less-major questions.

The Roman church has recently been viewed by Westerners in a few respects as more flexible than the Orthodox. While it is unquestionably more legalistic in its approach, Rome, since Vatican II and before John Paul II, has seemed more willing to bend with the times. Witness the *aggiornamento* in adoption of vernacular languages in the mass, restoration (in some cases) to the laity of communion in two kinds, standing while receiving communion, etc. It is rather the Orthodox church which to some appears more intransigent. Not in its basic dogma (which has and should remain unchanged) but in its apparent opposition to finding new modes of expression in worship, perhaps to new types of prayers, and in certain other respects. As the archbishop of Smyrna some fifty years ago put it to his flock—and this statement with its surrounding context is claimed by some Orthodox to have led the way to the formation of the ecumenical movement—"Do not be afraid to cast aside worn out ecclesiastical garments and to put on new ones."[57] The same spirit could well apply today. G. Florovsky put it well in various discussions of his on the "spirit of the Fathers" (and I paraphrase his remarks): "To retain the spirit of the Fathers of the early Church is not to deny all change. The Fathers themselves lived in an age of tremendous social ferment and therefore had to entertain change with respect to ex-

55. For *economia,* see esp. Geanakoplos, *Byzantine East and Latin West,* 74, and *Byzantium,* no. 97; cf. H. Alivizatos, *Oikonomia kai to kanonikon dikaion tēs orthodoxou ekklēsias* (Athens, 1949). See also essay 11. In Syropoulos, 346, 414, etc., both emperor and patriarch make reference to the term *economia.* On *economia* in general see Geanakoplos, *Byzantium,* no. 98.

56. For texts relating specifically to Heraclius and Alexius, see Geanakoplos, *Byzantium,* nos. 98A and B.

57. Quoted in Geanakoplos, "The Greek Orthodox Church: Alive and Relevant," in *Orthodox Theology and Diakonia* (1981), 175.

ternal matters while preserving unchanged the *kerygma* of Christ and the Apostles."[58]

J. Meyendorff has recently suggested that in order to achieve reunion the Roman and Orthodox churches should revert to their respective positions at the time of the unionist council of 879–80, when Patriarch Photius was reinstated as patriarch of Constantinople after a serious schism between him and Pope Nicholas I. In accordance with papal instructions the papal legates had acquiesced in this action. Nor did the pope, as Meyendorff stresses, seem to mind that he was backtracking on his predecessor's excommunication of Photius.[59] The peace, *eirēne*—a word often used by the Byzantines also for religious reconciliation and union—prevailed with both sides feeling respect for each other. In the same manner, Patriarch Athenagoras and Pope Paul VI, meeting at Jerusalem in 1965, after almost ten centuries of schism, treated each other as brothers, prelates on the same level, despite their differing claims of jurisdiction and administration. More recently, Patriarch Demetrius I and Pope John Paul II met in Rome in 1987.

I now turn to the important matter of what modern ecumenists call "reception" *(hypodochē)* of the ecumenicity of a council. Some synods earlier designated as ecumenical, such as the Robber Synod of 449, the Constantinople Synod of 1215, and even that of Florence in 1438–39, were ultimately not accepted by the Orthodox as ecumenical. To be sure, none, as the Orthodox church insists is necessary, was proclaimed ecumenical by a later synod. Yet all (or most) other requisites for ecumenicity existed, especially in the case of Florence. Unlike Lyons, at Florence all five patriarchs or their representatives were present, there was prolonged discussion, and at the end the emperor, all the Orthodox clergy (except Mark of Ephesus), and the pope accepted the union. It was the Byzantine population, or as A. Khomiakov, P. Trembelas, and others have put it, "the conscience of the Church," who would not "receive" the union when the Orthodox legates returned home.[60] Hence, although

58. See G. Florovsky, "The Ethos of the Orthodox Church," *Ecumenical Review* 12 (1960): 183ff.; and Florovsky, "The Authority of the Ancient Councils and the Tradition of the Fathers," and "St. Gregory Palamas and the Tradition of the Fathers," both in vol. 1 of his collected works, *Bible, Church, Tradition* (Belmont, Mass., 1972), 93–120.

59. J. Meyendorff, "What Is an Ecumenical Council?" in *Living Tradition, Orthodox Witness in the Contemporary World,* (Crestwood, N.Y.: 1978), 71: "Can we today jointly accept the Photian Council of 879–880 as ecumenical?"

60. On these, see Geanakoplos, "Church and State in the Byzantine Empire," 80 n. 76. A. Khomiakov, *L'église lạtine et le protestantisme au point de vue de l'église d'Orient* (Lausanne, 1872); H. Alivizatos, *Hē syneidēsis tēs ekklēsias* (Athens, 1954); and Bishop of Meloa on the legitimacy of a council being dependent on the response of the laity, "Ecumenical Councils," 358.

Rome still today accepts Florence as an "ecumenical" council, the Orthodox list it with Lyons as a rejected council.[61]

But, I ask, could the Greek people, then so violently anti-unionist, ever have been persuaded to accept the ecumenicity of Florence? I think it would have been possible only if, as the Orthodox constantly urged, the council had been held in Constantinople itself, where the populace, so mistrustful especially of their own *Latinophrones* (Latinophiles), could follow the proceedings and thus have their suspicions allayed. As it was, on the return of the Orthodox legates the people demanded to know why their representatives had signed the document of union and thus betrayed the "purity" of the Orthodox faith, something they felt would bring down upon their heads the wrath of God, much as they believed had happened to them for their sins in 1204. Here again we see the near identification of Orthodox religious feelings with their ethnic sentiments—feelings which made them, they believed, quite different from the Latins.[62] This consideration made the achievement of union at Florence doubly difficult. Today, however, we are *all* more or less Western in culture, and such deep-seated cultural differences are less likely to be of real importance. Moreover, since 1821 there is (as in the present case of Israel) a solidly established Greek nation, and little danger exists that Greek culture will become attenuated. Nonetheless, national pride is still a factor that must at least be taken account of in any future council.

To return to the Council of Basel—which continued to sit during that of Florence—its minority ecclesiastical group had moved to Ferrara. Subsequently it moved to Florence with the pope, who had now succeeded in drawing the Greek delegation to himself. The consummation of union, however ephemeral, by the pope and the Greeks was the key factor (as Gill and J. Flick flatly and I believe correctly affirm) which gave the previously almost powerless Pope Eugenius new life, the ability to stand up to the majority group of conciliarists at Basel and, finally, the courage to abort the Western conciliar movement (although he himself had been excommunicated at Basel).[63] Of course, in the triumph of the papacy the fact that Cardinal Cesarini and other leading conciliarists, including

61. It appears that the Roman church accepts the initial twenty-five sessions of the Council of Basel as ecumenical but not the later sessions (that is, those held after the beginning of the Council of Ferrara-Florence). (But this point was variously regarded in the later fifteenth and early sixteenth centuries.) See *Lexicon für theologie und kirche* (1958), vol. 2, col. 25.

62. See on Greek fear of Latinization esp. essay 11, 244–45; Geanakoplos, *Interaction of the Sibling Cultures,* 46–48, 289–92; and *Byzantium,* nos. 161, 285.

63. Gill, *Council of Florence,* vii, 411; and Flick, "Decline of the Medieval Church," 2:202. Also Crowder, *Unity, Heresy, and Reform,* 159, 172–77. Pope Martin V crushed Conciliarism as an effective force.

Aeneas Silvius and above all Nicholas Cusanus, went over to the papacy was also vital. But that might well not have happened had not the Greeks, paradoxically enough, elected to go to the pope rather than to the conciliarists, whose tradition was far less familiar to them.

I mention here another point revealed by the sources on the proceedings at Florence—that the Greek emperor John instructed his bishops to preserve utter silence on the doctrines of Hesychasm.[64] After all, with the Latins considering the Hesychastic vision of the "divine light" to be a theological innovation (the Hesychasts believed it was an expression of the "energies" of God), the Latins might well have thrown this "innovation" back at the Greeks, who themselves were rejecting the Latin *filioque* addition to the creed as an interpolation.

As noted earlier, after the convocation of the first Western conciliarist council at Pisa in 1409, there was raised to the papal throne the Greek Alexander V. Although Latin in faith, he was born of a Greek family on Venetian Crete as Peter Philarges. And, as mentioned above, when Jean Gerson, one of the great conciliarist thinkers and rector at the University of Paris, heard of Peter's election, he read a jubilant speech before the French king and University of Paris professors, praising the election not only because Peter had been a student and then a noted Scholastic professor "at our University of Paris," not only because most of Europe—England, where Peter had earlier studied at Oxford; France; parts of Germany and Italy, especially Venice (though not at first)—"seem to support him, but especially because it bodes well for the unity of the Roman Church and, most significant of all, for the reunion of the two ancient branches of Christendom." Peter had been archbishop of Milan, probably the leading conciliarist activist just before Pisa, and he had pressed for a council primarily because of the evil of having two rival popes.[65] Peter, to some degree at least, may consciously or not have been influenced by certain Byzantine or patristic conciliar ideas. I am not, incidentally, proposing the election of a Greek pope to promote union (!), though it should be recalled that in the early church many Greeks and Syrians became popes. (Indeed, next to Italians, more Greeks have been pope than any other people.)[66]

As we know, with the papal triumph at Florence—many of the Byzan-

64. Gill, *Council of Florence,* 206. On Hesychasm at Florence, and Hesychasts and Bernardino of Siena, see Geanakoplos, *Interaction of the Sibling Cultures,* chap. 11, 219–24.

65. Discussed in my forthcoming biography of Pope Alexander V. For speech, see text above and n. 14.

66. It has been estimated that most popes have been Italian, then come Greeks (and Syrians), then French, Spaniards, and one English and one Polish pope.

tines in effect begging for help against the Turks and the emperor constantly seeking to press the issue of religious union[67]—the conciliarists sitting at Basel finally accepted the new pope Nicholas V and declared their council dissolved. The conciliar pronouncements of Constance and Pisa seemed a dead letter, but there can be little doubt that they did affect, theoretically, the views of certain German reformers of the Reformation period. As to the Council of Florence, it has been considered by the Roman church as the continuation of the Council of Basel.[68] Rome in fact terms Florence—though, as we have noted, there are questions about Basel—an ecumenical council.

The most important legacy of Florence is that virtually every possible issue between Constantinople and Rome was discussed and some logical solutions, some compromises, or even *modi vivendi* on many questions were suggested or adopted. In my view any future council to be held between Orthodox and Roman churches—and let us not forget that Armenians, as well as Monophysites, Nestorians, and other dissident Eastern churches then also signed union with Rome—could do no better than to regard this council and its deliberations as a, indeed *the,* point of departure. Study of its deliberations will help ecumenicists not only to avoid the mistakes made but also to draw lessons from what was accomplished, and thus to permit ventures into certain pressing questions of our much more secular world: in the sphere of ecclesiology, social ethics, and of course the difficult question of which churches should (or perhaps should not) be invited to an ecumenical council.[69]

May I say in conclusion that, although I do not envision or perhaps even really desire an *institutional* merger of the Orthodox and Latin churches, in conformity with immemorial Orthodox belief I would accept the pope as president, honorarily, of a united Christian church. But I would hope above all for acceptance of each other's sacraments—that is, for a *spiritual* union. For though the Latins accept the efficacy of Orthodox sacraments, the Orthodox do not do the same for the Latins—a consideration which I believe can be overcome without insurmountable

67. See above, essay 11, n. 82.

68. See Flick, "Decline of the Medieval Church," vol. 2; also Haller, *Concilium basiliense.* As noted, the first twenty-five sessions at Basel are considered ecumenical by the Roman church. See also Crowder, *Unity, Heresy, and Reform,* 166; and Schmidt, "The Problem of Papal Primacy, 35–49, expressing the Roman view.

69. Presumably the Catholics (including the old Catholics) and Orthodox (probably including the "dissident" Orthodox) would come, and somewhat later at another council also the Anglicans and Episcopalians and, possibly, still later, the Lutherans. But should other Protestants, especially those not accepting the theory of apostolicity as handed down by tradition, attend a modern ecumenical council? I believe this question can be settled only after an initial council of the Greek and Roman churches.

difficulty, especially in the light of the common experience of Florence. As Patriarch Athenagoras of Constantinople, that sage and beloved prelate, said to me in 1965 in Istanbul, "My one ambition now is to go to Rome and to take communion from the same cup as the pope." To which one can only add, in something of the manner in which the decrees of the first seven ecumenical synods began: "May the many, spiritually at least, become one under the guidance of the Holy Spirit."[70]

70. It should be noted that a commission of the various Orthodox churches has had meetings to reach agreement among themselves before a future council with Rome: see *Towards the Great Council: Introductory Reports of the Interorthodox Commission in Preparation for the Next Great and Holy Council of the Orthodox Church* (London, 1972). Meantime, a joint commission of Roman and Orthodox representatives has also met looking toward a possible convocation of the Orthodox and Roman Catholic churches. Finally, see G. H Williams, "The Ecumenism of John Paul II," *Journal of Ecumenical Studies* 19 (1982). And Pope John Paul II's work on a council, titled *Sources of Renewal* (New York, 1980).

Additional Bibliography for Essay 12

J. Gill, *Constance et Bâle-Florence,* Histoire des conciles oecuméniques, vol. 90 (Paris, 1965). J. Hussey, *The Orthodox Church in the Byzantine Empire* (Oxford, 1986), 271–72, on Basel. G. Christianson, *Cesarini: The Conciliar Cardinal: The Basel Years, 1431–38* (St. Ortilien, Germany, 1979). H. Müller, "Zur Prosopographie des Basler-Konzils: Französisches Beispiel," *Annuarium historiae conciliorum* 14 (1982): 140–70. My *Byzantio kai dysē*, the Greek translation of *Interaction of the "Sibling" Byzantine and Western Cultures,* with revisions, corrections, and updated bibliography. A. Leidel, "Die Primatsverhandlungen auf dem Konzil von Florenz als Antwort auf die ostliche Pentarhietheorie," *Annuarium historiae conciliorum* 7 (1975): 272–89. S. Agourides, ed., *Deuxième congrès de theologie orthodoxe à Athènes, 19–29 Août 1976* (Athens, 1978), papers on modern Orthodoxy delivered at a panorthodox conference. J. Meyendorff, *The Byzantine Legacy in the Orthodox Church* (New York, 1982). My *A Short History of the Ecumenical Patriarchate of Constantinople: "First among Equals" in the Eastern Orthodox Church.* J. Stieber, *Pope Eugenius IV, The Council of Basel and the Secular and Ecclesiastical Authorities in the Empire* (Leiden, 1978), which contains virtually nothing on the Byzantine church.

Appendix
Selected Works
Index

Appendix

Some Observations on the Problem of the First Printed Editions of the Greek Church Fathers in the Italian and Northern Renaissance

Much intensive research has been done in the fields of humanism and religion in the Renaissance. And in particular, investigation continues to be devoted to the revival of specific classical works, both Latin and Greek. But there is still no work of synthesis on the first printed editions of the Greek Fathers in the period from 1470, the probable date of the earliest edition, to the latter part of the sixteenth century, by which time virtually the entire corpus had been disseminated in the West. Linguistic considerations apart, there are several reasons for this lack: the difficulty of assembling complete data on widely scattered editions, our inability to date some of the earliest *incunabula,* and, not least, the inadequacy of our tools for research. Aside from E. Legrand's *Bibliographie hellénique* and P. Meyer's *Die theologische Literatur der griechischen Kirche im sechszehnten Jahrhundert,* both concentrating on editions done by Greeks not Westerners, almost nothing of a synoptic nature exists, certainly nothing comparable to R. Sabbadini's or J. Sandys's work on the discovery of classical manuscripts and their first editions.[1]

1. The very few works even touching on the recovery and publication of the Greek Fathers in the Renaissance include E. Legrand, *Bibliographie hellénique ou description raisonnée des ouvrages publiés en grec par des grecs au XVe et XVIe siècles,* 4 vols. (Paris, 1885–1906); Legrand, *Bibliographie hispano-grecque* (New York, 1915–17); P. Meyer,

Although Greek was largely lost to the medieval Western world, some works of the Greek Fathers were known in Latin translation. (Indeed, one may suspect that the medieval West knew more patristic Greek works than has been realized. On this question A. Siegmund's *Die Überlieferung der griechischen cristlichen Literatur in der lateinischen Kirche bis zum zwölften Jahrhundert* is valuable.[2] It extends only to 1200, however, thus omitting the important Scholastic period.) Among the best known were certain sermons and commentaries of Chrysostom, Basil, and Origen.[3] Origen, of course, was suspect in medieval eyes because of certain of his doctrinal views, that is, the preexistence of souls and the *apokatastasis.* Also well known in translation were Greek ascetic and moral discourses of Basil and Ephraem and especially Chrysostom's *De patientia Job,* as well as the history of the Christian church by Eusebius. In pure theology only two Greek patristic works seem to appear repeatedly in the medieval West: that of John of Damascus in the twelfth century (with his Aristotelian approach) and the Neoplatonic mystical writings of Pseudo-Dionysius, whose corpus had been widely circulated from John Scotus Erigena's time onward.[4] But Dionysius was, technically at least, not viewed in the same light as the other Greek Fathers, since he was believed (wrongly) to have been a disciple of St. Paul.

Renaissance humanists naturally drew heavily on this earlier medieval Greek tradition. Yet though humanist interests, in particular those of the editors of the Greek first editions, were often similar to those of the Scholastics, they were in some ways quite different. A few theories may be adduced for the changes wrought by and in Renaissance attitudes toward these works. Early Italian humanist translators of the Greek

---

Die theologische Literatur der griechischen Kirche im sechszehnten Jahrhundert (Leipzig, 1899); R. Sabbadini, *Le scoperte dei codici latini e greci nei secoli XIV e XV,* 2 vols. (Florence, 1905–14; rpt. 1967); J. Sandys, *A History of Classical Scholarship,* 3 vols. (Cambridge, 1903–8; rpt. 1958). See now the article of E. Rice, Jr., "The Renaissance Idea of Christian Antiquity: Humanist Patristic Scholarship," *Renaissance Humanism: Foundations, Forms, and Legacy,* ed. A. Rabil, vol. 1 (Philadelphia, 1988), 17–28, especially for its interpretation of the various motivations of the Italian (and other) humanists in reviving study of the Latin (especially) and Greek Fathers, and its discussion in particular of the patristic scholarship of the Florentine Dominican Zanobi Acciaiuoli in the early sixteenth century.

2. A. Siegmund, *Die Überlieferung der griechischen cristlichen Literatur in der lateinischen Kirche bis zum zwölften Jahrhundert* (Munich–Pasing, 1949).

3. On Origen see M. Schär, *Das Nachleben des Origens Zeitalter des Humanismus* (Basel, 1979).

4. On John of Damascus (who though Aristotelian in his form of argument was often Platonic in spirit) see Geanakoplos, *Interaction of the Sibling Byzantine and Western Cultures,* 62–63.

Fathers—with the possible exception in certain ways of Ambrogio Traversari—were in general more interested in the style of the works than medieval scholars had been. Whereas the medieval translator (William of Moerbeke, for instance) had produced word-for-word versions, the Renaissance humanists, in an effort to reproduce the eloquence of the original, made freer translations, which, in many cases (though not always), were more faithful to the content of the text. One may recall in this respect the dispute involving the Bishop of Burgos in Spain, who, lacking any knowledge of Greek, in 1430 criticized the humanist Leonardo Bruni's translation of a classical Greek text, preferring instead the Scholastic, more literal rendering of William of Moerbeke.[5]

The humanists in some instances also effected a change in attitudes toward certain works of the Greek Fathers which had for centuries been considered heretical. Notable is the case of Origen—some of his biblical commentaries had always been widely read—many more of whose works now became popular in the Renaissance largely because of the Neoplatonic ideas embodied therein and because of his felicitous manner of expression.[6]

To take another example, the humanists also reoriented medieval views toward the Byzantine Eusebius's *Praeparatio evangelica,* in which Eusebius had sought to point out the Hebrew precursors of the Christian Gospel.[7] However, humanistic attitudes toward certain other Greek Fathers, Chrysostom and Basil in particular, differed little from the Scholastic, since their "orthodoxy" had never been questioned, as reflected by the many translations of their works.

The leading advocate of the revival of Christian antiquity in the early Italian Renaissance was certainly the Florentine Ambrogio Traversari. It is to him that we owe the translation into Latin of more than twenty Greek patristic works, many for the first time. As a monk (later minister-general of the order) of the Camaldolese convent of Santa Maria degli Angeli in Florence, Traversari early became fascinated by ancient learning, both Greek and Latin, but with particular interest in the Greek patristic writings. According to his own testimony, he began to learn

5. On this episode see G. Holmes, *The Florentine Enlightenment* (New York, 1969), 115–17. It must be noted that the bishop preferred the literal translation in part at least because he was vitally interested in theological terminology, which required a verbatim approach.

6. See E. Wind, "The Revival of Origen," in *Studies in Art and Literature for Bella da Costa Greene,* ed. D. Miner (Princeton, N.J., 1954), 412–24. D. Walter, "Origène en France au debut du XVIe siècle," *Courants religieux et humanisme à la fin du XVe et au début du XVIe siècle* (Paris, 1959); and Schär, *Nachleben des Origens.*

7. For the finding of the *Praeparatio evangelica,* see n. 23.

Greek on his own, not through formal study with the humanists, but simply by comparing individual words from the Greek Psalter and the New Testament with their corresponding Latin versions.[8]

A Byzantine refugee from Constantinople, Demetrius Scaranus, who has been largely neglected by historians, was of considerable help to Traversari in his work on the patristic Greek texts.[9] Scaranus, who spent the last decade or more of his life at Ambrogio's monastery, performed for him the difficult but fundamental task of transcribing the sometimes almost undecipherable manuscripts of centuries past. These Traversari had managed to secure either directly from the Greek East or from the libraries of Italian or Byzantine humanists in Italy, such as Manuel Chrysoloras, Guarino, Corbinelli, or Francesco Filelfo.[10] But Scaranus was probably more than a scribe, if we can believe a letter of Traversari to his supporter in his patristic venture, the humanist Niccolò Niccoli.[11]

Contrary to what is sometimes believed, Traversari did not study Greek with the Byzantine Manuel Chrysoloras.[12] Nonetheless, the two did eventually meet, and the famous Byzantine professed much esteem for Traversari's learning. Indeed, because of Chrysoloras's similar interests in Greek patristic writings as well as the classics, he encouraged Traversari in his project of translating the Fathers. Traversari, it seems, unlike many other Italian humanists, was interested in the Greek Fathers not for antiquarian reasons but, more important as he saw it, for the light they could cast on beliefs and practices of the early period of Christianity when the Eastern and Western churches were still one, ecclesiastically and culturally. Indeed, in 1424 he even translated a late Byzantine treatise, which he dedicated to the pope—the *Adversus Graecos* of the four-

8. On Traversari see C. Stinger, *Humanism and the Church Fathers: Ambrogio Traversari (1386–1439) and Christian Antiquity in the Italian Renaissance* (Albany, 1976). Also A. Dini- Traversari, *Ambrogio Traversari e il suo tempo* (Florence, 1912), old but still of some value; and for his correspondence see L. Mehus, *Ambrosii Traversarii latinae epistolae* (Florence, 1959). Traversari translated into Latin more than twenty Greek patristic works. Of his favorite, Chrysostom, he possessed some 17 to 18 manuscripts: see B. Ullman and P. Stadter, *The Public Library of the Renaissance: Niccolò Niccoli, Cosimo de' Medici and the Library of San Marco* (Padua, 1972), 25. For Traversari's reference to his Greek see L. Bertalot, "Zwölf Briefe des A. Traversari, *Römische Quartalschrift* 29 (1915): 101–2. Cf. Holmes, *Florentine Enlightenment,* 56.

9. On Scaranus see esp. Mehus, *Ambrosii Traversarii epistolae,* 8:365; and G. Mittarelli and A. Mittarelli, *Annales Camaldulenses* (1755), 6:270; cf. G. Cammelli, *Manuele Crisolora* (Florence, 1941), 66, 143; and Stinger, *Ambrogio Traversari,* 20, 28.

10. On libraries used by Traversari see R. Blum, *La biblioteca della Badia fiorentina . . .,* in *Studi e testi* (Vatican, 1951); Cammelli, *Manuele Crisolora,* 185; and Holmes, *Florentine Enlightenment,* 92.

11. See Mehus, *Ambrosii Traversarii epistolae,* esp. 8:46.

12. See Cammelli, *Manuele Crisolora,* 66–67.

teenth-century Latinophile Byzantine Manuel Calecas. Evidently, it was Traversari's intention to promote the union of the churches by expounding a near-contemporary Byzantine theologian's support for the Latin view of the double procession of the Holy Spirit.[13]

Among some notable Latin translations of the Greek Fathers made by Traversari—treatises, letters, and sermons—were works of Basil, Athanasius, Gregory of Nazianzus, Ephraem the Syrian, the Pseudo-Dionysius, and his favorite, John Chrysostom, whose eloquence especially attracted him. He also translated (apparently at Chrysoloras's suggestion) a very important work of early Byzantine monasticism, sixth-century John Climacus's *Ladder of Paradise.*[14] As a participant in the theological disputations at the Council of Florence, Traversari acted as an official interpreter and sometimes, because of his known sympathy for and understanding of the Byzantines, was called upon to serve as a kind of mediator or conciliator between the two parties.[15] His knowledge of Byzantine theology, derived from his study of the Greek Fathers, thus had its pragmatic side. Of course, his allegiance at the council was entirely to the papacy.

Having discussed the work of the initiator of Renaissance interest in the Greek Fathers, let us turn to the printing of the first editions of these works—an undertaking that would enable them to be more easily and more widely disseminated. What was the chief criterion of selection for the first Greek patristic works to be printed, at least in the case of the first that seems to have appeared, Basil's famous *Discourse to Christian Youth on Studying the Greek Classics?* This work, discovered—or rather rediscovered—in the West about 1400, was first translated into Latin (after 1410) by Leonardo Bruni of Florence, pupil of the Byzantine professor Manuel Chrysoloras.[16]

Where could the humanists, whose zeal for classical learning was frequently under attack, find more powerful vindication for study of the classical, that is, the pagan Greek literary heritage than in this work of Basil's? Indeed, St. Basil's prime purpose in writing the *Discourse* had been precisely to justify (with distinct qualification) the study of the pagan Greek classics by showing their utility for the Christian believer of

13. On Calecas see Dini-Traversari, *Ambrogio Traversari,* 124; and J. Gill, *The Council of Florence* (Cambridge, 1959), 164. On the *filioque* see essay 11, above.

14. See L. Hain, *Repertorium bibliographicum in que libri omnes ab arte typographica inventa,* 4 vols. (Stuttgart, 1826–38). Stinger, *Ambrogio Traversari,* 15–16, 110–12. Also Holmes, *Florentine Enlightenment,* 96–99, 122–24; and Cammelli, *Manuele Crisolora.*

15. Gill, *Council of Florence,* 141, 169, etc. See above essay 11.

16. On Bruni see now essays 1 and 2 above; and Holmes, *Florentine Enlightenment,* passim, with bibliography.

his own time.[17] The work thus gave cogent support to the Renaissance humanist emphasis on the *studia humanitatis,* a curriculum of study that stressed, among other things, classical literature as a preparation for the study of sacred Scripture. It could hardly have been coincidental, then, that Basil's work, which had circulated widely in manuscript, was (apparently) the first Latin translation of a Greek Father's work to be printed, in 1470 (or possibly 1471) in Venice,[18] soon to become the center of printing in Italy.

Basil's *Discourse* was enormously popular, not only because of its vindication of classical pagan learning, but also because of its emphasis on the similarity of Christian and classical moral precepts and its praise for the classical literary style (especially its simplicity, directness, and eloquence). This popularity is indicated by the many *incunabula* editions of the *Discourse* (in Latin) printed before 1500, including several Italian, German, Spanish, and even a Hungarian one.[19] It may in fact have been the first and only Greek patristic work published in fifteenth-century Spain.[20] The Hungarian edition attests as well to the range of King Matteo Corvinus's humanistic patronage.[21] A chief source of information on

17. See esp. W. Jaeger, *Early Christianity and Greek Paideia* (Cambridge, 1961). Also Geanakoplos, *Byzantium: Church, Society, and Civilization Seen through Contemporary Eyes,* document no. 296. On Basil's *Discourse* see above, essays 1 and 2.

18. Since most early editions were undated, it is often difficult to know exactly when Greek patristic works were first printed, but this seems to have been the first. See *Gesamtkatalog der Wiegendrücke,* vol. 3 (Leipzig, 1928), no. 3700.

19. Gathered from *Gesamtkatalog,* vol. 3, nos. 3700–18; Sabbadini, *Scoperte;* V. Scholderer, *Catalogue of Books Printed in the Fifteenth Century now in the British Museum* (London, 1908– 49); B. Botfield, *Praefationes et epistolae editionibus principibus auctorum veterum praepositae* (Cambridge, 1861); and J. Graesse, *Trésor de livres rares et précieux* (Dresden, 1859–69); and J. Erickson, "The Greek Fathers of the Church and Their Printed Editions," a paper written for my seminar at Yale in 1968 from which I have profited. In 1499 in Spain the humanist Rodrigo de Santaella published a letter from St. Basil in his *Vocabularium ecclesiasticum:* see M. Bataillon, *Erasmo y España* (Mexico City, 1970), 1:56–57.

20. For Spain see Legrand, *Bibliographie hispano- Grecque.* In 1519 Hernan Nuñez prepared an interlinear edition of Basil's *Discourse to Christian Youth* for his students (Legrand, ibid., 43), and in 1524 Francesco de Vergara at Alcalà University made a translation and edition of a theological treatise of the Greek Father Gregory of Nyssa, who was largely bypassed by the Renaissance Christian humanists, especially in France, in part, perhaps, because he was confused with Nemesios of Emessa (E. Rice, "The Humanist Idea of Christian Antiquity: Lefèvre d'Etaples and His Circle," in *French Humanism,* ed. W. Gundersheimer [New York, 1969], 179–80).

21. On Corvinus see *Mathias Corvinus König von Ungarn, 1458–90,* ed. W. Fraknól (Freiburg, 1891). And now M. Birnbaum, "Humanism in Hungary," in *Renaissance Humanism: Foundations, Forms, and Legacy,* ed. A. Rabil, vol. 2 (Philadelphia, 1988), esp. 297–300.

which Greek patristic works were first printed and why, is the prefatory letter of dedication customarily inserted at the beginning of each work by the editor or publisher. Such prefatory letters to printed editions naturally express praise for the person to whom the work is dedicated and, of course, explain the significance of the work printed. These letters, along with the text itself, are our main evidence for the attitudes of the editor and, perhaps, the publisher. In his prefatory letter to his translation of Basil's *Discourse,* which was dedicated to the Florentine chancellor Coluccio Salutati (and which was repeatedly printed), Bruni clearly indicates that his main purpose in making the translation is to justify Christian study of the pagan classics.[22]

The second most popular Greek patristic work published was, it seems, Eusebius's *Praeparatio evangelica,* and this again evidently for practical reasons. Eusebius's remarkable affirmation that the Neoplatonic ideas of the Greeks were derived from the Hebrews, provided, for the humanists, still another argument for study of the classics. Eusebius's case differed from Basil's, however, in that he had long been subject to accusations of Arianism. In any event, the first to translate the *Praeparatio* into Latin was the ubiquitous and irascible Cretan émigré George of Trebizond, who had the work printed in Venice in 1470. In his prefatory letter, George, after praising his patron, Pope Nicholas V, tells us that, because of Eusebius's Arian proclivities, he has in his translation "cut off the thorns from the work and left only the roses."[23] That George's translation, with its "corrective" editorial comments, was reprinted in numerous *incunabula* editions seems to indicate the great popularity of his edition. Still, certain Renaissance editors preferred the original text to George's "rectified" version.[24]

George of Trebizond became deeply involved in the philosophic dispute over the respective merits of Plato and Aristotle, begun by the Greeks, especially Gemistos Pletho, at the Council of Florence. George made use, at least indirectly, of Eusebius's *Praeparatio* to support the Aristotelian faction. Specifically, he tried through his edition of the *Praeparatio* to demonstrate that the "wretched" Platonists had borrowed

22. For Bruni's preface see *Gesamtkatalog,* vol. 3, no. 3711. Also Basil, *De legendis libris gentilium* (Leipzig, ca. 1490–94).

23. On the discovery of Eusebius and his *Praeparatio evangelica* see George of Trebizond's preface (Venice, 1470, printed by Nicholas Jenson), in Legrand, *Bibliographie hellénique* 3:8–9: "in Urbe [Rome] forte reperta est." On George of Trebizond's career see now J. Monfasani, *George of Trebizond: A Biography and a Study of His Rhetoric and Logic* (Leiden, 1976). George's preface is reprinted in Legrand, *Bibliographie hellénique* 3:8–10.

24. Cf. an edition published at Treviso in 1480, from Hain, *Repertorium bibliographicum,* 6702.

their "little wisdom" from the Hebrews.[25] How widespread this erroneous belief was in the Renaissance is not clear; nor is the opposite view of some later humanists—that the Greeks were older than Moses and could not, therefore, have borrowed from him. But a continuing repugnance for the Byzantine "schismatics" on the part of some Western humanists cannot be ruled out as a factor here.

Despite his heterodox views, Origen, as we have noted, came to enjoy considerable popularity in Renaissance Italy and also, later, in the North. However, researchers investigating the first editions of Origen must exercise caution in generalizing about the Renaissance treatment of his views, especially the heretical ones, in the first printed versions. For although the humanist Marsilio Ficino and others particularly fond of Origen were evidently discriminating in their use of his philosophy and theology, others, like Matteo Palmieri and Leonardo Dati, seem clearly (if secretly) to have accepted certain of his heretical views, such as the preexistence of souls.[26]

In 1475 a Latin version of Origen's *Homilies* appeared, and a few years later the Byzantine Theodore Gaza had Origen's *Contra Celsum* brought from Constantinople for Pope Nicholas V. The edition was dedicated to Pope Sixtus IV and the Venetian doge.[27] In his preface of 1481, the translator of the work, Christopher Persona, compared Sixtus to Origen in virtue and learning.[28] The attractiveness of Origen's views on such questions as the preexistence of souls for humanist proponents of Neoplatonism and of the esoteric and occult is understandable. But the fascinating question this brings up of the so-called rehabilitation of the (heretic) Origen is not without difficulties. We may recall, for example, the case of Pico della Mirandola, whose arrest in Paris was in part occasioned by several suspect theses he propounded, one of which affirmed that it was more reasonable to believe in Origen's salvation than in his damnation.

In their eagerness to disseminate knowledge of the Greek Fathers through the medium of the press and also to further acceptance of the classics in their educational and philosophical program, the Italian

25. V. Rossi, *Il quattrocentro* (Milan, 1897), 68–69; and esp. Monfasani, *George of Trebizond.*

26. On all this see esp. Wind, "Revival of Origen"; and Holmes, *Florentine Enlightenment,* 97.

27. See Hain, *Repertorium bibliographicum,* 7947, for dedication to doge and pope. On recovery of the *Contra Celsum* see Legrand, *Bibliographie hellénique* 3:51–52. See also essay 3 above.

28. See Wind, "Revival of Origen," 414–15. Letter of Persona in *Origenis Contra Celsum libri octo* (Rome, 1481), 20.

humanists gradually gained a more accurate view of the Greek Fathers in their historical context. Here one recalls the great Lorenzo Valla, whose critical acumen permitted him to demonstrate not only the spuriousness of the Donation of Constantine and even to point out errors of translation in the Latin version of Jerome's Vulgate Bible, but also, more pertinently still, to air his suspicions, on philological-historical grounds, of the common Western view of Dionysius as the disciple of St. Paul. Work recently done on Valla's philological method and the new edition of his *Annotationes* indicate how the new type of philological analysis enabled Italian humanists gradually to come to a greater understanding not only of the text of many Greek patristic works but also of the cultural ambience in which they were written.[29] As a result in no small part of the dogmatic disputes at the Council of Florence and of his contact with the Greek representatives there, Valla had become convinced of the inadequacy of the Scholastic method and the need to substitute an exegetical theology based primarily on philological and rhetorical analysis of the biblical text and derived, in the Byzantine manner, from the patristic commentaries. In this development Byzantine influence, as has recently been shown, played an important but hitherto overlooked role.[30]

To turn briefly to northern Europe, the patristic Greek editions of only two, but two of the greatest, humanists will concern us here—Lefèvre d'Etaples and Erasmus. The French-born Lefèvre differed from the earlier Italian humanists in that he was more concerned with the Greek Apostolic Fathers of the first and second centuries A.D. than with the later, better known figures of the fourth and early fifth centuries. As he affirms in his prefatory letter to his *Theologia vivificans* (containing letters of Polycarp and Ignatius and Ambrogio Traversari's translation of the Dionysian corpus—not, perhaps not surprisingly, that of Ficino), he preferred the Apostolic Fathers because they lay at or near the very sources of the Christian faith.[31] Lefèvre, who seemed to dislike Neoplatonism, viewing it as a corruption of Christianity, disputed Ficino's view that

29. On Valla's philological method see S. Camporeale, *Lorenzo Valla: Umanesimo e teologia* (Florence, 1972), 234–76; also essays 1 and 3 above for additional bibliography. And A. Perosa's edition of Valla's *Collatio Novi Testamenti* (Florence, 1970).

30. See Stinger, *Ambrogio Traversari,* 66, 205; also essay 3 above.

31. Perhaps he preferred the style of Traversari to that of Ficino. Although cf. Stinger, *Ambrogio Traversari,* 161–62. For Lefèvre see esp. A. Renaudet, *Préreforme et humanisme à Paris pendant les premières guerres d'Italie* (Paris, 1916), passim; and C. Graf, *Essai sur la vie et les écrits de J. Lefèvre d'Etaples* (Geneva, 1970). On the *Theologia vivificans* see edition of J. Higman and W. Hopyl (Paris, 1498–99). For background see esp. E. Rice, *The Prefatory Epistles of Jacques Lefèvre d'Etaples and Related Texts* (New York, 1972); and for his Greek learning, Rice, "The Humanist Idea of Christian Antiquity," 163–80 (cf. n. 20, above).

Dionysius was the "crown of Christian theology" and the "summit of Platonic learning."[32] It is interesting, nonetheless, that he believed that Dionysius should be considered not so much a Platonist as an immediate follower of Jesus and Paul—and in that lay his importance. Which raises the question whether, or to what extent, Lefèvre knew Byzantine theology (actually he knew little Greek), and, in particular, whether or not he used the Byzantine Maximos the Confessor's exegesis of Dionysius, with its more systematic organization of Dionysius's thought and grater emphasis on the person of Christ.[33]

For the cosmopolitan Erasmus, the Greek Fathers were especially important in furthering his cherished program of "Christian humanism." Remarkably, they were of greater significance in his mind than the Latin Fathers. It appears that he even borrowed his famous phrase "philosophy of Christ" from the Greek Fathers, the Apologists and Alexandrians.[34] Like Lefèvre, Erasmus was vitally interested in the question of Christian origins and especially in the original teachings of Christianity. And yet again, rather like Lefèvre, he was not particularly drawn to Dionysius. Indeed, in 1505 he arranged to have published a work of Valla, who earlier had impugned the authenticity of the Dionysian writings.[35] Erasmus's views of the relative importance of the principal Greek and Latin Fathers show surprising perspicacity as well as an independence of judgment remarkable for his time.[36] Of the greatest Greek Fathers (for whom

32. See Marsilio Ficino, *Opera omnia* (Basel, 1576), vol. 2, pt. 2, p. 1013; also Renaudet, *Préreforme et humanisme à Paris,* index under Lefèvre.

33. See Geanakoplos, *Interaction of the Sibling Cultures,* chap. 6, "Maximos the Confessor and His Influence on Eastern and Western Theology and Mysticism."

34. L. Spitz, *The Religious Renaissance of the German Humanists* (Cambridge, Mass., 1963), 214, says, correctly, that Erasmus placed the Latin Fathers below the Greek in exegetical skill, a talent much admired by him. See also Spitz, 235, for the phrase "philosophy of Christ."

35. Valla, *Annotationes in Novum Testamentum* (Paris, 1505), published by Badius. On Valla and Dionysius see 21 above and 86 below.

36. Little has been done on Erasmus and his editions of the Greek Fathers (I have been working on this subject for many years), but see esp. R. Peters, "Erasmus and the Fathers: Their Practical Value," *Church History* 36 (1967): 254–61; R. Pfeiffer, "Erasmus und die Einheit der klassischen und der cristlichen Renaissance," *Historisches Jahrbuch* 74 (1954): 175–88; and C. Hekethorn, *The Printers of Basel in the 15th and 16th Centuries* (London, 1897). Fundamental is *Opus epistolarum Erasmi*, ed. H. S. Allen and P. S. Allen (Oxford, 1906–47). Erasmus prepared editions of thirteen Fathers; the Greeks included Irenaeus, Chrysostom, Athanasius, Basil, sermons of Gregory of Nazianzus, and Origen. Other editors of Greek Fathers were Agricoloa and Pirckheimer in Germany. Erasmus edited Chrysostom (of which his *De sacerdotio* in Greek was the *editio princeps*), and Basil, the *editio princeps* in Greek of many writings. It is striking that with regard especially to Chrysostom, Erasmus feared not only that the manuscripts available

Erasmus had only the highest esteem), he calls Basil clear and natural, Chrysostom persuasive, and Gregory of Nazianzus, a writer with finesse. On the other hand, though he had tremendous regard and affection for Jerome in particular, Erasmus criticized the Latins Ambrose as obscure, Tertullian as difficult and gossipy, and Augustine as too digressive, "like the Africans in general."[37]

Erasmus read the Greek Fathers, Chrysostom for instance, not only for their moral teachings but also, it seems, for their portrayal of a united Christendom, particularly at a time when the unity of Christendom was in grave jeopardy. (We may recall the parallel views of the earlier Byzantines Demetrius Cydones and Maximos Planudes with respect to the Latin Fathers Augustine and Thomas.)[38] Knowledge of the Greek Fathers was particularly useful to Erasmus in his dispute with Luther. Indeed, it seems safe to say that, in his view, the writings of the Greek Fathers, many of whom were even closer in time than the Latins to the fountainhead of Christianity, strongly exemplified and reflected the unity of the church. Why, then, should Luther be permitted to shatter this traditional unity, especially when several of his chief views were based directly on certain ideas of Augustine of which, or at least of Luther's use of which, Erasmus did not approve?

Erasmus, moreover, seemed to have found in the Greek Fathers confirmation for his condemnation of papal claims to temporal power and for his views on the nature and unity of the church.[39] Strikingly, he considered Origen, that is, the "rehabilitated Origen," to be the greatest of the Greek Fathers. (One may recall Erasmus's remark that one page of Origen is worth more for Christian philosophy than ten of Augustine.)[40] Nevertheless, despite his enthusiasm for the ancient Greek Fathers, Erasmus probably did not have too high a regard for the late Byzantine theologians, whose empire he, like other humanists of the West such as Reuchlin, believed had fallen to the Turks as divine punishment for breaking away from the Roman church. And yet when he defines the

---

contained scribal errors (a constant preoccupation) but also that certain Greek editors (after the signing of religious union between the Greek and Roman churches in 1439) might have made changes in the Greek sacred texts in order better to conform to Latin teachings (*Opus Epistolarum Erasmi,* letter 2340).

37. Quoted in Peters, "Erasmus and the Fathers," 254, who refers to Erasmus's *De ratione concionande,* in *Opera omnia* (Leiden, 1703–6), 5:857. New English translation to be printed in Toronto.

38. See Geanakoplos, *Interaction of the Sibling Cultures,* chap. 4.

39. Spitz, *Religious Renaissance of the German Humanists,* 325.

40. See Erasmus's letter to John Eck, 15 May 1518, in *Opus epistolarum Erasmi* 3:337 (cited in Wind, "Revival of Origen," 422).

church as "the consensus of the Christian people throughout the world," he seems, at least by implication, to include the Greeks.[41]

In any synoptic treatment of Greek patristic first editions, Erasmus must occupy an important, if not the chief, place. For his editions mark, in certain ways, the climax to the entire movement. Although scholars have carefully investigated some aspects of his work in this regard, the results have not always been used, as they should be, to throw light on the sources of his Christian humanism. Nor have they been integrated into a larger, comprehensive account of Greek first editions. This is significant, for when viewed in the light of the whole development, research on individual Greek Fathers takes on an added, sometimes even a rather different, meaning.

After Erasmus's death in 1536, and especially during the last part of the sixteenth century, his aim of furthering Christian humanism seemed to predominate in the printing of patristic Greek editions. More complete texts were sought out, greater textual accuracy was striven for, and editions of hitherto unprinted Fathers appeared: Gregory of Nyssa, Clement of Alexandria, Epiphanius, and others.[42] Soon even certain late Byzantine theologians began to be published, for example, George Scholarios (Gennadios), the first post-Byzantine patriarch under the Turks.[43] (As we have seen, already in the early fifteenth century Traversari had translated the work of the fourteenth-century Byzantine Latinophile theologian Manuel Calecas on the procession of the Holy Spirit *[filioque],* but this had been largely in order to help refute the Orthodox position.)[44] By the late sixteenth century, however, with publication of most of the corpus of the Greek Fathers, the chief criterion for publication seems to have become less the consideration of utility than scholarship, that is, philology.

It should be noted that not until the 1550s did publication of the Fathers in the original Greek text become general; previously, almost everything published had been in Latin translation. (No part of Origen's work, for example, appeared in Greek until 1602.) This may most easily

41. See R. Bainton, *Erasmus of Christendom* (New York, 1969), 193, who also has some discussion of Erasmus and the church fathers.

42. For these editions see handbooks listed in n. 19, esp. Graesse, *Trésor de livres rares.*

43. Gennadios was earlier much attracted to Thomas Aquinas. See A. Papadakes, "Gennadius II and Mehmet the Conqueror," *Byzantion* (1972): 89–90. Cf. now Zisis, *Gennadios Scholarios.* Also my forthcoming book, "The Ecumenical Patriarchate of Constantinople through the Centuries," 14 essays.

44. See Holmes, *Florentine Enlightenment,* 96–99, 122–24.

be explained by the greater exigencies of Greek scholarship. But it is interesting to note that in 1567 Pope Pius V declared St. Thomas a Doctor of the Church, and shortly thereafter (in 1568) he also officially exalted four Greek Fathers—Basil, Gregory of Nazianzus, Chrysostom, and Athanasius—declaring them Doctors of the Church.[45]

To turn, in conclusion, exclusively to the role of the Byzantine scholar-exiles in the West: how they catered to Western humanist tastes by translating, editing, and publishing first editions of classical Greek works is by now reasonably well-known. But given the increasingly strong (but still insufficiently appreciated) Western humanist interest in the Greek Fathers, it was only logical that these exiles would have published patristic writings in addition to classical works, not only to cater to rising interest among Latin readers, but also for the benefit of their own fellow Greeks. Thus, as early as 1499, the Cretan scholar Musurus had edited for Aldus several letters, in Greek, of St. Basil. These, published as part of a collection of classical and early Christian epistles, constitute, so far as I can determine, one of, if not the very first, work of a Patristic Greek author to be printed entirely in Greek. Later, in 1516, one year after the death of his patron and close friend Aldus, Musurus edited for the Aldine press, in Greek, sixteen *Logoi* (*Orations*) of another major Greek Father, Gregory of Nazianzus.[46]

With regard to the printing of Greek Patristic literature for Greek consumption, one is reminded here of the prophetic words of the Byzantine cardinal Bessarion, who left his great library of Greek manuscripts to Venice not only for the use of Western scholars but, as he elsewhere so clearly implied, to benefit his own countrymen, who, under Turkish domination, were in grave danger of becoming culturally barbarized.[47] There is no doubt that a feeling of patriotism also motivated other Greek exiles of the late fifteenth and early sixteenth centuries—such as George of Trebizond and Zacharias Calliergis in Italy and Demetrius Ducas in Spain and Italy—to edit and publish first editions of Greek Fathers, of the Greek New Testament text (recall Ducas's vital role in editing the

45. *New Catholic Encyclopedia* (1969), s.v. "Doctor of the Church."

46. For Basil see Geanakoplos, *Greek Scholars,* 122 and Legrand, *Bibliographie hellénique* 1, cxviii. In 1471, in Venice, Francesco Filelfo published a Latin translation of Basil's *Epistola ad Gregorium Nazianzenum de officiis solitarie* (*Gesamtkatalog der Wiegendrucke,* vol. 3, no. 3699), and in 1515 Giacomo Mazzocchi published the *Hexameron* and commentary by Argyropoulos of St. Basil (in Latin): M. Manoussakas and K. Staikos, *The Publishing Activity of the Greeks during the Italian Renaissance* (1469–1523) (Athens, 1987) 52.

47. See Geanakoplos, *Interaction of the Sibling Cultures,* 162, and above 80–81.

New Testament Greek text for Cardinal Ximenes's Polyglot Bible), and of Orthodox liturgical books for the practical, daily worship of their fellow Greeks in the West.[48]

Of cardinal importance, then, during the last phase of the relations between the Byzantine Palaeologan and the Western Renaissance worlds, was the rising interest among Western humanists in the Greek church fathers. Not only did this indicate increasing Western appreciation for a neglected but fundamental aspect of their own Christian heritage, but it also demonstrated that even in the religious sphere, so long marked by controversy, some theologians and humanists of both Latin and Greek cultures, by emphasizing translations and original Greek texts of the Church Fathers, were able to foster a deeper awareness of the underlying ecclesiastical and cultural unity of the two great halves of Christendom.[49]

48. On Demetrius Ducas in Spain see Geanakoplos, *Greek Scholars in Venice,* chap. 6. Liturgical works were needed by Orthodox Greeks in the West and East for purposes of worship. Venice was the primary, almost exclusive, center for liturgical Greek publication for centuries. See N. Tomadakes, "The Publications in Italy of Greek Ecclesiastical Works (Primarily Liturgical)" (in Greek), *Epeteris Hetaireias Byzantinōn Spoudōn* (1969–70): 3–22, which deals with publication only by Greeks. Cf. Also Geanakoplos, *Greek Scholars in Venice,* 247–49, on Demetrius Ducas's printing of the liturgies of Basil and Chrysostom in Italy, ibid, and 212, 219, for Zacharias Calliergis's *Octoechos.* Cf. above on George of Trebizond's Eusebius, n. 23.

49. For a somewhat parallel development with respect to diffusing knowledge of the Greek Church Fathers in early 16th-century Muscovite Russia, see my study, "The Post-Byzantine Athonite Monk Maximus 'the Greek': Reformer of Orthodoxy in Sixteenth-Century Russia," *Greek Orthodox Theological Review* (in press).

Selected Works of Deno J. Geanakoplos

Books

Emperor Michael Palaeologus and the West, 1258–1282: A Study in Byzantine—Latin Relations. Cambridge, Mass.: Harvard University Press, 1959. Reprint. Hamden, Conn.: Shoestring Press, 1974. Also published in Greek, *Ho Autokratōr Michaēl Palaiologos kai hē dēsis.* Athens, 1969. And in Italian, with an updated bibliography, *L'imperatore Michele Paleologo e l'Occidente, 1258–1282.* National Academy of Palermo, 1985.

Greek Scholars in Venice: Studies in the Dissemination of Greek Learning from Byzantium to Western Europe. Cambridge, Mass.: Harvard University Press, 1962. Also published in Greek, *Hellēnes logioi eis tēn Benetian,* translated by Ch. Patrinelis. Athens, 1965. Republished as *Byzantium and the Renaissance*, Hamden, Conn.: Shoestring Press, 1972. An Italian edition, somewhat revised, is *Bisanzio e il rinascimento: Umanisti greci a Venezia e la diffusione del greco in Occidente (1400–1535).* Rome, 1967.

Byzantine East and Latin West: Two Worlds of Christendom in Middle Ages and Renaissance: Studies in Ecclesiastical and Cultural History. Oxford: Blackwell Press, 1966. Reprint. New York: Harper Torchbooks, 1967. Published in Greek, *Byzantinē anatolē kai latinikē dysē.* Athens, 1974.

With P. MacKendrick, J. Hexter, and R. Pipes. *Western Civilization.* 2 vols. New York: Harper and Row, American Heritage, 1968. 2d ed. rev., 1975. Also published in shortened, one-volume form.

Interaction of the "Sibling" Byzantine and Western Cultures in the Middle Ages and Italian Renaissance (330–1600). New Haven, Conn.: Yale University Press, 1976. A revised and corrected version published in Greek, *Byzantio kai dysē: Hē hallēlepidrasē tōn amphithalōn politismōn ston mesaiōna kai stēn italikē anaggenēsē, 330–1600.* Athens: Hestia, 1985.

Medieval Western Civilization and the Byzantine and Islamic Worlds: Interaction of Three Cultures. Lexington, Mass.: D. C. Heath, 1979.

A Short History of the Ecumenical Patriarchate of Constantinople: "First among Equals" in the Eastern Orthodox Church. New York: Cosmos Press, 1983.

Byzantium: Church, Society and Civilization Seen Through Contempor-

ary Eyes. Chicago: University of Chicago Press, 1984; paperback edition, 1985.

"The Ecumenical Patriarchate of Constantinople through the Centuries. 14 Essays." Submitted to press.

Constantinople and the West: Essays on the Late Byzantine (Palaeologan) and Italian Renaissances and the Byzantine and Roman Churches. Madison: University of Wisconsin Press, 1989.

Articles

Review article (in Greek) on J. Starr's *Jewish Life in Crete under the Rule of Venice. Krētika chronika,* 4 (1950): 363–68.

"Greco-Latin Relations on the Eve of the Byzantine Restoration: The Battle of Pelagonia, 1259." *Dumbarton Oaks Papers,* no. 7 (1953): 99–141, with two appendices.

"Michael Palaeologus and the Union of Lyons." *Harvard Theological Review* 46 (1953): 79–89.

"The Nicene Revolution of 1258." *Traditio* 9 (1953): 420–30.

"On the Schism of the Greek and Roman Churches: A Confidential Papal Memorandum for Union." *Greek Orthodox Theological Review* 1 (1954): 16–24.

"The Council of Florence and the Problem of Union between Greek and Latin Churches." *Church History* 24 (1955): 324–46.

"A Byzantine Looks at the Renaissance: The Views of Michael Apostolis toward the Rise of Italy to Cultural Eminence." *Greek, Roman and Byzantine Studies* 1 (1958): 157–62.

"Erasmus and the Aldine Academy of Venice: A Neglected Chapter in the Transmission of Greco-Byzantine Learning to the West." *Greek, Roman and Byzantine Studies* 3 (1960): 107–34. Also in shortened form in *Greek Heritage* 2 (1965): 102–12.

"Church and State in the Byzantine Empire: A Reconsideration of the Problem of Caesaropapism." *Church History* 34 (1965): 381–403.

"Church Building and Caesaropapism, A.D. 312–565." *Greek, Roman and Byzantine Studies* 7 (1966): 167–86.

"La colonia greca di Venezia e il suo significato per il rinascimento." In *Venezia e l'Oriente fra tardo medioevo e rinascimento.* Florence: Sansoni, 1966. 183–203. ed. Fondazione Cini.

"Edward Gibbon and Byzantine Ecclesiastical History." *Church History* 35 (1966): 170–85.

"Pletho, Giorgius Gemistus." In *Encyclopedia of Philosophy,* edited by P. Edwards, vol. 6, 350–51. New York, 1967.

Twelve articles on Renaissance and Byzantine history: Arsenius Apostolis, Michael Apostolis, John Argyropoulos, Zacharias Calliergis, Demetrius Chalcondyles, Manuel Chrysoloras, Demetrius Ducas, John Lascaris, Marcus Musurus, George of Trebizond, Michael VIII Palaeologus, Sicilian Vespers. In *The New Catholic Encyclopedia.* New York, 1967.

"The Library of the Cretan Humanist-Bishop Maximos Margounios, especially His Collection of Latin Books Bequeathed to Mt. Athos," including a catalog of books. In *Acts of III International Cretological Congress,* 75–91. Heraklion, 1968.

"Some Aspects of the Influence of the Byzantine Maximos the Confessor on the Theology of East and West." *Church History* 38 (1969): 150–63.

"Byzantium." In *Perspectives on the European Past,* edited by Norman F. Cantor, 137–65. New York, 1971.

"The Patriarchal Order of the Knights of St. Andrew: Historical Background and Offices of the Archons." Greek Orthodox Archdiocese, New York, 1971, 1–10.

"The Transmission of Greek Learning from Byzantium to the West in the Renaissance." *Alumni Lectures* (Hellenic College), 1 (1971): 5–29.

"Saint Nicholas of Myra: A Saint for All Seasons." *Alumni Lectures* (Hellenic College), 3 (1973): 101–12.

"Archbishop Iakovos: Prelate, Educator, and Leader of the People." *Orthodox Observer* (1974): 11–14.

"The Discourse of Demetrius Chalcondyles on the Inauguration of Greek Studies at the University of Padua in 1463." *Studies in the Renaissance* 21 (1974): 18–44.

"The Ecumenical Patriarchate." In *22nd Biennial Clergy-Laity Congress, Chicago, 1974,* 36–41. Greek Orthodox Archdiocese, Chicago, 1974.

"The Italian Renaissance and Byzantium: The Career of the Greek Humanist-Professor John Argyropoulos in Florence and Rome (1415–1487)." *Conspectus of History* 1 (1974): 12–28.

"Michael VIII Palaeologus." In *Encyclopaedia Britannica,* 14th ed., 1974.

"Some Observations on the Problem of the First Printed Editions of the Greek Fathers in the Renaissance." Paper presented at Professor R. Bolgar's conference at King's College, Cambridge University, 1974. Published as "Western Recovery and Translation of the Greek Church Fathers and their First Printed Editions in the Renaissance." Chap. 12 in *Interaction of the Sibling Byzantine and Western Cultures,* 254–64.

"Byzantium and the Later Crusades, 1261–1453." Chaps. 2 and 3 in *A History of the Crusades,* edited by K. Setton, vol. 3, 27–103. Madison: University of Wisconsin Press, 1975.

"Bonaventura, the Two Mendicant Orders, and the Greeks at the Council of Lyons (1274)." In *The Orthodox Churches and the West,* edited by D. Baker, 183–211. Oxford: Oxford University Press, 1976.

"The Diaspora Greeks: The Genesis of Modern Greek National Consciousness." In *Hellenism and the First Greek War of Liberation: Continuity and Change,* 59–77 Thessalonica, 1976.

"Religion and 'Nationalism' in the Byzantine Empire and After: Conformity or Pluralism?" *Greek Orthodox Theological Review* 22 (1977): 98–116. Also published in *Ecumenical Review* 29 (1977): 614–32. Paper originally read at the Orthodox- Jewish Colloquium, New York: January, 1972.

"The Little-Known Greek Aristotelian Humanist at Padua: Nicolaus Leonicus Tomaeus." Paper presented at the World Aristotle Congress, Thessalonica, 1978. Published in *Proceedings* of the congress, vol. 2, 15–20. Athens, 1981. A related version of this article is "The Career of the Little-Known Renaissance Greek Scholar Nicholas Leonicus Tomaeus and the Ascendancy of Greco-Byzantine Aristotelianism at Padua University (1497)," in Festschrift for J. Karagiannopoulos, *Byzantina* 13 (1985): 357–72.

"A Reevaluation of the Influences of Byzantine Scholars on the Development of the *Studia Humanitatis,* Metaphysics, Patristics, and Science in the Italian Renaissance (1361–1531)." In *Proceedings of the Patristic, Medieval and Renaissance Conference,* vol. 3, 1–25. Villanova, Pa., 1978.

"The Byzantine Recovery of Constantinople from the Latins in 1261: A Chrysobull of Michael VIII Palaeologus in Favor of Hagia Sophia." In *Essays for George H. Williams, Continuity and Discontinuity in Church History,* edited by F. Church and T. George, 104–17. Leiden, 1979.

"The Reign of Emperor Michael VIII Palaeologus" (in Greek). In *Historia tou hellenikou ethnous,* vol. 9, 116–37. Athens, 1979.

Review article on J. Monfasani's *George of Trebizond: A Biography and a Study of his Rhetoric and Logic. Renaissance Quarterly* 32 (1979): 355–62.

"Important Recent Research in Byzantine-Western Relations: Intellectual and Artistic Aspects, 500–1500." In *Essays in Honor of P. Charanis,* ed. A. Laiou, 60–78. New Brunswick, N.J.: Rutgers University Press, 1980.

"St. Basil, Christian Humanist of the 'Three Hierarchs' and Patron Saint of Greek Letters." *Greek Orthodox Theological Review* 25 (1980): 94–102.

"The Greek Orthodox Church: Alive and Relevant." In *Orthodox Theology and Diakonia: Essays Honoring Archbishop Iakovos,* edited by D. Constantelos, 175–96. Brookline, Mass., 1981.

"Die Konzile von Basel und Florenz (1431–49) als Paradigma für das Studium moderner ökumenischer Konzile aus orthodoxen Perspektive." *Theologische Zeitschrift* 38 (1982): 330–59.

Six articles on the Palaeologan Renaissance, Manuel Chrysoloras, Bessarion, Pelagonia, Gemistos Pletho, and Emperor Michael VIII Palaeologus. In *Dictionary of the Middle Ages,* edited by Joseph Strayer. New York, 1982–.

"The Second Ecumenical Synod of Constantinople (381): Proceedings and Theology of the Holy Spirit." *Greek Orthodox Theological Review* 27 (1983): 207–29.

"The Greek Population of South Italy and Sicily and Its Attitudes to Charles of Anjou and Michael Palaeologus before and during the Early Phase of the Sicilian Vespers." In *XI Congresso di Storia della Corona d'Aragona,* April 1982, vol. 3, 177–82. Palermo, 1984.

"Italian Renaissance Thought and Learning and the Role of the Byzantine Emigré Scholars in Florence, Rome, and Venice: A Reassessment." In festschrift for A. Pertusi, *Rivista di studi bizantini e slavi* 3 (1984): 129–57.

"Theodore Gaza, a Byzantine Scholar of the Palaeologan Renaissance in the Italian Renaissance." *Medievalia et humanistica,* n.s. 12 (1984): 61–81. Earlier published in *Hē Thessalonikē Metaxy Anatolēs kai Dyseōs* (Thessalonica, 1982): 43–58.

"An Orthodox View of the Councils of Basel (1431–49) and of Florence (1438–39) as Paradigm for the Study of Modern Ecumenical Councils." *Greek Orthodox Theological Review* 30 (1985): 311–34.

"How Well did the Cretan-born Pope of the Italian Renaissance, Alexander V (Peter of Candia) Know Greek?" Paper presented at the International Byzantine Congress, 1986.

"Introduction." In *All That A Greek Orthodox Should Know: Answers to Questions and Problems of Today's Living,* by Rev. N. D. Patrinacos, 7–11. New York, 1986.

"Italian Humanism and the Byzantine Emigré Scholars." In *Renaissance Humanism: Foundations, Forms, and Legacy,* edited by A. Rabil, vol. 1, 349–81. Philadelphia: University of Pennsylvania Press, 1987.

"Patriarch Athenagoras and the 50th Anniversary of the Founding of Holy Cross Orthodox School of Theology in America: The Patriarchal Academy of Constantinople." Orthodox Perspectives on Pastoral Praxis, Papers (24–25 September 1986) celebrating the 50th anniversary of Holy Cross Orthodox School of Theology (Brookline, Massachusetts, 1988) 1–12.

"The Post-Byzantine Athonite Monk Maximos 'the Greek': Reformer of Orthodoxy in Sixteenth Century Russia." *Greek Orthodox Theological Review.* In press.

"The Discourse of Peter of Candia (Pope Alexander V) on Giangaleazzo Visconti's Assumption of the Title Duke of Milan, 1395." Paper read at Cretan Congress. Submitted to press.

"Some Western Influences on Byzantine Society and Culture." Paper prepared for Dumbarton Oaks. Submitted to press.

Index